Four Letters of Pelagius

Studies in Pelagius

PELAGIUS: INQUIRIES AND REAPPRAISALS
by Robert F. Evans

Four Letters of Pelagius

ROBERT F. EVANS

THE SEABURY PRESS · NEW YORK

Library of Congress Catalog Card Number:
68 - 11594

Printed in Great Britain

ROBERTO LOWRY CALHOUN

VIRO DOCTISSIMO
MAGISTRO SEVERO
PHILOSOPHO ACUTO
THEOLOGO CHRISTIANO

Preface

THIS book has been a long time in the making. It incorporates material from a dissertation presented in 1959 to the graduate faculty of Religion at Yale University for the degree of Doctor of Philosophy. Since that date the material has undergone much revision and expansion. This reworking has been accompanied by critical reflection on the methods here employed toward the solution of the problem of Pelagius' authorship. The last decade has seen advance in the use of computers and of modern statistical theory for the solution of problems of authorship in general. These new approaches have not been employed in the present study, and I have reached the conclusion that whatever contributions the newer methods will make to the solution of this particular problem, the more traditional methods here employed have produced evidence both impressive in its diversity and permanent in its importance. As I suggest in the introductory chapter, the flexibility of the older and slower methods is well adapted to the special problems posed by the character of Pelagius' undisputed extant works.

Of many acknowledgments that could be made, I wish to record my special gratitude to the following for help, encouragement, and advice given at various stages in the evolution of the manuscript: Professor J. H. Baxter, of St. Andrews University; Professor Robert L. Calhoun, formerly of Yale University; Professor Henry Chadwick, of Oxford University; Professor Robert A. Kraft, of the University of Pennsylvania; Professor Edmund Silk, of Yale University.

A very special expression of thanks is due to Mrs. Hilda H. Rifkin for her unstinting labour in the typing and revising of a difficult manuscript.

R. F. E.

University of Pennsylvania
June 1, 1967

Contents

Abbreviations

EDITIONS OF TEXTS, JOURNALS, AND REFERENCE WORKS

C.C.	*Corpus Christianorum: Series Latina* (Turnhout, Belgium, 1953–)
C.S.E.L.	*Corpus Scriptorum Ecclesiasticorum Latinorum* (Vienna, 1866–)
J.T.S.	*Journal of Theological Studies* (London, 1899–)
P.B.A.	*Proceedings of the British Academy* (London, 1903–)
P.L.	*Patrologiae Cursus Completus: Series Latina*, ed. J. P. Migne (Paris, 1878–90)
P.L. Sup. i	*Patrologiae Cursus Completus: Series Latina, Supplementum*, Volumen I, ed. A. Hamman (Paris, 1959)
Souter, i	Alexander Souter, *Pelagius' Expositions of Thirteen Epistles of St. Paul*, vol. I (Cambridge, 1922)
Thes.	*Thesaurus Linguae Latinae* (Leipzig, 1900–)

WORKS AND FRAGMENTS ASSUMED TO BE BY PELAGIUS

(for further bibliographical details, see pp. 34 f.)

Dem.	*Epistola ad Demetriadem*
Exp.	*Expositiones XIII Epistularum Pauli*
Lib. Fid.	*Libellus Fidei*
C. Arr.	*Contra Arrianos*
de Div. Fil.	*De Divinitate Filii*
de Div. Spir. S.	*De Divinitate Spiritus Sancti*
C. Apoll.	*Contra Apollinaristas*
De Nat.	*De Natura*
De Lib. Arb.	*De Libero Arbitrio*
Lib. Ecl.	*Liber Eclogarum*

THE FOUR LETTERS HERE UNDER STUDY

Cel.	*Epistola ad Celantiam, C.S.E.L.* lvi, pp. 329–56
De Lege	*De Divina Lege, P.L.* xxx, 105–16
Virg.	*De Virginitate, C.S.E.L.* i, pp. 225–50
Vita	*De Vita Christiana, P.L.* xl, 1031–46

Four Letters of Pelagius

Chapter I

INTRODUCTION

EVIDENCE will be presented in these pages to support the thesis that Pelagius is the author of four letters.[1] These writings, in addition to some fifteen others, were attributed to Pelagius over thirty years ago by Georges de Plinval.[2] The world of Pelagius scholars has been ever since in a state of confusion and disagreement over the correctness of Plinval's attributions. John Ferguson, in his general study[3] of Pelagius, accepts them without discussion. Torgny Bohlin, in his important book[4] on Pelagius' theology, ignores them. Serious attacks upon Plinval's argument have come from Ivo Kirmer[5] and John Morris.[6]

Plinval left himself open to serious criticism for his manner of supporting such a revolutionary hypothesis. His treatment was at best suggestive, certainly not conclusive. It is not enough to set a few parallel passages beside one another, to take note of striking similarities, and then to add some general remarks about tone and method of composition.[7] But over and above this all too cursory way of establishing the authorship of single documents, there was a second fault in Plinval's method. Having "vindicated" one document for Pelagius in the manner just indicated, he would then go on to draw material from this writing to establish Pelagius' authorship of further works. The end result was a chain with some very weak links.[8] And there was a third and crucial weakness in Plinval's argument, to which Morris has recently called attention.[9] Plinval wished to assign to Pelagius five of the six documents in the Pelagian Corpus published by Caspari in 1890.[10] To do this it was necessary to wrest away the first of the Caspari documents from the other five; this first letter contains biographical details about its author such that he could not possibly be Pelagius.[11] Plinval attempted this operation by the most dubious of arguments,[12] whereas the material presented by Caspari (pp. 304–16) ought to be sufficient to warn us off any easy attempt to dislodge the first letter from the other five documents. On the basis of evidence so far presented, all of the writings in the Caspari corpus belong together, and their author is not Pelagius.[13]

In two books[14] written since his 1934 article, Plinval has virtually assumed his original list of Pelagius' writings as standing intact, with some few doubtful exceptions. He has, no doubt, hoped that the total effect of these books, in which his new attributions are freely employed, would be to produce an impression of a unified body of writings. One's judgment must be, however, that his argument for Pelagius as the author of these works has not moved materially beyond the degree of strength that it possessed in 1934.

Plinval, however, had a sure instinct in the case of at least four of his documents. In order to defend this judgment it is necessary to consider the contrary arguments of Kirmer and Morris. Kirmer attempted a rigorous application of statistical analysis with respect to language and style, and with results which do not agree with Plinval in the case of a single document. Those aspects of the writings which are decisive for Kirmer's judgments and which he subjects to the closest scrutiny are vocabulary, the use of particles, and figures of rhetoric. The great bulk of his dissertation is thus devoted to series and lists. For each single work that is considered, the examples which he culls from that work under each of his categories are brought forward and compared with a list culled from the assured writings of Pelagius.

Four general criticisms of Kirmer's treatment may be made.

1. Kirmer is often mistaken in his enumerations, as when he claims that word *x*, occurring in one of Plinval's documents, is not to be found in Pelagius, or as when he asserts that figure of rhetoric *y* is found only *z* number of times in one of the questionable writings, whereas it appears a larger number of times in Pelagius' letter to Demetrias. Examples of such oversights will be offered in the body of material presented below.

2. Kirmer's judgments are often based upon numerical ratios

which are not impressive, and he does not allow for the very wide differences in style and language which can be found within the works of single authors. Consider, for example, the matter of particles. Kirmer presents a table (pp. 28 f.) of particles found in the work *De Vita Christiana* and in Pelagius' letter to Demetrias, listing in parallel columns the number of times each particle occurs in each of the two writings. In evaluating such a table one does well to heed the sort of wise warning issued over sixty years ago by Eduard Wölfflin that we should not even speak of differences until something occurs five or ten times more often in A than in B. Statistical ratios such as 10:25 hardly deserve to be mentioned.[15] There is a wide degree of fluctuation in the use of particles to be discovered in Latin Christian authors of the time of Pelagius. In the case of *atque*, for example, Jerome's frequency varies from 33 to 105 within the same number of lines; in the case of *-que* Ambrose varies from 24 to 110.[16] We may now look at Kirmer's table, excluding for a moment the copulative particles (considered in the next item of criticism). The figures in parentheses beside the right hand column indicate, in Kirmer's view, the number of times the particles would have been used in Pelagius' letter (hereafter cited as "Dem.") if that document had come from the same author as the *De Vita Christiana* (hereafter cited as "Vita"). It is to be borne in mind that the Pelagius letter is half again as long as the other work.

	Vita	Dem.
aut	19	26 (28)
vel	8	38 (12)
sed	52	44 (78)
autem	10	14 (15)
vero	15	22 (22)
tamen	6	21 (9)
itaque	3	12 (5)
ergo	14	11 (21)
igitur	3	6 (5)
unde	4	18 (6)
hinc	0	9
nam	10	10 (15)
enim	36	58 (54)
namque	0	3

	Vita	Dem.
quia	14	10 (21)
quoniam	0	2
idcirco	0	8
utique	2	8 (3)
ut . . . ita	1	10 (5)
sicut	20	0 (30)
prout	4	0 (6)
potius . . . quam	4	0 (6)
tam . . . quam	3	8 (5)

There are first two corrections to be made in this table. Whereas Kirmer indicates no example of *idcirco* in Vita, there are in fact three.[17] The table records ten occurrences of *ut . . . ita* in Dem., but I have been able to count only eight,[18] and in any case this particular figure is of only rare occurrence in Pelagius' other assured writings. Apart now from *sicut* and perhaps *hinc*, this table does not, I think, constitute a serious argument against Pelagius as author of Vita. The figures are just not striking enough to arrest attention, and Kirmer's right hand column of figures in parentheses serves only to suggest his undue insistence upon precise numerical correlation. *Sicut* would be troublesome if it were not for the fact that Pelagius uses that word repeatedly in his Expositions (hereafter cited as Exp.) of Paul's epistles.[19] Its absence from Dem. is but one of the literary peculiarities of that letter, as is also the relatively frequent occurrence of *hinc*. This latter word is to be found only once in the fragments, running to some seventeen Migne columns, of Pelagius' work *De Fide Trinitatis*.[20] Vita, in which *hinc* does not occur, is of approximately equal length.

Similar observations might be made about other sets of statistics which Kirmer supplies.[21]

3. Kirmer relies much too heavily upon the letter to Demetrias as representative of Pelagius' writing. A very large part of his case rests upon a comparison of certain select features of Plinval's documents with those same features in the Pelagius letter, and his uniformly negative judgments as to Pelagius' authorship derive much of their support from the observation that the new writings do not employ certain rhetorical devices with the same frequency and with the same degree of artfulness

as does the letter to Demetrias.[22] I have argued elsewhere[23] that this letter is stylistically peculiar among Pelagius' writings and have suggested reasons for this peculiarity. Here it will be enough to illustrate the point by reference to the remaining items in Kirmer's table not reproduced above. If the letter to Demetrias were the only extant document from Pelagius, then the differences between that letter and the other documents in respect of copulative particles would weigh very heavily against most of Plinval's attributions. But this letter is not all that we have. I have counted the copulative particles on 104 of Souter's pages[24] of the Pauline commentary. The number of times *et* appears in these pages is approximately the same as in the whole of Dem., thus giving a fairly accurate gauge by which to note the relative frequency of each of the other particles. Below now is the remainder of Kirmer's table, showing copulative particles in Vita and Dem., and beside the two columns of Kirmer's table is a third column showing the incidence of the same particles counted in Exp.

	Vita	Dem.	Exp.
et	245	279	275
-que	18	114	5
atque	5	19	7
ac	4	48	6
etiam	15	30	58
quoque	3	11	1

The kind of evidence provided by the second and third columns above might serve to make one doubt that Dem. and Exp. both come from Pelagius. Contemporary evidence for Pelagius as author of Dem., however, is far too strong to allow us to take this suggestion seriously. Pelagius himself in his letter to Pope Innocent specifically calls attention to his letter to Demetrias, and both Augustine and Orosius cite the letter as belonging to Pelagius and provide quotations from it.[25] The stylistic contrasts between Dem. and Pelagius' other writings do encourage us, on the other hand, to take seriously the jibe of Orosius that Pelagius, coming from a relatively humble personal background, had the help of others in writing his letter to the young noble virgin.[26] In any case, Kirmer's many tables showing statistics from Dem. alone among Pelagius' writings give a thoroughly misleading picture. It is not too much to say that the stylistic elegance of the letter to Demetrias is not typical of Pelagius.[27]

4. Kirmer selects for attention those aspects of the writings which at best would serve either to confirm or to refute a view concerning their authorship held on other grounds. It is true of course that he was responding to Plinval's argument and intending to refute it. The point here is that if Kirmer's dissertation is viewed as a comprehensive treatment of the problem of the authorship of Plinval's documents, it then becomes a piece of extended special pleading. In the case of vocabulary, for example, he is content for the most part to take note of particular words which are *not* found in both Pelagius and the new documents, not noting the wide and very interesting agreement in vocabulary that is to be found in the case of at least four of the questionable works. Much evidence in favour of Pelagius' authorship of four of Plinval's attributions can be brought forward, as will here be shown—evidence which neither Plinval nor Kirmer considered.

The *De Vita Christiana* is a writing which contemporaries of Pelagius thought was his. He was required to answer for some lines in it at his trial at Diospolis in December, 415, and denied that the words were his.[28] I have treated elsewhere[29] the external evidence relating to this work, with the following conclusions: (1) The most impressive lines of external evidence link the Vita both with the Synod of Diospolis and with Pelagius; (2) the objections which critics have raised against the possibility of Pelagius as author will not bear examination; (3) there is no good reason for holding on to the notion that the author of the Vita is the fifth century British Bishop Fastidius;[30] (4) the general reliability of Pelagius' testimony at Diospolis is not such as would make it improbable that he denied his authorship of a work that was in fact his.

Caspari (p. 360, n. 1) has set out grounds for considering the general thought of the Vita to be Pelagian in character, a judgment with which we may readily agree, though disagreeing with his case for Fastidius as author. Morris[31] is sufficiently doubtful about Fastidius as to be willing to refer to the author as "Fastidius," in inverted commas. Morris, however, has produced an ingenious suggestion as to the date of composition of the Vita. The author in chapter 3 describes magistrates (*iudices*) who cruelly misused their power when alive and who now have been forced to spill their own blood, lying unburied and torn limb from limb, their families dispossessed. This passage describes, thinks Morris, the recent violent overthrow of a government of magistrates, a government over which stood no emperor, prefect, or vicar. "There is one recorded set of circumstances which fits this abnormal situation," argues Morris (p. 35): the British *civitates* of 410–11, which had renounced their allegiance to Constantine and applied to Honorius for military and financial assistance and which "acknowledged no superior prefect or emperor." The Vita, then, comes from Britain and cannot have been written by Pelagius, who in 410 had lived for at least a decade in Rome.

One might reply that ch. 3 of the Vita *may* refer to some one concrete political disturbance, but that there is nothing in the chapter that requires this interpretation. The terms in which the author writes make it in fact more probable to interpret him as reflecting in general upon the violent end to which evil men come. Referring to diverse times and diverse judges, he opens his treatment of the subject with the observation, "*Sed hoc ille facilius intelligere potest, qui per diversa tempora diversorum iudicum impie scelerateque conversantium expectavit interitum.*" It is not necessary, furthermore, to interpret his phrases "*dum alterius iudicium non timent qui alios iudicant,*" and "*qui hominis non timent in delinquendo iudicium*" as referring to governing magistrates who acknowledge no superior human governor. They are to be understood in the light of the immediately prior, more general statement," "*Quorum quo potestas sublimior est, eo ad peccandum maior audacia, quae totum sibi licere credit quod potest.*" His point is, more naturally, that magistrates as such do not have the judgments of men to fear and are thus likely to rush headlong into sin ("*ad peccandum praecipites sunt*"), whereas they will sooner or later know that God is their judge.

But further, the evidence to be presented below, particularly in the sections on parallel passages, on the use and context of biblical quotations, and on vocabulary, is such as to make Morris' hypothesis difficult. If one is not inclined to accept this evidence as establishing Pelagius' authorship, one would then have to conclude that there is literary dependence of the Vita upon Pelagius, in particular upon his Pauline expositions. The *terminus ad quem* of the expositions is 410.[32] Assuming, as one reasonably might, that Pelagius wrote his comments on the Epistle to the Romans first, one can suppose that he did not begin the work until 405, a date earlier than which he would not have had the Origen-Rufinus commentary on Romans available as a source.[33] One would thus have to suppose that a copy of the expositions, written sometime during the period 405–10, made its way to Britain, where "Fastidius" then read it and became sufficiently familiar with it to draw upon scattered passages in the composition of his letter to the widow in the period 410–11. This letter then made its appearance by 413[34] in the Mediterranean world (why?), where it was both copied out[35] and attributed to Pelagius. One can say about this projected course of events that it is not impossible. A simpler hypothesis is to attribute the *De Vita Christiana* to Pelagius.

The work *De Virginitate* (hereafter cited as "Virg.") is a letter on the vocation of Christian virginity addressed concretely to a particular woman. One of the MSS., Codex Vindobonensis, gives us evidence that the original letter was in all probability written soon after the year 404.[36] If Pelagius is its author, one would understand that he might naturally use his own identical words in two works written at approximately the same time. Thus we find in ch. 8 of Virg. a passage of some sixty words (cited below as Parallel Passage 8) in almost identical agreement with some lines from his exposition of I Corinthians. The general Pelagian character of the letter has been treated by Plinval[37] and by Kirmer.[38]

Morris (p. 36) has found a quotation[39] from Virg. in Gildas,[40] preceded by the introductory words "*ut bene quidam nostrum ait.*"

This Morris prefers to take as meaning that Gildas was quoting "a work written in Britain and preserved in Britain," on the ground that it is unlikely that Gildas would have known that Pelagius, "a long-dead heretic once active in Italy, had been British by birth." Though Morris admits that this is only a subjective and personal opinion, one may question the grounds for it. We know that Pelagianism gained considerable momentum in Britain in the fifth century and can suppose that this Pelagian movement was not without its traces in the middle of the sixth century; we know that the name of Pelagius as belonging at least to the Pauline commentary was known in Ireland as late as the ninth century[41] and that Gildas twice visited Ireland; and we know that Gildas had once gone to Rome, where he might well have been reminded of Pelagius' British origin. Pelagianism was still cause for some concern in Rome, as one may gather from the action of Boniface II in confirming the *capitula* of the Second Synod of Orange. The official cloud over the name of Pelagius, added to a certain national pride in the work from which he quotes, might well account for the precise words with which Gildas introduces the quotation.

It must be further remembered that an important scrap of external evidence bearing on the date of composition suggests that Virg. is to be placed at a time such that someone copying out the letter could still regard Pope Innocent I's *Liber Regularum* of 404 as having been issued "*nuper*".[42] This should tell us that the letter was probably written not later than 406. Its author, moreover, if he is not Pelagius, draws upon Pelagius' expositions of Paul; of that there can be no doubt. It is an improbable supposition that an author writing in Britain would have had the Pauline commentary in 406.

The letter *Ad Celantiam* (hereafter cited as "Cel.") is one of spiritual and moral direction addressed to a married woman. Over two-thirds of it concerns Christian life and faith in general, the remainder being occupied with specific instructions on the life proper to a married woman, the management of her household, and the relation of the woman to her husband. Kirmer has sufficiently indicated points of contact between the contents of the letter and Pelagian teaching in general, and has also well pointed out the many similarities in subject matter between this letter and Pelagius' letter to Demetrias.[43]

Seven of the ten manuscripts assign Cel. to Jerome, two lack any title or ascription, and in the twelfth century Codex Berolinensis the title is crossed out, and in the margin is written by a later hand *apocipha*. Criticism since the sixteenth century has variously attributed it. Erasmus suggested Paulinus of Nola; Vallarsi pointed to Sulpicius Severus.[44] The Migne editors thought Pelagius likely,[45] and a like judgment was taken up somewhat hesitantly in the Teuffels history of Roman literature.[46] Cel. is the first of the documents which Plinval in his 1934 article attributed to Pelagius.[47] The plentiful parallels which will be noted between Cel. and Dem. make it seem likely that Cel. belongs to the approximate time of the letter to Demetrias, i.e., 414, whereas the striking relation of the Pauline commentary to Virg., in addition to the MS. evidence, places the latter work some seven years earlier.

The small treatise *De Divina Lege* (hereafter cited as "De Lege") is one of the works in the pseudo-Jerome collection which forms a part of vol. xxx, *P.L.*, a volume including also Pelagius' letter to Demetrias, an interpolated recension of his Pauline expositions, and the *De Virginitate*. The work is addressed to a man of senatorial background who apparently is a recently converted and baptized Christian.[48] Its primary theme from beginning to end is a right understanding of certain aspects of Christian belief and practice, including baptism,[49] knowledge of the divine law,[50] the keeping of the divine commandments,[51] the heavenly reward,[52] the threat of the final judgment,[53] and miscellaneous ethical matters[54]—all of which are themes highly characteristic of Pelagius. The Pelagian cast of thought which characterizes this writing has been attested by Caspari and Kirmer.[55] Vallarsi, in a brief notice,[56] suggested Faustus of Riez as its author. No detailed attention in modern criticism was paid to the document until Caspari noted certain parallels between it and the works in his

Pelagian corpus, as well as three striking parallels between the De Lege and another work which he published in the same volume, an admonition on the ascetic life.[57] Caspari rightly saw that in spite of these parallels the author of De Lege is not the author either of his Pelagian corpus or of the other letter, although he did not consider the possibility that the De Lege might have Pelagius as its author.

Morris (pp. 36–7) suggests two reasons from the contents of the De Lege for our thinking that this letter does not come from Pelagius. Neither of these reasons is firmly grounded. The De Lege, he thinks, comes "from a senatorial milieu," and to support this view he adduces three quotations from ch. 6:

> In nostra classe viri fortes opprobria sciunt portare, non munera.
>
> Retrahit quidem verecundia senatorem, ne sequatur pauperem Christum.
>
> Turpe est inter parentes senatores atque grammaticos scholasticum pro Christo voluntaria humilitate deiectum verbis simplicibus esse contentum.

The second and third of these may be quite adequately interpreted by supposing that the person to whom the letter is addressed is of senatorial background and that the author is showing his awareness of the personal and social problems which are posed when such a person becomes a Christian. It is no surprise that Pelagius should be writing to such a person, as is attested by the request of the Aniciae women that he write to Demetrias, the youngest and last member of that illustrious family. The first quotation requires its context for its proper understanding. The author is employing an ironic military metaphor to characterize the rigours and lowliness of the Christian life. Immediately before the above quotation are these clauses:[58] "*Christianis vexilla crucis sunt deliciae; trophaea nostrae vitae non pompis, sed miseriis reportantur.*" The words "*in nostra classe*" in this case mean "in our army," i.e., in the Christian "army," the phrase clearly standing as a parallel to the "*nostrae vitae*" of the preceding clause.

Nor are we to suppose, with Morris, that the author of the De Lege expresses views on monasticism that could not have been views of Pelagius. He writes to his correspondent: "*Ego te Christianum volo esse, non monachum dici, et virtutem propriae laudis possidere magis quam nomen alienum; quod frustra a Latinis in turba commorantibus imponitur, cum a Graecis solitarie viventibus legitime deputetur.*[59] The author seems chiefly concerned here with the application of a name, the name of *monachus*, and prefers that the name be restricted to its older Eastern application to those leading solitary lives. It has become common to speak of Pelagius as a monk, but the term is applied to him in our sources only by persons other than himself.[60] For all his recurring preoccupation with ascetic principles, Pelagius in his writings does not associate those principles with the term *monachus*. He apparently wants his Christian ascetics to remain "*in turba commorantes*," after his own manner.

If the De Lege, Virg., and the Vita are from Pelagius, then a likely historical possibility opens up with respect to the literary relations among those three documents, the Pauline commentary of Pelagius, and Caspari's Pelagian corpus. Let us accept Morris' very likely thesis[61] that the author of the Caspari corpus is to be fittingly described as the "Sicilian Briton," whose views were the subject of a letter[62] of alarm addressed to Augustine in 414 by the Sicilian Hilarius.[63] The parallels cited by Caspari (p. 395, n. 7)[64] and by Morris (p. 36) for De Lege and Virg. respectively, suggest that the "Sicilian Briton" was familiar with both of those documents. Although Caspari took the literary dependence to be the other way, it seems more likely that the "Sicilian Briton" took ideas and Biblical references making brief appearances in De Lege and developed them both in length of treatment and in severity of thought. One might cite as a notable example the first in Caspari's list of parallels. The author of De Lege at the end of ch. 4 and the beginning of ch. 5 is supporting with biblical references his points, 1) that disobedience of divine prohibitions is as serious as failure to obey positive commandments, and 2) that disobedience of the more "minor" commandments is not to be thought of no consequence. His biblical references include Adam, Samuel, Ananias and Sapphira, Saul and Jehoshaphat, and Oza (and others). In chs. 13 and 14 of *De Operibus* (pp. 90–92) the "Sicilian Briton" has assimilated the first point above to the second and in a very much more extended fashion reproduces most of the examples given in the De Lege passage and adds a few of his own. He makes virtually the same observations about his biblical figures but in more extended, intensified, and terrifying language. We may illustrate by the comments of the two authors on the man of God (called *Sameias* by De Lege) in I Kings 13:

De Lege 4 (109, D) Sic Sameias eadem die, qua mirabilia fecerat gratia prophetali, a leone deiectus occiditur.

De Operibus xiii, 2 (p. 91) Et, ut addo, ille homo dei et propheta, qui, eodem die, quo per dei spiritum futura praecinuerat et multa admiranda fecerat signa virtutum quia cum indigno cibum sumpsit, saevissimis leonis dentibus deputatus est.[65]

One might say, more generally, that the "Sicilian Briton" took the ascetic and rigourist ideas of Pelagius and developed them to a degree of acerbity that goes beyond Pelagius' own writings. Thus Pelagius is always quick to encourage the vocation (*propositum* is his word) to continence and apparently accepts the notion that those who have adopted the life of sexual abstinence have as their special reward the *regnum coelorum*. He does not, however, share the view of the author of *De Castitate* that *castitas* is the "*fundamentum . . . sanctitatis atque iustitiae*,"[66] a view which sets the latter author's treatment of the subject quite apart from the opinion of Pelagius that the fulfillment of *iustitia* is the common vocation of all Christians and that the continent accomplish something over and above this, the *consilium perfectionis*.[67] The "Sicilian Briton" is even of the opinion that something like freedom of choice is to be found in the animal world.[68]

Now the "Sicilian Briton" was familiar not only with De Lege, with Virg., and otherwise with Pelagian ideas in general. He knew and drew upon the Pauline commentary of Pelagius. This is evident at many places and may be illustrated by the following parallel passages, in which both authors are concerned to make the point that biblical writers sometimes identify people in terms appropriate to them only formerly.

De Div. xi, 6 (p. 46)	Exp. 125, 14 ff.
Sed, hanc esse scripturae consuetudinem, novimus, ut quosdam dicat esse, quod fuerant. sicut Abigail adhuc uxorem Nabal Carmeli nuncupat, cum, viro priore defuncto, ad David matrimonium transmigrasset, et sicut, qui ex gentibus Christo crediderant, etiam post fidem gentes appellat, et alios multos, quod nunc commemorare prolixum est.	Hic arcarium, ex-arcario dicit, sicunt gentes credentes ex-gentibus saepe vocavit, secundum consuetudinem legis, quae Abigeam exorem Nabal appellavit, cum iam illo mortuo in David matrimonium transmigrasset.

Furthermore, it is not at all difficult to find passages in Carpari's corpus which seem to bear the same kind of relation to the commentary of Pelagius that has already been suggested as obtaining between that corpus and the De Lege. A passage in *De. Cast.* ix, 2 (p. 137), running to some 135 words, concerning marriage as a remedy for the incontinent, and using the analogy of the good doctor willing to allow the less harmful fruits to a convalescing patient who refuses to abstain from all fruits, is most naturally to be seen as an expansion of a passage in Exp. (159, 13–17) of some thirty-five words which employs the same precise analogy. In arguing for Old Testament support of the notion that a state of sanctity includes abstention from carnal relations, Pelagius very briefly alludes to Exod. 19:15 ff. and to I Sam. 21:4 f., whereas the author of *De Cast.* (v, 1–3, pp. 131 f.) develops these Old Testament incidents at much greater length to make the same point. Commenting upon I Cor. 11:21 and 12:13, Pelagius makes the very characteristic observation that those who are made one by the sacraments in the one body of Christ have no business looking upon earthly goods as belonging to themselves individually, a theme taken up with great vigor in ch. 8 of *De Divit.* (viii, 3 f., pp. 35 f.).

The "Sicilian Briton," then, was acquainted with De Lege, with Virg., and with Exp. It remains to be said that he was also acquainted with the Vita. Here again it was Caspari (pp. 376–8 and 378, n. 1) who set out the telling parallels. He also made the observation, parallel to similar judgments made here, that the author of the work *De Operibus* gives a most detailed and thoroughgoing treatment to a theme which makes a brief appearance in ch. 13 of the Vita (and, one might add, in various places[69] throughout the commentary of Pelagius): Bare faith without performance of the commandments of Christ is not enough. I should want to interpret this fact about the *De Operibus* as indicating the same kind of relation to the Vita and to Exp. as has been argued for the "Sicilian Briton's" relation to the De Lege and to Pelagius at other points.

Caspari was of the opinion (p. 382) that his very striking parallels were not sufficient to bring one to the necessary conclusion that one of the authors had influenced the other, and this on the grounds that the two were handling the same themes, were both of an ascetic cast of mind, and were both Pelagians. Why he was content with this sort of judgment in the case of the Vita but not in the case of De Lege is not clear, particularly in view of the fact that the parallels for the Vita are even more striking than those for De Lege. Though individual judgments will differ, I should think that the very grounds which Caspari suggests, in view of many precise verbal parallels, would argue for literary dependence. Consider, for example, two instances of the close association of biblical texts: 1) Tobit 4:16 and Mt. 7:12 quoted in immediate succession in passages making the same point (Caspari, p. 18 and Vita 10 [1039]); 2) the same precise conflation of John 14:21 and Mt. 7:24 (Caspari, p. 4 and Vita 9 [1038]). Or consider Kirmer's surprisingly long list,[70] running to nineteen separate items, of synonymous word combinations common to the Vita and to the "Sicilian Briton." The following are drawn from one item in that list.

Vita 3 (1034) nemo idcirco *securus* delinquat et *liber*.

Vita 13 (1042) ergo *securi* peccamus et *liberi*.

De Operibus ii, 2 (p. 70) ut sub obtentu fidei *liberius securiusve* delinquerent.

De Operibus xvi, 7 (p. 99) ut *securius liberiusque* peccemus.

De Cast. x, 8 (p. 144) *liberi* degimus ac *securi*.[71]

But there is one important parallel between the "Sicilian Briton" and the Vita which Caspari did not notice, and this one cannot with plausibility be accounted for on the basis of common ascetic and Pelagian outlook, even if all the rest of his parallels could be. It will be recalled that ch. 3 of the Vita contains a passage calling attention to the violent deaths of cruel and unjust magistrates (*iudices*). The author's intent in this passage is primarily to illustrate the way in which wicked men often meet untimely and unpleasant deaths. Ch. 6 of the *De Divitiis* also discusses the cruelties and deaths of magistrates, with the different purpose of denouncing anyone who thinks he can be both a Christian and a magistrate. The whole passage in *De Divitiis* offers a splendid example of the way in which the "Sicilian Briton" develops, intensifies, transforms the materials in his sources. The author of the Vita makes a passing observation to the effect that men in positions of such power tend to rush headlong into misuse of power, whereas the author of *De Divitiis* looks upon the magistrate as such as beyond redemption, and argues at tedious length and with much scorn that the Christian life and the office of a magistrate cannot be combined. As both authors describe the deaths brought upon the magistrates by the judgment of God, the following parallels emerge.

Vita 3 (1035)

Alii vero qui similia commiserant, sic dei indignatione prostrati sunt, ut insepulti iacerent, et esca feris et coeli volucribus fierent. alii autem qui innumerabilem hominum multitudinem iniuste peremerant, membratim particulatimve concissi, ut non minor fuerit concisura membrorum quam quos interimi fecerant, numerus punitorum.

De Divitiis vi, 2 (p. 32)

Tot necesse est sub iudice suppliciorum mortes evenire, quot poenae sunt. et hinc christianis multiplex ad pietatis officium angor innascitur, dum se vident in cognato corpore ab avibus et feris, sepultura quodammodo denegata, lacerari atque discerpi.

In addition to the physical details of death, there is a particular parallel between the final clauses of the passage from Vita and the first clause from *De Divitiis*, although the author of the latter changes the point slightly.

The "Sicilian Briton," then, used as source materials Pelagius' *Expositiones*, the *De Vita Christiana*, the *De Virginitate*, and the *De Divina Lege*. He did this to his own ends, developing and expanding certain lines of thought and particular passages from his texts. He did not copy slavishly,[72] although he did often copy. He had an independent cast of mind that often moved beyond the thought of his sources, but he was not afraid to exploit the sources from which he had drunk deeply.

It has been commonly held[73] that Pelagius in about 409 or 410 stopped for a time in Sicily on his way to Africa, where he was in 411.[74] I have found no evidence for this in the sources. It is, in particular, nowhere stated that James and Timasius, friends of Pelagius and correspondents of Augustine, were residents of that island, as Hedde and Amann suggest. The reason for the notion of Pelagius' sojourn in Sicily was probably that of accounting easily and naturally for that outbreak of Pelagianism in Syracuse which was the subject of Hilary's letter[75] to Augustine in 414. I believe we now have concrete evidence that Pelagius did stop in Sicily. He gave to the man whom we are calling the "Sicilian Briton" copies of four of his works: The *Expositiones*, the *De Vita Christiana*, the *De Virginitate*, and the *De Lege*.

This conjecture has more to commend it than its simplicity in accounting for data so far considered. It helps also to explain smaller points of connection between the writings of the "Sicilian Briton" on the one hand and Vita, Virg., and De Lege on the other while avoiding the assertion of identity of authorship. Although I shall not use the space to attempt a demonstration here, I am convinced that a balanced examination of content of thought, vocabulary, and style would lead to the conclusion that the "Sicilian Briton" cannot be the author of Vita, Virg., and De Lege, and would lead to this conclusion, furthermore, even if there were no works of Pelagius extant to draw these three documents towards the great heretic. If there were no such works of Pelagius extant, we would not know who the author of Vita, Virg., and De Lege was. But there are, nonetheless, a striking number of synonymous word-combinations common to one or more of these three documents and to the writings of the "Sicilian Briton." Kirmer has already performed the task of laying them out for us to see.[76] Particularly in the case of the Vita is the list so long that something more than merely literary dependence of one work upon another seems to be indicated, particularly since most of these parallel word-combinations occur in contexts in which there is no question of the "Sicilian Briton's" copying or even closely paraphrasing the Vita.[77] Most of these word-combinations, moreover, have more than a purely ornamental significance; they emphasize ideas highly characteristic of Pelagius, e.g., *sanctitas et iustitia*, *misericordia pietasque*, *securus et liber*,[78] *fallit ac decipit.*[79]

If we suppose Pelagius to have met the "Sicilian Briton," and to have been responsible for the latter's possession of four of his own writings, we may also suppose that the two spent some time in conversation. The Sicilian was attracted to Pelagius' teaching, and they were both, after all, Britons residing for the present in Sicily, a circumstance that would not tend to keep them apart, to say the very least. From these conversations, the "Sicilian Briton" acquired for himself features of Pelagius' own vocabulary and manner of expression relative to matters of characteristic importance to Pelagius himself and to the Sicilian.

Such a suggestion may seem a bit unusual, but literary critics, after all, only betray their narrowness by confining attention to relations among documents and excluding relations among persons.[80]

The present study employs methods which have long been familiar to scholars. The approach to problems of authorship which has been opened up by the modern science of statistics is of unquestioned value, but its value is not of a sort that will render otiose the kind of study here undertaken. At least some practitioners of the new method are explicitly aware that statistics offers one kind of evidence which needs to be complemented by other and more traditional kinds of evidence.[81] But in the case of the present study in particular it is not yet clear just what relevance the new statistical methods might have. Those methods have been of use where works of roughly like nature and of continuous prose writing have been compared. In the case of Pelagius the two complete and extant works which we can assume to be his and which are of use to us[82] present special problems. The expositions on Paul, running to over 530 pages in Souter's edition, do not contain continuous prose writing but rather consist of expository comments on individual verses and parts of verses, the comments ranging in length for the most part from a few words to a few lines, with occasional exceptions going as high as some twenty lines. The letter to Demetrias, on the other hand, contains stylistic peculiarities of such a sort as to make the conclusion probable that Orosius was right when he suggested that Pelagius had the benefit of literary assistance in its composition.[83] The individuality of this letter is apparent on comparison not only with the Pauline commentary but with Martini's fragments, running to thirteen Migne columns, from Pelagius' work on the Trinity.[84] The extant writings which are assumed in the present study to come from Pelagius do not therefore possess the unity and continuity which must be presupposed in the application of such new statistical methods of which I am aware. We do however possess works and fragments of works by Pelagius which are the equivalent in length of some 13,000 Migne lines. This study is based upon the assumption that a volume of material of this magnitude does offer sufficient ground at the present time for assigning the four letters in question to Pelagius.

Chapter II

PARALLEL PASSAGES

THE form of presentation of the evidence to follow will be necessarily a bit arbitrary and artificial. Items in the section on biblical quotations might have appeared in the section on parallel passages, and vice versa. Hopefully my reasons for putting one item in one section and not in another will be sufficiently apparent, and in any case it doesn't matter. In particular it is to be noted, however, that many items in the vocabulary chapter could have been included as parallel passages. The latter section might well have been much longer than it is. For the sake of completeness and in order to present the full range of evidence as persuasively as possible, I have included not only parallels which I have discovered but some also which Plinval has pointed out.

A word needs to be said about the relevance of parallel passages. Some interpreters are of the opinion that a passage in work *a* which is an exact or nearly exact quotation from work *b* is enough to instill the strong suspicion that works *a* and *b* are not from the same author. This is absurd. There is no *a priori* reason why Latin authors of the fifth century should be less inclined to quote themselves than are authors of the twentieth century. In fact one would suppose that they would be more inclined to do so, with less stringent standards of annotation. The Pauline expositions themselves are not without evidence that Pelagius quoted or very closely paraphrased himself,[1] that he returned often to quote or allude to favourite verses of scripture for the purpose of supporting some of his characteristic themes,[2] and that he had highly characteristic ways of saying certain things which reappear throughout the expositions.[3] When a close parallel is found between two works, then, this is simply an invitation to further exploration. One looks for parallels which are less exact, parallels which might indicate neither quotation nor close paraphrase of a passage immediately before the eyes, but the less conscious reproduction of habitual ways of thought and manners of expression. And one looks for particular items of vocabulary and of style.

It is my conviction that this kind of investigation will lead to the judgment that Pelagius is the author of these four letters.[4] The preceding essay has attempted to show that, by reason of the relation of three of these letters to the writings of the "Sicilian Briton," and by reason of a similar relation of the Pelagius expositions to the same writings, the three letters find a natural and plausible "placing" as letters of Pelagius used by the writer in Sicily. There is thus an argument in two parts—one which sees the three letters in relation parallel with the expositions to the "Sicilian Briton," and the other which sees them as internally related to Pelagius' own writings.

For Cel. there is unfortunately now lacking an argument of the first kind, and we must rely entirely on internal evidence linking this letter to the works of Pelagius. Cel. has another peculiarity in that the obvious parallels bind it closely to Pelagius' letter to Demetrias. I interpret these facts as meaning that whereas the other three were all written by, say, 410, when Pelagius was presumably in Sicily, Cel. comes from a time closer to that of the writing of Dem., *viz.* 414.[4a] Whether Cel. borrows from Dem. or Dem. borrows from Cel. is impossible to say with any assurance.

I have decided to accept the thesis of Dom Celestin Charlier that the manuscript of Pelagius' *Expositiones* containing the text closest to the original of Pelagius is Paris 653, styled V in Souter's apparatus.[5] Souter provides a description of this manuscript in vol. i of his edition,[6] but Charlier offers, I think, a better interpretation of the data which Souter collected. It was the judgment of E. A. Lowe that Paris 653 is "a north Italian MS. of about 800 A.D.",[7] and that it probably issued from a Verona scriptorium. Although Charlier's article is only a brief summary of a larger body of evidence which he has not yet published, his conclusion is confirmed by a consideration of the textual evidence at many places in the commentary.

It has seemed advisable at this point to avoid a comparison of the Biblical texts common to the letters and to Pelagius. For two of our letters, the Vita and De Lege, there is not yet available a modern critical edition, and one knows that Biblical texts were of all things the most subject to alteration. Charlier and others[8] have shown that Souter was needlessly and wrongly biased against readings agreeing with the Vulgate in his Pauline text of Pelagius, and further investigation may show that some such bias was at work in the *C.S.E.L.* editions of Virg. and Cel.

In every section below, the evidence is cited in the following order: Vita, Virg., Cel., De Lege.

The following works and fragments of works are assumed to be by Pelagius.

1. *Expositiones XIII Epistularum Pauli.* Page and line references are to Alexander Souter's edition (Cambridge, 1931), vol. ii.

2. *Epistola ad Demetriadem* (*P.L.* 30, 15–45).

3. *Libellus Fidei* (*P.L.* 45, 1716).

4. Fragments published by P. C. Martini in *Antonianum* xiii (Rome, 1938), pp. 319–34.

(a) *Contra Arrianos.*

(b) *De Divinitate Filii.*

(c) *De Divinitate Spiritus Sancti.*

(b) *Contra Apollinaristas.*

5. Fragments of *De Natura* in Augustine, *De Natura et Gratia*, vii–lxvii.

6. Fragments of *De Libero Arbitrio*, as follows:

(a) in Augustine, *De Gratia Christi*, iv–xliii, and *De Peccato Originali*, xiii and xv.

(b) fragments published by A. Souter in *Proceedings of the British Academy* (London, 1906), pp. 437–39, and in *Journal of Theological Studies*, O.S., xii (Oxford, 1911), pp. 34–5.[9]

7. Fragments of *Liber Eclogarum* (called also *Liber Capitulorum* and *Liber Testimoniorum*) in Augustine, *De Gestis Pelagii* 7 and 54 f. and *Contra Duas Epistolas Pelagianorum* 4.21; and Jerome, *Dialogus Adversus Pelagianos* 1.25–32. These fragments have been

collected and set down in such order as is possible by J. Garnier, *P.L.* 48, 594 f.

"Pelagius" in the following means Pelagius the author of the above undisputed works.

In the parallel passages below the more notable points of correspondence are set in italics, whether they be precise verbal parallels, common scriptural texts, or interesting parallels in clause structure, syntax, etc.

1. Both Dem. and Vita have passages in which a series of Old Testament figures are discussed. The purpose of the series in each work is different. In the Vita it is to indicate the divine pleasure at human righteousness and displeasure at unrighteousness. In Dem. it is to prove that there were righteous men between Adam and Moses who lived holy lives and pleased God. The series and discussion in Dem. is longer than in the Vita. Dem. includes mention of Melchizedek, Joseph, and Job, who are not discussed in Vita. But both of them include Abel, Enoch, Noah, Lot, and Abraham, and the relative order of these figures is the same in both. The order in Vita is Abel, Enoch, Noah, Abraham, Lot, while in Dem. Melchizedek is inserted between Noah and Abraham. In the cases of Noah and Lot there are no particularly striking parallels in expression, but there are the following parallels for the other three.

Vita	Dem.
Vita 7 (1037) ... in exordis mundi Cain et Abel fratres fuisse germanos; e quibus unus Deo placuit, eo quod innocens esset et *iustus* ...	Dem. 5 (19, D) Quem (Abel) *iustum* in Evangelio Dominus ipse commemorans breviter perfectionem eius exposuit.
Vita 7 (1037) ... *Enoch*[10] satis iustum fuisse Scriptura designat, cui tantum iustitia contulit, ut nec praesentem mortem sciret, sed et ad immortalitatem *de medio* omnium *mortalium* singulariter *raperetur*.	Dem. 5 (19, D) Beatum *Enoch*[10] ita placuisse Deo legimus, ut eum *e medio mortalium raperet*.
Ibid. Abraham quid per fidei et iustitiae meritum consecutus sit, scriptura testatur, ut illo in tempore solus *amicus*[11] *Dei* esset in terris.[12]	Dem. 5 (20, C) Quid Abraham *amicum Dei*, quid Isaac et Jacob memorem?

Notable about the entire series in Vita is the appearance of one or the other of the words *iustus* and *iustitia* in relation not only to Abel, Enoch and Abraham, as above, but to Noah and Lot as well.[12a] This is of special interest when it is remembered that one of Pelagius' recurring arguments concerns the *iustitia* of certain Old Testament figures. For him this term is a comprehensive one denoting the possession of all virtues incumbent upon all men; it means full obedience to all the divine commandments.[12b] Because scripture gives us warrant for applying this term to certain individuals in the Old Testament, Pelagius appears to argue, we may draw the conclusion that these ancient worthies were without sin, and thus we have concrete scriptural evidence that man possesses the capacity to be without sin, or to put the point another way, that man possesses a natural goodness sufficient to preserve him from disobeying the law of God.[12c] The particular point in ch. 7 of the Vita is that God blesses the righteous man and works his wrath upon the unrighteous. If the Vita is by Pelagius, he is here taking up a highly characteristic theme, *viz.*, the *iustitia* possessed by a number of biblical figures, and employing it for a purpose somewhat different from his more usual one.

2. Vita and Exp. both have discussions of the patience of God which show striking parallels.[13]

Vita 2, 1033

Sed plerosque incredulos et impudentes et perfidos misericordis Dei longa patientia peccare facit intrepidos; ut ex hoc peccatorum suorum Deum non arbitrentur ultorem, quod *non statim* venit *punire peccantes*. miseri et ingrati, suae salutis improvidi, quia hoc etiam Deo imputant, quod eorum *differatur* interitus, ignorantes Dei providentia duplici ratione servari, ut et humano generi longa eius patientia consulatur; et ne ille iudicetur impatiens, si illico voluerit damnare peccantes. nam si tam patiens

Exp. 20, 8–16

Multum enim se homines per patientiam Dei seducunt, et quia *non* vult *statim punire peccantes*; putant eum aut res humanas minime curare aut *donare* quid *differt*, plerique etiam calumniantur, quare in praesenti non reddit, non intelligentes quia si statim redderet, nullus paene iam hominum remansisset, nec de iniustis fierent iusti. ideo autem hominibus videtur deus diu *exspectare peccantes*, quia nos, cum parvi temporis simus, centum annos aeternitatem putamus.

non esset, iam diu humani generis origo desiisset, nec iustos de peccatoribus haberemus, si confestim Deus vellet punire qui peccant . . . Deus enim non *donat* peccata, sed differt; nec perseverantem peccatorem a morte liberat, sed ut vel sero convertatur et vivat, patienter *exspectat*; sicut beatus Petrus apostolus ait, "*Non tardat Dominus promissis sed patienter agit propter vos, nolens aliquos perire, sed omnes ad paenitentiam converti* (2 Pet. 3:9)." Ille enim te quasi pius, benignus, et clemens, illico idcirco non percutit, ut tu quanta illius erga te sit pietas, quanta clementia sit recognoscas, qui te peccatorem et impium *expectare* mavult, et servare conversum quam punire *peccantem*.

Ibid., 19, 25—20, 3

Sed secundum *beati petri*, "*Non tardat dominus promissis, sed patienter agit propter nos, nolens aliquos perire sed omnes ad paenitentiam reverit* (2 Pet. 3:9)."

Ibid., 3 (1034)

Nemo ergo *sibi* ideo *blandiatur*, nemo se stulta et vana suspicione decipiat, nemo idcirco securus delinquat et liber, quod super peccatores confestim Dei ira *iudiciumque* non veniat, ut ex hoc opinetur se impune peccasse, quod non illico perimatur; sed hoc magis *differre* Deum, quam dissimulare congnoscat . . . sicut scriptum est, "*Ne dixeris, Peccavi, et quid accidit mihi triste? est enim Altissimus redditor patiens* (Eccli. 5:4)."

Et alibi, "*Ne tardes converti ad dominum, neque differas de die in diem; subito enim veniet ira eius* (Eccli. 5:7)."

Ibid., 19, 22–25

Aut numquit propterea *tibi* de impunitate *blandiris*, quia semper in praesenti non reddidit, et longitudinem temporis considerans, putas non esse *iudicium*.

Ibid., 20, 3–7

Bonus enim (Deus) *exspectando*, iustus est puniendo, unde dicit salomon: "*ne tardes converti ad deum, neque differas de die in diem; subito enim venit ira eius, et in tempore vindicata disperdit* te. (Eccli. 5:7)" et iterum: "*Ne dixeris, Peccavi, et quid accedit mihi triste? est enim altissimus patiens redditor* (Eccli. 5:4)."

Summary of above evidence:

(a) non statim venit punire peccantes (Vita) = non vult statim punire peccantes (Exp.).

(b) Both use the contrasting verbs *differre* and *donare* of God's action with respect to punishment and sin.

(c) Both give the same two reasons for God's delay in judgment:
   (i) if there were no delay, the human race would have ceased to exist;
   (ii) there would have been no opportunity for conversion.[14]

(d) Both use the verb *exspectare* to indicate God's "waiting" for sinners to turn to him.

(e) Both use 2 Pet. 3:9.

(f) Both use Eccli. 5:4 and 5:7 closely together, but in reverse order.

(g) Both use the verb *sibi blandiri* in identical contexts.

3. Vita and Exp. have a doctrine of the filling up of the measure of sins expressed in similar terms, with allusions to the Sodomites and Amorites, and with the noun *modus*.

Vita 4 (1035)

Esse autem certum peccatorum *modum* atque mensuram, Dei ipsius testimonio declaratur. *Et quod unusquisque* vel celerius vel tardius, prout peccatorum suorum *modum* expleverit, iudicetur, evidentissime demonstratur, quando de *Sodomorum* et Gomorrhaeorum interitu atque incendio . . . Deus loquitur, dicens (then quote of Gen. 18:20). De *Amorrhaeis* vero quid dicit (Deus), qui sua nondum peccata finierant, quos post multos annos quam supra dictae civitates crematae sunt, constat esse deletos?

Exp. 76, 20–22

Quod unusquisque modo et fine peccatorum suoram impleto puniatur, sicut *Sodomitae* et *Amorraei*.[15]

4. Vita and Exp. have parallel passages on the meaning of justification by faith and the proper interpretation of Rom. 3:28.

Vita 13 (1043)

Justificari hominem Apostolus per fidem sine operibus legis dicit, sed non sine illis operibus, de quibus alterum apostolum audio dicentem, "*Fides sine operibus mortua est* (James 2:20)." Paulus enim apostolus de operibus legis locutus

Exp. 34, 9–19; 32, 4–6

Abutuntur quidam hoc loco (i.e., Rom. 3:28) ad destructionem *operum iustitiae*, solam fidem baptizato posse sufficere adfirmantes, cum idem alibi dicat apostolus . . . (quotes of I Cor. 13:2 and Rom. 13:10 in favour est, hoc est, de *circumcisione* carnali et neomenia, et *sabbato*, et *huiusmodi caeteris*, quae lex fieri ante praeceperat, et iam Christi tempore non erant necessaria, iste vers (James 2:20) de *operibus iustitiae* loquitur, quae qui non fecerit mortuus est, quamvis se simulet esse fidelem.

of *caritas*) . . . quod si haec eorum sensui videntur esse contraria, sine quibus operibus apostolum iustificari hominem per fidem dixsise credendum est? scilicet *circumcisionis* et *sabbati*[16] et *ceterorum huiuscemodi* non absque *iustitiae operibus*, de quibus beatus Jacob dicit, "*Fides sine operibus mortua est* (James 2:20)."

Exp. 32, 4 ff.; on Rom. 3:20.

Opera legis *circumcisionem* dicit, *sabbatum* et *caeteras* caerimonias, quae non ad iustitiam sed ad carnis laetitiam pertinebant.

5. The concluding chapter of Vita, 15 (1045–46), concerns widows, their differing classifications and the life that is appropriate to them. The argument is supported by quotations from I Tim. 5:3–6, 10. There are interesting parallels between this chapter and Pelagius' comments on these verses in Exp.

(a) In Vita 15 (1045) we read the following:

> Tria autem esse vidvarum genera non ignorare te credo. unum quod perfectissimum, coelesti praemio destinatum, quod, ritu illius de Evangelio vidvae, Deo orationibus et ieiuniis die noctuque deservit.

This is a manifest reference to the widow Anna in Luke 2:37,[17] as well as to I Tim. 5:5. The text of the latter verse in Pelagius reads, "*Quae autem vere vidva est et desolata, speravit in deum et instat obsecrationibus et orationibus nocte ac die.*" The subject is the same as in the quotation above—the best widows, those who are "widows indeed." Pelagius' comment on this verse is as follows: "Qualis erat *Anna* filia Fanubel, tales praecipit honorari."

(b) Vita (15, 1046) quotes I Tim. 5:10 and inserts into the text of the verse an interpolation almost identical with an interpolation which Pelagius inserts into the same verse.

Vita 15 (1046)

"Vidva eligatur quae fuerit in operibus bonis testimonium habens. Si filios educavit," *quod subintelligitur, Deo;* "si hospitio recepit, si sanctorum pedes lavit."

Exp. 495, 1 f.

"Si filios edocavit," *subauditur*, a *Deo*, "si hospitio recepit, si sanctorum pedes lavit."

Plinval was the first to point out this parallel.[18] If the Vita is by Pelagius, this passage will be the only instance in his known works in which the passive verb *subintelligitur* is found. When in the commentary he wishes to make a comment such as the above, he always uses the verb *subauditur*.[19] Kirmer asserts that far from supporting the thesis that Pelagius is the author of the Vita, this passage proves the contrary.[20] This is a striking instance of Kirmer's misuse of statistics. One might say at most that the change in verb neutralizes the evidence, but it proves nothing. Pelagius was familiar with both of these verbs used in just this kind of context. Ambrosiaster used both of them frequently for this purpose,[21] and it has been shown that Pelagius knew and used Ambrosiaster for his own exegesis.[22] The verb *subintelligere* with this meaning does not fall into the class of rare words in ecclesiastical Latin from the third century on. Besides its use by Ambrosiaster it is found in Tertullian,[23] Augustine,[24] and, later, in Gregory the Great.[25]

6. Vita and Exp. show a noticeable parallel of expression in discussing those who do not see the judgment of God in suffering and death. The comment from Exp. forms part of Pelagius' remarks on I Cor. 11 : 31, where the discussion concerns those who are sick and dead through unworthy participation in the sacrament.

Vita 3 (1034)

Sed hoc (i.e., the working of God's wrath) nemo intelligit, nemo cognoscit; nec quisque adversa sustinens malis suis aestimat irrogari; sed quod portulerit, *consuetudinis* potius *putat esse* quam criminis.

Exp. 194, 3–5

Erat praesens correptio et nunc est, sed quia talia patiuntur, *putamus consuetudinis esse* quod culpae est.

7. The following is really an example of the same paronomasia in Pelagius and Vita. Pelagius in two places achieves a certain effect by using the verb *vindico* and the noun *vindicta* in close proximity.

Exp. 467, 4–6. The text under consideration is Col. 3:13: "Sicut et dominus donavit vobis, ita et vos." Pelagius' comment reads: "Si ille indulsit qui potuit *vindicare*, quanto magis vos, quorum *vindicata* aut nulla aut satis est parva."

Also from a fragment of the *De Natura* we find the following: "Non debuit sic *vindicari* peccatum, ut peccator per *vindictam* plura commiteret."[26]

In Vita 5 (1036), the discussion concerns the question, "Why do we see good men perishing along with evil men?", and reads in part: "Illi (the good men) enim vadunt ut iudicent, isti (the evil) ut iudicentur; illi ut *vindicentur*, isti ut in eos *vindicta* celebretur."

8. The one major and rather breathtaking parallel cited by Plinval for Virg. in his original article[27] we reproduce below. In the middle of the letter the author is discussing the manner of life proper to a true Christian virgin. He quotes I Cor. 7:34 and follows this quotation with several sentences that correspond almost exactly to Pelagius' comments on the same verse in Exp.

Virg. 8 (235, 9–14)	Exp. 169, 5–11
Nuptam viro placere adserit (i.e., Paul), cogitando quae mundi sunt, innuptam vero Deo, eo quod nulla cura illi sit saeculi. dicat ergo mihi, quae virum non habet et tamen quae mundi sunt cogitat, cui placere desiderat? nonne incipiet illi nupta praeponi? quia illa cogitando quae mundi sunt complacet vel marito, ista vero nec marito, quem non habet potest placere nec Deo.	Nuptam viro placere adserit cogitando quae mundi sunt; innuptam vero Deo eo quod illi nulla cura sit saeculi. Quae ergo virum non habet et tamen quae mundi sunt cogitat, cui placere desiderat? nonne incipiet illi nupta praeponi, quae cogitando quae mundi sunt complacet vel marito, cum haec nec marito, quem non habet, nitatur placere nec Deo.

Two possibilities now suggest themselves: this is a lost writing of Pelagius, or this is a writing of a Pelagian copying the master. Comparison of the letter as a whole with the works of Pelagius points to the first of these alternatives.

9. Virg. and Exp. show similarities in passages where both of them discuss the unlikelihood of our being easily forgiven now, if those of old time were not so forgiven. The exegesis in Exp. concerns I Cor. 10:11, which itself is a conclusion to be drawn from God's judgment upon the children of Israel in three different incidents in Exodus and Numbers. In Virg. the reference is to the sin of Adam. It is to be noticed that both of

these passages belong to a type of argument highly characteristic of Pelagius, that of establishing a moral obligation for Christians now on the basis of Old Testament incidents. A characteristic of this kind of argument is the either implicit or explicit thought that because of the Christian dispensation our obligation is even greater now. The words *quanto magis* often appear in the argument, as they do in the passage from Exp.

Virg. 7 (234, 1–7)

Quem (Deum) si in aliquo contempseris, *si pepercit* Adae, parcet et tibi. immo illi magis *parcendum* fuerat, qui *adhuc rudis et novellus erat*, et nullis ante peccantis. et propter peccatum suum morientis retrahebatur exemplo. tibi vero post tanta documenta, post legem, post prophetas, post Evangelis, post apostoles, *si delinquere volueris*, quomodo indulgeri possit, ignoro.

Exp. 182, 12–17

Omnia quae illis (children of Israel in the wilderness) contingerent, secundum facta quidem sua receperunt, sed tamen ideo scripta sunt, ne nos putemus impune peccare. *si* enim *adhuc parvolis et rudibus* non *pepercit*, quanto magis nobis, qui legem perfectionis accepimus, non parcit, *si talia fecerimus*.

The form of the argument is virtually the same in both, and many common words are present. Yet it is applied to two different Old Testament contexts, and there is not that extent of agreement that would make copying or "quotation" the most likely hypothesis for explaining the agreements. Rather it might well be the sort of argument that was part of one author's regular equipment and that could be brought out on more than one occasion and applied to more than one biblical incident.

10. Consider now two extended sections in Virg. and Dem. in which the theme treated is the same: Virginity is of no avail if that which is enjoined on *all* Christians is not also kept. The sections are too long to quote in full at once, and we shall consider smaller parts of them separately. The passages in question are as follows: Virg. 4 (228, 14)—6 (231, 7) and Dem. 9 (24, C) (nec ulli omnino)—10 (26, B) (. . . perfectio subsequatur).

(a) In both we have the injunction to keep the general commandment while also following the counsel of perfection, and this idea is expressed in grammatically parallel constructions.

Virg. 4 (229, 14): Cupiens divinum implere *consilium*, ante omnia *serva mandatum*.

Dem. 10 (25, A): Perfectionis igitur secuta *consilium*, beatitudinem specialis agressa propositi, *serva* generale *mandatum*.

In both cases the idea of following the *consilium* is expressed in a participial clause, followed by the main clause with the imperative of *servo*.

(b) In both, that which is commanded to all is *iustitia*, which is defined as a twofold requirement, to refrain from that which is forbidden and to execute those positive acts that are commanded.

Virg. 6 (230, 24—231, 1): Iustitia ergo non aluid est quam non peccare, non peccare autem est legis praecepta servare. praeceptorum autem observatio duplici genere custoditur, ut nihil eorum quae prohibentur facias, et cuncta quae iubentur implere contendas.

Dem. 9 (24, B): Prohibentur mala, praecipiuntur bona, conceduntur media, perfecta suadentur. in duobus illis quae priori loco sunt, peccatum omne concluditur; in utroque enim dei continetur imperium. et non solum praecipere, sed et prohibere ipsum, iubentis est. generaliter namque omnibus mandatur iustitia.

(c) In Virg. 4 (229, 6), *virginitas* is *supra mandatum vel praeceptum*, and in Dem. 10 (25, B) she who practices chastity is acting *supra legem* and *supra mandata*.

(b) In both, I Cor. 7:25 is used with the same intent, *viz*., to remind the reader that virginity is not required of a Christian but is undertaken as a vocation in addition to that which is required of all.

Virg. 4 (229, 6–9): supra mandatum vel praeceptum esse virginitatem sapiens ex lege nullus ignorat, Apostolo dicente: "de virginibus autem praeceptum Domini non habeo, consilium autem do."

Dem.9 (25, A): et apostolus de virginibus praeceptum quidem se dicit non habere domini, sed dat consilium.

In the latter case, the verse is not quoted, but the reference is clear.

(e) Virg. and Dem. both teach that reward awaits the virgin higher than that awaiting other Christians, and in both the noun *gloria* appears in relation to this distinction. In Virg. the distinction is further specified as between *vita aeterna* for Christians in general and *caeleste regnum* for virgins.

Virg. 4 (288, 19—229, 3): vitam ergo non habet nisi qui cuncta legis mandata servaverit, et qui vitam non habuerit, caelestis regni non potest esse possessor . . . nihil ergo virginitas sola proficiet, quae caelestis regni *gloriam* sperat, nisi et illud habuerit cui perpetua vita promittitur, per quam caelestis regni praemium possidetur.

Dem. 9 (24, C): . . . ut aut cum minori *gloria* concessis utamur, aut ob maius praemium etiam ea, quae nobis permissa sunt, respaumus . . . Maioris praemii amore flagrans, vovisti Deo non imperatam, sed laudatam virginitatem.

11. In Dem. and Virg. we find extended comparisons between the bride of Christ and a young lady of the world striving to please the young man to whom she is engaged.

Virg. 12 (241, 21—242, 9)

Quaecumque ergo humanorum sponsaliorum pigneribus subarratur, statim a domesticis, a familiaribus, ab amicis sponsi sollicite et diligenter requirit et servulis quales iuvenis habeat mores, quid potissimum diligat, quid accipiat, quo usu vivat, qua se consuetudine regat, quibus utatur dapibus, in quibus praecipue rebus delectetur et gaudeat, quae cum didicerit, ita se in omnibus temperat, ut sponsi moribus suum obsequium, sua iucunditas, sua diligentia, sua vita concordet. *et tu, quae Christum sponsum habes,* a domesticis et familiaribus eius sponsi tui mores interroga, et strenue ac sollerter inquire in quibus praecipue delectetur, qualem compositionem in te vestium diligat, cuiusmodi concupiscat ornatum.

Dem. 24 (38, B–D)

Saeculi vero virgines, quae se nuptiis praeparant, et indulgentiam magis Apostoli quam consilium sequi malunt, magisque amplectuntur incontinentiae remedium, quam praemium continentiae, ut sponsis placeant, eosque in amorem sui magis incitent, mira se sollicitudine formare student, et naturalem corporis pulchritudinem, ornandi arte commendant. haec est illis per dies singulos cura pracipua: decentibus fucis colorare faciem, implicare auto crinem, et ardentes concharum lapides, capitis honorem facere, suspendere ex auribus patrimonia, brachia ornare monilibus ac latera, et inclusas auro gemmas a collo in pectus demittere. *non minorem sponsus tuus requirit ornatum* . . .

. . . assume ergo omnem illum ornatum, per quem placere Christo potes.

There is of course considerable difference in detail between these two passages. In Dem. the girl's activity is entirely concerned with her personal adornment, while the bride-to-be in Virg. inquires in addition about such matters as what kind of food pleases her fiancé. But the form of the two discussions is quite similar.

(a) Quaecumque ergo humanorum sponsaliorum pignoribus subarratur (Virg.) = Saeculi vergo virgines quae se nuptiis praeparant (Dem.)

(b) Both have parallel but different accounts of the girl busying herself for the pleasure of her future husband.

(c) Et tu quae Christum sponsum habens, etc. (Virg.) = Non minorem sponsus tuus requirit ornatum, etc. (Dem.).

(d) After the quotation in (c) above, Dem. continues with an enumeration of those personal and spiritual ornaments pleasing to Christ. We do not have here such an enumeration in Virg., but in this treatise we do find immediately after the above passage two quotations from the New Testament: I Pet. 33:1–4, and I Tim. 2:9. These fairly lengthy quotations concern that very sort of replacement of jewelled ornaments by spiritual ornaments which are the subject of Pelagius' own remarks in Dem. The quotations from I Pet. and I Tim. in Virg. are then followed by discussion of the contrast between outer and inner adornment. This parallel between the "end-points," so to speak, of the two arguments is particularly striking in that the description of the activities of the worldly bride-to-be in Virg. is *not* centred on her personal apparel. In both passages we see a common progression of thought that begins with the "fiancées of the world" and ends with the substitution of spiritual ornaments for ornaments of gold, silver and pearls.

But Virg. does offer from an earlier part of the treatise a passage having precise verbal parallels with these lines in Dem. on spiritual and worldly ornaments. I should argue that a powerful suggestion of common authorship is forthcoming from the fact that close verbal parallels to the passage in Dem. are found in Virg. in a section which lies quite outside that in which the close parallel in progression of thought was discerned above, although there is clearly a general parallel in thought also between the passages to which we now turn attention. Ch. 10 of Virg.[28] is occupied with an exposition of the meaning of bodily holiness in the virgin. This exposition is accomplished by means of a series of imperative sentences exhorting the reader to cleanse various parts of the body to make way for appropriate virtues. The parts of the body included in this series are head, forehead, neck, eyes, tongue, ears, hands, and feet. That this chapter is concerned with the substitution of spiritual for worldly ornaments will be made clear from the following typical exhortation:

Virg. 10 (237, 20 ff.): Munda collum, ut non aurea reticula capillus portet et suspensa monilia, sed illa potius ornamenta circumferat, de quibus scriptura dicit: "misericordia et fides non deficiant a te" (Prov. 3:5, LXX). suspende autem illa in corde velut in collo tuo.

We shall now place in parallel columns the relevant lines from chapter 10 of Virg. with the lines from Dem. which immediately follow the passage quoted above.

Virg. 10 (237, 11—239, 2)	Dem. 24 (38, D)
Munda ab omni inquinamento caput, quia crimen est illud post *chrismatis* sanctificationem aut croci aut alterius cuiuslibet pigmenti suco vel pulvere sordidari, aut auro vel gemmis vel qualibet alia terrena specie comi, quod iam *caelestis ornatus splendore refulget* . . . Munda aures, ut *nonnisi sermonibus sanctis et veris auditum praebeant*, ut numquam obscena aut turpis aut saecularia verba suscipiant . . .	Satis pulchram Deo crede faciem tuam, si hominibus pulchra apparere non studeas. istud ornamentum serve capitis, quod acquisivisti *chrismatis* sacramento, cum tibi in coelestis regni mysterium, diadema quoddam regalis unctionis impositum est. Optima ornamenta sunt aurium, *verba Dei. Ad ea sola paratus esse debet auditus virginis;* eaque pretiotissimis lapidibus anteferre. omnia prorsus membra decorentur operibus sanctitatis; totaque virginalis animi pulchritudo, gemmati monilis instar, *vario virtutum fulgore resplendeat.*

Summary of above evidence:

(a) With reference to the adorning of the head, both make

specific reference to the inappropriateness of worldly jewellery after the sacraments of baptism, and both use the work *chrisma* in this connection.

(b) In Dem., *verba Dei* are the appropriate ornaments for ears, corresponding to the *sermonibus sanctis et veris* of Virg.

(c) *ut nonnisi sermonibus sanctis et veris* auditum *praebeant* (Virg.) = *ad ea sola paratus esse debet* auditus *virginis* (Dem.).

(d) The clause, *Omnia prorsus membra decorentur operibus sanctitatis* after the mentioning only of face, head and ears in Dem. is a summary parallel to the other members of the body specified in the whole of ch. 10 of Virg.

(e) The clause, *caelestis ornatus splendore refulget* (Virg.), represents the same idea and uses two of the same word roots as a clause found in the passage from Dem.: *vario virtutum fulgore resplendeat.*[29]

12. This item concerns the same general idea as the above, but the lines in question are from different sections of the letters.

Virg. 13 (243, 12 f.)	Dem. xvi, 30, A
Resplendeat (i.e., the virgin) auro iustitíae et gemmis refulgeat sanctitatis ac *pretiosissimo* pudicitiae *margarito* coruscet.	Remoremur hic, virgo, paulisper, et *pretiosissimas margaritas*, quibus exornanda est sponsa Christi, per singula Apostoli verba pensemus (i.e., the words of Phil. 2:41 f. quoted just before).

13. Pelagius twice in Exp. makes the point that the sacraments are given to all Christians equally. In one instance this is said in the course of the exegesis of I Cor. 11:21. The point here is that to go ahead and consume one's own food and drink is not in accord with the communal character of the sacrament.

Exp. 190, 22 ff.: . . . dominica cena omnibus debet esse communis, quia ille omnibus discipulis suis qui aderant aequaliter tradidit sacramenta.

In the other instance it is the Pauline statement, "For by one Spirit we were all baptized into one body—Jews or Greeks, slaves or free" (I Cor. 12:13) that is under discussion, and Pelagius in characteristic fashion makes the verse support his ascetic preoccupations.

Exp. 197, 17 ff.: quorum spiritalia communia sunt, hi debent et carnalia communiter possidere, secundum sententiam viri sapientis et sancti qui dixit quorum unus est deus idemque pater eorum nisi et possessio communis est iniqui sunt.

In the opening lines of Virg. we meet with the thought that the sacraments are the possession of all, this time by way of qualifying the notion that virgins have "something special over and above others" (*proprium aliquid prae ceteris habent*) and are themselves "as if holier and purer sacrifices."

Virg. 1 (225, 6–10): nam cum universa turba credentium paria gratiae dona percipiat et isdem omnes sacramentorum benedictionibus glorientur, istae proprium aliquid prae ceteris habent, cum de illo sancto et immaculato ecclesiae grege quasi sanctiores purioresque hostiae ... eliguntur.

Clearly the basic point that is made in the two passages from Exp. and that in Virg. are different. But one could see the matter as follows: In Exp. the giving of the sacraments to all directly supports the author's contention that worldly goods are to be shared equally; in Virg. the same author, in admitting a certain kind of *inequality* among Christians, asserts this inequality to be the case *although* the sacraments are given equally.

14. On Gal. 5:17, Pelagius' comment begins as follows:

Exp. 336, 5 f.: Haec facit ratio, ut *voluntatem non sequatur effectus.*

With no reference to the verse from Galatians, the author of Virg. uses an identical verbal formula in warning his reader against security in abstaining from sin in act only and not in thought.

Virg. 11 (240, 8–11): nolo existimes te crimen fugisse peccati, si *voluntatem non sequatur effectus,* cum scriptum sit; "quicumque viderit mulierem ad concupiscendam eam, iam moechatus est in corde suo (Matt. 5:28)."[30]

This parallel might well offer an example of the automatic repetition of a verbal formula by one and the same author in different contexts. Although the words fit appropriately enough into the context of the passage in Virg., there is in the surrounding lines no hint of Galatians 5 or of Romans 7.

15. In ch. 11 of Virg. we find some lines which, in a manner characteristic of Pelagius, link baptism and the church

together with moral considerations. There is a clear reference, without quoting, to Eph. 5:27, and by implication membership in the Church is made conditional on moral behaviour. We shall place these lines beside two passages from Pelagius. The first extract from Pelagius is from his comments on Eph. 4:4 f., and the second from his exegesis of Eph. 5:27, the text echoed but not quoted in the passage from Virg.

Virg. 11 (241, 8–12)
Quamquam enim nulli Christianorum *peccare liceat* et omnes quicumque spiritualis lavacri sanctificatione purgantur, immaculatam decurrere conveniat vitam, ut ecclesiae, quae sine macula, sine ruga, sine aliquo eiusmodi esse discribitur, possint visceribus intimari . . .

Exp. 363, 3–6 (on Eph. 4:4)
. . . potest hoc et contra illos dici qui sibi putant *licere peccare* et aliis non licere, cum et ipsi in unum corpus baptizati eundem spiritum acceperint. . . .

Exp. 378, 4 f. (On Eph. 5:27)
Si omnibus membris immaculata est (i.e., "ecclesia"), maculati in ea non esse censentur.

Summary of above evidence:

(a) Baptism is linked to the idea expressed, in both cases, by the words *licet peccare*.

(b) Eph. 5:27 is linked to the notion of moral criteria for membership in the Church. Perhaps it bears pointing out that this notion of moral criteria for membership in the Church is at least not explicitly suggested by the text of Eph. 5:27, itself. Pelagius' comments on the verse are typical of many other places in Exp. where moralistic preoccupations are imported into the commentary. The verse was apparently of some importance for Pelagius. Apart from the above, he refers to it at three other places —Exp. 128, 12; 484, 3; 515, 12. It is to be remembered also that his interpretation of this verse was at issue in one of the charges brought against him at Diospolis.[31]

16. In Virg. and Dem. occur passages in which it is momentarily suggested or admitted that the life of a Christian virgin is difficult. But in both works these remarks are followed by a reminder of the greatness of the heavenly *praemium*. The adjective *grandis* is common to the opening words of both passages.

Virg. 2 (226, 6–21)

Grande est enim et immortale, paene ultra naturam corpoream, sopire luxuriam et concupiscentiae flammam adolescentiae facibus accensam animi virtute restinguere . . . magnus quidem est pudicitiae *labor*, sed maius est *praemium*; temporalis custodia, sed remuneratio aeterna.

Dem. 27 (42, D)

Dicas forsiten: *grandis labor* est. sed respice quod promissum est . . . considera, quaeso, magnitudinem *praemii* tui, si tamen considerari potest quidquid immensum est . . . quid tanto remuneratore durum putabis, cuius tanta sunt *praemia* . . . quid enim dignum vel facere, vel pati possumus in brevi hoc tempore vitae nostrae, cum id immortalitate si compensandum.

17. At the beginning of ch. 9 of Virg. the author quotes some words from I Cor. 7:34 concerning the unmarried woman and her being holy "in body and spirit"—*ut sit sancta et corpore et spiritu.*[32] The next three chapters are then taken up with an exposition of the meaning of holiness in body and spirit. Chs. 9 and 10 concern bodily holiness and ch. 11 spiritual holiness.[33] This theme is obviously of considerable importance to the author of Virg. It is of great concern to him to say that a virgin must not pride herself on the bare fact of her virginity, but that all parts of her body must be free of worldly adornment and that she must seek purity of will and of mind.

A recurring thought in Pelagius is that moral qualities or virtues must be possessed in mind and body—*et mente et corpore.* If we look first at ch. 12 of Dem.[34] we find Pelagius there quoting I Cor. 7:32–34, the same passage from which Virg. quotes at the beginning of ch. 9. Some relevant lines which Pelagius writes after this quotation are as follows:

> Quae corpore et spiritu sancta est, nec in membris, nec in mente delinquit. . . . Quamvis enim virgo corpore, virgo sit spiritu; et nihilominus aut manibus, aut oculis, aut auribus, peccet, aut lingua, quomodo corpore sancta dicenda est?[35]

It is to be noticed first of all that when Pelagius begins to comment on the verse he uses the words *in mente* as an equivalent of the *spiritu* of the verse from I Cor. This we find also in Virg.:

> Illa est sancta tam corpore quam spiritu, quae nec *mente* nec corde delinquit.[36]

Then we see that Pelagius finds an immediate synonym for the *corpore* of the text in the word *membris*. The author of Virg. also uses this synonym. His immediate remark after quoting the scriptural verse is the following:

> Non dixit, ut sit *sancta membro* aut corpore tantum, sed ut sit sancta corpore et spiritu.[37]

But we discover also in the words above from Dem. that Pelagius in this connection has a brief enumeration of various "members" of the body in which it is possible for a virgin to sin—hands, eyes, ears, and tongue. Now this brief enumeration here, I should say, finds a parallel in the much more extended discussion noted earlier which runs through chs. 9 and 10 of Virg. In these two chapters, also after quoting I Cor. 7:34, the author exhorts to the cleansing of head, forehead, neck, eyes, tongue, ears, hands, and feet, and specifies appropriate virtues for each member of the body.

This concern for virtues which are possessed *et mente et corpore* meets us at many places in Pelagius' commentaries. When the author of I Tim., for example, says that a bishop ought to be sober and chaste,[38] Pelagius' only comment reads, *Et mente et corpore.*[39] And more examples could be cited.[40]

Of course other authors wrote in a similar vein. The point here has been to show that a persistent concern of Pelagius is reproduced in extended form in Virg., and that the section in Virg. shows parallels with Pelagius' own pattern of thought (the association of the virgin's sinning in various members of the body with I Cor. 7:34) and vocabulary.

17a. One of the theses in Pelagius' book of testimonies (called variously *Liber Eclogarum*, *Liber Capitulorum* and *Liber Testimoniorum*)[40a] asserts that a Christian ought gladly to give up his possessions to anyone who would rob him of them. With striking parallels a similar point is made in Virg.

Virg. 7 (233, 17)	Lib. Ecl. (in Jerome, *Dialogus adversus Pelagianos* 1.29)
. . . *ut si quis* tua *auferre voluerit, gratanter amittas* . . .	Christianum illius debere esse patientiae, *ut si quis auferre voluerit, gratanter amittat.*

18. Cel. and Dem. identify *iustitia* as consisting in the observance of the twofold commandment enjoined upon all Christians in quite similar ways.

Cel. 5 (333, 11–15)

Duo autem sunt genera mandatorum, in quibus clauditur toto iustitia. prohibendi unum est, iubendi alterum. ut enim mala *prohibentur*, ita *praecipiuntur* bona. ibi otium imperatur, hic studium. ibi coercetur animus, hic incitatur. hic fecisse, hic non fecisse, culpabile est.

Dem. 9 (24, B)

Prohibentur mala, *praecipiuntur* bona, conceduntur media, perfecta suadentur. in duobus illis quae priori loco sunt peccatum omne concluditur. in utroque enim Dei continetur imperium. et non solum *praecipere*, sed et *prohibere* ipsum, iubentis est. generaliter namque omnibus mandatur iustitia.

The one important difference between these two passages can be accounted for by the different circumstances of the respective persons to whom the letters are addressed. Dem. is written to a recently professed virgin, which makes it appropriate that Pelagius should mention those *media*, e.g., marriage, which are permitted, and those *perfecta*, e.g., virginity, which are subjects of *persuasio*. Cel., on the other hand, is addressed to a married woman who by excess of zeal has taken to renouncing the marriage bed without the consent of her husband. The author of Cel., while stating clearly that sexual abstinence is *magni . . . animi signum et perfectae virtutis indicium*, is upset by the woman's action in this regard and cautions her against it.[41] Understandably he does not here raise the subject of the *media* and the *perfecta*.

19. The twofold commandment is defined in closely parallel terms.

Cel. 5 (333, 20 f.)

Hoc itaque *duplex* diversumque praeceptum, *prohibendi* scilicet et *imperandi*, aequo omnibus iure mandatum est.

Dem. 15 (29, D)

. . . lex Dei *duplici* mandatorum genere distincta sit, et mala *prohibens*, bona *imperet*, atque ab utraque parte contemptum sui vetet.

20. There are moreover, no exceptions to this general requirement either for *virgin*, *widow*, or *married* woman.

Cel. 5 (333, 20–24)

Hoc itaque duplex diversumque praeceptum . . . aequo omnibus

Dem. 10 (25, A–B)

. . . serva generale mandatum. dixi, idemque nunc repeto; in iure mandatum est. non *virgo*, non *vidva*, non *nupta* ab hoc imperio liberata est. in quovis proposito, in quovis *gradu aequale* peccatum est vel prohibita admittere vel iussa non facere.

causa iustitiae unum debemus. *virgo*, *vidva*, *nupta*, summus, medius et imus *gradus aequaliter* iubentur implere praecepta.[42]

21. Dem. and Cel. both use the image of the mirror in similar but not the same contexts. In Cel. the specific text Mt. 7:12 (quoted before the passage set out below) is to be the mirror for all of the woman's actions, while in the letter of Pelagius it is the reading of Scripture in general that is to provide such a mirror.

Cel. 15 (341, 19–23)
Ad omnem igitur actum, ad omne verbum, ad omnem etiam cogitatum haec sententia (i.e., Mt. 7:12) retractetur, quae tibi quasi speculum quoddam paratum et ad manum semper positum qualitatum tuae voluntatis ostendat atque etiam vel de iniusto opere coarguat vel de iusto laetificet.

Dem. 23 (37, C)
Optime uteris lectione divina, si eam tibi adhibeas speculi vice, ut ibi velut ad imaginem suam anima respiciat, et vel foeda quaeque corrigat vel pulchra plus ornet.[43]

In addition to the general similarity provided by the image, there is a closer structural similarity to be observed, although the vocabulary does not correspond: the clause *atque etiam vel de iniusto opere coarguat vel de iusto laetificet* (Cel.) is equivalent to the clause *et vel foeda quaeque corrigat vel pulchra plus ornet* (Dem.).

22. Close parallels in vocabulary are to be found in two passages in which human complaint at the severity of the divine law is depicted.

Cel. 15 (341, 26—342, 5)
En totum illud *arduum* divinae legis totumque difficile, en ob quam *dura* imperia domino *reclamamus et dicemus* nos vel difficultate vel impossibilitate mandatorum premi. nec sufficit, quod iussa non facimus, nisi etiam iubentem iniustum pronuntiemus,

Dem. 16 (30, C)
. . . in os domini *reclamamus et dicimus: Durum* est, *arduum* est, non possimus, homines sumus, fragile carne circumdamur. o caecam insaniam! o profanam temeritatem! duplici ignorantia accusamus deum scientiae, ut videatur nescire quod fecit, nescire

dum ipsum aequitatis auctorem non modo *dura* et *ardua,* sed *impossibilia* etiam *praecepisse conquerimur.*

quod iussit; quasi oblitus fragilitatis humanae, cuius auctor ipse est, imposuerit homini mandata quae ferre non possit. simulque (proh nefas!) ascribimus iniquitatem iusto, pio crudelitatem. dum eum primo *impossibile* aliquid *praecepisse conquerimur* . . .[44]

We have here a most striking case of two passages that contain identical turns of phrase but that do not suggest copying of one author by another.

23. Chapter 4 of Dem. contains a passage of some forty lines in which the subject of the internal judgment of conscience is treated at some length. At the end of ch. 14 of Cel. we find in a few lines a much briefer treatment of the same subject. The difference in size between these two passages and the diffusion over many more lines of the points of contact in the longer passage add to the interest and impressiveness of the parallels that emerge. These are as follows:

(a) In Cel. we find the phrase *secreto animi iudicio*[45] in reference to that internal court by which man is judged, while Dem. speaks of the *animae nostrae secreta*[46] and the *secreta mentis poena.*[47]

(b) Both passages use the same present participle to refer essentially to the same thing—the "concealment" of guilt known only to conscience.

(i) Cel. 14 (341, 17 f.): . . . latentem *hominum conscientiam secreto animi iudicio aut absolvit aut damnat.*

(ii) Dem. 4 (19, B): . . . *et* latentem *reum, secreta mentis poena persequitur.*

(c) Both use similar but not identical verb patterns to indicate that the verdict of conscience can be favourable or unfavourable, and in both cases this verb combination comes at a concluding point in the discussion.

(i) Cel. 14 (341, 17 f.): . . . *et latentem hominum conscientiam secreto animi iudicio* aut absolvit aut damnat.

(ii) Dem. 4 (19, C): . . . *ipsis nos cogitationibus fidelissimis et integerrimis sane testibus* aut arguit aut defendit.

24. Both Pelagius' letter to Demetrias and Cel. exhort their respective readers to refrain from the sin of defaming other people. Among other parallels of expression we find in these passages almost exact verbal agreement running to two clauses.

Cel. 16 (342, 18—344, 4)

Ac semper *scripturae memor esto* dicentis, "Noli diligere detrahere, ne eradiceris (Prov. 20:13)." pauci admodum sunt, qui *huic vitio* renuntient, rarumque invenias, qui ita inreprehensibilem suam vitam exhibere velit, ut is non libenter reprehendat alienam ... Tu vero ita hoc malum ita effuge, ut *non modo ipsa non detrahas, se ne alii quidem detrahenti aliquando credas* nec obtractatori auctoritatem de consensu tuo tribuas eiusque vitium nutrias *annuendo*. "*Noli,*" inquit scriptura, "*consentaneus esse cum derogantibus adversum proximum tuum et non accipias super illum peccatum* (Lev. 9:18);" *et alibi*, "*Sepi aures tuas spinis et noli audire linguam nequam* (Eccli. 28:28)" ... est sane *hoc vitium*, quod vel in primis extingui debeat et ab his, qui se sancte instituere volunt, prorsus excludi ... quodsi esset in nobis haec diligentia, ne passim obtrectatoribus credemus, iam omnes detrahere timerent, ne non tam alios quam se ipsos *viles* detrahendo *facerent*.

Dem. 19 (33, D)

Numquam detractio ex ore virginis procedat. Villium satis hominum est, et suam laudem quaerentium, alios *viles facere;* quia alterius vituperatione se laudari putant, et qui suo merito placere non possunt, placere volunt in comparatione peiorum. parum diximus, *non solum ipsa non detrahas, sed ne detrahenti quidem aliquando credas*. pessimum est *hoc vitium*, quod alterum *vilem facit* videri. non minus auribus quam lingua fugias detractionem. *scripturae memor esto*, quae dicit, "*Non eris consentaneus derogantibus adversus proximum tuum, et non accipies super illo peccatum* (Lev. 9:18)." *et alibi*, "*Sepi aures tuas spinis, et noli audire linguam nequam* (Eccli. 28:28." accusator est enim auditor, qui facit detractorem, qui se avertat aures, et vultum contrahat ac oculos abnuendo contineat, male loquentem etiam tacens arguit, ut discat non libenter dicere, quod didicerit non libenter audiri.

Summary of above evidence:

(a) *non modo ipsa non detrahas, sed ne alii quidem detrahenti aliquando credas* (Cel.) = *non solum ipsa non detrahas, sed ne detrahenti quidem aliquando credas* (Dem.).

(b) Both quote Lev. 9:18 and Eccli. 28:28 (LXX) in immediate succession and separated by the words *et alibi*.

(c) Both speak of the sin of defaming as *hoc vitium.*

(d) *viles ... facerent* (Cel.) = *viles facere* and *vilem facit* (Dem.).

(e) The injunction in Cel. not to nourish the defamer's sin, using the ablative gerund *annuendo*, is a kind of parallel to the exhortation in Dem. to positive discouragement, using the ablative gerund *abnuendo*.

(f) Identical formulae occur—*scripturae memor esto*—but introducing different scriptural texts.

25. In ch. 20 the author of Cel. takes up the theme of true Christian humility, which is also the subject of ch. 20 of Dem. There is much common thought between these two chapters. Both give mention of hypocritical movements and poses of the body which simulate humility but hide pride and arrogance.[48] Common to both is the assertion that no virtue is more acceptable to God than true humility.[49] There occurs also the following close parallel in expression.

Cel. 20 (346, 22 ff.)	Dem. 20 (34, C–D)
Aliud est enim virtutem habere, aliud virtutis *similitudinem*; aliud est rerum *umbram sequi*, aliud *veritatem*.	Quam multi . . . . fallaci ac pessima decepti *similitudine*, vitiis pro virtutibus gloriantur . . . multi enim huius virtutis *umbram*, *veritatem* eius *sequuntur* pauci.

26. The true nobility of Christians as against false standards of high birth and wealth is the common theme of ch. 21 of Cel. and part of ch. 22 of Pelagius' letter to the young noble virgin. Identical sentiments are expressed, and there is noticeable common vocabulary.

Cel. 21 (347, 4–8)	Dem. 22 (36, C–D)
Nescit religio nostra personas nec condiciones hominum sed animos inspicit, servum et nobilem de *moribus* pronuntiat. sola apud Deum libertas est non *servire peccatis*, summa apud eum nobilitas *clarum* esse virtutibus.	Nobilitatis ad hoc tantum, memineris, ut cum claritate generis, *morum* sanctitate contendas; et cum nobilitate corporis, animi virtute nobilior proficias . . . ille *clarus*, ille sublimis, ille sit nobilis, ille tunc integram nobilitatem suam servare se putet, si dedignetur *servire vitiis*, ab eisque non superari.

27. Both Cel. and Pelagius' letter devote attention to the theme, highly typical of Pelagius, that Christians are not to pick and choose among Christian precepts with a view to

deciding which ones they wish to obey, but are rather to consider the majesty and authority of Him who is the author of *all* the commandments. Pelagius' letter to Demetrias elaborates the theme with a comparison: the more powerful are earthly lords, the more ready are slaves to obey them; therefore should we be most eager to obey that most powerful of all lords.[50]

Cel. 5 (333, 24—334, 2)

Neque vero eorum te seducat error, qui *ex arbitrio suo* eligunt, quae potissimum dei mandata *contemnant* quaeve quasi *vilia ac parva* despiciant, nec metuunt, ne secundum divinam sententiam minima contemnendo paulatim decidant.

Cel. 6 (334, 9–13)

Et sane nescio, an possimus leve aliquod peccatum dicere, quod in dei *contemptum* admittitur. estque ille prudentissimus, qui non tam considerat, quid issum sit, quam illum, qui iusserit, nec quantitatem imperii, sed *imperantis cogitat dignitatem.*

Dem. 16 (30, A–B)

Non enim quasi *ad arbitrium nostrum* quaedam ex mandatis dei debemus *eligere,* sed generaliter universa complere. nec aliqua praecepta eius quasi *vilia* minuscula *ac parva contemnere,* sed *imperantis* in omnibus *maiestatem* aspicere. nullum quippe mandatum dei *contemptibile* nobis videri potest, si eius semper *cogitemus* auctorem, sine murmuratione et haesitatione . . . quantoque potentiores domini, tanto servi ad obedientiam proniores sunt . . . et non solum bene merituros esse se credunt, si iussa fecerint, sed tamquam iam meruissent quod iussi sunt, ita pro *dignitate praecipientis* servitium beneficii loco ducitur.

28. A section in Cel. on the Two Ways occupies a space equivalent to one half of a Migne column. In Pelagius' letter to Demetrias we find two sentences devoted to the Two Ways, occupying three lines of one Migne column. Here again we have a case of striking agreements in expression between a short passage and points scattered over a much longer passage.

Cel. 10 (337, 7–22)

Illa (i.e., via) ad vitam, haec tendit ad mortem, illa celebratur et *teritur* a multis, haec vix invenitur a paucis . . . haec (i.e., the narrow way) vero insueto *calle* virtutum tristior atque horridior ab his tantum eligitur, quibus non tam delectatio itineris

Dem. 10 (26, A)

Fugienda tibi lata illa via est, quam multorum ad mortem euntium *comitatus terit.* et ad vitam aeternam, *angusti* illius *itineris,* quod pauci reperiunt, *callis* tendendus est.

cordi est quam utilitas mansionis . . . si cum paucis *angustum iter* et subtilem quandam semitam invenimus, ad vitam tendimus; sin vero multorum *comitamur* viam, secundum domini sententiam imus ad mortem.

The common use of the verb *tero* and of the root *comit-* are particularly notable, as well as the appearance of *angustum iter*.

29. The final pair of parallel passages to be noted between the letter to Celantia and the works of Pelagius has for its subject matter the avoidance of flatterers and flattery.

Cel. 17 (344, 6–23)

Adulatorum quoque assentationes et noxia blandimenta fallaciae velut quasdam pestes animae fuge. nihil est, quod tam facile corrumpat mentes hominum, nihil, quod tam *dulci et molli vulnere* animum feriat . . . in multis *isto maxime tempore regnat hoc vitium*, quodque gravissimum est, humilitatis ac benivolentiae loco ducitur. eo fit, ut iam, qui adulari nescit, aut invidus aut superbus putetur. et sane grande et persubtile artificum laudare alterum in commendatione sui et decipiendo animum sibi obligare decepti, quodque hoc maxime vitio agi solet, *fictas laudes* certo pretio vendere. quae autem haec tanta est *levitas animi*, quae tanta vanitas relicta propria *conscientia* alienam *opinionem* sequi et quidem fictam atque simultatam, rapi vento falsae laudationis, gaudere ad circumventionem suam et illusionem pro beneficio accipere?

Dem. 21 (35, B–D)

Adulatores ut inimicos cave, quorum sermones super oleum molles, et ipsi sunt iacula. corrumpunt *fictis laudibus leves animas* et male credulis mentibus *blandum vulnus infligunt*. crevit *hoc in nostra aetate vitium*, et in ultimo fine stetit, nec iam augeri potest. in hanc omnes nos scholam studiumque dedimus, ut officium putemus illudere. quodque ipsi ab aliis libenter accipimus, id aliis quasi quoddam munus offerimus. et spe recipiendae laudis, eos a quibus laudari volumus, ante laudamus. saepe adulantium resistimus verbis ad faciem, et in secreto mentis favemus, maximumque fructum cepisse nos ducimus, si vel *fictis laudibus* praedicamur . . . unde eo perducta res est, ut, neglecta veritate meriti, de sola *opinione* curemus, qui testimonium vitae nostrae, non a *conscientia* nostra, sed a fama petimus. Conscientiam tuam, quae certe deo semper patet, in multitudine versari puta.

Summary of above evidence:

(a) *fictas laudes* (Cel.) = *fictis laudibus* (twice—Dem.).

(b) With respect to the very same idea both passages have an example of oxymoron: *dulci et molli vulnere* (Cel.) = *blandum vulnus* (Dem.).

(c) Both make the remark, in different words, that *hoc vitium* has become particularly prevalent recently: *in multis isto maxime tempore regnat* hoc vitium (Cel.) = *crevit* hoc *in nostra aetate* vitium (Dem.).

(d) Both contrast the currying of *opinio* with the deliverances of *conscientia*.

(e) *leves animas* (Cel.) = *levitas animi* (Dem.).

30. One of the most striking of all the parallels to be found between De Lege and Pelagius' works has apparently escaped Plinval unnoticed. About one third of the way through ch. 7 the author of De Lege begins the familiar Pelagian theme that *all* of the commandments of God are intended for *all* Christians. There are, to be sure, many heavenly mansions, but these many mansions will separate those who have achieved *differing grades of righteousness*, not sinners from the righteous. In the course of the remarks the author makes a clear reference, without quoting, to I Cor. 15:41. In Pelagius' comments on this same verse we find thought identical with that expressed in De Lege and some identical vocabulary.

De Lege 7 (113, A–B)

Scimus quidem multas esse apud patrem in coelestibus mansiones. sed mansionum iustitia *iustiores* mansiones *differre*; sicut et stellam stella dixit apostolus, esse clariorem. sed stellam cum stella, non lapidem comparavit; quia terrenus lapis inter coelestes stellas esse non poterat; sicut nec peccator inter iustos in regno coelorum. sed sunt quidam *gradus gloriae* inter iustos in coelo, sicut et inter peccatores gradus *poenae.*

Exp. 223, 5–8 (on I Cor. 15:41 f.)

Stellarum diversitati *iustorum differentiam* comparavit (i.e., Paul), quos *gradus* virtutum, non peccata, *in gloria* facientes sed diversos; nam peccatorum diversitas in coelo non erit, sed *in poena.*

Summary of above evidence:

(a) *iustiores mansiones differre* (De Lege) = *iustorum differentiam* (Exp.).

(b) *gradus gloriae* (De Lege) = *gradus . . . in gloria* (Exp.).
(c) *inter peccatores gradus poenae* (De Lege) = *peccatorum diversitas . . . in poena* (Exp.).
(d) In both the point is made that the difference in glory among the stars in the Pauline text really refers to the future differences in grade among the righteous in heaven.
(e) In both the especial point is clear that there are no sinners in heaven.[51]

We find I Cor. 15:41 f. quoted also in Pelagius' letter to Demetrias. Immediately before the quotation, Pelagius has been exhorting Demetrias to spurn the example of wicked people and to turn her thoughts to the future reward and the heavenly state of the just. This thought apparently brings to mind the brightness of the stars referred to in the Pauline text, which Pelagius then quotes. On citing the passage from Paul, however, Pelagius leaves the theme he has been discussing and immediately turns to the notion of the future disparity in reward among the righteous. It is clear that the text was important for Pelagius in supporting this notion of which he was so fond. The quoted lines below begin immediately after Pelagius' quotation of I Cor. 15:41 f.

Dem. 17 (31, C): Dispares sunt in regno coelorum per singulorum merita mansiones. diversitas enim operum, diversitatem facit praemiorum; quantumque aliquis hic in sancitate fulserit, tantum ibi fulgebit in honore.

Apart from the relation of this characteristic theme to the text from I Cor., we notice that the language of Pelagius' comments here includes what is certainly a reference to the "many mansions" of John 14:2 (*dispares . . . mansiones.*). On referring back to the quotation from De Lege we notice that reference to the same text is included there also (*scimus . . . multas . . . mansiones*). The one passage in De Lege, therefore, is related differently to two passages in separate works of Pelagius, a fact that immediately arrests attention.

31. De Lege and Dem. both tell us, with some identical vocabulary, that knowing the divine law necessarily precedes doing it.

De Lege 4 (108, D)

Ne qui forte existimet nos contra apostolum, doctorem legis praeferre factori, suo ordine respondebimus, oportere *prius* nosse quid iussum sit, quidve prohibitum, et scientes utrumque servemus; alioqiun ante scientam mandati *impossibile est* nosse quid fiat.

Dem. 9 (24, A)

Impossibile est enim ei quemque placere, cui quid placeat, ignorat. fierique potest, ut etiam obsequendi voto offendat, cui quomodo obsequi debeat, ante non didicit. et ut maius est, voluntatem domini facere quam nosse; ita *prius* est *nosse* quam facere.

In addition to the more obvious parallels in expression and thought, we note that in Dem. the point is made explicitly, and in De Lege implicitly, that doing the law *is* greater than knowing it.[52]

32. De Lege presents us with some lines on a theme highly typical of Pelagius—the fleeting character of this world and the futility of becoming enmeshed in its cares. A point is made that is identical with a point in a similar passage in Dem.—anything that comes to an end is not worth our striving to possess. Parallels in vocabulary and in construction are present, though in a way which does not, I submit, suggest the copying of one author by another. The passages are different in their vasic form. In De Lege the author describes the typical hectic behaviour of a man who is suddenly visited with some slight indisposition and who is prepared to make great sacrifices for the restoration of the health of his body, whereas everyone is neglectful of his eternal well being. In Dem. Pelagius is concerned to urge his reader that riches and public honours be despised in favour of an eternal reward which will not pass away.

De Lege 8 (114, A)

Curritur ad medicos, et pro remedio carnali promittuntur munera, aurum, argentum; interdum etiam mancipia traduntur, et pene totum patrimonium aut negligitur aut donatur, ut consulatur vitae *quandoque periturae*; et *pro aeterna salute* omnis admodum homo negligens est, omnis avarus . . . nemo ad brevitatem temporis,

Dem. 29 (43, B)

Respuantur honores, despiciantur divitiae. ipsa quoque vita nostra martyrii amore contemnatur. et haec omnia etiam si *pro aeternitatis praemio* non darentur, essent tamen *quandoque peritura* . . . quid porro non breve et incertum, et causi non serviens? quale istud bonum est, quod semper timeas amittere? . . . et, si vita nostra nemo ad naturae respicit conditionem, nemo considerat, nemo retractat vana esse omnia, *quae aliquo fine* clauduntun.

tendatur per mille annos ... quale hoc, quaeso, diu est, *quod fine deletur*.[53]

33. As does Pelagius' letter to Demetrias, so De Lege contains a vivid account of the coming of the Lord and the cataclysms of the last day. We have here a splendid example of the appearance of one or two features bearing important similarity to a passage in Pelagius but which do not give the impression of having been copied from Pelagius. The entire account of the last day in De Lege possesses a literary vigour not at all unequal to that of Pelagius and is far from giving the appearance of patchwork. If it had been another author using Pelagius, one would have expected more extensive use than the small but telling similarities indicate.[54] We quote only a small part of the discussion in each case.

De Lege 7 (113, C)

... pavemus, contremiscimus, et proni ad terram, deposita superbia, cervices submittimus. *quid faciemus* in illa die miseri, quando revoluto coelo cum angelicis virtutibus, igneus Dominus totus adveniet, quando cadentibus desuper stellis, sol in tenebras, et in sanguinem luna mutabitur, ... quando peccatores dicent montibus, "*Cadite super nos, et collibus, tegite nos?* (Luke 23:30)."

Dem. 30 (44, B–C)

Si ita mortalis timemus hostis humanam manum, *quid faciemus* cum clangore terribili tuba intonare de caelo coeperit et ad illam archangeli vocem omni buccina clariorem, totus simul remugiet mundus? cum viderimus super nos non manufacta arma concuti, sed et virtutes coelorum commoveri ... "Tunc," inquit (i.e., Dominus), "plangent super se omnes tribus terrae, et videbunt filium hominis renientem in nubibus coeli cum virtute multa et maiestate (Mt. 24:30)." *Cadite super nos; et collibus*, Operite nos' (Luke 23:30).[55]

34. After the vigorous lines on the cataclysms of the last times, the author of De Lege warns his reader not to regard the biblical accounts of the terrible judgment awaiting sinners as having been written only to excite fear and not as pointing to things that will really happen. We are to consider the divine judgment made known in the flood, on the Sodomites, on the Egyptians, and on the inhabitants of Jerusalem; thus we are to

gauge the future by the past. We find Pelagius saying strikingly similar things in two places in the Expositions as he comments on two similar verses which speak of the coming of the wrath of God—Eph. 5:6 and Col. 3:6.

De Lege 8 (113, D)
Verum ne ex suggestione diaboli haec (i.e., the violent events and the judgment of the last times) ad terrorem, non ad veritatem dicta credentur, *de praeteritis futura probantur*, quando talia *in diluvio*, *in Sodomis*, in Aegypto, in Ierosolymis saepe ob delicta hominum facta referuntur.

Exp. 374, 7 ff. (on Eph. 5:6)
Ex praeteritis futura cognoscite; si *Sodomitis* pepercit et his qui *in diluvio* perierunt, parcet et vobis.

Exp. 465, 4 f. (on Col. 3:6)
Super *Sodoma* et eos qui *in diluvio* perierunt; *ex praeteritis ergo exemplis futura timenda sunt.*

There are further interesting parallels in thought between De Lege and Pelagius' writing which do not, however, contain close similarities in expression and are therefore not of decisive value as evidence for Pelagius as author. So long as we have found close verbal parallels in some instances, however, such parallels in thought can only tend to strengthen the case, and certainly do not weaken it. The most interesting of these are as follows:

(1) De Lege 8 (114, A) and Exp. 42, 9–18, on human willingness to endure much for the sake of bodily health but not for the sake of eternal salvation.

(2) De Lege 6 (111, D) and Exp. 392, 13—393, 1, on the apostles' zeal in suffering for the faith and our lack of the same.

(3) De Lege 4 (109, B) and Dem. 9 (24, B), on the whole meaning of sin as included in disobedience to the two-fold commandment.

(4) De Lege 5 (110, A) and Dem. 16 (30, B), on not despising even the smallest of the divine commandments, out of respect for the person of Him who commands.

Chapter III

VOCABULARY

Simplicity and directness characterize the prose of Pelagius. There are few rare words, and with the exception of some passages in the letter to Demetrias there is little by way of *color poeticus*. The words listed below are largely ordinary words, and each has been selected for attention for one or more of the following reasons: (a) noticeable frequency of occurrence in the assured writings; (b) use in a particular way, e.g., in conjunction with a certain other word or words; (c) use of a common word to the exclusion or near exclusion of equally common synonymous words; (d) correction of published misinformation concerning the usage of Pelagius. An asterisk beside a word indicates that Souter has already called attention to it and that further examples culled from the Pauline commentary may be found in the word list on pp. 93–115 in Vol. I of his edition. In the case of several such words I have called attention to peculiarites not noted by Souter.

*ADSUMO, -ERE. Pelagius often makes brief mention of the Incarnation using this verb, almost always with the appropriate form of *homo* as direct object.[1] Exp. 70, 6 *secundum -pti hominis loquitur formam, qui mortuus est atque resurrexit;* 138, 14 f. *et perfectam -pti hominis naturam destruat.*

Virg. 3 (327, 5) *dominus et salvator noster Deus cum propter humani generis salutem hominem dignaretur -ere.* De Lege 1 (105, D) *dominum et dei verbum descendisse de coelis, ut -pto naturae nostrae homine, humanum genus . . . erigeretur in Christo.*

*ANTE. This form of the adverb is much more frequent than *antea* in Pelagius.[2] *Ante* is found in Virg. 7 (234, 3) and in Cel. 18 (34, 5, 9) . . . *Antea* does not occur in the four works in question.

*ALIQUANTI, -AE, -A, used instead of *aliqui*, and usually in contrast to *omnes*. Exp. 86, 7 *sicut ergo tunc omnes perierunt, ita et nunc -i salvantur;* 69, 21 (on Rom. 8:32 *sed pro nobis omnibus tradidit illum*) *non pro -is.*

Vita 1 (1033) *non -i, sicut sub lege prius fuerat, sed omnes in prophetis et sacerdotibus unguntur et regibus.*

*ARGUO, -ERE, a frequent verb in Pelagius, used almost always with a personal direct object without accompanying genitive or ablative.[3] Exp. 86, 19 *a salvatore -untur culiem liquantes.*[4] Dem. 19 (34, A) *male loquentem etiam tacens -it.*

De Lege 6 (111, C) *stulti et inutiles et tenuis fidei*[5] *-untur.*

*AUCTORITAS, -TIS. Souter was right in calling attention to Pelagius' frequent use of this word but was inaccurate in stating that it occurs "usually with reference to St. Paul's apostolic authority." For cases in which it does have this reference, see Exp. 128, 1; 151, 16; 231, 8 and 15; 474, 2; C. Apoll. 333, 1. But in the following it does not: Exp. 6, 19; 107, 4; 108, 21; 126, 2; 271, 19; 276, 4; 277, 12; 290, 2; 306, 9.

Virg. 1 (225, 19) *Christi sponsas virgines dicere ecclesiastica nobis permittit —;* 17 (248, 93) *absentium obtrectatores quasi malignos scripturae -e deterre.* Cel. 28 (352, 7) *cum hic apostolica omnino interdicat —.*

*BAPTISMUM, -I. Pelagius only three times uses the a-stem, *baptisma, -atis.*[6] In addition to the examples of the o-stem in Souter, there is the following in Dem: 19 (33, A). It is the o-stem that we find four times in Vita 13 (1043 *tris* and 1044) and once in De Lege 2 (107, B). The a-stem occurs once in Vita 1 (1033).

MIHI BLANDIOR, -IRI. Pelagius' use of this verb has interesting parallels in the four works under examination. He does not use it often; only four instances have been counted. In all of these it is false boasting which brings guilt before God, that is in question. In the case of two of them there is a clear reference in the surrounding text to the judgment of God or to man's condemnation because of boasting falsely based, and in one of these the idea is that we are not to think that because the judgment of God has not yet descended we may sin with impunity, an idea present also in one of the instances from Vita. Exp. 19, 22 f. *aut numquit propterea tibi de impunitate -ris, quia semper in praesenti non reddidit . . . et putas iam non esse iudicium?*[7] Dem. 15 (29, D) *et -mur nobis si malis fructibus non gravemur qui damnandi sumus, si a bonis steriles manserimus.*

Vita 3 (1034) *nemo ergo sibi ideo -atur, nemo se stulta et vana suspicione decipiat, quod super peccatores confestim Dei ira iudiciumque non veniat;* 6 (1036) *nec in hoc nobis nomine tantum, quod Christiani dicimur, -amur, sed propter hoc etiam nos iudicandos credamus.* Virg. 7 (232, 23) *nolo enim tibi in hoc -aris, si aliqua non feceris, quia aliqua feceris, cum scriptum sit: "qui universam legem servaverit, offendat autem in uno, factus est omnium reus."*[8] *Adam enim semel paccavit et mortuus est;* 8 (234, 8) *an tibi de virginitatis praerogativa -ris? memento Adam et Evam virgines deliquisse.* Cel. 32 (355, 28) *beati sunt qui . . . ita illum speculantur diem* (i.e., judgment day), *ut se ad eum cotidie praeparent, qui non de praeterita sibi iustitia -entes. . . .* De Lege 4 (109, C) *non nobis -ri debemus in factis iussorum, si in prohibitorum transgressionem peccemus, cum transgressionis crimen benefacti meritum tollat.*[9]

A further close parallel is to be seen in the following. Dem. 22 (27, A) *non est quod sibi aliquis de nobilitate generis -atur.* Virg. 16 (246, 10) *quid tibi, o stulta, in generis nobilitate -ris et complaces.*

*BREVITER, with *quidem* and *plene*. Dem. 9 (24, C) *mandatur iustitia, quam salvator in evangelio—quidem sed plenissime comprehendens.* Epist. ad Innoc. (in Aug. de grat. ch. 36, 39)—*quidem sed plane*[10] *libero hominis arbitrio dei gratiam . . . coniunxi.*

Virg. 11 (239, 18) *quid sit sanctam esse corpore—quidem sed plene exposuisse me arbitror.*

*CAUSA, -AE. This word is very frequent in Pelagius and characteristically has the meaning "subject," "matter," "case." Note the parallels below in the use of the word with *talis* and with *dumtaxat*. Exp. 107, 20 *unus quisque id faciat in tali -a dumtaxat quod melius iudicarit;* 109, 1 . . . *aliquit . . . in talibus -is* *arbitratur immundum;* 426, 1 *in hac -a dumtaxat.* Dem. 10 (25, A) *in -a iustituae omnes unum debemus;* 12 (27, C) *delinquere autem non in -a castitatis tantum esse potest.*

Vita 7 (1037) *de cuius -a nunc dicendum non est.* Virg. 6 (230, 20) *-a de qua agimus talis est;* 6 (231, 14) *nec aliquod eis in his . . . -is praebemus auxilium.* Cel. 1 (329, 9) *mihi tamen nescio quomodo in praesenti -a propius innotuit;* 28 (352, 7) *in hac dumtaxat -a;* 28 (352, 9) *in tali -a;* 28 (352, 21 f.) *super hac -a;* 28 (352, 28) *in hac -a;* 29 (353, 2) *totamque hanc -am a sui principio retractemus.* De Lege 1 (105, C) *si me non et tempus et -a simulque tuerentur et caritas;* 6 (112, C) *talis -a est virginum de evangelio quinque stultarum;* 8 (114, D) *aptum huic -ae quaeremus exemplum;* 10 (116, B) *et qualiter de iuramenti -a brevi sermone satisfactum est.*

*COMPREHENDO, -ERE, used characteristically to mean "I include" or "I sum up." Pelagius is fond of saying that all instances of a general category are "included" under one heading or in one sentence, or that members of a series are "summed up" in a single item. The adverb *breviter* often modifies the verb, to which cf. *brevis* in the example from Cel. below. It will be noticed further that Pelagius in Dem. says that the Lord "sums up" the meaning of *iustitia* in Mt. 7:12, an idea, in relation to the same scripture text, reproduced in the quotation from Cel. Exp. 368, 1 *omnia crimina totius immunditiae et avaritiae nomine -it;* 413, 6 *ad extremum, ut omnia breviter -am.* Dem. 10 (26, D) *considera, quaeso, quantum a consilio distet imperium. ibi aliquos excipit; hic generaliter omnes -it;* 9 (24, C–D) *generaliter namque omnibus mandatur iustitia, quam salvator in evangelio quidem, sed plenissime -ens, ait* (followed by quotation of Mt. 7:12).

Cel. 14 (341, 15 ff.) *infinitae namque sunt species partesque iustitiae, quas omnes una hac brevis sententia* (i.e., Mt. 7:12, quoted immediately before) *-it.*

*COMPROBO, -ARE. Pelagius uses the word consistently as an equivalent of *probo,* with the meaning "I prove," and not the meaning "I approve" or "I acknowledge." Note parallels below in the use of the gerundive and of *testimonium.* Exp. 29, 25 *quod* *non ratiocinatione sola collegimus, sed etiam de Iudaeis testimonio -amus;* 189, 11 *sicut et ex multis aliis -atur.* Dem. 8 (23, B) *nec illud est parvum argumentum ad -andum naturae bonum.* de div. Spir. S. 486, 12 f. *quod evidentius illo evangelico testimonio -atur.* de div. Fil. 134, 23 *illud sane ad veram deitatem fillii -andam inter cetera demonstrandum est.*[11]

Vita 8 (1038) *et quid . . . praeceperit, tam veteris quam novae legis testimoniis -emus;* 9 (1039) *et Deus verus esse servorum actu et opere -etur;* 10 (1040) *prophetae David testimonio -atur;* 12 (1042) *illam eleemosynam Deus -at, quae de iustis laboribus ministratur* (here the meaning is clearly "approves," which is at variance with Pelagius' normal usage). Virg. 3 (227, 16) *eius beatitudinem manifestissimis rationibus -asse;* 7 (232, 9) *quod illo vel maxime testimonio -atur.*

*CONSISTO, -ERE, used with *in* and the ablative. Note the parallel between *fides* as "subsisting" in the mind and *pietas* as "subsisting" in the heart. Exp. 35, 21 *nam fides in mente -it;* 60, 5 *legi divinae quae in mente -it;* 72, 1 *deum diligebat in Christo, cuius dilectio -it in custodia mandatorum.* De Natura (in Aug. de nat. et grat. 45, 53) *dicimus possibilitatem non tam in arbitrii humani potestate quam in naturae necessitate -ere.* See also ibid. 47, 55.[12]

Vita 6 (1037) *cuis in pectore sola pietas -it.* De Lege 4 (109, B) *peccatum non in uno tantum mandatorum genere, sed in utroque -it.*

*E CONTRARIO, Pelagius' normal way of saying "on the contrary" or "on the other hand." For this purpose he does not use *contra, e contra, in contrarium,* or *per contrarium.* In addition to the instances cited by Souter for Exp., see Dem. 4 (19, B), 7 (22, B), and 16 (30, C).

Vita 10 (1040). Virg. 4 (229, 17). Cel. 11 (338, 10). De Lege 5 (110, B). However, the following are found in De Lege: *e contra* (5, 110, C), and *contra* (7, 112, D).

CUMULUS, -I, and CUMULO, -ARE. In his infrequent use of these cognate words Pelagius gives them an exclusively unfavourable colouring, associating them with sins. Exp. 39, 3 *per scientiam -ando delicta;* 391, 22 *mihi -etur invidia vel pressura;* 424, 14 *gentibus invident ad suorum -um peccatorum.*

Vita 4 (1036) *quam diu -um suorum non habuerint delictorum.* De Lege 8 (114, D) *peccata non poenitendo -amus.* In Cel. the word is found once and has precisely the opposite reference: Cel. 18 (345, 15) *numquam maledictio ex ore tuo prodedat, quae ad -um benignitatis iuberis etiam maledicentibus benedicere.*

*DEPUTO, -ARE. Souter overstated the case when he suggested that this verb is used "always with accusative and dative." In seven instances out of nine is this so (to Souter's references add the following: Dem. 23 (37, B) and De Lib. Arb. [Souter, P.B.A., 1906] p. 438). The two instances with prepositional phrases (Exp. 6, 19 and 21, 20)[13] are in the passive, which corresponds to the case below from Virg. Exp. 345, 3 *salutem vestram non vestris meritis -es;* 430, 13 *etiam nimia incontinentia potest immunditiae -ari;* 6, 19 *in proselytorum locum ex legis auctoritate et consuetudine -emini.*

Virg. 4 (229, 19) *qui per praevaricationem in mortem fuerit -atus.* De Lege 9 (115, C) *quod . . . a Graecis solitarie viventibus legitime -etur.*

DESCENDO, -ERE, metaphorically with *ex* or *de* but not *ab*, as an equivalent of *orior.* Exp. 6, 5 *nos circumcisi ex genere Abraham ex stirpe sancta -imus.* De Nat. (Aug. de nat. et grat. 64, 76) [*peccatum*] *de arbitrii libertate -it.* C. Arr. 15, 13 *quia usus omnis ex veritate -at, et quidquid ex veritate -it posterius esse non dubium est.*[14]

Vita 1 (1033) *ex sacramento enim unctionis huius . . . vocabulum -it et nomen.* Virg. 16 (246, 13) *duos homines in exordio fecit Deus, ex quibus totius humani generis silva -it.* Cel. 22 (348, 11) *de quodam fastigio contemptus sui atque arrogantiae -at ad implendam dei voluntatem.*

*DISTRAHO, -ERE, the normal verb for "I sell." *Vendo* is almost entirely absent from Pelagius and is in fact absent from the four works in question.

Vita 6 (1036) *ut negotians nuncupetur quis, carius quod vilius emerat -it.*

*DIVERSUS, -A, -UM, a very frequent word in Pelagius and used in many connections. Exp. 95, 21 *ne vel hinc commoveantur quia dona accepere -a;* 223, 7 *quos gradus virtutum, non peccata, in gloria facientes sed -os;* 358, 7 *id est, unius corporis, non solum coheredes, quod potest -i esse generis.*

Cel. 1 (330, 6) *cumque sic animum in utroque nutantem cogitatio -a libraret;* 5 (333, 20) *hoc itaque duplex -umque praeceptum, prohibendi scilicet et imperandi;* 8 (336, 4) *debet enim vita . . . -am religionem per -a opera monstrare;* 16 (343, 9) *unde et beatus David -as innocentiae species iustitiaeque dinumerans.*

*DUPLEX, -ICIS. Pelagius is very fond of saying such things as that there is a twofold commandment, or that someone is guilty of a twofold sin, or that there is a twofold reward. Note the parallels below in the use of *genus*, *impero*, and *prohibeo.* Exp. 283, 12 *-em potestis habere mercedem;* 155, 6—*peccatum est.* Dem. 15 (29, D) *cum lex dei -i mandatorum genere distincta sit, et mala prohibens, bona imperet;* 16 (30, D) *-i ignorantia accusamus deum scientiae.*

Virg. 6 (230, 25) *praeceptorum autem observatio -i genere custoditur, ut nihil eorum quae prohibentur facias, et cuncta quae iubentur implere contendas;* 17 (248, 16) *et -is peccati reatus est.* Cel. 5 (333, 20) *hoc itaque — diversumque praeceptum, prohibendi scilicet et imperandi, aequo omnibus iure mandatum est;* 30 (354, 10) —, *ut vides, malum, aequale et anceps periculum est.*

*EFFICIO, -ERE. The passive form of this verb is used widely by Pelagius and equals *fio*, which is found far less often. Exp. 50, 8 *quia unum membrum de corpore eius effectus es;* 364, 12 *dum iam humanitas cum divinitate unum effecta est.* Dem. 17 (31, B) *ipse -atur vitii servus.* Also De Nat. (in Aug. de nat. et grat. 10, 11 [*bis*] and 11, 12).

Vita 9 (1039) *his . . . conversando -atur aequalis;* 10 (1040) *sed ut -amur boni;* 13 (1044) *qui peccando iam filii perditionis effecti sunt;* 14 (1045) *qui pauper mundo -tur, ut Deo locuples fiat.* Virg. 16 (246, 14) *certe omnes per divini lavacri gratiam aequales -mur;* 16 (246, 17) *tam nobilis quam ignobilis Dei -tur filius.* Cel. 32 (356, 8) *nec de praeterita iustitia confidens remissior -aris.*

*ME EXHIBEO, -ERE. Pelagius shows two highly characteristic and apparently rather rare uses of this reflexive form: (1) with an appositive direct object *talem* or *qualem* having a pronomial force; (2) with no direct object other than the reflexive pronoun but with the adverb *ita* or *qualiter*. For the first of these the Thes., among Christian authors,[15] gives one reference from Pelagius and Virg. 18 (249, 11), the latter under the name of Sulpicius Severus. The epistle of Uranius to Pocatus is wrongly cited.[16] For the second use the Thes. gives three references from Pelagius; Virg. 14 (244, 16), again under the name of Sulpicius Severus; Caes. Arel. serm. 225, 4; and Bened. reg. 63, 14.[17] Incorrect reference is made to a fragment of a Pelagian letter edited by Dom Morin.[18] Exp. 88, 18 *si quo me talem -eam ut me desiderent imitari;* 94, 8 *modo docet quales se -ere debeant;* 44, 14 *ut qualiter se -ere debeant recognoscent;* 119, 4 *ita vos -etis ut* ... Also 513, 18 and 532, 18.

Vita 9 (1039) *nam si se talem -eat Dei servus;* 9 (1039) *ita se homo Dei -ere debet;* 9 (1039) *nam si se talem -eat Christianus, si se talem -eat Dei servus.* Virg. 14 (244, 16) *ita te -e, ut in te caelestis nativitas appareat;* 18 (249, 11) *talem te -e, quasi sis cum Domino locutura.*[19]

*EXORO, -ARE. In Pelagius this verb never means "I prevail upon" but always simply "I pray," with the sense of intercessory prayer, usually but not always without *Deum* as direct object. Exp. 121, 2 *caritas spiritus ut pro invicem -emus;* 413, 2 *pro suis persecutoribus -abat.*

Vita 6 (1037) *pro persecutoribus suis et hostibus -are.*[20]

*EX HOC. This adverbial phrase is characteristic and is usually followed by a clause beginning with *quia, quo, quod* or *ut*. Dem. 5 (20, A) *cuius meritum facile — intelligi potest, quod multo post futurum Domini sacramentum ante signavit.*

Vita 2 (1033) *ut — peccatorum suorum Deum non arbitrentur ultorem, quod non statim venit punire peccantes.*

FACIO, -ERE. Pelagius shows a tendency to use this verb with a complementary infinitive. Exp. 65, 22 *serpens spe divinitatis vanitati subiectos corruptioni fecerit deservire;* 68, 10 *ut scire nos -at (Deus) quales simus.*[21]

Vita 3 (1035) *quos ecfen interimirat;* 3 (1035) *quod fecissent occidi;* 12 (1042) *melius est enim te non -ere eleemosynam, quam unde paucos tegis, inde plurimos, -as denudare.*

FALLO, -ERE; FALLAX, -ACIS; FALLACIA, -AE. These words in combination with *decipio, seduco* and *sermo* show interesting parallels. Exp. 294, 1 *ne forte . . . satanas . . . decipiat et -at incautos;* 443, 4 *nec sermo dialecticae -aciae seducat* (cf. Exp.369, 18). Dem. 30 (44, A) *qui multos -aci securitate deceptos . . . comprehendit.*

Vita 13 (1042) *quos ita insipientiae et imprudentiae tenebrosa ignorantia -it ac decipit.* Virg. 15 (245, 12) *nemo -aci sermone seducat.*[22]

*FORMA, -AE, a characteristic word in Pelagius, meaning "pattern" or "example" in conduct, and placed frequently in conjunction with *exemplum.* Exp. 45, 11 (on Rom. 5:12, explaining briefly how sin and death came into the world by one man) *exemplo vel -a;* 47, 19 *Adam solam -am fecit delicti, Christus vero et gratis peccata remisit et iustitiae dedit exemplum vivendi;* 232, 17 *ita -am nobis dat alios consolandi.*

Virg. 19 (250, 8) *esto ergo omnibus -a vivendi, esto exemplum.* Cel. 12 (338, 1) *sin vero ea vel deficiunt vel deficere putantur, apostolorum -a universis proposita est.*

*GENERO. Pelagius shows a rather frequent use of this verb in a metaphorical sense. Exp. 110, 18 *ex dissensione semper tristitiae et molestiae -antur;* 368, 2 *notandum quia contemptum dei ignorantia -avit;* 509, 4 *doctrina sua et conversatione destruxit peccata quae mortem hominibus -abat* (note parallel with *mortem below*).

Virg. 4 (229, 17) *ita eorum e contrario -at praevaricatio mortem.* De Lege 1 (105, D) *incorporalia ex corporalibus -ari omnino non possunt.*

GENUS, -ERIS. In a highly typical passage on the twofold commandment to avoid evil and to do good, Pelagius uses this word with the genitive plural of *mandatum* (an equivalent of *praeceptum* in his vocabulary) and with the adjective *duplex*. Dem. 15 (29, D) *cum lex Dei duplici mandatorum -e distincta sit, et mala prohibens, bona imperet.*

Virg. 6 (230, 25) *praeceptorum autem observatio duplici -e custoditur, ut nihil eorum quae prohibentur facias, et cuncta quae iubentur implere contendas.* Cel. 5 (333, 11) *duo autem sunt -a mandatorum, in quibus clauditur tota iustitia: prohibendi unum est, iubendi alterum.* De Lege 4 (109, B) *et peccatum non in uno tantum mandatorum -e, sed in utroque consistit.*

GRANDIS, -E. Pelagius has a certain fondness for this adjective, using it not with the meaning "full-grown" or "advanced in years," nor as applied to bodies and physical objects, but as a synonym of *magnus* and applied to such things as offences, rewards, tasks, etc. Exp. 48, 7 *-e ergo crimen inoboedientia est* (note parallel with *crimen* below in third example from Virg.); 160, 12 *plus diligat castitatem, cui et -e praemium repromittit.* Dem. 25 (39, B) *-i tibi opus est vigilantis -ique cura;* 28 (42, D) *dicas forsitan, -is labor est.* C. Apoll. 334, 22 *hinc -e ridiculum.* See also Exp. 67, 8; 402, 1; 487, 17. Dem. 19 (33, B); 24 (38, A); 24 (38, B).

Virg. 2 (226, 6) *-e est enim et immortale . . . sopire luxuriam et concupiscentiae flammam . . . restinguere;* 4 (228, 2) *res quae et -i virtute constat et ingenti praemio destinatur;* 7 (233, 5 f.) *an -e illum commisisse crimen putas;* 10 (237, 15) *-is quippe divinae gratiae contumelia est.* Cel. 4 (333, 5 f.) *-em vim obtinet vera dilectio;* 17 (344, 16) *et sane -e et persubtile artificium laudare alterum in commendatione sui.*

HUIUSMODI, one of Pelagius' most widely scattered pronomial forms. It is used in conjunction with nouns of all cases, and occasionally, by ellipsis, without accompanying noun. Exp. 136, 10 *humilient ergo se Deo* —. Dem. 7 (22, D) *plena sunt utriusque testamenti volumina huiuscemodi testimoniis.* De Nat. (in Aug. de nat. et grat. 7, 8) — *enim exemplis ostenditur.*

Vita 3 (1035) *Deus — crudelitatibus et impietatibus commovetur;* 6 (1036) — *enim exemplis agnoscimus;* 10 (1040) — *enim homines*

Deus honorat et diligat; 14 (1045) *absit ut — christianus dicatur.* Virg. 1 (225, 13) *de — enim apostolum praecipue dixisse reor;* 3 (227, 8) *virtutem — plurimum sibi complacere monstraret;* 14 (244, 3) — *Deus quaerit ornatum.* Cel. 28 (352, 15) *multa iam per huiuscemodi ignorantiam et audivimus et vidimus scissa coniugia.*

IMPLICO, -ARE, with regular a-stem in all parts. Pelagius uses this verb five times, in four of which the sense is metaphorical and unfavourable, with specific reference to hindrances to true Christian life and faith. The construction is with a dative or ablative, not a prepositional phrase. Cf. the text of 2 Tim. 2:4. Apart from that verse, this particular use finds only two parallels among the instances cited in the Thes.[23] Exp. 49, 25 *vitae veteris erroribus -antur;* 166, 15 . . . *sollicitudinem, quae multum potest obesse iustitiae, et qua praecipue iuncti matrimoniis -antur;* 333, 7 *qui vos legis oneribus -avit, ut cursum vestrae fidei praepediret;* 534, 4 *non vult nos superfluis contentionibus -ari.*[24]

Vita 13 (1042) *et eiusmodi* (i.e., those who say, "*sola fide*") *suis nituntur laqueis -are.* Virg. 5 (230, 6) *qui saecularium bonorum cupiditatibus et mundanarum voluptatum negotiis -antur.* Cel. 9 (336, 14) *illi brevi huic se vitae totos -ent qui aeterna nesciunt.*[25]

*INDIGEO, -ERE, the normal verb for "I need," much more frequent than *egeo.* Exp. 93, 3 *omnes misericordia -erent.* Dem. 25 (39, B) *unde tuae quoque divitiae, coelestis thesaurus, ista cautione -ent atque custodia.*

Vita 8 (1037) *nisi ut qui ante -uit alieno;* 14 (1045) *qui -entibus succurrit.*[26] Cel. 4 (332, 8) *neque enim obsequii nostri deus -et, sed nos illius -emus imperio;* 15 (342, 14) *si nobis ea praestemus invicem, quorum vicissim -emus.*

*INEBRIO, -ARE. Pelagius uses this verb metaphorically five times, and of these five instances two are with the noun *ira*, producing the image of being drunk with anger. Exp. 370, 3 *non mentem ira inebriet;* 465, 9 *ira est quae -at mentem.*

Cel. 22 (348, 5) *quid virtutis habet vinum non bibere et ira atque odio -ari.*[27]

INIURIA, -AE, in the notable locution *in -am ire*. The Thes. gives only the instance cited here from Cel., but under the name of Paulinus of Nola. Note in both cases here the genitive referring to God. De Lib. Arb. (in *J.T.S.*, old series, xii, p. 34) *hinc iam imus in creatoris -am*.

Cel. 4 (332, 4) *eiusque imperia superbissime contemnendo in tantae maiestatis imus -am*.

*IS, EA, ID. Various forms and constructions with this pronoun form some of the most characteristic particles in Pelagius.

(a) EO ... QUO, with comparatives. Dem. 8 (23, D) *eo facilius currere possis, quo in ea nihil asperum;* 18 (32, A) *eo difficilius est, quo eis uti dulcius est;* also 18 (32, A) and 18 33, A).

Vita 3 (1035) *quo potestas sublimior est, eo ad peccandum maior audacia*. Virg. 19 (249, 20) *fides eo perfectior videatur esse quo senior es*.

(b) *EO QUOD. Exp. 26, 13 *invisibilia non indigent visibilibus, eo quod visibilia imago sunt invisibilium*.

Vita 7 (1037) *unus Deo placuit, eo quod innocens esset et iustus*.

(c) EO ... UT. Dem. 21 (35, C) *unde eo perducta res est, ut, neglecta veritate meriti, de sola opinione curemus*.

Cel. 17 (344, 15) *eo fit, ut iam, qui adulari nescit, aut invidus aut superbus putetur*.

(d) *IDCIRCO ... QUIA. Exp. 40, 7 *idcirco de Sarra non genuit, quia et senex erat et sterilis*.

Vita 3 (1034) *idcirco Deus ... non videtur punire peccantes, quia cum punit non cognoscitur;* 13 (1044) *nec idcirco illis coelestis regni ianua panditur, quia illum ore ... confitentur*. Cel. 4 (332, 12) *idcirco magis illa immensitas, illa dei bonitas offenditur, quia eum per tanti etiam praemii detrimenta contemnimus;* 16 (344, 4) *idcirco in multis fervet hoc vitium, quia paene ab omnibus libenter auditur*.

(e) *IDCIRCO ... UT. Exp. 57, 4 *idcirco lex litterae superducta est ut commemoraret oblitos*.

Vita 2 (1034) *idcirco non percutit, ut tu quanta illius erga te sit pietas ... recognoscas*. Virg. 11 (239, 23) *et idcirco satisagit, ut ... animum ... mundum habeat;* 11 (241, 4) *idcirco ... virgo nuptias spernit ut . . . ab omni se delicto custodiat.* Cel. 22 (348, 12) *idcirco a variis ciborum desideriis mentem retrahunt, ut totam eius vim occupent in cupiditate virtutum;* 32 (356, 12) *et idcirco satagit, ut animam mundam habeat a peccato;* 32 (356, 16) *idcirco age, ut ordines reliquum tempus vitae tuae sine offensa.*

(f) *IDEO . . . QUIA. Dem. 15 (30, A) *Non ideo aliqua putes contemnenda esse mandata, quia leviora sunt.*

Cel. 4 (332, 12) *et ideo nobis irascitur . . . quia eum per tanti etiam praemii detrimenta contemnimus;* 16 (344, 4) *sed ideo hoc malum celebre est . . . quia paene ab omnibus libenter auditur.*

(g) *IDEO . . . QUO. Exp. 109, 15 *non hoc ideo dico quo putem aliquit esse commune.* This is the only intance of this particular combination of particles in Pelagius, which makes its similarity to the following sentence from Cel. all the more striking.

Cel. 24 (350, 15 f.) *nec hoc ideo dicimus, quo te retrahamus a tuis.*

(h) *IDEO . . . UT. Exp. 183, 11 *ideo primum calicem nominavit, ut possit de pane latius disputare.*

Cel. 4 (332, 7) *qui ideo aliquid imperat, ut causa habeat remunerandi;* 14 (341, 1) *sed ideo illa cognosce, ut facias quicquid faciendum didiceris;* 23 (349, 7) *et ideo sicut luminaria in mundo lucere nos iubet . . . ut incredulae mentes . . . ignorantiae suae tenebras deprehendant.*

IUSTITIA, -AE, Pelagius' characteristic and all-embracing word for the complete obedience to all that God commands. It includes both "not sinning" in the negative sense of refraining from all that God forbids, and the doing of those good works enjoined upon all Christians. A highly characteristic phrase is *opera iustitiae*, particularly in polemic against wrong interpretations of the doctrine that man is justified *sola fide*. Instances of the latter from Exp. 34, 9 and Vita 13 (1034) have already been given above in the parallel passages. Exp. 150, 10 *ostendit hic nihil prodesse absque -ae operibus scientam et doctrinam;* 103, 20 (after Paul's statement in Rom. 13:9 that the commandment to love neighbour as oneself sums up the commandments not to commit adultery, not to kill, etc.) *recapituatur omnis iustitia. in proximi dilectione consistit;* 332, 17 *speramus nos -ae moralis accepturos esse mercedem.* Dem. 5 (19, D) *omnis enim virtutum species uno -ae nomine continetur.*[28]

Vita 13 (1042) *si sola sine -ae operibus fides prodest;* 2 (1034) *maiores adhuc operas fecisse -ae;* 15 (1045) *misericordiae et -ae opera indesinenter exerce.* Virg. 5 (229, 24) *tres enim species sunt virtutum, ... prima pudicitia est, secunda mundi contemptus, tertia vero -a* (here the distinction is manifest between that which is enjoined upon all Christians, i.e., *iustitia,* and other special good works which may be undertaken by a Christian; see the surrounding context); 5 (230, 4) *mundi vero contemptus exposcitur, ut -a conservetur, quam implere difficile possunt qui saecularium bonorum cupiditatibus ... implicantur;* 6 (230, 24) *-a ergo non aliud est quam non peccare, non peccare autem est legis praecepta servare.* Cel. 2 (331, 10) *manifeste illud ostenditur nos non sola dei confessione tanti praemii magnitudinem promereri, nisi fidei -ae opera coniuncta sint.*

LEGO, -ERE. Pelagius shows a characteristic use of this verb in referring to biblical incidents, most often with a perfect infinitive in indirect discourse, and more often than not without quoting the relevant biblical text. Exp. 151, 3 *cum bonos pastores semper -amus magis deflesse peccata, ut Hieremiam, qui ait* (then follows a quotation of Jer. 9:1); 152, 10 *sed et per unius delictum in omnem populum Iudaeorum iram dei -imus advenisse.* Also Exp. 394, 10; 395, 8; 419, 4; 468, 10.

Vita 13 (1043) *universus hic mundus ut diluvio interiret, non perfidiae causam, sed criminum -o fuisse;* ibid. *ipsum qui hoc dicit, -o hominem absentem etiam condemnasse;* 13 (1044) *et salvatorem nostrum quodam loco dixisse -o* (followed by a quotation). De Lege 8 (114, D) *-amus Isaiam prophetam, et necessarium Ezechiae regis aptum huic causae quaeramus exemplum.*

*NECESSE EST. I include this here only for the purpose of correcting Souter, who wrote that the construction "seems always to take *ut* with the subjunctive."[29] It does take this complement in some instances: Exp. 227, 15; 332, 11; 368, 6. But it takes also the dative with infinitive (Exp. 289, 4 and C. Appol. 334, 20), infinitive without dative (Exp. 227, 14), accusative and infinitive (Exp. 385, 13), infinitive and noun clause (Exp. 225, 18), and simple noun clause without introductory conjunction (Exp. 293, 5 [app. crit., MS. V] and 323, 6).

Vita 6 (1036) (with *ut* and subj.). Virg. 15 (245, 9) (with dative and inf.); 15 (245, 14) (with accusative and inf.).

*NITOR, -I, almost always in Pelagius with an infinitive and meaning "I strive," "I exert myself."[30] Exp. 46, 26 *hi autem qui contra traducem peccati sunt, ita illam impugnare -untur;* 466, 2 *cum cognoverit cuius imago est, ei, in quantum debet et potest, -itur similare.* Also Dem. 11 (27, A) and C. Arr. 11, 24.

Vita 13 (1042) *et eiusmodi ... alios ... suis -untur laqueis implicare.* Cel. 2 (330, 23) *teque paratam ad implendam dei voluntatem ipsius -ar incitare sententiis.* The following instance in Cel. is without infinitive: 11 (338, 13) *per angustam viam -imur.* The context makes it likely, however, that an infinitive *ire* or *incedere* is to be understood (cf., on line 3 of the same page, *per spatiosam viam incedimus*).

*NOBILITAS, -ATIS. Pelagius uses this word in his rather frequent disparagement of those who boast of noble birth, and, by contrast, to point to that other nobility wherein Christians are sons of God and co-heirs with Christ. Note in particular parallels below with *terrenus*, *genus*, *blandior*, and *glorior*. Exp. 7, 16 *sic autem vos de generis -e iactatis;* 148, 14 *nec non et -em terrenam vobis vindicatis.* Exp. 295, 1 *in -e terreni generis gloriari;* 363, 8 *nolite vobis de terrena -e aliquit adrogare.* Dem. 22 (37, A) *non est quod sibi aliquis de -e generis blandiatur;* 22 (36, D) *magisque illa -e glorieris, quae filios Dei et cohaeredes Christi facit.* For other instances in Dem. see 1 (15, C), 11 (26, C–D), 22 (36, C, *bis*), 30 (44, B).

Virg. 14 (244, 16) *agnosce te non hominis tantum, sed et Dei filiam et divinae nativitatis -e decoratam;* 16 (246, 7) *non Christi sunt virgines quae ... in opibus delectantur et corporeae -is origine gloriantur;* 16 (246, 10) *si patrem Deum se habere sentirent, -em carnis non amarent;* 16 (246, 11) *quid tibi ... in generis -e blandiris;* 16 (246, 17) *terrena — splendore caelestis gloriae obumbratur;* 16 (246, 20) *caelestis et divinae -is gloria aequaliter vestiuntur.* Cel. 21 (347, 3) *nulli te umquam de generis -e praeponas nec obscuriores quasque et humiliore loco natas te inferiores putes;* 21 (347, 7) *sola apud Deum libertas est non servire peccatis, summa apud eum — clarum esse virtutibus;* 21 (347, 14) *nam et alias frustra sibi aliquis de -e generis applaudit.* De Lege 6 (111, A) *paupertati, non -i, futurorum beatitudo promittitur.*

*NOVI, -OSSE. Pelagius shows a widespread use of this perfect tense as an equivalent of the present tense of *scio*. See examples given in Souter, to which add Exp. 24, 23; 171, 7; 205, 15; 207, 3; 211, 17; 261, 1.

Virg. 17 (248, 2) *pretiosa Deo lingua est, quae nonnisi de divinis rebus -it verba construere.*

*NULLUS, -A, -UM, in the phrase, *in nullo*, to express the idea, "in no respect." The phrase *nulla in re* occurs neither in Pelagius nor in the four works in question. Exp. 193, 4 *si in nullo nos reprehendit;* 241, 2 *oboedientia enim illa perfecta et vera est quae in nullo contemnit.*

Vita 14 (1044) *cuius* (i.e., *Dei*) *misericordiam nemo cognoscit, qui in nullo imitatur bonos.* Virg. 6 (231, 13) *si in nullo eorum necessitatibus participamus.*

*NUNCUPO, -ARE. Souter noticed that this word does not occur in Exp., whereas *nomino*, *appello*, and *voco* do. Kirmer uses this fact as evidence for his case against Pelagius' authorship of Vita. The word does occur, however seven times in Martini's fragments as follows: C. Arr. 11, 29; 11, 31. de div. Fil. 133, 12; 133, 6; 134, 19. de div. Spir. S. 485, 31. C. Appol. 332, 12.

Vita Praef. (1033), 13 (1044), 15 (1045). De Lege 5 (110, C).

*OCCASIO, -NIS, used in Pelagius generally of the opportunity to do something evil or otherwise undesirable.[31] The parallels below with *aufero*, with *perditio*, and with genitive gerunds are to be noted. Exp. 52, 21 *qui non solum peccata sed etiam -es auferri docuit delictorum;* 186, 8 *ut sub libertatis specie -em demus infidelibus blasphemandi;* 335, 14 *dum alter alteri — perditionis exsistit;* 423, 1 *-em auferre cupiebat vel accipiendi vel de se aliquit* *suspicandi;* 493, 18 *ne eis ipsa -em det saeculo serviendi.* De Nat. (in Aug. de nat. et grat. 27, 30) *ad auferendam superbiae vel gloriae -em.*

Virg. 6 (232, 5) *hoc fuit pie cum flentibus flere, -em fletus auferre;* 17 (247, 10) *discordiarum quoque et litium -es subterfuge;* 19 (250, 6) *cave ergo ne cui vel concupiscendi -em tribuas.* Cel. 23 (349, 21) *ne malae mentes -em inveniant detrahendi;* 23 (349, 28) *cum ne -em quidem male de se sentiendi dedit;* 28 (352, 17) *-e castitatis adulterium perpetratum;* 30 (353, 26) *sine ullius -e scandali magister firmaverit de castitate sententiam.* De Lege 2 (107, A) *et fiat ei causa salutis interitus et perditionis —.*[32]

OMNINO. One of Pelagius' interesting peculiarities is his almost complete restriction of this word to negative clauses, as Martini was first to point out.[33] Exp. 168, 23 *unitas divisionem — non recepit;* 199, 9 *sine intestinis — non vivitur.* Dem. 3 (17, D) *nec esset — virtus ulla in bono perseverantis.*[34] It will be seen below that of the seven occurrences of the word in Cel., four are in clauses that are not formally negative. It might be argued that the verbs in two of these four clauses have quasi-negative meanings (*interdicere* and *contemnare*). Further, Pelagius does show an occasional use of *omnino* in formally non-negative clauses: De Nat. (in Aug. de nat. et grat. 19, 21) *unde ante omnia quaerendum puto quid sit peccatum; substantia aliqua, an — substantia carens nomen.* Dem. 18 (32, C–D) *in quibusdam ostendimus quamdam vim naturae nostrae, in aliis — torpescimus.*

Vita 5 (1036) *non oportet nos — peccare;* 14 (1045) *christianus est qui — non movetur iniuria.* Virg. 7 (233, 13) *ut — non iures;* 16 (246, 18) *et nusquam — iam comparet.* Cel. 1 (330, 10) *ut peccare me — crederem, si tacerem;* 4 (333, 9) *nihil — debemus agere;* 13 (339, 24) *nihil — agimus;* 16 (342, 16) *nulli umquam — detrahas;* 22 (348, 18) *sed omnibus — virtutibus abstinentia opitulatur;* 28 (352, 7) *cum huic apostolica — interdicat auctoritas;* 30 (354, 12) *contemnare — virum atque despicere aperte contra apostoli sententiam est.* De Lege 1 (105, D) *quia incorporalia ex corporalibus generari — non possunt.*

PARCO, -ERE. Pelagius repeatedly employs this verb in expressing the thought that just as persons in a previous, similar situation were not "spared," so neither will one be "spared" now if one does not do better than they. In this usage he is undoubtedly reflecting the language of Rom. 11:21 and of 2 Pet. 2:4 f., but he extends the usage beyond that of these texts, twice making the subject of the verb to be St. Paul himself. Exp. 180, 13 *ne quis confidens . . . putet sibi deum -ere, si peccaverit, tale patrum proponit exemplum;* 302, 17 *qui postmodum peccaverint, nec ipsis -am* (i.e., St. Paul); 314, 5 *Galatarum infirmitas compulit eum narrare quod nec ipsi Petro pepercerit;* 374, 8 *si Sodomitis pepercit et his qui in diluvio perierunt, -et et vobis.* Also Exp. 19, 15; 90, 6; 182, 15; 497, 11.

Virg. 7 *quem si in aliquo contempseris, si pepercit Adae, -et et tibi* (note parallels in sentence structure and word order between this and the instance cited above from Exp. 374, 8).

*PERFICIO, -ERE. Pelagius uses this verb very widely referring to that "accomplishment" of good works and that "perfecting" of the lives of Christians in virtue which are such prominent aspects of his teaching. Exp. 365, 4 *ut -iantur sancti;* 131, 8 *si unum sentiatis et proferatis, tunc vere poteritis esse perfecti.* Dem. 19 (33, C) *dominus ipse, ad perfectam nos benignitatem vocans, ait;* 24 (38, B) *singulasque virtutes animi formare in se atque -ere.* De Lib. Arb. (in Aug. de grat. chr. 4, 5) *quod vero potest homo velle bonum atque -ere, solius Dei est.* See also Dem. 19 (34, A), 24 (38, A), 28 (42, B).

Virg. 7 (232, 9) *non sufficit christiano a malis se abstinere, nisi etiam bonorum operum officia perfecerit;* 11 (241, 6) *ab omni se delicto custodiat et universa legis mandata -ait;* 17 (248, 14) *tantum te a Domino recepturam esse mercedis, quantum eius timoris et dilectionis causa perfeceris;* 19 (250, 4) *coeptum virginitatis propositum ad finem usque conserva, quia non inchoasse tantum, sed perfecisse virtutis est.* Cel. 22 (348, 12) *quae* (i.e., *voluntas dei*) *maxime in humilitate -itur;* 30 (354, 5) *hoc* (i.e., *castitas*) *enim sicut alia quoque bona non tantum coepisse sed perfecisse laudandum est;* 32 (356, 20) *non inchoasse sufficit, sed perfecisse iustitia est.* De Lege 1 (105, C) *aut per te aut per alios eruditus in virum perfectum.*

*POSTMODUM. Pelagius uses this form and not *postmodo*. Exp. 180, 21; 245, 5. *Postmodo* does not occur in any of the four documents in question.

Vita 1 (1034), 3 (1035), 8 (1037), 8 (1038), 10 (1040), 10 (1041). De Lege 1 (105, C).[35]

PRAECIPIO, -ERE, used frequently with accusative and an active or passive infinitive.[36] Exp. 266, 18 *sacerdotes in doctrina suo exemplo -epit dilatari;* 380, 10 *parentibus filios -epit oboedire.* See also Exp. 281, 10; 379, 9; 416, 8; 429, 10; 494, 2; 497, 1. Dem. 6 (21, C).

Vita 8 (1037) *quid . . . eum observare praeceperit;* 8 (1038) *et quid crebrius fieri et observari praeceperit.* Vita also has dative construction in the following: 7 (1037), 10 (1041).

*PRAESENS. The adverbial phrase *in praesenti* occurs very frequently in Pelagius, while *in praesens*, *in praesentia*, and *in praesentiarum* do not occur at all. The phrase *in praesenti* as Pelagius uses it is almost always contrasted, either explicitly or implicitly, with things as they will be at the last judgment or in the future life. The contrasting phrase *in futuro* is often present. Exp. 18, 19 *et si non in praesenti, tamen in futuro esse puniendos;* 19, 23 *aut numquit propterea tibi de impunitate blandiris quia semper in praesenti non reddidit, et . . . putas non esse iudicium;* 233, 1 *in futuro remuneret (deus) quos etiam in praesenti non deserit.*

Vita 3 (1034) *deus in -ti non videtur punire peccantes;* ibid. *et in -ti dei ira superveniet et in futuro servatur;* 3 (1035) *ante iudicii diem in -ti etiam iudicantur;* ibid. *in -ti etiam dei iudicium evadere posse existemus;* 15 (1046) *sed nec dignae erunt tales in futuro tempore sanctorum esse consortes, quos ita in -ti spreverunt.*

*PROFECTUS, -US, used often and meaning "progress" in the Christian life, a recurring theme in Pelagius. Exp. 10, 13 *prudenter laudat* (i.e., Paul) *ut provocet ad -um.* Dem. 11 (26, D) *et cum in omnibus mundi studiis -u non satientur homines, hic tantum coepisse sufficet?* 26 (40, D) *et si a proposito non revocat* (i.e., the devil), *certe retineat a -u.* Also Dem. 11 (26, D) and 26 (40, C).

Cel. 2 (330, 22) *cui tam sanctae petitioni tamque pio desiderio non satisfacere, quid aliud est quam -um alterius non amare.* De Lege 10 (115, D) *sed quoniam aput christianos non tam ordo quaeritur quam —.*

*PROFICIO, -ERE, a very frequent verb in Pelagius and used in several constructions, of which only those are noted here which have parallels in the four works in question. When it is used absolutely, it means either "to make (moral and spiritual) progress," an idea highly important to Pelagius, or "to be of (moral and spiritual) advantage." When used with *ad* or *in* and the acc., it means "to progress" toward some good end or "to regress" toward some bad end. Souter did not note the instance in Exp. with *in* and the abl., which finds a parallel in one of the examples below from De Lege. Exp. 8, 3 *qui in virtutibus -ientes mutato nomine sunt vocati;* 206, 16 *hoc opus est caritatis unde multi -iunt;* 334, 6 *si enim expoliatio membri -it, multo magis ablatio;* 492, 17 *poterunt et tuo exemplo ad meliora -ere.*

Virg. 5 (230, 17) *quae (iustitia) si non fuerit, nec prima (pudicitia) nec secunda (contemptus mundi) -iet;* 19 (249, 21) *Iesus . . . -iebat non aetate tantum corporea, sed et sapientia et gratia spirituali coram Deo et hominibus.* Cel. 23 (349, 6) *vult* (i.e., Paul) *enim etiam extraneos ad fidem homines per fidelium opera -ere.* De Lege 2 (107, B) *tum demum -iet ad vitam, quae per praesumptionem forte praecipitasset ad mortem;* 9 (114, D—115, A) *age, ut in spiritualitate -ias.*

PROPOSITUM, -I. This word in Pelagius has a tendency to mean the resolve to lead the "religious" life, including in particular sexual continence.[37] Exp. 430, 10 *non solum de fornicatione, sed etiam de transgressione -i: quisque enim continentiam deo voverit, fecit sibi inlicitum quod licebat.* Dem. 10 (25, A) *perfectionis igitur secuta consilium, beatitudinem specialis agresse -i.* See also Exp. 496, 10 and Dem. 13 (27, D), 14 (28, C), 19 (33, A), 21 (35, D), 21 (36, A), 22 (36, C), 24 (38, B) (*bis*), 26 (40, C) (*bis*), 26 (40, D) (*bis*), 27 (42, B).

Virg. 12 (241, 16) *o virgo, serva -um tibi magno praemio destinatum;* 12 (241, 19) *agnosce statum tuum, agnosce locum, agnosce*

-um; 16 (246, 5) non Christi sunt virgines, quae -i sui et professionis immemores gaudent in deliciis; 19 (250, 3) *coeptum virginitatis -um ad finem usque conserva.* Cel. 5 (333, 23) *in quovis -o, in quovis gradu aequale peccatum est vel prohibita admittere cel iussa non facere.*

*PROVOCO, -ARE. Of thirty-four instances of this verb in Pelagius, twenty-four are with *ad* and an accusative. Of these accusatives one is the gerundive *dicendum*, for which cf. the instance from Vita below; twice the accusative is *iracundiam*, for which cf. the instance from Cel. below.

Exp. 10, 12 *prudenter laudat ut -et ad profectum;* 120, 13 *quantum proficit discipulus, tantum ad dicendum -atur et doctor;* 471, 2 *nolite illos ultro ad iracundiam -are;* also 338, 8 with *ad iracundiam*. Dem. 14 (29, A–B) *tuoque exemplo ad perpetuam -es castitatem*. Also Dem. 5 (20, D), 5 (21, A), 9 (25, A).

Vita praef. (1031) *me peccatorem et ignarum ad dicendum hortatur et -at;* 11 (1041) *quid ad -andam celerius eius iram . . . sceleratas ad deum porrigis manus;* 14 (1045) *qui ad fletum fletibus -atur alienis.* Cel. 1 (329, 9) *-atus enim ad scribendum litteris tuis;* 4 (332, 3) *clementissimum dominum ad iracundiam -amus;* 28 (352, 27) *ad praemium -et continentiam.*

PUTO, -ARE. As Martini was first to point out, Pelagius shows a certain fondness for employing this verb with a gerundive in indirect discourse. Exp. 12, 3 *nobis erubescendum -ant*. Dem. 2 (16, D) *observandum -o*. To the other four examples given by Martini (p. 312) should be added the following: Dem. (30, A) *aliqua -es contemnenda esse mandata;* De Natura (in Aug. de nat. et grat. 19, 21) *quaerendum -o quid sit peccatum.*

Virg. 2 (227, 1) *quod ita intellegendum -o;* 16 (247, 2) *qui non -ant humanis caelestia praeponenda.* Cel. 23 (349, 19) *quod a nullo -at esse credendum.*

*PUTOR, ARI. There is a noticeable use in Pelagius of passive forms of *puto*, seventeen instances in all. Of this number, all but one (C. Arr. 12, 29) are in contexts in which that which "is thought" to be the case is unfavourable or undesirable, or in which the subject of the verb is either undesirable in itself or is being cast in an unfavourable light. Exp. 41, 25 *ne non spes sed blasphemia -aretur;* 135, 10 *quod stultum -atur dei;* 214, 7 *ne apostoli -arentur mentiti.* See also the following: Exp. 73, 16; 151, 11; 175, 6; 220, 12; 236, 11; 263, 11; 297, 6; 302, 4; 307, 9; 310, 1; 527, 17. Dem. 3 (17, C) and 7 (22, B).

Cel. 12 (338, 21) *sin vero ea* (i.e., *exempla*) *vel deficiunt vel deficere -antur;* 17 (344, 16) *aut invidus aut superbus -etur.* De Lege 2 (106, C) *ut hoc quod dico, non ex humano sensu inventum, aut ingenio proprio excogitatum -etur, sed divinis sententiis videatur constructum.*

*QUALITAS, -ATIS, a noticeably frequent word, used to designate the particular character of an act, of an age, or of some other entity. Note parallels below with *peccatum.*

Exp. 324, 5 (*elementa*) *quae fuerant eorum infirmitati necessaria pro temporis -e;* 370, 19 *non silentium imposuit, sed -em loquendi.* de div. Spir. S. 484, 26 *cum . . . -em suae pollicitationis exigeret.* De Nat. (in Aug. de nat. et grat. 37, 44) *scriptura . . . non modo peccata, verum etiam peccatorum indicat -em.* From the same work, see also the instances at 10, 11 and 11, 12. Also Dem. 2 (16, C).

Vita 1 (1033) *huic ergo iudicium geminum servatur; et pro dei subsannatione, quem sine causa dominum appellavit, et pro -e peccati.* Virg. 7 (233, 10) *non agitur de -e peccati, sed de transgressione mandati.* Cel. 15 (341, 21) *quae tibi quasi speculum quoddam paratum et ad manum semper positum -em tuae voluntatis ostendat.* De Lege 2 (106, D) *ut corporis -e manente, homo vetus in novam animi mutetur volentatem;* 5 (110, A) *qui* (i.e., *deus*) *non tantum ad -em peccati respicit, sed ad personae contemptum.*

RUDIS, -E, found five times in Pelagius. On one occasion the adjective is applied to the Jews, as in the instance below from Cel. Twice in Pelagius it is found in close relation to *novellus*, as in the instance below from Virg. Noteworthy also is the parallel in thought and in the use of *parco* in the quotations from Exp. and Virg. below: if the "untutored" of the Old Testament were not "spared," one may scarcely expect more leniency now, after having been much more fully informed concerning the divine will than was the case then.

Exp. 182, 15 *si enim adhuc parvolis et -ibus non pepercit, quanto magis nobis qui legem perfectionis accepimus, non parcit.* Dem. 26 (40, C) *fatigare cogitationibus -es animas, et novellis in proposito mentibus . . . afferre moerorem.* de div. Spir. S. 486, 18 *novellis ac -ibus filii nomen insinuari crebrius oportebat.* Also Exp. 4, 23; 175, 13.

Virg. 7 (234, B) *illi* (i.e., Adam) *magis parcendum fuerat, qui adhuc -is et novellus erat . . . tibi vero post tanta documenta, post legem, post prophetas, post evangelia, post Apostolos si delinquere volueris, quomodo indulgeri possit ignoro.* Cel. 13 (340, 8) *-i adhuc populo et hominibus ad oboedientiam insuetis per Moysen imperatur a domino . . .* Cf. Vita praef. (1032).

*SAEPE. Souter recorded an erroneous impression when he wrote that this adverb "is entirely absent, I think." It is found as follows: Exp. 21, 18; 81, 11; 163, 19; 164, 5; 171, 16; 212, 24; 321, 21; 495, 11. Dem. 18 (33, A), 21 (35, C), 27 (42, A), 30 (44, C). De Lib. Arb. (in Aug. de grat, Chr. 4, 5). De Nat. (in Aug. de nat. et grat. 12, 13 and 54, 63).

Virg. 7 (233, 4). Cel. 4 (332, 15), 13 (340, 1), 16 (343, 20). De Lege 5 (110, B), 8 (113, D), 8 (114, C), 10 (116, A).

SATIS. As Martini pointed out, Pelagius uses this word characteristically to modify adjectives and adverbs. He does not use the word in its minimizing sense of "tolerably," "passably," but rather employs it to give a slight but positive accent to the adjective or adverb which it modifies. This will be found to accord with the instances recorded below from Vita, Virg., and De Lege.[38]

Exp. 77, 13 *quod — iniquum est.* Dem. 19 (33, D) *vilium — hominum est, et suam laudem quaerentium, alios viles facere;* 24 (38, D) *— pulchram Deo crede faciem tuam;* also 19 (34, A). C. Apoll. 333, 23 *— iustum est;* 333, 30 *quae utique cum — longe distent ab eius rei veritate cui comparata sunt.* See also ibid. 332, 7; 334, 27 and 32. De div. Spir. S. 487, 20.

Vita 1 (1033) — *deo dignos;* ibid. — *pauci de plurimis mererentur accipere;* ibid. *hoc* — *foedum et miserum est;* 7 (1037) *Enoch* — *iustum fuisse scriptura designat.* Virg. 4 (228, 16) — *certum est;* 10 (239, 8) *ad omnia misericordiae et pietatis opera* — *promptae;* 18 (249, 4) — *tranquillam et quietam esse convenit mentem.* De Lege 4 (108, D) *temerarium* — *est;* 5 (110, C) *iuste* — *et recte.*

*SECUNDUM (preposition with accusative). Souter wrote misleadingly that whereas *secundum* is scattered widely in Pelagius' Expositions, *iuxta* "is very rare in this author." The following seven instances of *iuxta* do not constitute great rarity for the volume of Pelagius' assured writings: Exp. 4, 2; 55, 5; 114, 16; 261, 18. Dem. 15 (29, D). de div. Sp. S. 487, 1. de lib. arb. (*J.T.S.* p. 34, 1.29).

Secundum occurs in the four letters as follows: Virg. 17 (247, 19), 10 (237, 10), 14 (244, 4). Cel. 32 (355, 30), 32 (356, 5). De Lege 6 (112, C), 10 (116, C). *Iuxta* occurs in the four letters as follows: Virg. 17 (247, 10). De Lege 1 (106, A), 2 (107, B), 3 (108, B), 6 (112, A), 9 (115, A).[38a]

SECURITAS, -ATIS, and SECURUS, -A, -UM. In about half the instances of one or the other of these words in Pelagius, the sense is ironic, referring to the false security of those who think they can continue to sin with impunity, or of one who thinks he can be secure in good works already performed or in reliance upon the Jewish law. Exp. 24, 9 *confidis vel securus es* (on the words in Rom. 2, 17 *et requiescis in lege*); 433, 17 *quando omnes scierit dormire securos* (i.e., when the day of the Lord will come as a thief in the night); 521, 16 *ut securi deliquant.* Dem. 27 (42, B–C) *cesset omnis ignavia, et inutilis de praeterito labore securitas.* See also Exp. 271, 14; Dem. 18 (32, D) and 30 (44, A); Ep. ad Liv. (in Mar. Merc., comm. super nom Cael. 4, 3). For non-ironic uses, see Exp. 67, 9; 121, 9; 179, 5; 378, 12; 471, 16. Dem. 4 (19, B), 25 (39, B), 25 (40, A).

Vita 3 (1034) *nemo . . . securus delinquat et liber;* 13 (1042) *nam si nullum crimen, sed sola perfidis condemnatur, ergo securi peccamus et liberi.* Cel. 4 (332, 1) *et nos securo et bono animo sumus, qui pers ingula quaeque peccata inhorantes deum clementissimum dominum ad iracundiam provocamus;* 22 (348, 1) *magisque id providendum est, ne tibi hoc, quod licita contemnis, securitatem quandam illicitorum faciat;* 31 (355, 19) *ita se curis vitae praesentis involuunt, ut obliviscentur futuram, quos somno quodam ignorantiae et malae securitatis oppressos fluctibus domini comprehendet adventus;* 32 (356, 3) *nec sanctus ergo securus esse debet, quamdiu in huius vitae agone versatur.* For non-ironic uses see Virg. 11 (241, 4); Cel. 23 (349, 28) and 32 (356, 17) (*secure*); De Lege 8 (114, A).

*SENSUS, -US. Besides occurring in other connections, for which Souter may be consulted, this word occurs a noticeable number of times in Pelagius in conjunction with the adjective *proprius*, or with the verb *loquor*, or with both of them together. The meaning in each case is to express or to rely upon an interpretation of one's own, without the support of sacred authority. Exp. 95, 8 (the text of part of Rom. 12:3 reads, *dico enim per gratiam dei quae data est mihi*, on which Pelagius' comment follows immediately) *prohibiturus humanam sapientiam quae per legem est, non -u proprio loqui se dicit, sed auctoritate gratiae spiritualis;* 175, 22 (the text of 1 Cor. 9:8 reads, *numquid secundum cor meum haec dico, an et lex haec non deicit?*) *id est numquid proprio tantum -u loquor?* 171, 8 *huiusmodi scientia quae ex -u proprio et humano descendit, eos qui praeter eam divinam non habuerint, inflat;* 260, 1 (on 1 Cor. 5:13[a]) *ita sive in exstasi sumus, deo, sive nostro -u loquimur, vobis.*

Vita 7 (1937) *sed ne me ex -u proprio loqui quis arbitretur aut credat . . . tam veteris quam novae incipiam exempla proferre;* 10 (1040) *nemo, inquam, -u proprio se decipiat et illudat.*[39] De Lege 2 (106, C) *praefatiunculae meae verba verbis dominicis probabo, ut hoc quod dico, non ex humano -u inventum, aut ingenio proprio excogitatum putetur, sed divinis sententiis videatur esse constructum;* 4 (109, C) *quod non mei -us assertio, sed utriusque testamenti exempla probant.*

*NON SOLUM — SED ETIAM. Souter wrote inaccurately that this formula is "almost invariable" for "not only — but also" and that *non solum — sed et* is found "once or twice." The latter occurs more often than Souter suggested, and other formulas are found as well.

non solum — sed etiam: Exp. 7, 10; 25, 8; 42, 3; 45, 3; etc. Dem. 23 (37, C). Cel. 2 (330, 20), 4 (332, 14) (*nec solum*), 16 (343, 12).

non solum — sed et: Exp. 66, 3; 76, 8; 102, 14; 352, 4; 384, 1; 404, 6; 501, 5; 511, 6; 520, 1; 530, 18. Dem. 15 (29, D) (*nec . . . solum, sed et*). Vita 13 (1042).

non modo — sed etiam: Exp. 390, 12. Dem. 27 (42, B) (*non solummodo*). Cel. 14 (341, 15), 15 (342, 4), 28 (352, 7).

non . . . tantum — sed etiam: Dem. 12 (27, C).

non . . . tantum — sed . . . quoque: Dem. 6 (22, A).

non solum — verum etiam: Exp. 16, 2. De Nat. (Aug. de nat. et grat. 10, 11).

non modo — verum etiam: De Nat. (Aug. de nat. et grat. 10, 11; 36, 42; 37, 44).

SPECIES, -EI. In seven out of sixteen instances of this word in Pelagius, it is used either with the genitive *virtutum*, or with some other genitive denoting a particular state of moral excellence, in accord with Pelagius' fondness for talking about "virtues" and contemplating their various "kinds." Exp. 204, 1 *modo describit ipsa membra et -es caritatis;* 264, 8 *notandum quod conscientia -es sit virtutum;* 369, 14 *hinc describit ipsas -es sanctitatis;* 384, 1 *iustitia diversis virtutum conectitur -ebus.* Dem. 2 (16, C) *ac iam inde audientis animum ad -es incitare virtutum;* 5 (19, D) *omnis enim virtutum — uno iustitiae nomine continetur.* De Lib. Arb. (fragment ed. Souter in *Proceedings of the British Academy*, 1905–6. Hereafter this reference will be given as P.B.A. with page numbers). *duas enim . . . -es perfectionis ostendit.*

Virg. 5 (229, 21) *tres enim -es sunt virtutum;* 5 (230, 7) *quisquis ergo pudicitiae primam -em possidet et secundam . . . non obtinet;* 5 (230, 15) *quia ut prima — propter secundam est* (see 5 [229, 21] for context). Cel. 14 (341, 15) *infinitae namque sunt -es partesque iustitiae;* 16 (343, 4) *beatus David diversas innocentiae -es iustitiaeque dinumerans.*[40]

SPLENDOR, -ORIS, found six times in Pelagius. In four of the six, the word is found with the noun *sol*, and in five of the six the reference is to that "splendour" with which the saints will shine at the last day. The biblical source of this usage is probably Mt. 13:43: *tunc iusti fulgebunt sicut sol in regno patrias sui.*[41] But neither *splendor*, nor any cognate thereof, appears in this text, either in the Vulgate or in any variants listed in the *Editio Maior* of Wordsworth and White.[42] Exp. 65, 12 — *solis et cetera quae sanctis legimus repromissa;* 223, 12 (on 1 Cor. 15:43, where the reference is obviously to the resurrection) *in gloria -is ut sol;* 248, 2 (here the reference is to the transfiguration of Christ) *cum ascendens montem solus -e solis visus est radiasse;* 441, 15 *ipse* (i.e., *Christus*) *in suis glorificandus est membris, quae solis -e fulgebunt.* Dem. 30 (44, D) (with reference to the last day) *et incorruptionis -e donanda es.*

Virg. 8 (236, 4) *domini est — solis qui sanctis promittitur* (followed by quotation of Mt. 13:43).[43]

*SUPERFLUE. It is this form of the adverb that Pelagius uses, never *superfluo*. Likewise Vita 13 (1044).

*TERRENUS, -A, -UM, usually in an unfavourable sense, designating the kind of cares and goals with which a Christian should not be concerned. It is found with notable frequency, and often contrasted specifically to *caelestis*. *Terrestris* is rare in Pelagius. Exp. 486, 14 *turpe lucrum est de caelestibus mysteriis -a sectari;* 512, 15 *quae salus in Christo est, non nuda, sed gloria vestita, nec -a gloria, sed caelesti.* Dem. 11 (26, D) *ferventissimi in is,- frigidissimi in caelestibus sumus.* C. Apoll. 333, 32 *quis enim dubitet nihil omnino -um aequari posse caelestibus.*

Vita 14 (1044) *nisi quis -a despexerit, divina non capiet, nisi humana contempserit, non potest possidere coelestia;* 14 (1045) *qui coelestia potiusquam -a desiderat.* Virg. 10 (237, 14) *crimen est . . . aut vel gemmis vel qualibet alia -a specie comi, quod iam caelestis oranatus splendore refulget;* 13 (243, 5) *carnalia ornamenta et -a praesumerent;* 14 (244, 24) *caeleste mihi aliquid in -o corpore redolet;* 16 (246, 17) *-a nobilitas splendore caelestis gloriae obumbratur.* Cel.

9 (336, 13) *illi -a sapiant, qui caelestia promissa non habent.* De Lege 3 (108, C) *quanto a -a cogitatione remotior est, tanto deo vicinior et coelo est;* 6 (112, C) *his qui in -is magis negotiis quam in coelestibus laboraverunt;* 7 (113, B) *quia -us lapis inter coelestes stellas esse non poterat;* 9 (115, B) *ambiant -a gentiles, quibus coelestia non debentur;* 10 (116, C) *iussum est imaginem -i hominis deponere, et assumere formam coelestis.*

TRANSGRESSOR, -ORIS. Kirmer was mistaken in asserting that this word does not appear in Pelagius.[44] In fact it appears in the same combination as in Virg. Exp. 295, 21 *quinque vicibus tricenas et novenas quasi — legis accepit.*

Virg. 6 (231, 5) *si a malo recesseris et non feceris bonum, — es legis.*

VAS, -IS. Pelagius three times employs the designation *vas electionis* as a way of referring to the apostle Paul. Dem. 27 (42, C) *si beatus Paulus — electionis . . . adhuc tamen se extendit.* De Lib. Arb. (*J.T.S.* [old series] xii, 34) *ergo ne apostolus Paulus —electionis . . .;* ibid. *quod si ipse — electionis et ecclesiarum magister . . . ad malum se dicit inpelli.*

Cel. 12 (339, 1) *clamat — electionis nosque quasi ad angustum hoc iter convocans dicit;* 22 (348, 15) *nam et — electionis, . . . hoc efficit castitatem;* 27 (357, 21) *de quo et — electionis ait* (followed by quotation of 1 Tim. 2:9–10); 28 (352, 25) *ita — electionis ac magister gentium inter utrumque temperatus incedit ac medius.*

Possibly the most immediately striking aspect of the vocabulary of Pelagius is the proliferation of adverbs in *-ter.*[45] Plinval has published a list[46] of some of these, to which we may add the following:

abundanter: Exp. 385, 9; 468, 3
diligenter: Exp. 280, 7
evidenter: Exp. 249, 14
firmiter: Exp. 348, 14; 427, 3; 455, 16
generaliter: Exp. 329, 5
hilariter: Exp. 281, 7
inpudenter: Exp. 288, 16
mediocriter: Dem. 23 (37, D)
negligenter: Dem. 8 (23, C)
patienter: Exp. 204, 18.
peculialiter: Exp. 358, 10
sapienter: Exp. 196, 9

similiter: Exp. 325, 10
simpliciter: Exp. 290, 3
spiritaliter: Exp. 405, 7; 524, 14
velociter: Exp. 439, 4
viriliter: Exp. 228, 12; 383, 16

Adverbs in *-ter* are generously represented in the four works in question, as the following list will testify.

acriter: Cel. 1 (330, 4)
aequaliter: Virg. 16 (246, 20). Cel. 21 (347, 17); 30 (354, 7). De Lege 6 (111, D); 7 (113, A)
audenter: Vita 11 (1041); 15 (1046); Cel. 7 (334, 20)
breviter: Vita 10 (1039); Virg. 6 (230, 19); 11 (239, 18)
carnaliter: Virg. 16 (246, 20)
clementer: Vita 2 (1034); De Lege 6 (112, A)
diligenter: Vita praef. (1032); Virg. 12 (241, 23); Cel. 23 (349, 25)
evidenter: Vita 9 (1039); De Lege 2 (106, D)
fideliter: De Lege 6 (112, A)
fiducialiter: Vita praef. (1032)
fortiter: De Lege 6 (112, B)
frequenter: Cel. 14 (340, 20)
generaliter: Vita 15 (1045); De Lege 6 (111, D)
gratanter: Virg. 7 (233, 18)
graviter: Vita 10 (1040)
incessabiliter: Vita 15 (1046)
indesinenter: Vita 14 (1045); 15 (1046)
instanter: Vita 15 (1046)
iugiter: Cel. 14 (340, 22)
leniter: Vita 2 (1034)
libenter: Vita praef. (1031); 8 (1037); Cel. 11 (338, 7); 16 (342, 21); 16 (344, 5)
mediocriter: Cel. 28 (352, 5)
negligenter: Cel. 30 (354, 27)
qualiter: De Lege 10 (116, B)
patienter: Virg. 17 (248, 7)
probabiliter: Cel. 22 (348, 8)
scienter: Cel. 22 (348, 8)

simpliciter: Cel. 7 (334, 20); De Lege 10 (115, D)
sollerter: Virg. 12 (242, 7)
spiritaliter: Virg. 1 (226, 4); Cel. 14 (340, 19)
terribiliter: De Lege 7 (113, B)
vigilanter: Cel. 2 (330, 16)

We find also in Pelagius a certain fondness for putting more than one of these adverbs in the same sentence. Note particularly the parallel below for the contrast of *spiritaliter* and *carnaliter*. Exp. 338, 3 *si per spiritum vitam habemus, spiritaliter conversemur, et non legi carnaliter serviamus;* 440, 14 *nam sicut indubitanter pro nomine domini patientibus requiem, ita incunctanter tribulationem his qui eos tribulant, repromisit;* 468, 2 *et hic ostenditur verbum Christi non sufficienter, sed abundanter etiam laicos habere debere et invicem se monere atque docere, ut sapienter et rationabiliter proferatur.*[47]

Vita 15 (1046) *ante omnia incessabiliter domini tui meditare mandata, orationibus et psalmis instanter incumbe.* Virg. 13 (1043, 7) *ornetur plane, sed interioribus ornamentis et spiritaliter, non carnaliter componatur.* Cel. 7 (334, 10) *unde audenter ac simpliciter loquebatur ad dominum;* 14 (340, 19) *memoria spiritaliter excolenda est, cui non tam frequenter recordanda sunt praecepta;* 22 (348, 9) *qui probabiliter ac scienter abstinentiae virtutem tenet.*

Chapter IV

BIBLICAL QUOTATIONS

A. *INTRODUCTORY FORMULAE*

Pelagius, with notable frequency, refers to an entire quotation by the demonstrative pronoun *illud*.

Exp. 11, 6: secundum *illud* Jacobi (followed by quotation of James 4:15);
Exp. 237, 6: sicut *illud* Moysi;
Exp. 13, 8: ut *illud*.
Dem. 27 (41, D): ut *illud* in Evangelio legimus;
Dem. 6 (21, D): Necdum Evangelicum *illud* sonnerat.
C. Arr. 13, 19: *illud* . . . quo continetur dixisse deum.[1]
Vita 9 (1039): ut vere in eo propheticum *illud* impleatur (cf. Virg. 8 (236, 12) below);
Vita 13 (1043): sed dicit quis *illud* apostoli dicentis;
Vita 13 (1044): ubi est *illud* propheticum.
Virg. 1 (226, 15): in his quam maxime *illud* impletur apostoli;
Virg. 6 (231, 18): ita alteri ipse subvenias propter *illud*;
Virg. 8 (236, 12): et impletur in eis *illud* propheticum (cf. Vita 9 (1039) above);
Virg. 10 (239, 3): propter *illud* quod scriptum est.
Cel. 1 (330, 11): *illud* mecum scripturae reputans;
Cel. 1 (330, 14): et *illud* beati Petri.

Another mannerism is to place two verbs of speaking into an introductory formula, one of them *dico* in a participial form. The phenomenon itself is not unusual. What is notable is the frequency with which it appears in Pelagius, particularly in Exp. The brevity of most of his comments does not force out this kind of formula, contrary perhaps to expectation, although it does occur less often in the latter portions of the commentary, where his notes tend to be even shorter than in earlier sections.

Exp. 5, 24: apud ipsos quoque Hebraeos eadem *commemorat dicens*;

Exp. 6, 14: ad quos etiam ipse venisse *testatus est dicens*;

Exp. 76, 12: et alios ut currerent *adhortatus est dicens*;

Exp. 319, 15: salvator *edocuit dicens*.[2]

Dem. 20 (35, A): Aliam nos humilitatem Christus docuit, qui nos ad exemplum suum *hortatur, dicens*.

Vita 2 (1034): sicut et ipse *testatur* . . . *dicens*;

Vita 4 (1035): ad Abraham Deus *loquitur, dicens*;

Vita 9 (1038): Quid sit enim Deum diligere, Domini et Salvatoris doctrina *declarat, dicentis*.[3]

Virg. 2 (226, 18): de quibus spadonibus dominus in evangelio *repetit dicens*;

Virg. 7 (232, 10 ff.): *comminatur* dominus aeterni ignis reos fore . . . *dicens*;

Virg. 11 (240, 13): unde et beatus Petrus *praecipit dicens*;

Virg. 18 (249, 6): quod per prophetam *testatur dicens*.

Cel. 31 (355, 4): *vocatque* nos dominus in evangelio *dicens*;

Cel. 16 (343, 8 ff.): unde et beatus David . . . de hac quoque virtute *non tacuit dicendo*.

De Lege 1 (107, B): sicut Philippus eunocho in actibus apostolorum *probat dicens*;

De Lege 3 (108, C): quem . . . divinus sermo . . . vere ditiorem divitibus *praefert dicens*;

De Lege 4 (109, B): unde et beatus apostolus Ioannes paria *testatur dicens*;

De Lege 7 (113, A): sicut in fronte codicis ad Romanos *loquitur dicens*.

When he wishes to juxtapose two quotations which both support his point or are otherwise related to the subject under discussion, Pelagius usually separates the two by one of the following: *et*,[4] *et iterum*,[5] *et alibi*,[6] *alibi* as part of some longer phrase,[7] and much less often *et rursum*,[8] or *et rursum* as part of some longer phrase.[9] It is to be noted that the latter two occur only in Dem. Among our four letters it is only Cel. that has phrases with *rursum*, another fact which links that letter to Dem.

et iterum: Vita 2 (1034), 5 (1036) [*ter*], 8 (1038), 9 (1039), 13 (1044) [*bis*]. Virg. 11 (240, 2). Cel. 1 (330, 13), 3 (331, 16), 32 (356, 14), 32 (356, 19). De Lege 4 (109, B).
et alibi: Vita 2 (1034), 3 (1034), 13 (1044). Virg. 11 (240, 3). Cel. 23 (349, 12). De Lege 4 (108, D), 4 (109, C).
alibi in phrase: Vita 8 (1038), 10 (1040), 15 (1046). Cel. 7 (335, 4).
et rursum: Cel. 4 (333, 1) [*ac rursus*], 10 (337, 4), 31 (355, 26).
et rursum in phrase: Cel. 3 (331, 17).

Regarding clusters of biblical quotations, we may notice that De Lege 5 (110, D) contains a group of three texts (Mt. 16:24; Acts 14:22; Mt. 5:11 f.) run together, separated by no particles. It is not characteristic of Pelagius to do this, although such a cluster does occur in at least one place: Exp. 161, 15–18.

Pelagius frequently brings a biblical quotation to an end with the words *et cetera* or *et reliqua.*[9a] This we find in three of the letters as follows: Vita 13 (1044). Virg. 7 (232, 16); 13 (243, 17). De Lege 4 (109, B).

B. USE AND CONTEXT OF BIBLICAL QUOTATIONS

It is necessary in this regard to be highly selective and to choose only those instances which seem to recur or to be peculiar in Pelagius' use of quotations, and those whose context provides striking parallels in expression. More than seventy biblical quotations or clear allusions are common to the four letters and to Pelagius.

The section on Parallel Passages has already brought to light a number of striking similarities in use of Biblical tests.

We might well expect that in the case of Pelagius in particular, similar groupings of two or more quotations would appear in more than one of his writings. He compiled himself a book of testimonies, called by Gennadius *Liber Eclogarum*[10] and by Augustine *Liber Capitulorum*[11] and *Liber Testimoniorum.*[12] The obligations and sanctions of Christian morality were the centre of attention, and Pelagius intended his own book to be a supplement to the third book of Cyprian's *Testimoniorum Libri III ad Quirinum.*[13]

The fact that such a book existed has a twofold bearing upon our investigation. On the one hand it could have been used by Pelagians other than Pelagius, and thus the appearance in a questionable work of a given collocation of texts would not be strong evidence for Pelagius' authorship. This provides us with one reason for being severely selective in the citation of such evidence. On the other hand one would expect that if a disputed work is by Pelagius it would probably contain groupings of texts similar to some found in the undisputed works. In any case one need not assume that all "Pelagians"—e.g., Julian of Eclanum—were familiar at first hand with the written works of Pelagius.

Evidence cited below is of the use of single texts as well as of the collocation of two or more.

1. In the course of moral exhortation, Pelagius returns again and again to the threat of the last judgment and often quotes or alludes to certain Matthean passages.

(a) Mt. 7:22 f.:

> Exp. 212, 10: si quis autem haec ignorat, ignorabitur et a nobis et a domino dicente eis, qui se in eius nomine prophetasse dicebant: "nescio vos."[14]
>
> Exp. 202, 18: quid enim mihi proderit habere praesentiam et virtutes, si opera non habeam caritatis? dicitur enim mihi: "non novi te, operari iniquitatis."[15]

In Vita 13 (1044) the discussion concerns those who confess the Lord with their mouths but deny him in deed, and Mt. 7:22 f. is quoted in full.

(b) Mt. 25:41 ff.:

> Exp. 319, 14 ff.: et eos qui evangeli praecepta contemnunt, maledictor esse et salvator educuit dicens: "discedite a me, maledicti, in ignem aeternum."
>
> Exp. 373, 19–374, 3: (Pelagius is commenting on Eph. 5:5) Contra illos agit, qui solam fidem dicunt ducere ad regnum posse caelum, quia huiusmodi actus non ex deo, sed daemonibus exhibentur; *hereditas autem regni caelorum dei filiis, non diaboli praeparatur*.
>
> Vita 10 (1040): qui etiamsi nihil mali fecerit nec boni, tamen ad aeternae vitae praemium non admittitur, sed gehennae ignibus mancipatur; sicut Evangelio Dominum dixisse legimus . . . (then follows complete quotation of Mt. 25:41–43).

Virg. 7 (232, 8): Sed ut dicere coeperamus, non sufficit Christiano a malis se abstinere, nisi etiam bonorum operum officia perfecerit, quod illo vel maxime testimonio comprobatur, quo comminatur Dominus aeterni ignis reos fore, qui quamvis mali nihil gesserint, non fecerint omne quod bonum est, dicens: "Tunc dicet rex his qui ad sinistram sunt," etc.

At the end of Dem. we find, as a kind of conclusion to the letter, an extended section on the last day,[16] which follows immediately after mention of the admitted difficulty of the life of chastity and an exhortation to consider the heavenly reward and the fleeting and temporal character of this-worldly existence.[17] This structural feature of Pelagius' letter finds a parallel in the concluding section of Cel. At the opening of ch. 31 we discover mention of the arduousness of the life of chastity,[18] followed by immediate reference to the heavenly reward,[19] followed in turn by a consideration of the last day in which quotations of Mt. 25:34 and 25:41 as well as other texts are brought forward. We have here, then, not only the appearance of a favourite theme of Pelagius supported by one of his favourite texts, but also a marked structural similarity between the concluding sections of Cel. and Pelagius' letter to Demetrias.

2. Next we have an example of the way in which certain thoughts and words may become associated in the mind of one author with certain texts. At the end of ch. 4 of the Vita the author discusses those whom God loves and those whom he does not love, and follows with quotation of Ps. 5:4–6.

Malos non amat Deus, peccatores non amat, iniustos non mat, rapaces, crudeles, impios; sed amat bonos, iustos, pios, humiles, innocentes, mites, sicut scriptum est, "Quoniam non Deus volens iniquitatem tu es. Non habitabit iuxta te malignus, neque permanebunt iniusti ante oculos tuos. Odisti omnes qui operantur iniquitatem, perdes omnes qui loquuntur mendacium."

In commenting on part of Rom. 13:4 (*Dei etenim minister est, vindex in iram ei qui malum agit*), Pelagius writes the following (Exp. 102, 11):

Quia deus non diligit malos, qui "*odit omnes qui operantur iniquitatem.*"

The words *deus non diligit malos* are clearly parallel to the more extended discussion in the passage from the Vita, and Pelagius closes the sentence with a clear (and accurate) reminiscence of part of Ps. 5:5, changing only the *odisti* of the psalm text to the third person singular *odit*, to agree with *deus*. It is to be noticed further that the phraseology *deus non diligit* (*amat*) *malos* is not found in the surrounding verses of the psalm.

3. There is a very interesting use of a verse from the Song of Songs (5:16) in both Vita and Exp. In the former[20] the author is engaged in describing the kind of man that a Christian ought to be, and writes that there should be no one who does not desire to see and hear him, no one who will not believe he is a son of God. In him ought to be fulfilled *propheticum illud:* "*Fauces eius dulcedinis, et totus desiderium.*"

In commenting on a phrase from 2 Cor. 6:6, which is in the middle of Paul's exhortatory list describing those qualities which he desires the Corinthians to have, Pelagius writes the following on the words, "in suavitate": *Ut nulli verbis nostris amaritudinem generemus, et ut dicatur de nobis: "fauces eius dulcedines," et reliqua*,[21] a clear reference to the verse in Song of Songs. The general context in both Vita and Exp. is similar, although there are no striking verbal similarities apart from the reference to the Old Testament verse.

4. There appears in Pelagius' Expositions and in Vita a fascinating and elusive combination of sayings which may be traced in Christian literature back to the Apostolic Fathers. The combination may be seen in its clearest form in 2 Clement 13, 2. The author of that tract exhorts his readers not to be pleasers of men, lest the name of God be blasphemed among those "outside" on account of what Christians do. He then quotes Isaiah 52:5b, which he follows by another saying whose written source is at present unknown: "For the Lord says, 'Every way is my name blasphemed among all the Gentiles (Isaiah 52:5b),' and again, 'Woe unto him on whose account my name is blasphemed'." It is possible that this combination existed, at one stage, in Jewish and Jewish-Christian collections of messianic testimonies concerning the Name of the Lord.[22] See also Ignatius, Trall. 8:3; Polycarp, Phil. 10.2 f.; Apostolic Constitutions 1.10.1 and 3.5.6; and cf. Justin Martyr, Dial. 17.

The context of thought as between Pelagius and Vita is somewhat different. Pelagius is commenting on St. Paul, who in Romans 2:25 quotes Isaiah 52:5b as part of his discussion of the *Jews*, who by their boasting in the Law blaspheme the Name of God. Vita quotes the same verse in the context of a discussion of *Christians* who blaspheme by their actions. The text common to them both is in this case identical with the Vulgate, except that for Pelagius there is no *sicut* before *scriptum* after St. Paul's quotation of the verse from Isaiah. The future perfect *fuerit blasphematum* in both is to be noted,[23] as well as the genitive *domini* (cf. *dei* in the scriptural text).

Vita 9 (1039)

. . . cuius vita tam impia, tam scelesta, tam luxuriosa, tam sordida. et erit illius prophetiae reus, "Nomen enim dei per vos blasphematur inter gentes (Rom. 2:24 = Is. 52:5b)." sed *vae* illis per quos *nomen domini fuerit blasphematum.*

Exp. 25, 18 ff. (on Rom. 2:25 = Is. 52:5b)

"Nomen enim dei per vos blasphematur inter gentes, scriptum est enim." Praeposterato ordine ante posuit testimonium quam diceret scriptum: ita enim dicentis sermo delapsus est. *vae,* quorum actibus *nomen domini fuerit blasphematum.*[24]

5. Pelagius quotes or refers four times to Mt. 13:43—"Then the righteous will shine like the sun in the kingdom of their Father"—when the subject of the heavenly reward of the righteous is under consideration, as it often is in Pelagius. He quotes it, for example, in commenting on 1 Cor. 2:3, and again in his exegesis of Rom. 2:4. In the letter to Demetrias the same text is employed in urging the reader to be mindful now of the heavenly reward in spite of the trials imposed upon Christians by sinful men.[25]

In ch. 8 of Virg. the author exhorts the virgin to keep her mind fixed not on the things of the world but on the things of God, to think on things holy and virtuous, and to consider the heavenly reward. In the middle of this exhortation we find the following lines.

> Domini est resurrectio mortuorum, Domini est immortalitas, Domini est incorruptio, Domini est splendor solis qui sanctis promittitur, sicut in Evangelio scriptum est: *tunc iusti fulgebant sicut sol in regno Patris eorum* (Mt. 13:43).[26]

6. In Dem. 27, Pelagius quotes Mt. 5:28—"Every one who looks at a woman lustfully has already committed adultery with her in his heart." The quotation occurs in the midst of a discussion of the necessity to care for one's thoughts—*cogitationes*. The author of Virg. uses the same quotation while discussing the same subject. This is not an unusual topic, and the biblical verse is a fairly obvious one to support the point in question. But the sentences before and after the quotation in both cases contain parallels in thought, vocabulary, and word-roots which make the comparison valuable as evidence.

Virg. 11 (240, 8 ff.)	Dem. 27 (41, D)
Nolo existimes te *crimen* fugisse peccati, si *voluntatem* non sequatur effectus, cum scriptum sit: (quotation of Mt. 5:28). Nec dicas, "*cogitavi* quidem, sed non perfeci." quia etiam concupiscere nefas est quod fieri nefas est.	Huiusmodi *cogitatio* etiamsi ex aliquo impedita casu, non impleat *voluntatem*, nihilominus actione *criminis* condemnatur a Domino, ut illud in Evangelio legimus: (quotation of Mt. 5:28). Apud Deum, cui nota sunt omnia etiam antequam fiant, *voluntas* perfecta faciendi, reputatur pro opere facti.

In addition to the common vocabulary and thought, it is not too much to say that the clause, *si voluntatem non sequatur effectus* (Virg.) is parallel to the clause of which *cogitatio* is the understood subject—*etiamsi, ex aliquo impedita casu, non impleat voluntatem* (Dem.).

7. In the discussion in Virg. of keeping the tongue from evil the author quotes Rom. 12:14 and follows this immediately with a conflation of I Thess. 5:15 and I Peter 3:9.

Et memor esto dicentis Apostoli: "benedicite et nolite maledicere" (Rom. 12:14). sed et illud crebrius recordare: "videte ne quis malum pro malo alicui reddat neque maledictum pro maledicto, sed e contrario benedicentes, quia in hoc vocati estis, ut benedictionem hereditate possideatis (Thess. 5:15 and I Pet. 3:9)."[27]

Pelagius, in commenting on Rom. 12:14, almost immediately quotes I Pet. 3:9.

Ne utrumque nos facere debere putaremus, sicut et Petrus ait: "non reddentes maledictum, sed e contrario benedicentes (I Pet. 3 : 9)."

8. We may detect a parallel in the association of Mt. 25:41 with James 2:10. One recalls from the quotation of Mt. 25:41 in Virg. (under no. 1, above) that it occurs, in a manner highly typical of Pelagius, as scriptural support for the thesis that it will not be enough at the last day simply to have abstained from evil. After the quotation there are some few lines expounding the meaning of this text, and then the author, more fully to support the argument, moves to a quotation of James 2:10.

> Nolo enim tibi in hoc blandiaris, si aliqua non feceris, qui aliqua feceris, cum scriptum sit: "qui universam legem servaverit, offendat autem in uno, factus est omnium reus."[28]

Now we find this same combination of texts in Pelagius' exegesis of Gal. 3:10, which verse itself is in line with Pelagius' preoccupation in its quoting of Deut. 27:26—"Cursed be every one who does not abide by all things written in the book of the law, and do them." In the body of Pelagius' comments on the verse from Galatians, we find the following lines.

> Eos qui evangelii praecepta contemnunt, maledictos esse et salvator edocuit dicens: "discedite a me, maledicti, in ignem aeternum (Mt. 25:41)," et Iacobus apostolus, qui unius mandati transgressorem omnium reum esse monstravit.[29]

Pelagius does not quote James 2:10, but mentions James by name, and the reference is clearly to that verse.

9. In both Cel. and Dem., Mt. 7:12 is quoted in contexts in which it is said that this command comprehends what is meant by *iustitia*.

Cel. 14 (341, 11 f.)	Dem. 9 (24, B–C)
Mt. 7:12 is first quoted followed by: Infinitae namque sunt species partesque *iustitiae* . . . quas omnes una hac *brevi* sententia *comprehendit* (i.e., *Dominus* subject understood).	Generaliter namque omnibus mandatur *iustitia*, quam Salvator in evangelio, *breviter* quidem, sed plenissime *comprehendens*, ait: (quotation of Mt. 7:12).

10. Cel. and Dem. both quote Phil. 3:13–14. There are striking parallels of expression in the remarks preceding the quotation in both letters, and both make essentially the same points—that we are to be renewed daily in virtue and that we

are not to be confident in virtue already achieved. The parallels below are not derived from the text of the verses in Phil.

Cel. 32 (355, 28—356, 11)

Beati sunt qui ita expectant, ita illum speculantur diem, ut se ad eum *cotidie* praeparent, qui non *de praeterita* sibi *iustitia* blandientes secundum apostolum *per dies singulos* in virtute *renovantur* . . . totum quo tenditur spatium vitae tua est, ut peragere possis iustitiam; nec *de praeterita iustitia* confidens remissior efficiaris, sed sicut dicit apostolus: (quotation of Phil. 3:14–15).

Dem. 27 (42, A–C)

Excitandus est enim spiritualibus stimulis semper animus, et maiori *quotidie* ardore *renovandus* . . . Cesset omnis ignavia, et inutilis *de praeterito labore* securitas. si volumus non redire currendum est. beatus apostolus *de die in diem* vivens Deo non quid ante fecisset, sed quid facere deberet semper attendens, dicebat (quotation of Phil. 3:13–14).

11. In contexts in which both Cel. and Dem. give miscellaneous instructions on the conduct of private life, Mt. 25:34 and 37 are quoted in succession without the intervening verses. Both letters are advising against lying and oath taking.

Cel. 19 (345, 20 ff.)

Mentiri vero atque *iurare lingua tua* prorsus ignoret tantusque in te sit veri amor, ut, quicquid dixeris, iuratum putes. de quo salvator ad discipulos ait: "Ego autem dico vobis non iurare omnino (Mt. 25:34);" et paulo post: "Sit autem sermo vester, est est, non non; quod autem his abundantius est, a malo est (Mt. 25:37)."

Dem. 19 (34, A–B)

Mentiri autem, maledicere atque *iurare lingua tue* nesciat . . . Et iurare ipse Christus prohibuit, qui dixit, "Ego autem dico vobis, non iurare omnino (Mt. 25:34)." et rursum: "Sit autem sermo vester, est est, non non; quod autem amplius est, a malo est (Mt. 25:37)."

12. De Lege 9 alludes to but does not quote Phil. 3:13. The allusion comes at the end of a series of exhortations to move on, to hurry on with progress in the Christian life, a theme highly typical of Pelagius. The two verbs which appear in the exhortations immediately preceding the quotation also appear in remarks of Pelagius in connection with the same Pauline verse. The extract below from Dem. is from a section of the letter in which Pelagius is making the same kind of exhortation as we find in De Lege: we are not to be idle and think we have ever attained perfection, but rather we are to hasten on to ever higher attainment. It is to be noted that the two verbs

in question are not derived from the Pauline verse or from the surrounding verses in Philippians, although they are perhaps words which not unnaturally might spring to mind in connection with Paul's thought.

De Lege 9 (118, D)	Dem. 27 (44, A)	Exp. 408, 4 f.
Curre, ut non negligas. *Festina*, ut celerius comprehendas. siquidem Paulus iam Christi catenam pro Evangelii annuntiatione circumferens, nondum se comprehendisse dicebat.	Si volumus non redire, *currendum* est. beatus apostolus de die in diem vivens Deo non quid ante fecisset, sed quid facere deberet semper attendens, dicebat: (quotation Phil. 3:13 f.).	(Comment on part of Phil. 3:13) Hoc solum scio quia cotidie proficio et praeteritum laborem non computans ad priora *festino*.

13. We find both Pelagius and De Lege referring to the same place in Hosea in relation to the symbolism of light and darkness, day and night. In both, light corresponds to knowledge (*scientia*) and darkness to ignorance. The same words are not quoted by each document. De Lege quotes Hosea 4:6b and Exp. quotes 4:5b–6a.

De Lege 3 (111, B)	Exp. 104, 15 ff.
... ostendens (dominus) in summa rerum salutarium nebula et tenebris constitutos eos, qui spiritualem lucernam, id est divinae legis scientiam habere nollent accensam. quam quidam repellentes, per prophetam a Domino repellentur, sicut scriptum est: "Quia tu scientiam repulisti, repellam et ego te (Hosea 4:6b)."	(Pelagius is commenting on Rom. 13:12: "Nox praecessit, dies autem appropriabit") Comparat diei scientam et ignorantiam nocti, propheta dicente: "nocti adsimilavi matrem tuam; factus est populus meus tamquam non habens scientiam (Hosea 4:5b–6a)."

Chapter V

SYNTAX AND STYLE

A. PARTICIPLES USED AS SUBSTANTIVES

One of the most marked features of the syntax of Pelagius is the extensive use of present participles as substantives. Comparison with Ambrose, for example, is striking. M. A. Adams[1] has culled from the letters of Ambrose about 100 present participles used in this way. These letters occupy a space of some 425 Migne columns,[2] which gives a frequency of about one to every four columns. The assured writings of Pelagius occupy a space equivalent to about 230 Migne columns.[3] I have counted 150 instances of these present participles in Pelagius, which gives an average of about one to every 1.5 columns, a frequency more than double that of Ambrose. Pelagius shows a particular fondness for the present participles of *credo*[5] and *pecco*.[5]

Investigation of our four letters yields the following results:

Vita: Twelve present participles used as substantives,[6] including one instance[7] of *credo* and one[8] of *pecco*. Average: one to every 1·2 Migne columns.

Virg.: Nineteen such participles,[9] including one of *credo*[10] and two of *pecco*.[11] Average: One to every ·7 Migne column.

Cel.: Ten such participles,[12] with no examples of *credo* or *pecco*. Average: One to every 1·5 Migne columns.

De Lege: Seventeen such participles,[13] including four of *credo* and none of *pecco*. Average: One to every ·6 Migne column.

It will have been noticed that the rate of frequency in Vita, Virg., and De Lege is higher than the overall average of Pelagius. This is not surprising. Pelagius is highly irregular in this regard, as can be seen from the fact that there is only one of these participles in Martini's fragments, which occupy seventeen Migne columns. In many sections of the Pauline commentary the frequency is well above Pelagius' overall average.

We may now give a few examples of this usage. Exp. 4, 28 *et non tam omnes increpat quam cur* peccantes *non increpaverint reprehendit;* 39, 19 *pater est omnium* credentium; 76, 13 *unde intelligitur quia hic* interrogantis *voce utitur et* redarguentis *potius quam* negantis. Dem. 22 (36, C) *illarum ait* esurientes *alere cibo.*

Vita 1 (1033) *in Christo* credentium *vocabulum descendit et nomen;* 8 (1037) *misereri* peregrinantibus *et* laborantibus. Virg. 7 (234, 3) *nullius ante* peccantis *et propter peccatum suum* morientis *retrahebantur exemplo;* 17 (247, 18) *qui aedificet semper magis quam aliquando destruat* audientes. Cel. 1 (330, 4) *pugnabatque acriter cum haesitatione mea humilitas* obsecrantis; 14 (341, 6) legentis *animum pascit ac refovet.* De Lege 9 (115, C) *cum sanctis et deum* timentibus *coronentur;* 10 (115, D) bellanti *dexteram pacis dare non poteram.*

B. USE OF THE GERUND

Souter called attention to another marked characteristic of the Latinity of Pelagius. In his own words, Pelagius "shows an extreme fondness for the ablative of the gerund, not as a mere substitute for the present participle, but with the earlier, instrumental force."[15] A few examples from Pelagius and all the instances from the four letters follow.

Exp. 133, 13 eligendo *piscatores artem retoricam et philosophiam reprobavit;* 417, 2 laudando *ergo illos apostolus ad maiora provocat et invitat.* Dem. 3 (18, A) *utriusque partis possibilitatem homini* inserendo, *proprium eius fecit esse quod velit.* De Nat. (in Aug. De Nat. et Grat. 11) *egone abnuo, qui rem* confitendo, *confitear necesse est et per quod res offici potest?*[16]

Vita 2 (1034) *qui patrem deum* peccando *perdiderunt;* ibid. peccando; 9 (1039) *his ...* conversando *efficiatur aequalis;* 9 (1040) *vitam ... perpetuam, quam bene* faciendo *non meruit;* 10 (1040) vivendo (*bis*); 12 (1042) sentiendo; 13 (1044) faciendo and peccando.

Virg. 8 (235, 9) *nuptam viro placere adserit,* cogitando *quae mundi sunt;* 8 (235, 12) *quia illa* cogitando *quae mundi sunt complacet vel marito.*

Cel. 4 (332, 3) *eiusque imperia superbissime* contemnendo *in tantae maiestatis imus iniuriam;* 5 (334, 1) contemnendo; 16 (343, 3) *eiusque vitium nutrias* annuendo; 6 (343, 10) dicendo; 16 (344, 3) *ne non tam alios quam se ipsos viles* detrahendo *facerent;* 17 (344, 17) decipiendo; 28 (352, 20) repellendo; 29 (353, 13) dicendo; 30 (354, 9) dicendo.

De Lege 8 (114, A) *qui* peccando *quotidie nosmetipsos occidimus;* 8 (114, D) *nec* poenitendo *pristina lacrymis peccata diluimus, sed peccata non* poenitendo *cumulamus.*

It needs to be pointed out that the only two ablative gerunds to be found in Virg. occur in those lines of ch. 8 which correspond precisely to the comments of Pelagius on 1 Cor. 7:34.[17] This fact will be grist for the mill of those who would prefer to see Virg. as coming from an author who copied from Pelagius. In view of all the other evidence bearing upon Virg., however, it is more plausible to interpret the fact as an instance of the irregularity in use of the gerund to be found in the assured writings of Pelagius. Virg. has a length of some nine Migne columns. In eight columns from the middle of Dem. there is not to be found one ablative gerund,[18] and in Martini's fragments, which run to seventeen columns, there are four.[19]

C. OBJECT CLAUSES

Souter noticed[20] that in the Expositions Pelagius, in addition to the classical construction with accusative and infinitive, employs for indirect discourse object clauses introduced by either *quod* or *quia*. *Quod* occurs more often than *quia*, and both are followed by either the subjunctive or the indicative, the subjunctive being more common with *quod* and the indicative more common with *quia*. Such clauses beginning with *quoniam* are entirely absent, and there is only one instance with *ut*.[21] These facts well agree with the object clauses in our four letters, all of which are listed below.[22]

Virg. 2 (226, 22): *Apostolus loquitur* quod sequantur.

Virg. 3 (227, 5): *illud cogitetur*, quod *dominus . . . virginalem* elegerit *uterum.*

Virg. 11 (241, 1): *vides ergo* quod *non in uno tantum membro dominicis* referantur *inhaerere vestigiis.*

Virg. 14 (224, 24): *puto* quod habitet *in quibusdam hominibus deus.*

Cel. 21 (347, 18): *obliviscimur* quia *ex uno omnes generati* sumus, *saltem id semper meminisse debemus* quia *per unum omnes* regeneramur.

De Lege 9 (115, B): *consideremus* quod *in hac terra hospites* sumus.

De Lege 9 (115, B): quia *non* quaerimus *hominum gloriam, deus testis.*

We thus have three clauses with *quod* and the subjunctive, two with *quod* and the indicative, three with *quia* and the indicative, and none with *quia* and the subjunctive.

D. *GENITIVE CONSTRUCTIONS*

Pelagius shows an occasional use of the genitive with an impersonal form of esse and an infinitive of some other verb, to express the idea that to do a certain thing belongs to the nature of, is appropriate to, or is habitually practiced by certain things or persons.

Exp. 64, 11 *timere enim servorum est, dilegere filiorum.* Dem. 9 (24, B) *non solum praecipere, sed et prohibere ipsum iubentis est.* De Nat. (in Aug., De Nat. et Grat. xlvii, 55): *audire, odorari, videre, potestatis nostrae sit.*[23]

Virg. 19 (250, 4) *non inchoasse tantum, sed perfessise virtutis est.* Cel. 6 (334, 3) *Stoicorum quidem est peccatorum tollere differentiam;* 7 (335, 2) *purissimae conscientiae est secure canere cum propheta* (followed by quotation of Ps. 100:2).

We find in Cel. also an instance of a more unusual use of the genitive with an impersonal form of *esse*, this time with an *ut* clause; it is paralled by a like instance in Exp.

Exp. 82, 2: *nemo ergo illorum vivet, quia in hoc tempore nemo perficit legem sine Christo, quia et* hoc legis est ut ipsi credatur.

Cel. 23 (334, 3): apostolici vero et praecepti est et exempli, ut curemus non conscientiae tantum sed etiam famae.[24]

E. *ABLATIVE ABSOLUTE*

Souter pointed out that a frequently occurring construction in Pelagius is that of the ablative absolute using a present participle with a noun, particularly an abstract noun, in the singular.[25]

Exp. 26, 8: *circumcisione cessante.*

Exp. 328, 14: *manente historiae veritate.*

Exp. 537, 16: *caritate faciente.*

Dem. 26 (40, D): *obsidente tristitia.*[26]

De Lege 2 (106, D): *corporis qualitate manente.*

De Lege 8 (114, C): *succendente oblivione.*

F. *USE OF THE COMPARATIVE*

Plinval discovered that when Pelagius uses a comparative with *ab* and the ablative instead of with *quam*, the comparative adjective or adverb is always *maius* or *minus*.[27] In our four letters there is only one comparative with *ab*.

Exp. 245, 18: *quanto maius est novum testamentum a lege.*

Exp. 290, 14: *ne putetis vos ab aliis ecclesiis . . . minus aliquid accepisse.*

Exp. 300, 2: *nihil minus fuerim a magnis apostolis.*

C. Apoll. 333, 38: *nihil minus habens ab eo.*

De Lege 9 (115, C): *quasi minus a ceteris habeant.*

G. *WORD ORDER*

A most important characteristic of the style of Pelagius and one, contrary to most that Kirmer selects for attention, that remains relatively constant through all his extant writings, is the particular form of hyperbaton in which a verb is placed between two related words, either between a substantive and its adjective or between one substantive and an accompanying substantive in the genitive. The order may be adjective–verb–noun or noun–verb–adjective, with the like alternatives in the case of the genitive construction. This figure pervades the writings of Pelagius as well as our four letters, and the following is only an illustrative selection of examples.

Exp. 42, 14 *a doloribus liberant sempiternis;* 240, 4 *qui paternum polluit thorum;* 476, 11 *occasiones fugere delictorum.* Dem. 1 (16, B) *nos morsibus tradamus invidiae;* 3 (18, D) *gratiae iuvantur auxilio;* 11 (27, A) *ad suas invitat epulas.* De Lib. Arb. (in Aug. De Grat.

Chr. 43) *ad perfectam incitat sanctitatem.* Lib. Fid. (1718) *ut semper nos liberi confiteamur substantiae.* C. Arr. 12, 23 *eiusdem cuius pater est substantiae.*[28]

Vita praef. (1031) *crebrioribus audeam litteris;* 4 (1036) *cumulum suorum non habuerint delictorum;* 10 (1040) *aliquid gesserint boni;* 13 (1042) *perpetuo tradebant interitui.* Virg. 1 (225, 3) *specialis est consecratio;* 2 (226, 11) *dulcedinem contemnere liberorum;* 7 (234, 4) *morientis retrahebatur exemplo;* 16 (246, 8) *nobilitatem admirentur humanam.* Cel. 4 (332, 7) *causas habeat remunerandi;* 6 (334, 13) *imperantis cogitat dignitatem;* 15 (341, 23) *in alterum habueris animum;* 27 (351, 20) *simplicemque commendat ornatum.* De Lege 2 (106, D) *in novam animi mutetur voluntatem;* 3 (107, D) *scientiam habere nollent accensam;* 4 (109, B) *vota reprobantur oblationum;* 9 (115, A) *languidumque vinceret teporem.*

Another feature of word order occurring with fair frequency in Pelagius is the separation by a verb of two coordinate words connected by *et* or some other copulative particle. Most often this works an effect of throwing emphasis upon the word appearing after the verb, an emphasis usually having an appropriateness for the context of the discussion.[29] The following, again, is only a selected list.

Exp. 40, 8 *et senex erat et sterilis;* 83, 17 *turpes sunt pedes atque deformes;* 90, 18 *apud deum autem omnia possibilia sunt atque facilia.* Dem. 25 (40, B) *dolo vincit ac fraude.*[30]

Vita 1 (1033) *vocabulum descendit et nomen;* 3 (1034) *nemo securus delinquat et liber;* 3 (1035) *deum iudicem sentiant et ultorem;* 7 (1037) *placatus fuerit vel offensus* (i.e., God).[31] Cel. 1 (329, 2) *gloria invenitur et gratia;* 28 (352, 7) *ita vas electionis ac magister gentium inter utrumque temperatus incedit ac medius;* 30 (354, 1) *et re vera quid ea castitate firmius est quidve tutius.* De Lege 1 (105, C) *si me non et tempus et causa simulque tuerentur et caritas;* 9 (115, B) *de his tantum sollicitudinem habere debemus et curam.*

H. ALLITERATION

Alliteration as a rhetorical figure is clearly present in the writings of Pelagius. One very notable feature emerges in this regard: the overwhelming preponderance of alliteration in *p* as compared to any other letter of the alphabet. I have attempted to count all the clear instances of alliteration in Dem., the Martini fragments, the fragments in Augustine, and 100 pages in Exp. (pp. 1–35, 255–87, and 500–32), as well as in the four letters. As a small effort toward correlating this data with the use of alliteration in two Latin Christian authors contemporary with Pelagius, I have counted the instances of alliteration in a roughly equal number of pages from the letters of Augustine and Jerome.[32] The figures from Pelagius, from the four letters, and from Augustine and Jerome are tabulated in the table below.

	Pel.	Vita	Virg.	Cel.	De Lege	Aug.	Jer.
A	27	1	5	1	4	41	28
B	0	0	0	0	0	1	1
C	35	6	13	9	9	61	55
D	32	1	2	4	2	32	26
E	5	1	2	2	1	33	9
F	10	1	1	1	0	12	16
G	1	0	0	0	1	1	0
H	2	1	0	0	1	5	5
I	7	4	2	3	2	22	21
L	6	1	0	0	0	10	9
M	11	1	0	6	4	29	18
N	9	2	2	1	1	10	8
O	5	0	0	1	1	5	5
P	65	25	17	11	23	52	59
Q	2	0	3	2	0	19	16
R	9	1	0	1	3	5	2
S	19	1	11	7	4	36	56
T	5	0	2	4	0	18	19
U	0	0	0	0	0	2	0
V	23	4	1	6	3	12	27

It will be seen that in Pelagius alliteration in *p* occurs almost twice as often as in *c*, the next highest letter. A similar ratio, 23/9, appears in De Lege. The ratio of *p* to *c* in Vita is 25/6, much more marked even than in Pelagius. In Virg. and Cel. the relation of *p* to *c* is not so striking: 17/13 and 11/9 respectively. But in Pelagius and in the four letters there are more instances of alliteration in *p* than in any other letter, and *c* is the next highest letter. Pelagius, moreover, is not regular in this regard, as one might expect. In thirty-three pages of Exp. (255–87) there occur exactly as many cases of alliteration in *p* as in *c*. In Augustine and Jerome *p* occurs with one of the highest frequencies also. But in both of these authors *c* appears with a frequency about equal to that of *p*, and in Jerome *s* occupies a place equal to *p* and *c*. One would not want to press these statistics unduly. I believe one could say, however, that the above table offers positive support to the case for Pelagius' authorship of the Vita and De Lege and that it does not offer negative evidence in the cases of Virg. and Cel.

I. METHODS OF ARGUMENT

Here we may bring together various miscellaneous items which have not found a convenient place in the foregoing.

1. FROM OLD TESTAMENT PARALLELS

Pelagius is fond of supporting a moral exhortation by reference to some incident or to some state of affairs in Old Testament times. The form of the argument is as follows: If *x* was true then, it is the case that *x* (or *y*) is even more true now. This general point underlies his discussion at many places where the argument does not emerge in this precise, succint form. But occasionally it does so emerge, and we find close parallels in Vita and Virg.

Exp. 182, 14 (the context is I Cor. 10:7–11) si enim adhuc parvolis et rudibus non pepercit, quanto magis nobis, qui legem perfectionis accepimus, non parcit, si talia fecerimus.

Dem. 8 (23, D) nam si etiam ante legem, ut diximus, et multo ante domini nostri salvatoris adventum iuste quidam vixisse et sancte referantur, quanto magis post illustrationem adventus eius, nos id posse credendum est qui instructi per Christi gratiam, et in meliorem hominem renati sumus.

Vita 10 (1041) Si illam (innocentiam) Iudaeis etiam sub veteri Lege degentibus, quando adhuc illis inimicum licebat odire, observare praeceptum est, quid te nunc agere convenit christianum, qui inimicum tuum iuberis amare.

Virg. 18 (248, 18) in ieiuniis magis quam in epulis delectare, illius vidvae (e.g., the Jewish widow Anna, Lk. 2:36–8) memor, quae non discedebat de templo ieiuniis et obsecrationibus deo serviens die ac nocte. et si vidva et quidem Iudaea talis fuit, qualem nunc virginem convenit esse Christi?

2. QUANTO MAGIS

A type of argument closely related to that above contains the words *quanto magis*. Here, however, we have arguments based not only on Old Testament models but on apostolic models, conclusions already reached in the course of an argument, etc. There is usually an introductory clause beginning with *si* and a second clause introduced by *quanto magis*. Pelagius is very fond of this rhetorical manner of argument, as Souter's long list[33] of occurrences of *quanto magis* indicates.

Exp. 132, 2 *si ergo* nec de veris apostolis dici hoc licet, *quanto magis* de falsis.

Exp. 245, 5 *Si ergo* illi inexcusabiles sunt qui legem in lapidibus acceperunt, *quanto magis* nos qui ex ore verba Christi suscepimus, si peccemus.

Virg. 9 (237, 5) *Ergo si* nec aliorum membrorum sanctificatio proderit, cum in uno sit vitium, *quanto magis*, si diversorum flagitio peccatorum omnia corrumpantur, unius nihil proderit integritas.

Virg. 17 (247, 10) nam *si* iuxta Apostoli doctrinam servum Domini litigare non oportet, *quanto magis* dei ancillam, cuius quo verecundior est sexus, animus debet esse modestior.

Cel. 26 (351, 5) *si ergo* etiam gentilibus maritis debetur honor iure coniugii, *quanto magis* reddendus Christianis.

3. GRADATIO

Pelagius does not make extended or even relatively frequent use of gradatio (argument of the form AB, BC, CD, etc.), and the examples which we do find are modest, but three instances of his use of it are of great interest for us here, precisely because the figure does *not* occur often. All three of these instances are concerned with sin—how it is to be defined, who are sinners and who are not sinners, and wherein lies the "possibility of not sinning." The first instance is concerned with Phil. 4:21, in which Paul gives instructions to "greet every saint." Pelagius wants to make clear what it means to say that they are saints, or that they are "holy."

Exp. 416, 10 et qui vere sancti erant, peccatores utique non erant, et qui non peccatores, sed sancti erant, quam poterant non esse quod non erant.

Two further instances we find in the fragments from the De Natura.

De Nat. (in Aug., De Nat. et Grat. 33) omne peccatum, nisi fallor, Dei contemptus est; et omnis Dei contemptus superbis est. quid enim tam superbum quam Deum contemnere?

De Nat. (in Aug., De Nat. et Grat. 59) ipsa non peccandi possibilitas non tam in arbitrii potestate quam in naturae necessitate est. quidquid in naturae necessitate positum est, ad naturae pertinere non dubitetur auctorem, utique deum. Quomodo ergo absque dei gratia dici existimatur, quod ad deum proprie pertinere monstratur?

Now in Virg. we find one example of gradatio, and it is again with reference to the subject of sin.

Virg. 6 (230, 24) Iustitia ergo non aliud est quam non peccare, non peccare autem est legis praecepta servare. praeceptorum autem observatio duplici genere custoditur.

4. MENTION OF HERETICS

A constantly recurring feature of the Expositions is the brief reference by name to certain heretics whenever it seems to Pelagius that Paul's words are of weight in refuting a particular heresy, or when an ambiguity in the apostle's words has been used to support heretical opinions. Manicheus and Jovinian are among those to whom Pelagius most often refers.[34] Very much in the spirit of Pelagius' references to these two is the following extract from Cel., where the author is commenting on Paul's teaching on marriage in I Cor. 7.

Cel. 28 (352, 23) apostolicae doctrinae regula nec cum Ioviniano aequat continentiae opera nuptiarum nec cum Manicheo coniugia condemnat. ita vas electionis ac magister gentium inter utrumque temperatus incedit ac medius, ut et remedium incontinentiae indulgeat et praemium provocet continentiam.

J. ADDITIONS TO KIRMER

Kirmer makes the recurring observation that certain figures of rhetoric do not occur in the documents which he examines as often as in Pelagius' letter to Demetrias. I have argued above that this letter cannot be taken as a reliable guide to the ordinary prose style of Pelagius. But the further point must be made that Kirmer overlooks examples of the rhetorical figures which he considers, examples which make the stylistic contrast between Dem. and our four letters a lesser one than he alleges it to be. I list below some examples which should be added to the relevant pages of Kirmer.

1. VITA

(a) Paronomasia

5 (1036) *illi ut* vindicentur, *isti ut in eos* vindicta *celebretur.*

ibid. vocanter *enim ante tempus boni, ne diutius* vexentur *a noxiis.*

7 (1037) *e quibus unus deo placuit eo quod* innocens *esset et* iustus; *alter vero, quia* iniustus *et* nocens, *deo placere non potuit.*

8 (1038) *in terram* aratris *et* rastris *domat.*[35]

(b) Polyptoton

8 (1038) *et illum legem* implesse *qui haec potuerit* implere.

13 (1043) *Adam a deo factus est homo* primus *in* primo *statu mundi.*

14 (1045) *qui ad* fletum fletibus *provocatur alienis.*

15 (1045) *qualem* tu te *vidvam debeas exhibere.*[36]

(c) Word-Antithesis

5 (1036) *illi enim vadunt ut* iudicent, *isti ut* iudicentur.

7 (1937) *e quibus unus deo placuit, eo quod* innocens *esset* et iustus; *alter vero, quia* iniustus *et* nocens, *deo placere non potuit.*[37]

(d) Chiasmus

9 (1038) *ut qui eum non velit videre, qui non audire desideret.*

14 (1044) *nisi qui Christi et doctrinam sequitur et imitatur exemplum.*

14 (1045) *qui pauper mundo efficitur, ut deo locuples fiat.*[38]

2. VIRG.

(a) Paronomasia

8 (234, 13) *et* inlicitum *aliquid incurrere quae se etiam a* licitis *castraverunt.*

8 (234, 19) *quae conubia deserunt non* inlicita *sed* licita *sperunt.*

10 (238, 3) *suspende autem illa in* corde *velut in* collo *tuo.*
16 (246, 17) *tam* nobilis *quam* ignobilis *dei efficitur filius.*[39]

(b) Polyptoton

3 (227, 9) virginem *habuit matrem* virgo *ipse permansurus.*
4 (228, 13) *tantus nihil* proderit *labor, dum vane* prodesse *creditur.*
5 (230, 13) *propter quod eam* habeas *non* habere.
15 (245, 4) *si vis ergo esse cum Christo et partem habere cum* Christo, Christi *tibi exemplo vivendum est.*
17 (247, 17) pudicae *mentis sermo etiam debet esse* pudicus.[40]

(c) Chiasmus

3 (227, 13) *dum totum in matre fuit quicquid habitabat in filio.*
16 (246, 6) *gaudent in deliciis in opibus delectantur.*[41]

3. CEL.

(a) Paronomasia

2 (330, 20) *ut possis in* coniugio *constituta non solum* coniugi *placere.*
6 (334, 12) *nec quantitatem* imperii *sed* imperantis *cogitat dignitatem.*
11 (338, 15) *et per* diversa *errorum* diverticula *ad viam multitudinis revertuntur.*
15 (342, 3) *nec sufficit,* quod iussa *non facimus, nisi etiam iubentem* iniustum *pronuntiemus.*
26 (350, 26) *tu magnum illum tua demonstra tanto ipsa* honoratior *futura, quanto illum amplius* honoraveris.[42]

(b) Polyptoton

4 (332, 21) *non aluid est quam eius praecepta* servare, *quae nobis ille* . . . servanda *mandavit.*
11 (338, 7) *si vel* adulamur *ipsi vel* adulantem *libenter audimus.*
11 (338, 8) *et magis offendere timemus* animos *hominum quam non ex* animo *loqui.*
12 (338, 20) *sin vero ea vel* deficiunt *vel* deficere *putantur.*
16 (343, 2) *ut non modo ipsa non* detrahas, *sed ne alii quidem* detrahenti *aliquando credas.*

17 (344, 16) *et* decipiendo *animum sibi obligare* decepti.

28 (352, 18) *utrum ille, qui* repulsus *a coniuge fornicatur, an illa, quae* repellendo *a se virum eum fornicationi quodam modo obiecit.*[43]

(c) Word-Antithesis

14 (341, 18) *aut* absoluit *aut* damnat.

15 (341, 22) *de* iniusto *opere coarguat vel de* iusto *laetificet.*

21 (347, 5) servum *et* nobilem *de moribus pronuntiat.*

22 (348, 22) *ne* perfectionis *magister* imperfectum *in se aliquid ostednat.*

28 (352, 17) *una pars se etiam* a licitis *abstinet, altera ad* illicita *delapsa est.*

30 (354, 15) *facile ex* amico inimicum *facies.*[44]

4. DE LEGE

(a) Paronomasia

1 (106, A) *colligimus* vocationem *nostram iuxta* vocantis *dignationem.*

5 (110, B) *qui dum* animali *sapienta occupant* animos.

5 (110, C) *vides quantum ab humanis* sensibus *per nostram imperitiam discrepat divina* sententia.

9 (115, A) *cave, ne quod accepisti bonum,* incautus *et negligens* custos *amittas.*

9 (115, C) *Christianis* divitiae *et haereditas sit* divinitas *Christi.*[45]

(b) Polyptoton

1 (105, D) *et si obedientiam* incorporalem, *quae inobedientiae remedium est, ex* incorporali *anima gigni ratione probabile est.*

3 (108, C) *propria* consilia *dei* consiliis *anteponat.*

5 (110, D) *quam damnationem* excepturos *credimus esse indevotos, cum tantam exprobationem devotus* exceperit.

7 (113, A) *sed* mansionum *iustitia iustiores* mansiones *differre, sicut* stellam stella.

9 (115, A) *donec qui* venturus *est* veniat.

10 (116, A) praesens *si iusseris cum* praesente.[46]

(c) Word-Antithesis

1 (105, D) *tantumque* novo *homini* per obedientiam *praestaretur* salutis, *quantum* veteri *per* inobedientiam perditionis *acciderat.*

3 (108, A) *una* suadet *ad* vitam, *alia* impellit *ad* mortem.

5 (110, D) *credimus esse* indevotos, *cum tantam exprobationem* devotus *exceperit.*

6 (111, D) *illi catenas baiulant* innocentes *nos aurum circumferimus* criminosi; *illi in* carceribus *vincti, nos im* tricliniis *delicati.*[47]

(d) Chiasmus

1 (105, D) *tantumque novo homini per obedientiam praestaretur salutis, quantum veteri per inobedientiam perditionis acciderat.*

9 (115, C) *honorent obsequiis, operibus colant.*

K. PARTICLES

For the sake of completeness I include below a table showing the occurrence of particles in the four letters under examination in this study, as well as in Dem., 104 pages[48] of Exp., and in the Martini fragments. With the exception of the data from Exp. and the fragments, and a few additions and corrections, the statistics below are taken from those supplied by Kirmer.[49] The works are measured in Migne lines.[49a]

	Vita (1100 lines)	Virg. (687 lines)	Cel. (800 lines)	De Lege (650 lines)	Dem. (1700 lines)	Exp. (1350 lines)	Mart. (714 lines)
Et	245	156	102	117	279	293	110
Que	18	1	45	10	114	3	5
Atque	5	1	28	1	19	4	6
Ac	4	7	20	2	48	4	8
Etiam	13	13	12	5	29	34	28
Quoque	3	1	4	1	11	1	12
Nam	10	8	4	2	10	5	7
Enim	36	28	40	2	58	34	13
Aut	19	34	14	13	26	10	20
Vel	8	7	12	3	38	44	13
Sed	52	45	30	26	44	79	14
Autem	10	4	7	4	14	10	9
Vero	15	8	15	0	22	7	7

	Vita (1100 lines)	Virg. (687 lines)	Cel. (800 lines)	De Lege (650 lines)	Dem. (1700 lines)	Exp. (1350 lines)	Mart. (714 lines)
Tamen	6	1	7	2	21	5	6
Itaque	3	0	4	0	12	0	5
Ergo	14	27	7	5	11	22	5
Igitur	3	0	6	1	6	3	8
Unde	4	5	13	5	18	8	3
Utique	2	1	2	0	8	2	2
Hinc	0	0	2	1	9	1	1
Ideo	0	0	8	0	8	11	1

If one understands that one's picture of the usage of Pelagius must be a composite one, drawn from the three last columns, it appears that the conclusion to be drawn from the table is that consideration of the relative frequency of particles does not offer evidence against Pelagius' authorship of the four letters, although neither does it offer positive evidence for it. A second conclusion is that the particles offer another line of evidence, along with the parallel passages, linking Cel. more closely to Dem. than to Exp. and the other three letters. It will be remembered also that Cel. does not show the relation to the writings of the "Sicilian Briton" that is to be seen in Exp., Vita, Virg., and De Lege. Cel. was written, I believe, after Pelagius had arrived in the Holy Land and at a date not distant from that at which he wrote Dem., i.e., 414.[49b] This leads to the further suggestion (see the copulative particles) that Pelagius had the same sort of literary assistance in the writing of Cel. as he very likely had for Dem. The last column of particles also links his work *De Fide Trinitatis* to the earlier period, a conclusion in line with the statement of Gennadius that that work was written before Pelagius was proclaimed a heretic.[50]

NOTES

Notes to Chapter I

1. *De Vita Christiana*, in *P.L.* xl, 1031–46; *De Virginitate*, in *C.S.E.L.* i, pp. 225–50; *Ad Celantiam*, in *C.S.E.L.* lvi, pp. 329–56; *De Lege*, in *P.L.* xxx, 105–16.

2. "Recherches sur l'oeuvre littéraire de Pélage," *Revue de Philologie* lx (1934), pp. 9–42, cited hereafter as "Recherches".

3. *Pelagius: A Historical and Theological Study* (Cambridge, 1956).

4. *Die Theologie des Pelagius und ihre Genesis* (Uppsala, 1957).

5. *Das Eigentum des Fastidius im pelagianischen Schrifttum* (St. Ottilien Oberbayern, 1937).

6. "Pelagian Literature," *Journal of Theological Studies*, N.S. xvi (1965), pp. 26–60.

7. See, e.g., "Recherches", pp. 15 f.

8. Cf. "Recherches," p. 15 with pp. 25 and 28; and cp. pp. 20–22 with pp. 23 f. and 29.

9. Morris, pp. 31 f.

10. C. P. Caspari, *Briefe, Abhandlungen und Predigten* (Christiana, 1890).

11. Caspari, pp. 3–13, and cf. Morris, p. 37.

12. "Recherches," p. 37, and "Le problème de Pélage sur son dernier état," *Revue d'Histoire ecclésiastique*, XXXV (1939), pp. 10 f.

13. See Caspari, pp. 223–329, and cf. Morris, pp. 37–41. I should not want to accept, however, Caspari's quite gratuitous attribution of his corpus to the British Pelagian, Agricola (pp. 386–9), and would prefer, with Morris (p. 40), to speak of him as the "Sicilian Briton."

14. *Pélage, ses écrits, sa vie et sa réforme* (Lausanne, 1943) and *Essai sur le style et la langue de Pélage* (Fribourg en Suisse, 1947).

15. *Archiv für Lateinische Lexikographie* xi (1900), pp. 577 f.

16. J. H. Gillis, *The Coordinating Particles in Saints Hilary, Jerome, Ambrose, and Augustine* (Washington, D.C., 1938), pp. 3, 24 f., 28.

17. 2 (1034), 3 (1034), and 13 (1044).

18. 1 (15, C), 4(19, B), 5 (20, B), 5 21, A), 8 (23, A), 9 (24, A), 10 (26, C), and 27 (41, C).

19. Alexander Souter, *Pelagius' Expositions of Thirteen Epistles of St. Paul* (Cambridge, 1922–31) ii, 5, 21; 8, 11; 11, 16; 15, 16; 42, 5; 48, 15 and *passim.*

20. These fragments, reproduced now in *P.L.* Sup. i 1544–60, were vindicated for Pelagius by C. P. Martini in his article "Quattuor Fragmenta Pelagio Restituenda," *Antonianum* xiii (1938), pp. 293–334.

21. Cf. his tables on metrical clausulae (pp. 45–8, 71–8, 99 f., etc.) with variations to be discovered in the sermons of Augustine recorded by M. Josephine Brennan, *A Study of the Clausulae in the Sermons of St. Augustine*

(Washington, 1947), pp. 18–25, and with similar variations in the works of Ambrose recorded by M. Rosella Delaney, *A Study of the Clausulae in the Works of St. Ambrose* (Washington, 1934), pp. 6–19. Cf. also Kirmer's tables on anaphora (pp. 37, 67 f., 96, etc.) with M. I. Bogan, *The Vocabulary and Style of the Soliloquies and Dialogues of St. Augustine* (Washington, 1935), p. 116.

22. See Kirmer, pp. 32, 33, 42, 43, 45, and *passim.*

23. R. F. Evans, "Pelagius, Fastidius and the Pseudo-Augustinian *De Vita Christiana*," in *Journal of Theological Studies*, N.S., xiii (1962), pp. 96 f.

24. Pp. 374–477.

25. Aug., *de Gratia Christi* i, 40–42, and Orosius, *Lib. Apol.* 29.

26. Orosius, *loc. cit.*: ". . . hoc quod neque apte neque decore dicitur, tibi imputare non debeamus, cui neque natales dederunt, ut honestioribus studiis erudireris, neque naturaliter provenit, ut saperes, sed illis dictatoribus tuis, qui miserum sensum miserrimo sermone conscribunt et te legendum cachinnis quasi titulum confusionis exponunt."

27. Morris (p. 28) glides too easily over the peculiarities of the letter to Demetrias.

28. Aug. *De Gest. Pel.* 16 and 19, and Jerome, *Dial. c. Pelag.* iii, 14 and 16.

29. R. F. Evans, "Pelagius, Fastidius and the Pseudo-Augustinian *De Vita Christiana*," *Journal of Theological Studies* N.S. xiii (1962), pp. 72–98, and "Pelagius' Veracity at the Synod of Diospolis," *Studies in Medieval Culture* (Kalamazoo, Michigan, 1964), pp. 21–30.

30. This was the view of both Caspari (pp. 374 f.) and Kirmer (p. 16). Morris (p. 28) is inaccurate in suggesting that Caspari assigned the Vita to the author of his six tracts; Caspari (pp. 386–9) assigned his corpus to Agricola.

31. Pp. 33, 35 f.

32. Marius Mercator, *Common. sup. nom. Cael.* ii, 1.

33. Cf. Souter, i, pp. 4 f. and 188 f.

34. Augustine wrote *De Gest. Pel.* in 417 and in ch. 19 tells us that "quidam sancti fratres" have had in their possession the work in question for "quattuor ferme annos" and have always understood the work as being by Pelagius.

35. The accusers at Diospolis (*Aug. de Gest. Pel.* 16), Augustine's "holy brethren" (*op. cit.* 19), and Jerome (*Dial. c. Pel.* iii, 14 and 16), were surely not all in possession of the same copy.

36. Cf. Vallarsi's discussion (*P.L.* xxx, 162) with the text and apparatus of Halm (*C.S.E.L.* i, p. 250).

37. "Recherches," pp. 24–6.

38. P. 87.

39. Virg. 7 (233, 10): "non agitur de qualitate peccati, sed de transgressione mandati."

40. *De Excidio Britanniae* 38.

41. Cf., for example, the table in Souter, i, p. 344.

42. See Vallarsi, *loc. cit.*

43. Kirmer, pp. 140 ff.

44. *P.L.* xxii, 1204.

45. *P.L.* Sup. i, 1103.

46. W. S. Teuffels, *Geschichte der römischen Literatur* (Leipzig, 1913) iii, p. 381.

47. "Recherches," pp. 14–16.

48. *De Lege* 1 (105, C–D) and 6 (111, A).

49. De Lege (1–2 (105–7).

50. De Lege 3–4 (107–8).

51. De Lege 4–5 (109–10).

52. De Lege 6 (111).

53. De Lege 7–8 (113–14).

54. De Lege 8–10 (114–16).

55. Kirmer, p. 104 and Caspari, p. 395, n. 7. Caspari terms the work "semi-Pelagian," but there is nothing in the evidence he adduces which Pelagius could not have said himself.

56. *P.L.* xxx, 105.

57. Caspari, pp. 392–7 and 395, n. 1. Caspari also shows the improbability of Vallarsi's suggestion of Faustus of Riez as the author of De Lege.

58. De Lege 6 (111).

59. De Lege 9 (115, C).

60. Aug., *De Gest. Pel.* 36; *De Haeresibus* 88; Mercator, *Lib. subnot. in verba Jul.* 11, 2.

61. Morris, pp. 37–41.

62. Aug., *Ep.* 156, to which *Ep.* 157 is Augustine's reply.

63. Morris goes too far, however, in suggesting (p. 38) that Hilarius sent a *work* to Augustine which is to be identified with the *De Divitiis* of the Caspari collection; nor did Caspari say precisely this, as Morris alleges. There is no evidence either in the letter of Hilarius or in Augustine's reply that the former sent more than his own letter reporting views, theses, held by some in Sicily.

64. To Caspari's parallels add the following: De Lege 9 (115, B–C) ("Nemo in deteriori . . . sit divinitas Christi") and De Divit. xix, 4 (p. 64) ("Nemo enim de India . . . locupletatione gaudere"), on fixing our desires only on those things which we can take with us to the next world.

65. It is surely not easy to suppose, with Plinval, that these two passages come from the same author.

66. Dem. 9 (24, C–25, A), 28 (43, A). *De Cast.* ii, p. 123.

67. See, e.g., Dem. 10 (25, A–D). Note that the extreme comments on I Cor. 7:3–5 in Souter's text, *Exp.* 159, 17–160, 20 and 160, 22–161, 8 are not in the Paris 653 ms. (V) and are not, I take it, part of the original text of Pelagius. See Celestin Charlier, "Cassidore, Pélage, et les origines de la vulgate paulinienne," *Studiorum Paolinorum Congressus Internationalis Catholicus* 1961 (Rome 1963), pp. 1–10.

68. Writing of various biblical instances in which men are compared to animals, he says (p. 58), "Ista non tam ad corporis habitudinem, quam ad morum similitudinem referentur, qui nec in ipsis animalibus absque aliquo naturalis motus gubernantur arbitrio."

69. See, e.g., Exp. 34, 9–22; 319, 7–18; 373, 19–374, 3.

70. Kirmer, p. 82.

71. To anticipate the argument a bit, I should suggest that the appearance in the "Sicilian Briton" of this particular combination of words, related to a subject of much concern to Pelagius, arises not only from the reading of the Vita but from conversation with Pelagius.

72. Consider in particular his use of Virg. That little treatise has a comparatively eirenic tone when compared to the "Sicilian Briton's" *De Castitate.* It is very suggestive that the one passage from Virg. of which the Sicilian writer makes any important use is the threatening section of ch. 7 (p. 233), in which the author treats the sin of Adam and Eve in relation to James 2:10. See Caspari, pp. 6–7 and 90, and Kirmer, pp. 89–92. The whole tone and cast of thought of the *De Castitate*, with its insistence that anyone with a serious interest in Christianity must abstain from marriage and carnal relations, is quite removed from Virg., with its characteristic emphasis that those who have chosen the special path of virginity must continue to live up to the requirements of *iustitia* incumbent upon all Christians.

73. For example, by Ferguson (p. 48) and by Hedde and Amann, "Pélagianisme," *Dictionnaire de Théologie Catholique* (Paris, 1933) xii, 685.

74. Aug., *De Gest. Pel.*, 46.

75. Aug., *Ep.* 156.

76. Kirmer, pp. 82–3, 102–3, 116. He interprets this data, of course, as evidence that Virg., Vita, and De Lege all have as their author Fastidius, who is also, according to Kirmer, the author of the Caspari corpus.

77. Kirmer, pp. 82–3.

78. See *securus* in Vocabulary section below.

79. See *fallo* in Vocabulary section, ch. 3 below.

80. Cf. comments recently made to similar effect by Robert M. Grant, *The Apostolic Fathers I: An Introduction* (New York, 1964), p. 62, concerning the possible relationship between Ignatius and the author of the Fourth Gospel.

81. E.g., J. H. I. Watt, "The Authenticity of the Writings Ascribed to Leontius of Byzantium, A New Approach by means of Statistics," *Studia Patristica* VII (*Texte und Untersuchungen* XCII, Berlin, 1966), p. 336, where the author quotes words to this effect by G. H. C. Macgregor and A. Q. Morton, *The Structure of the Fourth Gospel* (Edinburgh, 1961), p. 10.

82. I am leaving out of account here the very short *Libellus Fidei* which Pelagius sent to Pope Innocent.

83. See my remarks above in this chapter and notes 23 and 26.

84. See the table of particles at the end of ch. 5 in this book and note the disparity in use of *-que* as between *Dem.* and *Mart.*

Notes to Chapter II

1. See Exp. 374, 7 ff. and 365, 4 f.
2. See Souter, i, pp. 74–9.
3. See the evidence accumulated by Souter, i, pp. 85–115.

4. It is also my conviction that a similar investigation would lead indubitably to the judgment that the writings of the "Sicilian Briton" are not from Pelagius; it is beyond our scope here to undertake this latter enterprise.

4a. There is a further bit of evidence to suggest that Cel. comes from this later period of Pelagius' activity. In ch. 6 (p. 334) the author of Cel. makes a point of distinguishing his own position from the Stoic doctrine of the equality of sins. This point is to be understood as in all likelihood a response of Pelagius to Jerome's allegation that Pelagius did in fact teach the Stoic doctrine. Jerome makes this point in his anti-Pelagian dialogue, written in 415, after Pelagius has arrived in the Holy Land (see Jer., *Dial. adv. Pel.* 1.19).

5. Celestin Charlier, "Cassidore, Pélage, et les origines de la vulgate paulinienne," *Studiorum Paolinorum Congressus Internationalis Catholicus* 1961 (Rome, 1963), pp. 1–10.

6. Pp. 245–64.

7. Quoted by Souter, i, p. 249.

8. See H. Vogels, "Der Pelagius-Kommentar zu den Briefen des hl. Paulus," *Theologische Revue*, xxv (1926), pp. 121–26, and H. J. Frede, *Pelagius, der irische Paulus-text, Sedulius Scottus* (Freiburg, 1961).

9. The Souter and the Martini fragments are now available in *P.L.* Sup. i, 1539–60, where the page references used below are reproduced. The commentary on Paul is published in the same volume (1110–1374) and with Souter's pagination; Souter's apparatus is not included, however, which makes this edition of very much less value.

10. N.b. *Enoch*, accusative and uninflected.

11. Cf. Is. 41:8, 2 Chron. 20:7, Judith 8:22, and James 2:23 for Abraham as God's "friend."

12. Cf. Plinval, "Recherches," p. 19.

12a. Vita 7 (1037): "Noe quoque et ille iustus, cui iustitiae meritum quid praestiterit, novimus . . . Loth vero ut pereuntibus cunctis de Sodomitarum liberaretur incendio, quid aliud quam iustitiae meritum fuit?"

12b. See *iustitia* in vocabulary section below.

12c. Dem. 4–6; *De Nat.* (in Aug., *De Nat. et Grat.* 42–44); Aug., *De Gest. Pel.* 24; Jer., *Ep.* 133.13; *Dial. adv. Pel.* 1.12.

13. Cf. Plinval, "Recherches," p. 19, n. 3.

14. Cf. Wisdom of Solomon 12:10.

15. It is to be noted here that Pelagius is commenting on Rom. 9:17, and that he introduces these comments as representing the view of some commentators. Alfred J. Smith subjected Pelagius' commentary on Romans to a thorough source-investigation but did not find a source for the precise words quoted here. See his articles in *J.T.S.* (old series), xv, xix, xx, and xxxi.

16. Pelagius' specification of which works they are without which we are justified reflects Ambrosiaster; see *P.L.* 17, 87 and cf. Smith, *J.T.S.* xix (1917–18), 181.

17. The Vulgate text of Luke 2:37 reads as follows: *et haec vidva usque ad annos octoginta quattuor quae non discedebat de templo ieiuniis et obsecrattionibus serviens nocte ac die.*

18. "Recherches," p. 19, n. 3.
19. Cf. Exp. 11, 19; 34, 5; 48, 2; 55, 8 f.; 84, 4; 189, 24.
20. Kirmer, pp. 26 f.: "Man will mit dieser Parallele die These stützen, dass Pelagius beide Schriften verfasst habe. Wir glauben, dass diese Stelle das Gegenteil beweist."
21. Souter, *A Study of Ambrosiaster*, pp. 140, 142.
22. Souter, vol. I, pp. 176–183, and Smith's articles.
23. *Adv. Marc.* v, 3.
24. *Trin.* vi, 4, and *Serm.* civ, 3.
25. *In Job.*, xxxiii, 7. Cf. Lewis and Short, *Latin Dictionary*, Clarendon Press, Oxford, 1955. Souter's *Glossary of Later Latin* gives for this word only "Tert., *adv. Marc.* 5.3 on."
26. Aug. *De Nat. et Grat.*, xxii, 24.
27. Plinval, "Recherches," p. 26.
28. Virg. 10, pp. 237–239.
29. Part of this evidence is pointed to briefly in a footnote by Plinval, "Recherches," p. 25, n. 1, and the parallel passages above are quoted by Kirmer, pp. 88 ff., but with almost no development of the evidence, and an opposite interpretation given to it.
30. In commenting on Rom. 7:18 Pelagius also juxtaposes the two nouns, *voluntas* and *effectus*. Exp. 59, 5 f.: *Est voluntas, sed non est effectus, quia carnalis consuetudo voluntati resistit.* He apparently took this mode of expression from Origen-Rufinus; cf. Comm. on Rom., VI, 9: . . . *ut statim voluntatem sequatur effectus.* See Bohlin, p. 95.
31. Aug. *De Gest. Pel.* xi, 27 f.
32. Virg. 9 (236, 16).
33. Ibid., 9 (236)—11 (239 ff.).
34. Dem. 12 (27, B–D).
35. Dem. 12 (27, C).
36. Virg. 11 (239, 21 f.).
37. Virg. 9 (236, 16 f.).
38. I Tim. 3:2.
39. Ibid., 484, 6.
40. E.g., Exp. 492, 5; 493, 8; 530, 18.
40a. For this as a work of Pelagius, see Gennadius, *De Viris Illustribus* 43; Augustine, *De Gestis Pelagii* 7 and 54 f., and *Contra Duas Epistolas Pelagianorum* 4:21; and Jerome, *Dialogus Adversus Pelagianos* 1:25–32.
41. Cel. 28 (351 f.).
42. Plinval first pointed to this parallel, "Recherches," p. 15.
43. This parallel was first seen by Plinval, "Recherches," p. 15.
44. Part of this parallel was first pointed out by Plinval, "Recherches," p. 15.
45. Cel. 14 (341, 18).
46. Dem. 4 (19, A).
47. Ibid. (19, B).
48. Cel. 20 (346, 21) and Dem. 20 (34, D).
49. Cel. 20 (346, 14 f.) and Dem. 20 (35, B).
50. Cf. these passages with De Lege 5 (110, A–B).

51. It is very likely that Pelagius' emphatic rejection of the notion, that the differing glories of the stars refers to the presence of sinners in heaven, is at least partly in the interest of rejecting Ambrosiaster's exegesis of this verse. According to the latter, the stars are divided into three classes, each linked to a different "grade" of men as they will be in the resurrection: bright stars = those who have performed righteous works in this life; middle class stars = Christians who are sinners; the darker stars = unbelievers. *P.L.* xvii, 283.

52. This parallel was first cited by Plinval, "Recherches," p. 28.

53. The similarity of these two passages was first noticed by Plinval, "Recherches," p. 29. Cf. Exp. 167, 12 ff.; 168, 1–12; and Dem. 30 (44, C).

54. Cf. Plinval's remarks, "Recherches," pp. 30 f.

55. This parallel was first pointed out by Plinval, "Recherches," pp. 30 f.

Notes to Chapter III

1. The two exceptions to this are in C. Arr. 11, where Pelagius is arguing against the Arians and where it is thus natural for him to write as follows: *et vehementius constringendi sunt, ne quando velint de his, quae ad adsumptam substantiam pertinent, ei, quae illam adsumere est dignata, praescribere quandiu constet nos non de adsumpta, sed de adsumptirce substantia disputare.*

2. *Ante*, but not *antea*, occurs in Dem. as follows: 6 (21, C), 9 (24, A), 10 (26, C), 15 (29, D), 26 (41, B).

3. Exp. 5, 5 offers an exception: *Galatae iam nullius criminis arguuntur.*

4. Add also Exp. 528, 4 to the instances given by Souter.

5. The genitive *tenuis fidei* does not contradict the above rule. It obviously, by ellipsis, stands as a parallel to *stulti* and *inutiles*.

6. In addition to the two instances given by Souter, there is one in Lib. Fid. 10 (*P.L.* 45, 1718).

7. Another instance is in Exp. 22, 18.

8. James 2:10.

9. Christian writers by no means always, or even usually, use this verb in conjunction with some reference to the threat of judgment or to man's guilt. See the following, where such is not the case: Ambrst. in Rom. 3, 27; in I Cor. 15, 36; in Gal. 3, 14. Jerome, ep. 22, 8; 96, 14; 123, 5. Tert. mart. 4; ux. 2, 2, 1; pud. 3, 6; 19, 22; mon. 12, 2. Aug. in psalm 25, 14.

10. Codex Mediolanensis reads *plene*.

11. I do not understand Kirmer's contention (p. 26) that this word is not characteristic of Pelagius. It appears ten times in Exp. (see Souter), once in Dem., as above, twice in Pelagius' Libellus Fidei (*P.L.* XLV, 1718, 14), once in the extant fragments from De Natura (Aug. de nat. et grat. 10, 11), and three times in Martini's fragments (de div. Spir. S. 484, in addition to the two instances above).

12. For a use without *in*, see Exp. 513, 15.

13. Two other possible cases are spurious: Exp. 24, 8, where the Balliol MS alone reads *deputat*; and Exp. 42, 10, where V omits *se* and reads *depugnare*.

14. See also Exp. 73, 23; 171, 9; 372, 4; 507, 12. De Lib. Arb. (Aug. de grat. Chr. 4, 5). Martini (p. 31) was the first to notice this word, although he was misleading in implying that the preposition is always *ex*.

15. And among non-Christian authors only Claud. Don., Aen. 9, 645.

16. The relevant clause in Uran. epist. 7 (*P.L.* 53, 963) reads: *noluit talem se exhibere episcopum qui ab aliquo timeretur*. The noun *episcopum* makes this instance not fit the category.

17. Not 63, 27, as in the Thes.

18. The clause, in Rev. Ben. 34 (1922), p. 266, reads: *et soli nos faceret vitam exhibere iustitiae.*

19. There occurs the more usual use of an accusative noun or adjective with the reflexive pronoun. Dem. 10 (26, A) *apostolicam te exhibere vis virginem.* Vita 15 (1045) *qualem tu te vidvam debeas exhibere.* Virg. 19 (250, 10) *virginem te in omnibus exhibe*; 19 (250, 16) *cum quibus te tam sanctam in omnibus exhibeas.*

20. With these three parallels from Pelagius and Vita cf. the Vulgate text of Mt. 5 : 44: *orate pro persequentibus et calumniantibus vos.* Wordsworth and White give no variant readings showing *exorate.* Note that the "Sicilian Briton," in a passage showing striking parallels to ch. 6 of Vita, writes nonetheless "*pro . . . persecutoribus orat*" (Caspari, p. 377).

21. Plinval in *Essai*, p. 100, gives further examples.

22. Cf. Cel. 17 (344, 7).

23. Ps. Aug. serm. ed. Mai, 108, 3, and Cypr. epist. 4, 2.

24. Cf. the literal sense in Dem. 24 (38, C): *implicare auro crimen.*

25. Kirmer, who believes that both Vita and Virg. belong to Fastidius, is strangely inconsistent in his treatment of *implico.* In comparing its use in Vita to that in Pelagius he sees significance in the fact that the instances from Pelagius show the word used with abstract concepts while the one case in Vita shows it with the concrete image of the trap (see above; Kirmer, p. 50). In his list of metaphors in Virg., however, he includes without comment the above instances of *implico,* which on his analysis would surely be abstract and thus aligned with Pelagius and not with Vita.

26. *Egeo* appears in Vita 3 (1035); cf. Exp. 95, 22; 199, 15.

27. The image of drunkenness with anger appears not to be a frequent one in Latin Christian writings, although it occurs in the Latin version of Origen: in Jer. 2, 8: *inebriamur ira.* Cf. Origen in Lev. 7, 1: *iracundia inebriat animam.*

28. See also Exp. 110, 16; 167, 11; 342, 6; 383, 20; and Dem. 5 (20, B); 12 (27, C).

29. Souter, vol. I, p. 105.

30. One exception in Exp. 171, 11.

31. There are the following exceptions: Exp. 91, 6; 242, 8; 395, 6; 447, 9.

32. Pelagius' practice in the use of *occasio* finds a certain parallel, although not a precise one, in Priscillianus (*C.S.E.L.* 18): tract. 3, 46, 7 *alteris ad occasionem iustae damnationis adscribitur;* tract. 8, 89, 1 *et apparentiae malum occasionem praestat inimico;* tract. 10, 95, 4 *an persuasione felicium alienatae a deo vitae peccati occasio et materia praestetur.* Distinctly different uses

are found, for example, in the following: Tert. de anima 14, 1; herm. 19, 1; marc. 4, 9, 5 and 4, 38, 5; pat. 6, 4; pud. 16, 24; res. 63, 8. Optat. Mil. lib. 2 (*C.S.E.L.* 26) 62, 19, and 22; 63, 3 and 5. Paulin. Nol. *C.S.E.L.* 29) epist. 12, 106, 2; epist. 17, 125, 11. Caes. Arel. serm. 133 (523, 21).

33. Martini, p. 311.

34. Further examples not given by Martini: De Nat. (in Aug. de nat. et grat. 9, 10); 12, 13; 14, 15; 19, 21; 44, 52. Dem. 3 (18, B), 9 (24, C), 18 (32, C), 19 (34, D), 20 (34, C), 30 (35, B), 21 (35, D), 26 (41, B), 26 (41, C).

35. Kirmer (p. 25) finds evidence to support his thesis in the following: *postmodum* occurs twice in the presently assured works of Pelagius, whereas Vita uses it seven times; *postea* occurs not at all in Vita, whereas Pelagius *in his entire extant works and fragments* [italics mine] uses it eight times.

36. The more usual constructions with a dative are found, e.g., in the following: Exp. 162, 12; 435, 7; Dem. 6 (21, D).

37. Plinval went too far, however, in suggesting (*Essai*, p. 81) that this is always the meaning; in the following instances it is not: Exp. 106, 10; 177, 12; 235, 17. Moreover in some of the examples cited above from both Pelagius and Virg. the noun is modified by some particularizing adjective such as *specialis, suus, hic.* These by their very presence suggest that the noun itself is retaining a more generalized meaning, even though confined largely to contexts in which continence is under discussion.

38. In Pelagius the word can modify a verb, as at Exp. 85, 4 and Dem. 2 (17, A) and at the following: Vita praef. (1033). Cel. 1 (329, 7), 6 (334, 6). De Lege 6 (112, C).

38a. Four occurences of *iuxta* in De Lege as against two of *secundum* is admittedly surprising if this document is by Pelagius. Future investigation of the mss. of the De Lege may reveal that in some or all of these cases *iuxta* is not the proper reading. This is in fact the case at the following places in Exp., where Souter's text reads *iuxta*: 20, 21; 144, 2; 263, 8; 454, 8.

39. In this connection can be seen a striking instance of the unfortunate results produced by Kirmer's concentration upon the letter to Demetrias as criterion of Pelagius' authorship. Since no parallel to the locution *ex sensu proprio loqui* in Vita can be found in the letter to Demetrias, this fact then militates against Pelagius' authorship of Vita. (!) See Kirmer, p. 22.

40. For other uses and meanings of *species*, see the following: Exp. 143, 15: 186, 7; 203, 9; 241, 15; 258, 5; 334, 13; 463, 15. De div. Spir. S. 487, 23. De Lib. Arb. in *J.T.S.* [old series] xii, 34); Vita, Praef. (1032). Virg. 4 (228, 4), 4 (228, 7), 4 (228, 9). Cel. 20 (347, 2). De Lege 1 (106, B).

41. Text here according to Vulgate.

42. The only biblical occurrence of the combination *splendor solis* is in Acts 26:13, but this is in a context quite lacking in the significance given to the expression by Pelagius.

43. For other uses, see the following: Exp. 257 11. Virg. 10 (237, 15) and 16 (246, 18). De Lege 1 (106, B).

44. Kirmer, p. 92.

45. Cf. the remark of Plinval, *Essai*, p. 96; "L'originalité la plus frappante du vocabulaire de Pélage se marque par l'emploi intensif des adverbes en

-ter." By contrast, these adverbs are relatively rare in Jerome and in Ambrose. See H. Goelzer, *Etude lexicographique et grammaticale de la Latinité de saint Jérome* (Paris, 1884), p. 196, and M. F. Barry, *The Vocabulary of the Moral-Ascetical Works of St. Ambrose* (Washington, D.C., 1926), pp. 174–79. These citations in Plinval, *op cit.*, p. 97, n. 1.

46. *Op. cit.*, pp. 96 f.

47. Cf. also Exp. 196, 9 and 364, 6.

Notes to Chapter IV

1. See Martini, p. 305, for more examples. Also the following: Exp. 53, 10; 112, 16; 113, 2; 115, 16; 166, 12; 218, 15; 261, 18; 309, 2; 318, 8; 412, 9; 454, 8.

2. Also Exp. 11, 16; 28, 2; 34, 14; 72, 4; 73, 11; 76, 11; 82, 7; 130, 15; etc. De Div. Sp. S. 483, 21 and 486, 5.

3. Also the following: Vita 2 (1034), 8 (1038) [*bis*], 9 (1039), 13 (1044), 15 (1046).

4. Exp. 28, 14; 65, 14; 178, 20; 240, 9; 309, 2.

5. Exp. 5, 2; 9, 21; 20, 6; 27, 17; 105, 20; 130, 10; 131, 11; 175, 19; 192, 22; 341, 3.

6. Exp. 360, 17. Dem. 19 (34, A).

7. See evidence accumulated by Souter, i, p. 91.

8. Dem. 7 (22, 7); 19 (34, B).

9. Dem. 7 (22, B) and 18 (31, C).

9a. Examples of this are given in Souter, i, p. 92, and Martini, p. 306. Add the following: Exp. 14, 19; 67, 20. De Div. Fil. 135, 27.

10. *De Viris Illustribus* 43.

11. *De Gest. Pel.* 7, 54, and 55.

12. *Cont. Duas Epist. Pelag.* iv, 21.

13. Gennadius and Aug., *loc. cit.*, and Jerome, *Dial. cont. Pelag.* i, 32. The available fragments of Pelagius' book have been collected and set out in such order as is possible by Garnier, *P.L.* 48, 594–5.

14. In the above words Pelagius, to be precise, is conflating Mt. 7 : 22 f. with the *nescio vos* of Mt. 25:12. For those same two words extracted from the Mt. 25 passages, see Dem. 10 (25, D).

15. Further examples in Souter's index, ii, 544.

16. Dem. 30 (43–45).

17. Dem. 28–9 (42–3).

18. Cel. 31 (355, 3): Hoc sacramentum magnum est arduumque est iter castitatis.

19. Ibid., 1, 4: sed magna sunt praemia . . .

20. Vita 9 (1039).

21. Exp. 264, 10 f.

22. Cf. Jean Daniélou, *The Theology of Jewish Christianity*, trans. John A. Baker (London, 1964), pp. 145–63.

23. Cf. *blasphematur* in Polycarp, Phil. 10.3 and Didascalia 1.10.1.

24. Apart from Pelagius and Vita I have been able to find a similar "woe" saying in only one other Latin author of the fourth and fifth centuries.

In Sermon 60 of A. Mutzenbecker's recent edition of the sermons of Maximus of Turin we find the following (CC, xxiii, p. 242): "Quiquid autem pauper dominum benedicit, illi proficit quo faciente dominum benedicit. Et sicut scriptum est de illo: *Vae illi homini per quem nomen domini blasphematur;* ita et de isto scriptum est: *Pax huic homini per quem nomen domini benedicitur salvatoria.*" The combination of these two sayings here (both from an unknown written source or sources) would tend to lend credence to the suggestion above of an original collection of testimonies concerning the Name of the Lord.

25. Dem. xvii, 31. See also Exp. 441, 15.

26. Virg. 8 (236, 3 ff.).

27. Virg. 10 (238, 12 ff.).

28. Virg. 7 (232, 23–233, 3).

29. Exp. 319, 14 ff.

Notes to Chapter V

1. *The Latinity of the Letters of Saint Ambrose* (Washington, 1927), pp. 67–9.

2. *P.L.* 16, 913–1342.

3. To arrive at this figure I have subtracted one-third of the number of columns occupied by Exp., to allow for the Pauline text.

4. See Exp. 12, 18; 39, 11; 47, 2; 69, 11; 525, 103. *De Lib. Arb.* (in Aug. *De Grat. Chr.* 43).

5. See, e.g., Exp. 4, 28; 20, 9; 20, 19; 28, 20; 47, 15; 52, 15; 240, 5; 247, 14; 270 6; etc.

6. Vita 1 (1033), 2 (1033), 3 (1035), 8 (1037–8) [five], 9 (1039) [two], 13 (1043), 14 (1045).

7. Vita 1 (1033).

8. Vita 2 (1033).

9. Virg. 1 (225, 4), 3 (227, 17), 4 (229, 4) [two], 5 (229, 23), 6 (231, 9), 6 (231, 10), 6 (231, 11), 7 (233, 15), 7 (233, 16) [two], 7 (233, 22), 7 (234, 3), 7 (234, 4), 8 (234, 9), 11 (240, 22), 11 (241, 5), 17 (247, 19), 19 (249, 14).

10. Virg. 1 (225, 4).

11. Virg. 7 (234, 3) and 8 (234, 9).

12. Cel. 1 (330, 5), 4 (333, 6), 6 (334, 13), 11 (338, 5), 11 (338, 7), 14 (341, 6), 16 (343, 3), 18 (345 16). 23 (349, 9), 27 (351, 17).

13. De Lege 1 (106, A) [two], 2 (107, B) [three], 4 (109, B), 5 (110, D) [two], 9 (115, A) [two], 9 (115, B), 9 (115, C) [three], 10 (115, D), 10 (116, A) [two].

14. De Lege 1 (106, A) and 2 (107, B) [*ter*].

15. Souter, i, p. 80.

16. Further examples from Exp. in Souter, i, pp. 80 f. See also Martini, p. 309. For Dem. and other fragments, the following: Dem. 6 (21, C) ferendo and tolerando; 6 (22, A) carendo and possidendo; 10 (26, A) cogitando; 19 (34, A) abnuendo; 20, (34, D) insequendo; 24 (38, A)

praeferendo; 25 (40, A) faciendo; 25 (40, B) cogendo and suadendo; 27 (41, C) transeundo and fugiendo. De Nat. (Aug., De Nat. et Grat. 11) negando; 71, vincendo. De Lib. Arb. (Aug., De Grat. Chr. 24) adhaerendo.

17. Exp. 169, 5–11.

18. From Dem. 10 (26, A) *cogitando* to 19 (34, A) *abnuendo*.

19. Martini, p. 309.

20. Souter, i, pp. 82 f., with examples.

21. Exp. 47, 10. The absence of *quoniam* and *ut* is in contrast, for example, to the use of Ambrose. See M. A. Martini, *The Use of Indirect Discourse in the Works of St. Ambrose* (Washington, 1930), pp. 106–8 and 110 f.

22. The *ut* clauses in Virg. 7 (233, 11 ff.) and 9 (236, 16 ff.) are not exceptions. In ch. 7 *dixit* (233, 11) is simply a synonym of *praecipit*, as is apparent from the sentence itself and from the appearance on the next line, in parallel fashion, of *praecipit* with *ut* clauses. Pelagius does give us examples of *praecipio* with *ut* clause: Exp. 433, 12 and 491, 10. In Virg. 9 the author is commenting on part of I Cor. 7:34: "ut sit sancta et corpore et spiritu." The sentences which follow the quotation of this text (e.g., "cum ergo dicit ut sit sancta corpore") do not contain indirect discourse but direct.

23. Also the following: Exp. 194, 4. Dem. 19 (33, D), 24 (38, B).

24. Cf. Plinval, *Essai*, p. 104.

25. Souter i, pp. 81 f.

26. More examples for Exp. in Souter, i, pp. 81 f. For Dem., the following: 4 (19, A), 5 (20, A) [*bis*], 5 (20, B), 19 (33, D), 19 (34, B) [*bis*], 26 (40, D) [*bis*].

27. Plinval, *Essai*, p. 103.

28. Further examples in Souter, i, p. 83 and Martini, p. 298. For Dem. and De Lib. Arb. the following is only a selected list: Dem. 2 (16, C) ad species incitare virtutum; 5 (20, A) sanctitatis quaesivit exemplum; 8 (23, C) per multos corrupit annos; 16 (30, C) pro magno ducimus beneficio. De Lib. Arb. (in Aug. De Grat. Chr. 34) libero utentes arbitrio; 24 suam mortificat voluntatem.

29. I cannot agree with Kirmer in his contention (p. 57) that because many instances of this figure form metrical clausulae, the word order is therefore determined by the clausulae and has no other significance. There are far too many examples in which a particular poignancy attaches to the second of the two words separated by the verb, a poignancy made apparent, if not by the sentence alone, then by the context. Cf. Plinval's remarks on this subject, *Essai*, pp. 51 and 71.

30. Further examples for Dem. are given in Kirmer, p. 57. For Exp., the following: 70, 14; 94, 12; 97, 14; 165, 13; 187, 8; 191, 22; 245, 13; 378, 12; 379, 4; 388, 14; 413, 1.

31. There are some twenty additional examples to be found in Vita.

32. The letters of Augustine examined are the first twenty-nine letters, pp. 2–207, in *Augustine, Select Letters* (London, 1930) Loeb Classical Library, and those of Jerome are the first ten letters, pp. 2–227, in *Select Letters of Saint Jerome* (London, 1933), Loeb Classical Library.

33. Souter, i, p. 110.

34. Jovinian and the Jovinians: Exp. 142, 11; 281, 12; 409, 11; 421, 4. Manicheus and the Manichaeans: Exp. 8, 21; 53, 12; 56, 8; 62, 17; 73, 7; 189, 5; 224, 1; 246, 19; 302, 13; 336, 15; 454, 12; 499, 17; 503, 13.

35. Cf. Kirmer, pp. 34 f. Vita and Dem. are 1100 lines and 1700 lines in length respectively. The above four instances of paronomasia bring the total for Vita up to six, as against eight for Dem. Thus there is really no difference between the two letters in this respect. Kirmer does not follow any rigidly defined rules for determining instances of paronomasia. I have attempted not to allow any of my instances to go further afield than this.

36. Cf. Kirmer, p. 35, who gives only two instances as against thirteen for Dem.

37. Cf. Kirmer, p. 39, who says that this figure is not present at all in Vita and lists six examples from Dem.

38. Cf. Kirmer, p. 42, who lists only four instances.

39. Kirmer omits all mention of paronomasia in Virg. In discussing this figure in Dem. he notes (pp. 34 f.) that most of the examples there contain an antithesis in meaning between the two words of the figure, a feature which characterizes the above list from Virg.

40. Kirmer omits mention of polyptoton in Virg. The above list of five examples compares favourably with Kirmer's list of thirteen examples from Dem. (p. 35), in view of the fact that Dem. is two and one-half times as long as Virg.

41. These bring the total number of instances in Virg. up to six, as against sixteen for Dem. See Kirmer, pp. 42 f.

42. Kirmer alleges (p. 150) that paronomasia is virtually absent from Cel. and that this is one of many indications that this letter does not come from Pelagius.

43. Kirmer produces only eight instances of polyptoton from Cel. and remarks that it is not employed so copiously there as in Dem. pp. 150 f.).

44. Kirmer asserts word-anthesis to be absent from Cel. as opposed to its frequent use by Pelagius. See pp. 39 and 152 f.

45. Cf. Kirmer's *one* instance of this figure and his assertion that in De Lege it is "äusserst selten vorhanden" (p. 110).

46. Kirmer (p. 110) gives only four examples.

47. Kirmer claims (p. 111) that word-antithesis, as distinguished from antithesis of sense, is not present in De Lege.

48. Exp. 374–478.

49. Kirmer, pp. 93 f., 109 f., 145 ff.

49a. In the case of Exp., 1350 lines is an approximate number, allowance having been made for the Pauline text.

49b. See ch. 2 of this book, note 4a.

50. *De Viris Illustribus* 42: "Pelagius heresiarchus antequam proderetur hereticus, scripsit studiosis necessaria tres de fide trinitatis libros."

INDEX OF NAMES

S0-BYT-051

In God's Underground

By the same author

TODAY'S MARTYRED CHURCH

[*Frontispi*

In God's Underground

Richard Wurmbrand
EDITED BY CHARLES FOLEY

W. H. ALLEN
LONDON 1968

Printed and bound in Great Britain
by The Garden City Press Ltd., Letchworth, Hertfordshire
for the publishers W. H. Allen & Company
Essex Street, London WC 2
491 00220 3

First edition, April 1968
Reprinted, May 1968

Dedication

Dedicated to the Christian martyrs who sacrificed their lives in the service of God and died courageously following torture in Communist hands.

I cannot name all those to whom I am indebted for their kindness and help since my release from prison and my arrival in the West. But I do wish particularly to thank the Rev. Stuart Harris, director of the European Christian Mission, and the Rev. John Moseley of the Mission to Europe's Millions — missions which work to propagate the Gospel in countries under Communist rule, secretly sending in Bibles and other Christian literature, helping underground pastors and families of persecuted Christians. It was late in the night when they came first to the tiny attic in Bucharest where I lived with my family after release from jail. They brought us our first news from the West — that Christians there had not forgotten us, but included us daily in their prayers; and they brought the first relief for needy families. I, and many others, owe them much.

R.W.

PREFACE

I AM a Lutheran minister who has spent more than 14 years in different prisons because of my Christian belief, but that in itself is not the reason for the existence of this book. I have always disliked the idea that a man who has been unjustly imprisoned must write or preach about his sufferings. Campanella, the great author of 'City of the Sun' was kept in prison for 27 years; but that he was tortured and lay 40 hours on a bed of iron nails we know from his mediaeval biographers, not from him.

The prison years did not seem too long for me, for I discovered, alone in my cell, that beyond belief and love there is a delight in God: a deep and extraordinary ecstasy of happiness that is like nothing in this world. And when I came out of jail I was like someone who comes down from a mountain top where he has seen for miles around the peace and beauty of the countryside, and now returns to the plain.

First, I should explain why, more than two years ago, I came to the West. When I was released from jail in 1964 with several thousand other political and religious prisoners, it was because the Rumanian Popular Republic had adopted a more 'friendly' policy to the West. I was given the smallest parish in the country. My congregation numbered 35. If 36 people entered the church, I was told, there would be trouble. But I had much to say, and there were many who wished to hear. I travelled secretly to preach in towns and villages, leaving before the police could hear that a stranger was in their district. This, too, had to stop. Pastors who helped me were dismissed by the State, and I could become the cause of new arrests and confessions obtained by torture. I was a burden to those I wished to serve, and a danger.

Friends urged me to try to leave the country so that I might speak for the underground church in the West. It was plain, from the statements of Western Church leaders, that some did not know and others did not want to know the truth about religious persecution under the Communists. Prelates from Europe and America came on friendly visits and sat down to banquets with our inquisitors and persecutors. We asked them why. 'As Christians,' they said, 'we have to be friendly with everybody, you know, even the Communists.' Why, then, were they not friendly to those who had suffered? Why did they not ask one word about the priests and pastors who had died in prison or under torture? Or leave a little money for the families that remained?

The Archbishop of Canterbury came in 1965 and attended a service. Dr. Ramsey did not know that the congregation consisted of officials and secret police agents and their wives—the same audience that turns out on every such occasion. It had listened to visiting rabbis and muftis, bishops and Baptists. After they had returned home, we read of their approving comments on freedom in Rumania. A British theologian wrote a book in which he declared that Christ would have admired the Communist prison system.

Meanwhile, I lost my licence to preach. I was blacklisted and constantly followed and watched. I still sometimes preached at the homes of friends who did not count the danger, so I was not surprised when, some time after secret negotiations had begun for my departure to the West, a stranger asked me to his house. He gave the address, but no name. When I called he was alone.

'I want to do you a service', he said. I recognised that he was a secret police agent. 'A friend of mine says that the dollars have been received for you. Probably you'd like to leave the country at once. My friend is worried. You are a man who speaks his mind, and you are fresh from prison. They think it might be better if you were kept a while—or that a member of your family stays here to vouch for your good behaviour. Of course, your release will be unconditional . . .'

I gave him no assurances. They had the dollars and that must be enough. Christian organisations in the West had paid £2,500 in ransom money for me. Selling citizens brings in foreign currency and helps the Popular Republic's budget. A Rumanian joke says, 'We'd sell the Prime Minister if anyone would buy him.' Jews are sold to Israel at £1,000 a head, members of the German minority to West Germany, Armenians to America. Scientists, doctors and professors cost about £5,000 apiece.

Next I was summoned openly to police headquarters. An officer told me: 'Your passport is ready. You can go when you like, and where you like, and preach as much as you wish. But don't speak against us. Keep to the Gospel. Otherwise you will be silenced, for good. We can hire a gangster who'll do it for $1,000—or we can bring you back, as we've done with other traitors. We can destroy your reputation in the West by contriving a scandal over money or sex.' He said I could go. That was my unconditional release.

I came to the West. Doctors examined me, and one said: 'You're as full of holes as a sieve.' He could not believe that my bones had mended and my tuberculosis healed without medical aid. 'Don't ask me about treatment,' he said. 'Ask the One who kept you alive, and in Whom I don't believe.'

My new pastorate for the underground church began. I met friends of our Scandinavian Mission in Norway, and when I preached there, a woman in the front row began to weep. Later she told me that years ago she had read of my arrest and had prayed for me ever since. 'Today I came to church not knowing who would preach,' she said. 'As I listened I realised who was speaking, and I wept.' I learnt that thousands of people had been praying for me, as they still pray daily for those in Communist prisons. Children whom I had never met wrote, saying: 'Please come to our town—our prayers for you have been answered.'

In churches and universities all over Europe and America I found that people—although they were deeply moved, often, by what I said—did not believe that a danger really threatened them.

'Communism here would be different,' they said. 'Our Communists are few, and harmless.' We thought the same in Rumania, once, when the Party was small. The world is full of small Communist parties, waiting. When a tiger is young you may play with it: when it grows up, it will devour you.

I met Western Church leaders who advised me to preach the Gospel and avoid attacks on Communism; this advice I had also from the secret police in Bucharest. But wrong must be called by name. Jesus told the Pharisees that they were 'vipers', and for this, and not the Sermon on the Mount, he suffered crucifixion.

I denounce Communism because I love the Communists. We can hate the sin, while loving the sinner. Christians have a duty to win the souls of Communists, and if we fail to do so, they will overwhelm the West and uproot Christianity among us here as well. The Red rulers are unhappy and wretched men. They can be saved, and God's way is to send a man. He did not come himself to guide the Jews from Egypt, he sent Moses. So we must win over to God Communist leaders in every field—artistic, scientific and political. By winning those who mould the minds of men behind the Iron Curtain, you win the people they lead and influence.

The conversion of Svetlana Stalin, only daughter of the greatest mass-murderer of Christians, a soul brought up in the strictest Communist discipline, proves that there is a better weapon against Communism than the nuclear bomb: it is the love of Christ.

RICHARD WURMBRAND

PART ONE

THE first half of my life ended on February 29, 1948. I was walking alone down a street in Bucharest when a black Ford car braked sharply beside me and two men jumped out. They seized my arms and thrust me into the back seat, while a third man beside the driver kept me covered with a pistol. The car sped through the thin traffic of a Sunday evening; then, in a street called Calea Rahova, we turned in through steel gates. I heard them clang behind us.

My kidnappers belonged to the Communist Secret Police. This was their headquarters. Inside, my papers, my belongings, my tie and shoelaces, and finally my name were taken from me. 'From now on,' said the official on duty, 'you are Vasile Georgescu.'

It was a common name. The authorities did not want even the guards to know whom they were watching, in case questions should be asked abroad, where I was well-known. I was to disappear, like so many others, without trace.

Calea Rahova was a new jail and I was the first prisoner. But prison was not a new experience for me. I had been arrested during the war by the Fascists who ruled in Hitler's day, and again when the Communists took over. There was a small window high in the concrete wall of the cell, two plank beds, the usual bucket in the corner. I sat waiting for the interrogators, knowing what questions they would ask and what answers I must give.

I know what fear is well enough, but at that moment I felt none. This arrest, and all that would follow, was the answer to a prayer I had made, and I hoped that it would give new meaning to my past life. I did not know what strange and wonderful discoveries lay in store for me.

2

My father had a book at home which advised young people how to plan a career as a lawyer, a doctor, an army officer and so on. Once, when I was about five, he brought it out and asked my brothers what they would like to be. When they had chosen, my father turned to me, the youngest child. 'And what will you be, Richard?' I looked again at the title of the book, which was 'General Guide to the Professions', and thought about it. Then I replied 'I'd like to be a General Guide.'

Since then fifty years have passed, fourteen of them in prison, and I have often thought about those words. It is said that we make our choices early in life, and I know no better description of my present work than that of 'general guide'.

The idea of becoming a Christian pastor was, however, far from my thoughts, and from those of my Jewish parents. My father died when I was nine and our family was always short of money, and often of bread. A man once offered to buy me a suit of clothes, but when we went to the shop, and the tailor brought out his best, he said, 'Much too good for a boy like this'. I still remember his voice. My schooling was poor, but we had many books at home. Before I was ten I had read them all and become as great a sceptic as the Voltaire I admired. Yet religion interested me. I watched the rituals in Orthodox and Roman Catholic churches, and once in a synagogue I saw a man I knew praying for his sick daughter. She died next day, and I asked the rabbi, 'What God could refuse such a desperate prayer?' and he had no answer. I could not believe in an all-powerful being who left so many people to starve and suffer, still less that he had put on earth one man of such goodness and wisdom as Jesus Christ.

I grew up and went into the business world of Bucharest. I did well, and before I was twenty-five I had plenty of money to spend in flashy bars and cabarets and on the girls of 'Little Paris', as they called the capital. I did not care what happened so long as my appetite for fresh sensation was fed. It was a life which many envied, yet it left me in great distress of mind. I knew it to be counterfeit and that I was throwing away like trash something in me that was good and which could be put to use. Although I was sure there was no God, I wished, in my heart, that it was otherwise, that there should be a reason for existing in the universe.

One day I went into a church and stood with other people before a statue of the Virgin. They were praying, and I tried to say with them, 'Hail Mary, full of grace . . . ' but I felt quite empty. I said to the image, 'Really, you are like stone. So many plead, and you have nothing for them.'

After my marriage, I continued to pursue other girls. I went on chasing pleasure, lying, cheating, asking myself no questions, hurting others, until, at twenty-seven, these excesses combined with early privations to bring on tuberculosis. It was at that time a dangerous disease and it seemed for a while that I might die. I was afraid. At a sanatorium in the countryside I rested for the first time in my life. I lay looking out at the trees, and thought about the past. It came back to me like scenes from an agonising play. My mother wept for me; my wife had wept; so many harmless girls had wept. I had seduced and slandered, mocked and bluffed, all for a sham. I lay there and tears came.

In that sanatorium I prayed for the first time in my life, the prayer of an atheist. I said something like this: 'God, I know that You do not exist. But if perchance You exist, which I deny—it is for You to reveal Yourself to me; it is not my duty to seek You.'

My whole philosophy had been materialistic until then, but my heart could not be satisfied with it. I believed in theory that man is only matter and that, when he dies, he decomposes into salt and minerals. Yet I had lost my father, and had attended other funerals, and I could never think of the dead except as people. Who can think of his dead child or wife as a heap of minerals? It is always the beloved person who remains in the mind. Can our minds be so mistaken?

My heart was full of contradictions. I had passed hours in noisy places of amusement among half-naked girls and exciting music, but I liked also to take lonely walks through cemeteries, sometimes on winter-days when snow lay heavy on the graves. I said to myself: 'One day I, too, will be dead, and snow will fall on my tomb, while the living will laugh, embrace and enjoy life. I shall be unable to participate in their joys; I shall not even know them. I will simply not exist any more. After a short time, nobody will remember me. So what use is anything?'

In considering social and political problems I thought that perhaps one day mankind would find some system that would provide freedom, security and wealth for all. But when everybody is happy, nobody will want to die, and the thought that they will have one day to leave their happy life may make them unhappier than ever.

I remembered reading that Krupp, who had become a millionaire by creating weapons of death, was himself horrified of death. Nobody was allowed to speak the word 'death' in his presence. He divorced his wife because she told him about the death of a nephew. He had everything, but was unhappy because he knew that happiness could not last, that he would have to leave it behind and rot in a tomb.

Although I had read the Bible for its literary interest, my mind closed at the point where the adversaries challenge Christ: 'Descend from the cross if you are the son of God'; and, instead, He dies. It seemed to prove His foes were right, and yet, I found my thoughts going spontaneously to Christ. I said to myself, 'I wish I could have met and talked to Him'. Each day my meditation ended with this thought.

There was a woman patient in the sanatorium who was too ill to leave her room, but somehow she heard of me and sent a book about the Brothers Ratisbonne, who founded an order to convert Jews. Others had been praying for me, a Jew, while I wasted my life.

After some months in the sanatorium, I grew slightly better, and went to convalesce in a mountain village. Here I became friendly with an old carpenter, and one day he gave me a Bible. It was no ordinary Bible, as I learnt later: he and his wife had spent hours every day praying over it for me.

I lay on the sofa in my cottage, reading the New Testament, and in the days that passed Christ seemed to me as real as the woman who brought my meals. But not everyone who recognises Christ is saved; Satan believes, and is not a Christian. I said to Jesus, 'You'll never have me for a disciple. I want money, travel, pleasure. I have suffered enough. Yours is the way of the Cross, and even if it is the way of truth as well, I won't follow it.' His answer came into my head, like a plea: 'Come my way! Do not fear the Cross! You will find that it is the greatest of joys.'

I read on, and again tears filled my eyes. I could not help comparing Christ's life with mine. His outlook was so pure, mine so tainted; His nature so selfless, mine so greedy; His heart so full of love, mine filled with rancour. My old certainties began to crumble in the face of this wisdom and truthfulness. Christ had always appealed to the depths of my heart, to which my conscience had no access, and now I said to myself, 'If I had a mind like His, I could rely on its conclusions.' I was like the man in the ancient Chinese story, trudging exhausted under the sun, who came on a great oak and rested in its shade. 'What a happy chance I found you!' he said. But the oak replied, 'It is no chance. I have been waiting for you for 400 years.' Christ had waited all my life for me. Now we met.

3

This conversion took place six months after my marriage to Sabina, a girl who had never spared a thought for spiritual things. It was a terrible blow to her. She was young and beautiful, and she had lacked so much in her childhood. She hoped a happier life was beginning, when the man she loved, her partner in pleasure, changed into a devout believer who talked of becoming a pastor. She confessed to me later that she had even thought of suicide.

One Sunday, when I proposed going to evening service, she burst into tears. She said she wanted to see a film.

'All right,' I said. 'We'll go—because I love you.' We walked from one theatre to another and I chose the film which looked most suggestive. When we left I took her to a café and she ate a cream cake. I said, 'Now go home to bed. I want to look for a girl and take her to a hotel.'

'*What did you say?*'

'It is plain enough. You go home. I want to find a girl to take to a hotel.'

'How can you say such things!'

'But you made me go to the cinema, and you saw what the hero did—why shouldn't I do the same? If we go tomorrow and the day after to such films . . . every man becomes what he looks at; but if you want me to be a good husband, come to church with me sometimes.'

She thought about it. Then, quietly, gently she began to come more and more often to church. But she still hankered after the gay life and when she wanted to go out somewhere, I went too. One evening we went to a drunken party. The air was full of smoke. Couples were dancing and making love openly. Suddenly my wife was disgusted with it all and said, 'Oh, let's go! Now!'

I said, 'Why leave? We've only just come.' We stayed until midnight. Again she wanted to go home, and again I refused. It was the same at 1 a.m. And again at 2 a.m. When I saw she was thoroughly sickened by the whole affair, I agreed to go.

We came out into the cold air. Sabina said: 'Richard! I'm going straight to the pastor's house to make him baptise me. It will be like taking a bath after all this filth.'

I laughed and said, 'You've waited so long. You can wait until morning now. Let the poor pastor sleep.'

4

Our whole life changed. Before, we had quarrelled over nothing. I should have divorced Sabina with barely a second thought if she had interfered with my enjoyment. Now a son was born to us. Mihai was a gift from God, for in the old days we did not want a child that might have hampered our pleasures.

We were happy when the Rev. George Stevens, head of the Church of England Mission in Bucharest, asked me to become its secretary. I did my best to adapt my business instincts, but trouble arose when I persuaded an insurance agent to accept a bribe for dropping a claim against the Mission. To my surprise, Mr. Stevens did not seem to understand the arrangement I proposed. 'But who is right?' he asked. 'The Company or we?' I said that, in fact, the claim was justified. 'Then we must pay,' he said, closing what was to me an enlightening exchange.

In 1940, relations between Rumania and Britain were severed, and the English clergy had to leave. Since there was no one else, I had to try and carry on the Church work.

I studied and taught myself to preach, and was ordained as a Lutheran pastor. I had considered Rumania's rival denominations. The Orthodox church, to which four out of five people belonged, seemed to be overfond of outward show. I felt in the same way about the Catholic ritual: one Easter Sunday, after sitting through the Latin liturgy and a political address by the bishop, I left without even hearing in my own language that Christ was risen from the dead. I was attracted by the simpler Protestant services which made the sermon—in which one could teach and set a feast for the mind—its central part. And then, without his greatness, I had some spiritual kinship with Martin Luther. He was a choleric, quarrelsome man, but he also loved Jesus so deeply that he came to think man is saved not by his good deeds but by his faith. So I became a Lutheran.

I had always regarded clergymen with wariness, and above all those who might ask whether I was 'saved'. Now, although I wore no clerical garb, the impulse was all but irresistible to take the whole world as my parish. I could not make enough converts. I kept a list of my congregation and pulled it out in buses and waiting rooms to ask myself what each was doing at that moment. If one of them defected, I was sunk in misery for hours. It was a physical pain like a knife in my heart and I had to ask God to take it from me. I could not go on living with it.

5

Under Stalin's conditions for economic help to Hitler during the war there was a partitioning of Eastern Europe. One-third of our national territory was divided between Russia, Bulgaria and Hungary. Nazi influence supported the growth of an 'Iron

Guard' movement whose members tried to harness the Orthodox church to political terrorism. The night before assassinating Premier Calinescu, their chief opponent, nine fanatics spent the hours prostrate on a church floor, with their bodies forming a cross. After that, the Iron Guard helped Hitler's protégé, General Ion Antonescu, to seize power. King Carol was forced to abdicate in favour of his young son Michael, in whose name Antonescu ruled as a dictator.

Now the Iron Guard had a free hand to deal with Jews, Communists, Protestants. Murder walked the streets. Our mission was accused of treachery. I was threatened daily. One Sunday from the pulpit I saw a group of men in the green shirts of the Iron Guard filing quietly into the back of the church. The congregation, facing the altar, were unaware of the strangers, but I saw revolvers in their hands. I thought, if this were to be my last sermon, it should be a good one.

It was about the hands of Jesus. I told how they had wiped away tears, and lifted children, and fed the hungry. They had healed the sick, and been nailed to the cross, and they had blessed the disciples before He ascended to heaven.

Then I raised my voice. 'But YOU! What have YOU done with your hands?'

The congregation looked amazed. They were holding prayer books.

I thundered, 'You are killing and beating and torturing innocent people! Do you call yourself Christians? Clean your hands, you sinners!'

The Iron Guard men looked furious. Yet they did not care to break up the service. They stood with guns drawn while I said a prayer and the benediction, and the audience began to leave. When nearly all had safely gone, I came down from the pulpit and stepped behind a curtain. I heard running footsteps and shouts of 'Where's Wurmbrand? After him!' before I passed through a small door, turning the key behind me: this secret exit had been built many years before. Along corridors I found my way to a side street, and so escaped.

As the war progressed, many from the Christian minorities—Adventists, Baptists, Pentecostals—were massacred or driven into concentration camps with the Jews. All my wife's family were carried off—she never saw them again. I was arrested by the Fascists on three occasions; tried, interrogated, beaten and imprisoned. So I was well prepared for what was to come under the Communists.

6

Through the cell window at Calea Rahova I could see a corner of the yard. As I looked, a priest was let in through the gates. He moved quickly across the asphalt and through a door—an informer, come to report on his congregation.

I knew that I faced questioning, ill-treatment, possibly years of imprisonment and death, and I wondered if my faith was strong enough. I remembered then that in the Bible it is written 366 times—once for every day of the year—'Don't be afraid!': 366 times, not merely 365, to account for Leap year. And this was February 29—a coincidence which told me I need not fear!

The interrogators showed no hurry to see me, for Communist jails are like archives, to be drawn on at any time when information may be needed. I was questioned again and again over the whole fourteen and a half years I spent in prison. I knew that in the eyes of the Party my connections with the Western church missions and with the World Council of Churches were treasonable, but there was much else of importance which they did not know and must not learn from me.

I had prepared myself for prison and torture as a soldier in peace-time prepares for the hardships of war. I had studied the lives of Christians who had faced similar pains and temptations to surrender and thought how I might adapt their experiences. Many who had not so prepared themselves were crushed by suffering, or deluded into saying what they should not.

Priests were always told by interrogators, 'As a Christian you must promise to tell us the whole truth about everything.' For my part, since I was sure of being found guilty whatever I said, I decided that under torture I might incriminate myself, but never betray friends who had helped me to spread the Gospel. So I planned to leave my interrogators more confused at the end of their investigation than at the start. I would mislead them to the hilt.

My first task was somehow to get a message out to warn my colleagues and let my wife know where I was. I was able to suborn a guard to act as intermediary, for at that time my family still had money. He received about £500 for carrying messages over the next few weeks. Then everything we owned was seized.

The guard brought word that the Swedish Ambassador had protested about my disappearance, saying that I had many well-wishers in Scandinavia and Britain. The Foreign Minister, Mrs. Ana Pauker, replied that nothing was known of my whereabouts since I had secretly left the country some time ago.

7

The Ambassador, as a neutral envoy, could hardly press the matter further, least of all with Mrs. Pauker, a lady before whom strong men quailed. I had met her, and knew her father, a clergyman called Rabinovici, who told me sadly, 'Ana has no feeling for anything Jewish in her heart.' She studied medicine, then turned to teaching at the English Church Mission before embracing the Communist cause and marrying an engineer of similar views called Marcel Pauker. Both were in and out of prison for conspiracy, but Ana proved the more violent partisan. She went to live in Moscow and Marcel followed, with less enthusiasm. During one of Stalin's pre-war purges he was executed—shot, it was said, by his wife's hand, and few doubted the story. Ana was only outwardly a woman: inwardly she was 'topful', like Lady Macbeth, 'from crown to toe of direst cruelty'. After spending the rest of the war as a Soviet citizen in Moscow, with officer's rank in the Red Army, Mrs. Pauker returned in the role of Foreign Minister to become the dominating influence in Rumania.

Such was her loyalty to Russia that when, on a fine day, someone asked why she was walking through Bucharest with her umbrella up, Ana is said to have retorted, 'Haven't you heard the weather report? It's raining heavily in Moscow.'

After a group of political leaders, headed by young King Michael, had courageously deposed General Antonescu and ended his partnership with Germany, a meeting was summoned in Moscow to decide on the shape of the post-war world. Churchill said to Stalin, 'How would it do for you to have 90 per cent predominance in Rumania, while we have 90 per cent of the say in Greece?' And he wrote these words on a sheet of paper. Stalin paused. Then he made a large tick with a blue pencil on the paper and passed it back.

A million Russian troops poured into Rumania. These were our new 'allies'.

'The Russians are coming!' was no joke-phrase for us. The new occupiers had only one idea in life: to drink, rob and ravage the 'capitalist exploiters'. Thousands of women of all ages and conditions were raped by soldiers who burst into their homes. Men were robbed in the street of such novelties as bicycles and wrist-watches. When order in the Red Army was restored by shooting, and shops began to raise their shutters, the visiting troops were astonished by the goods on show, and even more when they learned that most of the customers were farmers and factory-workers.

The capitulation proclaimed on August 23, 1944, is still celebrated each year as the day when Rumania was freed. In fact, its terms were used to strip the country of its entire navy, most of its merchant fleet, half its rolling stock and every automobile. Farm produce, horses, cattle and all our stocks of oil and petrol were carried off to Russia. It was thus that Rumania, which had been known as the granary of Europe, became a starvation area.

8

On the day of my conversion I had prayed, 'God, I was an atheist. Now let me go to Russia to work as a missionary among atheists, and I shall not complain if afterwards I have to spend all the rest of my life in prison.' But God did not send me on the long journey to Russia. Instead, the Russians had come to me.

During the war, in spite of persecution, our mission's following had greatly increased, and many of those who had harried Jews and Protestants now worshipped side by side with their former victims.

After the war, my work for the Western church missions continued. I had an office, equipment, secretaries—a 'front' for my campaign.

I speak good Russian. It was easy for me to talk to Russian soldiers in streets, shops and trains. I did not wear clerical dress, and they took me for an ordinary citizen. The younger men, especially, were bewildered and homesick. They were pleased to be shown the sights of Bucharest, and invited to a friendly home. I had help from many young Christians who also spoke Russian. I told the girls that they could use their beauty to help bring men to Christ. One girl saw a soldier alone in a wine-shop. She sat beside him and accepted his offer of a glass, then suggested that they go somewhere quieter to talk. 'With you, anywhere!' said the Russian, and she brought him to my house. The soldier was converted, and brought others to us.

We secretly published the Gospel in Russian. More than 100,000 books were distributed in cafés, parks, railway stations, wherever Russians were to be found, over three years. They were passed from hand to hand until they fell to pieces. Many of our helpers were arrested, but none gave me away.

We were astonished not only by the number of conversions, but by their naturalness. The Russians were wholly ignorant of religion, but it was as if, deep in their hearts, they had been seeking truth; and now they recognised it with delight. They were mostly young peasants who had worked on the land, sowing and harvesting, and they knew in their bones that someone orders nature; but they had been brought up as atheists, and they believed that they were, just as many people believe themselves to be Christians, and are not.

I met a young painter from outer Siberia on a train journey, and told him about Christ as we travelled.

'Now I understand!' he said. 'I only knew what they taught us in schools, that religion is a tool of imperialism, and so on. But I used to walk in an old cemetery near my home, where I could be alone. I often went to a small, abandoned house among the graves.' (I understood that this was the cemetery's Orthodox chapel.)

'On the wall there was a painting of a man nailed to a cross. I thought, "He must have been a great criminal to be punished so." But if he were a criminal, why did his picture have the place of honour—as if he were Marx or Lenin? I decided that they had first thought him a criminal, and later found that he was innocent, and so put up his picture in remorse.'

I told the painter, 'You are half-way to the truth.' When we reached our destination, hours later, he knew all that I could tell him about Jesus. As we parted, he said: 'I planned to steal something tonight, as we all do. Now how can I? I believe in Christ.'

9

We worked among Rumanian Communists, too. Every book had to pass through their censorship. We presented books which had Karl Marx's picture as a frontispiece, and a few opening pages repeating his and Lenin's arguments against religion. The censor read no further—which was just as well, since the rest of the book was wholly Christian in content. The censor liked another of our titles—'Religion: an opiate for the people'. Faced with piles of old and new books to read, he did not trouble to look inside, where he would have found only Christian arguments. Sometimes a censor would pass anything for a bottle of brandy.

The number of Rumanian Communists had increased from a few thousands to millions, for a Party card could mean the difference between eating and going hungry. Stalin had installed a 'united front' government of his own choice with the leader of the 'Ploughman's Front', Groza, at its head. Apart from Ana Pauker, who is said to have 'invented' Groza, power was wielded by the Russians through three veteran Party comrades: Lucretiu Patrascanu, appointed Minister of Justice; Teohari Georgescu, who took over police and 'security' as Minister of the Interior; and Gheorghe Gheorghiu-Dej, a tough railway worker who was First Secretary of the Party.

I attended, in the role of observer, a meeting of Orthodox priests which Gheorghiu-Dej addressed after the Communist take-over. Jovial and stubby, he assured them all that he was prepared to 'forgive and forget'. In spite of their church's many links in the past with the Iron Guard and other Right-wing organisations, the state would go on paying their salaries as before. His concluding remarks about the similarity between Christian and Communist ideals won a cheer.

On informal occasions Gheorghiu-Dej was frank about his atheism and his conviction that Communism would spread over the world, yet he could speak indulgently of his old mother, who filled their home with icons and brought his daughters up as Orthodox believers. In eleven years in prison under the old régime, Dej had time to study the Bible and discuss religion with many imprisoned sectarians, with whom he expressed sympathy. Escaping from jail just before the Russians came, he would have been caught and killed by the dictator Antonescu if he had not been sheltered by a friendly priest. But if religion had touched Gheorghiu-Dej's life in his days of struggle, there was no room for it now that he was on top. The wife who had waited so long for his return was discarded, her place being taken by a film actress. The house was full of servants and suitors; Dej was rich and famous, and in no mood to listen to anyone.

When someone guided the conversation at his meeting with the priests into spiritual channels, he replied with standard Party arguments. He assured us that we would all have complete liberty of conscience in the new Rumania, and in return my colleagues promised to make no trouble for the state. I listened, and kept my reservations to myself. Many priests came forward at that meeting as champions of the Communist way of life, but sooner or later they stumbled over some Party doctrine and ended up in prison.

The campaign to undermine religion developed rapidly. All church funds and estates were nationalised. A Communist Ministry of Cults controlled the priesthood completely, paying salaries and confirming appointments. The ageing Patriarch Nicodim, a virtual recluse, was accepted as Orthodox figurehead, but the Party needed a more supple instrument and Dej decided that he knew the very man: the priest who had hidden him from the Fascists the year before. So Father Justinian Marina, an obscure seminary teacher from Rimincul-Vilcea, was made a bishop, and soon all Rumania's fourteen million Orthodox churchgoers knew that he was their Patriarch in everything but name.

The next task was to tear apart the Roman and Greek Catholics, of whom there were two and a half millions. The Greek Catholics, usually called Uniates, while keeping many traditions of their own (including the right of priests to marry), accepted the Pope's supremacy. Now they were taken over and forcibly 'merged' with the obedient Orthodox Church. Most of the priests, and all the bishops, who objected to this shotgun wedding were arrested, their dioceses abolished and their property seized. The Roman Catholics, ordered to break with the Vatican, refused; they, too, paid dearly for their resistance. With priests filling the jails and lurid stories of their treatment spreading through the country, the minority religions simply bowed the head and waited to hear their fate.

10

They did not have long to wait. In 1945 a 'Congress of Cults' was called in the Rumanian Parliament building, with 4,000 representatives of the clergy filling the seats. Bishops, priests, pastors, rabbis, mullahs applauded as it was announced that Comrade Stalin (whose vast picture hung on the wall) was patron of the congress—they preferred not to remember that he was at the same time president of the World Atheists' Organisation. The trembling old Patriarch Nicodim blessed the assembly and the Prime Minister, Groza, opened it. He told us that he was a priest's son himself, and his lavish promises of support, echoed by other personages who followed him, were appreciatively cheered.

One of the chief Orthodox bishops said in reply that in the past many political rivulets had entered the great river of his church—green, blue, tri-coloured—and he welcomed the prospect that a red one should join it, too. One leader after another, Calvinist, Lutheran, the Chief Rabbi, rose in turn to speak. All expressed willingness to co-operate with the Communists. My wife, beside me, could bear no more. She said, 'Go and wash this shame from the face of Christ!'

'If I do, you'll lose your husband,' I replied.

'I don't need a coward. Go and do it!' Sabina said.

I asked to speak and they were pleased to invite me to the rostrum: the organisers looked forward to publishing a congratulatory speech next day from Pastor Wurmbrand, of the Swedish Church Mission and the World Council of Churches.

I began with a brief word on Communism. I said it was our duty as priests to glorify God and Christ, not transitory earthly powers, and to support his everlasting kingdom of love against the vanities of the day. As I went on, priests who had sat for hours listening to flattering lies about the Party seemed to awake as from a dream. Someone began to clap. The tension snapped, and applause suddenly broke out, wave after wave, with delegates standing up to cheer. The Minister of Cults, a former Orthodox priest called Burducea who had been an active Fascist in other times, shouted from the platform that my right to speak was withdrawn. I replied that I had the right from God, and continued. In the end, the microphone was disconnected, but by then the hall was in such uproar that no one could hear anything.

That closed the congress for the day. I heard that the Ministry of Cults intended to cancel my licence as a pastor and was advised to seek the help of the influential Patriarch-elect. After several attempts I managed to reach Justinian on his return from a visit to Moscow, where a great fuss had been made of him. Black-bearded, smiling, full of his new dignity but no fool, this was the man who now had four-fifths of Rumania's church-going population under his care, and I suddenly decided that I might use my time with him better than to talk about my own affairs. So I said instead that, since his promotion, he had been constantly in my prayers. To have responsibility for fourteen million souls was truly a terrible load for one man to carry. He must feel like St. Ireneus, who wept when people made him bishop against his will, saying, 'Children, what have you done—how can I become the man this burden demands? The Bible saith that a bishop must be righteous.'

While I spoke, he said little, but after I had gone he asked about me among friends. For a time the talk about withdrawing my licence stopped. Later on, when I was held by the police for a six-week inquiry, Justinian was among those who helped to secure my release, and still later he invited me to Iashi, the seat of his bishopric, where we became friendly. His ignorance of the Bible was amazing, but not exceptional among Orthodox priests. He listened attentively when I reminded him of the parable of the Prodigal Son. Taking his hands in mine, I said that God welcomed back all who strayed, even Bishops. Other Christians besides myself used all the influence they could bring to bear on Justinian. He had begun a life of prayer and love for God when, regardless of his feelings, the Party launched a full-scale campaign against religion and I lost sight of him for several years.

The anti-God drive went hand-in-hand with the elimination of opposition parties, for after Stalin had all he wanted from his wartime allies, the last pretences of democracy were dropped. Rumania's great National Peasant leader, Iuliu Maniu, was put on trial with eighteen others on false charges and, at the age of over seventy, sentenced to ten years' imprisonment—he was to die in jail four years later. In the reign of terror which followed, it is estimated that some 60,000 'enemies of the state' were executed.

Ironically, the Minister of Justice who presided over this wholesale purge, forty-seven-year old Lucretiu Patrascanu, had received much help from Maniu in defending persecuted Communists before the war. The two men also worked together with King Michael to plan the armistice which Patrascanu then signed in Moscow in Rumania's name. Once Maniu was silenced, Patrascanu and other Party leaders forced our much beloved young king to abdicate.

So now a Popular Republic was proclaimed; but who would lead it? Not the puppet Groza, certainly. Ana Pauker was detested, even in the Party; the others were at odds. Many of Patrascanu's admirers saw in him a nationalist Communist who would guide the country away from Stalinist extremes. He was a 'Western'-type Communist from a landowning family, and everyone thought the better of him for saying that he was a Rumanian before he was a Red.

The problem of the leadership was the subject of hot debate in the Central Committee of the Party.

My life as a pastor, until this time, had been full of satisfaction.

I had all I needed for my family. I had the trust and love of my parishioners. But I was not at peace. Why was I allowed to live as usual, while a cruel dictatorship was destroying everything which was dear to me, and while others were suffering for their faith? On many nights, Sabina and I prayed together, asking God to let us bear a cross.

II

My arrest, in the widespread round-ups which were going on in this time, could have been considered an answer to my prayer, but never could I have supposed that the first man to join me in my cell would be Comrade Patrascanu himself.

When the door of my room in Calea Rahova opened, a few days after my arrival, to admit the tall Minister of Justice I supposed at first that he had come to question me in person. Why was I so honoured? Then the door was locked behind him: stranger still, his shirt was open at the neck and he wore no tie. I looked down at his highly-polished shoes—no laces! The second prisoner in my brand-new cell was the man who had brought Communism to power in our country.

He sat down on the other plank bed and swung his feet up; a tough-minded intellectual, he was not going to allow the transformation from Minister to jailbird to affect his poise. Wrapped in our greatcoats against the March chill, we began to talk. Although I knew Patrascanu's doctrines had shattered justice and caused so much destruction, it was possible to like him as a man and believe in his sincerity. He passed off his arrest with a shrug. It was far from being his first spell in prison. He had been arrested several times by the former rulers of Rumania. It seemed that his growing popularity had banded the other Party leaders against him. At a congress a few days earlier he had been denounced as a bourgeois traitor in the class war by his colleague Teohari Georgescu, Minister of the Interior. A second charge, that Patrascanu had been 'potentially helped by the imperialist Powers', was backed by Vasile Luca, the Minister of Finance, who had been in prison with him under the old régime. The accusations were driven home by Ana Pauker, another of his old friends.

They had been plotting against him for some time, Patrascanu said, but one incident in particular had told against him as a Communist. He had asked one of Georgescu's officials if there was any truth in the rumours that prisoners were being tortured. Why certainly, said the man from the Ministry; they were counter-revolutionaries who deserved no pity, especially if they held back information. Patrascanu was deeply disturbed. Was it for this, he demanded, that they had struggled all these years to bring the Party to power? His protest was reported to Georgescu, and the denunciation at the Congress followed.

'As I left the hall,' he said, 'I saw a new driver waiting at the car. He said, "Your chauffeur Ionescu has been taken ill, Comrade Patrascanu". I stepped in, two secret policemen got in after me—and here I am!'

He was sure that he would soon be reinstated, and when supper came I began to think he might. Instead of boiled barley, he was given chicken, cheese, fruit and a bottle of hock. Patrascanu took a glass of wine and pushed the tray over, saying he had no appetite.

While I tried not to eat too ravenously, he told amusing stories. One was about the Swiss senator who wanted to be Navy Minister. 'But we have no navy!' said the Prime Minister. 'What does that matter?' the senator asked. 'If Roumania can have a Minister of Justice, why shouldn't Switzerland have a Minister of the Navy?' Patrascanu laughed heartily at this anecdote, although it ridiculed the 'justice' he had created, and of which he himself was now a victim.

Next morning Patrascanu was escorted from the cell, I supposed for interrogation. He returned bad-temperedly in the evening to say he had not been answering questions but giving a lecture at the university, where he taught law. The Party wanted his arrest kept secret for the time being, and he, with thirty years of Communist discipline behind him, had to fall in with their wishes. He talked to me because he could talk, even outside prison, with nobody else. To reveal, even to his wife, that he was 'under examination', or to ask anyone's advice, would be a capital offence. This isolation preyed on his nerves, as it was intended to. He could be himself only with me, because he had reason to believe that I would never see the outer world again.

As Patrascanu told me something about his early life, I was interested to see that he had become a Communist not through any objective judgment, but in revolt against early troubles. His father, a well-to-do man, supported the Germans so enthusiastically in World War I that, after the victory of the Allies, the whole family was ostracised. Young Patrascanu had to go to Germany for a university education, and on his return joined the only political party which offered him a welcome. His first wife, a Communist, died in the Stalinist purges, and when he remarried it was to another Party member, who happened to be a school friend of my wife.

I tried to show Patrascanu the source of his convictions. 'You are like Marx and Lenin,' I said, 'whose ideas and actions were also the outcome of early suffering. Marx felt genius within him, but as a Jew in Germany when anti-semitism was rampant, he could find no outlet for it except as a revolutionary. Lenin's brother was hanged for an attempt on the emperor's life—rage and frustration made him want to overturn the world. It has been much the same with you.'

Patrascanu dismissed the idea. His nerves found an outlet in tirades against the wickedness of the church. The evil days of the Borgia Popes, the Spanish Inquisition, the savagery of the Crusades, Galileo's persecution, were all surveyed.

'But it's the crimes and errors of the Church which give us so much more to admire in it,' I said.

Patrascanu was startled. 'What do you mean?'

I said, 'A hospital may stink of pus and blood; in that lies its beauty, for it receives the sick with their disgusting sores and horrible diseases. The Church is Christ's own hospital. Millions of patients are treated in it, with love. The Church accepts sinners —they continue to sin, and for their transgressions the Church is blamed. To me, on the other hand, the Church is like a mother who stands by her children even when they commit crimes. The politics and prejudices of its servants are distortions of what comes from God—that is, the Bible and its teachings, worship and the sacraments. Whatever its faults, the church has much that is sublime in it. The sea drowns thousands of people every year, but no one contests its beauty.'

Patrascanu smiled. 'I could make much the same claim for Communism. Its practitioners are not perfect—there are scoundrels among them—but that doesn't mean there's anything wrong with our theories.'

'Then judge by results,' I said, 'as Jesus advised. Sad deeds have stained the history of the Church, but it has lavished love and care on people all over the world. It has produced a multitude of saints, and it has Christ, the holiest of all, at its head. Who are your idols? Men like Marx, who was described as a drunkard by his biographer Riazanov, director of the Marx Institute in Moscow. Or Lenin, whose wife tells us he was a reckless gambler, and whose writings drip with venom. "By their fruits ye shall know them." Communism has wiped out millions of innocent victims, bankrupted countries, filled the air with lies and fear. Where is its good side?'

Patrascanu defended 'the logic of Party doctrine'.

I said doctrines as such meant nothing. 'You can do atrocious acts under polite names. Hitler talked about a struggle for *Lebensraum* (vital space) and murdered whole populations. Stalin said "We must care for men like flowers", and he killed his wife and yours.'

Patrascanu looked uncomfortable; but he was frank. 'Our long-range purpose is to communise the world. There are few who want to go all the way with us, but we can always find some who are willing for their own reasons to go with us for a time. First we had the Rumanian ruling classes and the king, who backed the Allies against the Nazis. When they had served our purpose, we destroyed them. We won over the Orthodox church with promises, then used the smaller sects to undermine it. We used the farmers against the landlords and later the poor peasants against the rich farmers—and now all of them will be collectivised together. These are Lenin's tactical ideas, and they work!'

I said, 'Everyone knows that all your fellow-travellers have been jailed, executed or somehow destroyed in the past. How can you hope to go on using people and throwing them away?'

Patrascanu laughed. 'Because they are stupid. Here's an example. Ten years after World War I, the great Bolshevist thinker Bukharin opposed Trotsky's plans for making world revolution by force of arms. He argued that it was better to wait until the capitalist countries came to blows among themselves; Russia could then join the winning side and take the lion's share of conquered countries. A remarkable prophecy—but no one took it seriously. If the West had known that half Europe and two-thirds of Asia would become Communist as a result, the last war would never have taken place. Fortunately our enemies don't listen to our argument or read our books, so we can speak openly.'

I pointed out a flaw in his argument. 'Don't you see, Mr. Patrascanu, that as you used people and then cast them aside, so your comrades have used you and thrown you away? Haven't you blinded yourself to the evil logic of Lenin's doctrine?'

For once Patrascanu's bitterness was unconcealed. He said: 'When Danton was driven to the guillotine and saw Robespierre watching from a balcony, he called out, "You will follow me!" And I assure you now that they will follow me—Ana Pauker, Georgescu and Luca, too.'

So they did, within three years.

12

We spoke no more that evening, but at 10 p.m., after we had gone to bed, the door opened and my new name was called. Three men stood outside. One, whom I later knew as Appel, told me to dress. I did so, and Patrascanu whispered to put my greatcoat on as well: it might dull the blows. A pair of black goggles was put over my eyes so that I could not see where I was going, and I was led along a corridor to a room where I was put into a chair. Then the blindfold was taken off.

I sat before a table with a harsh, accusing light shining in my eyes. At first I saw only a shadowy figure opposite, but as I grew used to the glare I recognised a man called Moravetz. A former police inspector who had been in trouble for betraying secrets to the Communists, he had been rewarded now with the job of interrogator.

'Ah,' he said, 'Vasile Georgescu. You'll find paper and pen on that desk. Take your chair over and write about your activities and your life.'

I asked what interested him particularly.

Moravetz raised sarcastic eyebrows. 'As a priest, you've heard any number of confessions. We've brought you here to confess to us.'

I wrote an outline of my life up to the time of my conversion. Then, thinking the statement might come to the notice of Party leaders and have some effect, I explained at length how I—an atheist like themselves—had my eyes opened to the truth. I wrote for an hour or more before Moravetz took the paper and said, 'Enough for tonight'. I was led back to the cell where I found Patrascanu asleep.

Again several days passed without my being troubled. The Communists reverse normal police methods, which rely on the shock of arrest to make a prisoner talk. They prefer to let him 'ripen'. The interrogator never says what he wants; he merely approaches his prey suggestively from this direction and that so as to create anxiety and guilt. While the man is racking his brains for the reason of his arrest, tension is built up by other tricks: a constantly postponed trial, the tape-recorded sound of a firing squad, screams from other prisoners. He begins to make false judgments. One slip leads to another, until exhaustion forces him to accept his guilt. The interrogator becomes sympathetic. He offers hope and an end to suffering if the prisoner admits that he deserves punishment and tells all. So Appel returned in a few days and the first of my innumerable interrogations began.

I was taken this time to a basement room a few steps down from the cell by Appel, who gave me a chair, offered me a toffee from his briefcase and settled down on a sofa. One of his colleagues took notes. Chewing steadily, Appel checked points in my statement and commented that a man's thinking was decided by his class; not being of proletarian origin, I was bound to have reactionary views. I felt sure that Appel was no proletarian either, and I pointed out that none of the great Party thinkers were 'workers' in that sense. Marx was a lawyer's son, Engels's father was a man of property, and Lenin came from the nobility. Class alone never dictated a man's convictions.

Appel broke in. 'What were your connections with Mr. Teodorescu?'

'Teodorescu?' I said. 'That's a fairly common name. Which one do you mean?'

But Appel did not say. Instead he turned to discuss the Bible and the prophecies of Isaiah on the coming of the Messiah. From time to time, without warning, he mentioned the names of people who had helped in distributing my books to Soviet soldiers or in handling relief for the World Council of Churches. The shafts came seemingly at random. Appel was always polite and never persistent. He appeared to be more interested in my reactions to sudden questions than in my answers and, after another hour, I was taken back to the cell to think what it might mean.

13

Patrascanu tried to amuse himself at my expense by talking about the Party's plans to uproot and eradicate Christianity in Rumania. Already Ana Pauker, Georgescu and other Central Committee members had met Justinian in secret and decided he would serve their main purpose well.

'Justinian,' he said, 'has as much to do with God as I have with the Emperor of Japan. As for old Patriarch Nicodim, he's in his dotage. What respect can you have for a man who was issuing encyclicals at the start of the war calling on everyone to fight the seven-headed Bolshevik dragon and then, when we broke with Hitler, urged his flock to march with the glorious Red Army against the Nazi monster? That's what Patriarch Nicodim did, and the whole country knows it. These are the princes of the Church, and the rest aren't much better. They won't lead you far!'

I replied that if he did not leave prison as soon as he expected, he might come to meet more exemplary Christians.

'Patriarch Nicodim is a good man,' I said, 'but old and exhausted. Nor can I condemn the future Patriarch Justinian and those who have been tricked or forced into taking your road. It's too much like taking advantage of a girl and then calling her a harlot.'

I thought this dig might carry my point with Patrascanu, who was apt to speak with crudity and predilection about sexual matters. I tried, too, to tell him what Christian love meant. He was too engrossed in his own troubles to listen much at first; but he was a bookish man, at a loss with nothing to read, and argued for the sake of distraction. On religion, he said, 'I passed through all that at school. I used to pray, but later I gave it up.'

I asked him why.

'Your Jesus asks too much. Especially when one is young.'

I said, 'I've never thought myself that Jesus asks anything from men. When my son Mihai was small, I gave him money to buy me a birthday present. So Jesus gives the virtues he seems to ask for and makes us better characters. But perhaps you didn't have good religious teachers.'

'Probably. They're not too common.' Patrascanu sat up and yawned. 'Besides, there's a lot in Christianity I can't swallow.'

'For example?'

'Humility, and especially submission to tyranny. Take St. Paul's epistle to the Romans. It says all authority is from God, so we must behave ourselves, pay our taxes promptly and not kick against the pricks—this at a time when the ruler of the world was Nero!'

I said, 'Read the Bible again and you'll find it full of revolutionary fire. It starts with the Jewish slaves revolting against Pharaoh. It goes on with Samuel, Jael, Jehu and many other rebels against tyranny. Before going further, ask yourself how the authority approved by God came to power. It's usually the result of an upheaval—so submission to authority means submission to those who have made a successful revolution. Washington became an authority by overthrowing the English.'

'As Lenin overthrew the Tsars,' Patrascanu put in.

'Only to introduce a worse terror. The man will come who will end the Communist tyranny, too, and bring free government. Then he will be the authority from God. Then we should submit. The real teaching in this part of the Scripture is not submission to tyrants, but avoidance of useless bloodshed in revolutions which have no chance.'

Patrascanu said, 'What about "Render unto Caesar the things that are Caesar's"? With this axiom, Jesus was surely urging submission by the Jews to the Roman tyrant?'

'The first Caesar was a usurper,' I said, 'even in Rome. He was a general who had made himself dictator. His successors had no more right in Palestine, which became a Roman colony by force, than the Russians have here. So it's clear that Jesus meant, "Give Caesar what we owe him, a boot in the backside, and pitch him out." '

Patrascanu roared with laughter. 'If every priest explained the Bible like you do, we'd soon reach a better understanding,' he said.

I was not so sure.

One evening, he asked me to tell him the Christian belief in a nutshell. I recited the Nicean Creed and said, 'In return, you should tell me what the Communist creed really is.'

Patrascanu thought for a moment. 'We Communists believe that we will dominate the world', he said, and lay back on his grubby pallet.

Next morning he was taken from his cell. I never saw him again. We had become quite close in the week we had been together. I felt that he was moved by much of what I said, but it did not suit his plans to admit it, even to himself. It was years before I heard what became of him.

14

My next inquisitor, a little man called Vasilu who liked to talk out of the corner of his mouth, read from a typed list of questions. The first was also the hardest: 'Write down the names of everyone you know, where you met them and what your relations with them were.' There were many friends whom I wanted to shield, but if I left them out, and the police knew I had done so, they would be doubly suspect. As I hesitated, Vasilu snapped, 'Don't pick and choose. I said "everyone".'

To make a start, I wrote the names of my known assistants and parishioners. The list covered a page or two. I added Communist members of Parliament and every fellow-traveller and informer I could think of.

'Question Number Two,' said Vasilu, 'is to say what you have done against the state.'

'What am I accused of?' I asked.

Vasilu slapped the table. 'You know what you've done. Get it off your chest! Start by telling us about your contacts with your Orthodox colleague, Father Grigoriu, and what you think of him. Just write, and keep writing!'

Clergymen were always asked about one another—Protestants questioned about Orthodox priests, Catholics about Adventists, and so on, to stoke sectarian rivalries. Whatever you wrote might be used to trap you. A prisoner would be told, 'Sign with a nick-name—it's the way we work here'. When he had given several statements in different names, he would be asked to denounce a friend—with the warning that if he refused, everyone would be told he was an informer who had already given statements under false names. The threat was enough to make many real informers. During the long, solitary waits between interrogations, fresh questions were prepared and you tried to remember what you had said before, and what you had concealed. The inquisitors usually came in pairs, with their typed questions. If one went out, the other did not speak until he returned. Some interrogators, in those early days, were decent enough men who had to live somehow. One showed me, when his companion was out of the room, statements made against me. Several were signed by men I trusted, and I could guess the pressure that had been used on them.

I was still in the first stage of a long process. The number of prisoners was overwhelming, and qualified interrogators were few, but more were being trained in Soviet methods every day. At least, I had time to prepare myself, and I was put in good heart when a barber, while shaving me, whispered that Sabina was well and carrying on our work. My relief was beyond words. I thought my wife might have been arrested also and Mihai, my son, left to starve or rely on the charity of neighbours. Now I was ready to ream off as many chapters from my spiritual biography as the interrogators liked. On other matters I revealed as little as possible. The simple fact that a friend had once visited the West might get his family arrested and earn him a savage beating.

So interrogations continued, month after month. You had to be convinced of your criminal guilt before Communist ideals could be implanted, and they took root only when you had succumbed to the belief that you were entirely, endlessly in the Party's power and had surrendered every fragment of your past.

It was said now in Rumania that life consisted of the four 'autos': the 'autocriticism' which had to be recorded regularly in office and factory; the 'automobile' which took you to the Secret Police; the 'autobiography' which they made you write; and the 'autopsy'.

15

Knowing that torture lay ahead, I resolved to kill myself rather than betray others. I felt no moral scruples; for a Christian to die means to go to Christ. I would explain and He would surely understand. If St. Ursula had been canonised for killing herself rather than lose her virginity to the barbarians who sacked her monastery, then my duty to protect my friends was also higher than life.

The problem was to secure the means of suicide before my intention was suspected. Guards checked prisoners and their cells regularly for possible instruments of death: glass slivers, a piece of cord, a razor-blade. One morning, on the doctor's round, I said I could not remember all the details the interrogators needed because I had not slept for weeks. He ordered me a nightly sleeping pill and a guard peered into my mouth each time to see that it was gone. In fact, I held the pill under my tongue and took it out when he had left. But where to hide my prize? Not on my body, to which anything might happen. Not in my pallet, which had to be shaken and folded daily. There was the other pallet on which Patrascanu had lain. I tore open a few stitches and every day hid another pill among the straw.

By the end of the month I had thirty pills. They were a comfort against the fear of breaking under torture, but I had fits of black depression at the thought of them. It was summer. I heard homely noises from the world outside. A girl singing. A tramcar grinding around the corner. Mothers calling sons. 'Silviu, Emil, Matei!' Feathery seeds floated softly in to settle on my cement floor. I asked God what He was doing. Why was I being forced to put an end to a life which had been dedicated to His service? Looking up one evening through the narrow window, I saw the first star appear in the darkening sky, and the thought came to my mind that God had sent this light, which had begun its apparently useless journey billions of years ago. And now it passed through the bars of my cell, consoling me.

Next morning the guard came in and, without a word, picked up the spare pallet with my hoarded pills in it and took it for some other prisoner. I was upset at first. Then I laughed, and felt calmer than I had for weeks. Since God did not want my suicide, then He would give me strength to bear the suffering ahead.

16

The Secret Police had been patient, I was told, but now it was time for some results. Colonel Dulgheru, their grand inquisitor, never failed to get them. He sat at his desk, still and menacing, with delicate hands outspread before him. 'You've been playing with us', he said.

Dulgheru had worked before the war at the Soviet Embassy. Then, under the Fascists, he was interned and thus fraternised with Gheorghiu-Dej and other imprisoned Communists. They noted his tough qualities, intelligence and ruthlessness. So here he was, with delegated powers of life and death.

At once, Dulgheru began to question me about a Red Army man who had been caught smuggling Bibles into Russia. Until now the interrogators seemed to know nothing about my work among the Russians, but although the arrested soldier had not given me away, it was discovered that we had met. Now, more than ever, I had to weigh every word, for in fact I had baptised the man in Bucharest and so enlisted him in our campaign.

Dulgheru's questions were persistent. He thought he had scented something important. In the weeks that followed, I was worn down by a variety of means. The beds were removed from the cell and I had barely an hour's sleep a night, balanced on a chair. Twice every minute the spy-hole in the door gave a metallic click, and the eye of a guard appeared. Often when I dozed he came in and kicked me awake. In the end I lost all sense of time. Once I awoke to see the cell door ajar. Soft music sounded in the corridor: or was it an illusion? Then the sound became distorted and a woman's voice was sobbing. She began to scream. It was my wife!

'No, no! Please don't beat me. Not again! I can't bear it!'

There was the sound of a whip hitting flesh. The screams rose to an appalling pitch. Every muscle in my body was strained in a rictus of horror. Slowly the voice began to die away, moaning; but now it was the voice of a stranger. It faded into silence. I was left drained of feeling, trembling and drenched with sweat. Later I learnt that it was a tape-recording, but every prisoner who heard it thought that the victim was his wife or sweetheart.

Dulgheru was a refined barbarian, patterned on the Soviet diplomats with whom he had mixed. 'I order torture with regret', he told me. Being all-powerful in the prisons, he could dispense with notes and witnesses, and often came alone to my cell at night to continue interrogation. One critical session dragged on for hours. He asked about my contact with the Church of England Mission. What had I done there? I said that I'd visited Westminster Abbey. He became more and more incensed.

'Do you know,' he said with venom, 'that I can order your execution now, tonight, as a counter-revolutionary?'

I said, 'Colonel, here you have the opportunity for an experiment. You say you can have me shot. I know you can. So put your hand here on my heart. If it beats rapidly, showing that I am afraid, then know there is no God and no eternal life. But if it beats calmly, as if to say, "I go to the One I love," then you must think again. There *is* a God, and an eternal life!'

Dulgheru struck me across the face, and immediately regretted his loss of self-control.

'You fool, Georgescu!' he said. 'Can't you see that you're completely at my mercy and that your Saviour, or whatever you call him, isn't going to open any prison doors? You'll never see Westminster Abbey.'

I said, 'His name is Jesus Christ, and if He wishes He can release me, and I shall see Westminster Abbey, too.'

Dulgheru glared at me as if struggling for breath. Then he shouted, 'All right. Tomorrow you'll meet Comrade Brinzaru.'

I had been expecting this. Major Brinzaru, the colonel's aide, presided over a room where clubs, truncheons and whips were kept. He had hairy arms like a gorilla. Other interrogators used his name as a threat. The contemporary Russian poet Voznesensky writes, 'In these days of untold suffering, one is lucky indeed to have no heart', and Brinzaru was lucky in this way. He introduced me to his range of weapons. 'Is there any you fancy?' he asked. 'We like to be democratic here.'

He displayed his own favourite, a long, black rubber truncheon. 'Read the label.' It was inscribed, 'MADE IN U.S.A.'

'We do the beating,' said Brinzaru with a show of yellow teeth, 'but your American friends give us the tools.' Then he sent me back to my cell to think about it.

The guard told me that Brinzaru had worked before the war for a prominent politician and been treated as one of the family. After the Communist take-over which hoisted him up the ranks of the Secret Police, a young prisoner was brought to him for questioning. It was the politician's son, who had tried to start a patriotic movement. Brinzaru told him, 'I used to hold you on my knees when you were a baby!' Then he tortured the lad and executed him with his own hands.

Curiously, Brinzaru did not give me the threatened beating. On his nightly round of inspection, he flicked the spy-hole cover back to watch me for a moment. 'Still there, Georgescu? What's Jesus doing tonight?'

I said, 'He's praying for you.' He walked away without replying.

Next day he was back again. Under his supervision, I was made to stand facing a wall with my hands raised above my head so that my finger-tips just touched it. 'Just keep him there,' Brinzaru told the guard before leaving.

At last, the torture began. I do not want to make much of it, but it must be told because these things were common to all Secret Police prisons. First I stood for hours, long after my arms had lost all feeling, and my legs began to tremble and then swell. When I collapsed on the floor, I was given a crust and a sip of water and made to stand again. One guard relieved another. Some of them would force you to adopt ridiculous or obscene postures, and this went on, with short breaks, for days and nights. There was the wall to look at.

I thought of the walls referred to in the Bible, recalling a verse from Isaiah which saddened me: God says that Israel's wrongdoings put a wall between Him and the people. The failures of Christianity had allowed a Communist triumph, and that was why I had a wall before me now. Then I remembered a phrase, 'With my Lord, I jump over the wall.' I, too, might jump this wall into the spiritual world of fellowship with God. I thought of the Jewish spies who returned from Canaan to report that the cities were great and walled—but as the walls of Jericho came down, so the wall before me must also fall at the will of God. When pain was overwhelming me, I said to myself a phrase from the Song of Songs: 'My beloved is like a roe or a young hart; behold, he standeth behind our wall.' I imagined that Jesus stood behind my wall, giving me strength. I remembered that, as long as Moses held up his hands on the mountain, the chosen people went forward to victory; perhaps our sufferings were helping the people of God to win their battle, too.

From time to time, Major Brinzaru looked in to ask whether I was willing to co-operate. Once, when I was on the floor, he said, 'Get up! We've decided to let you see Westminster Abbey, after all. You start now.'

'Walk!' ordered the guard. I tried to pull my shoes on, but my feet were too swollen. 'Come on! Hurry! Keep going round! I'll be watching from outside.'

The cell was twelve paces round: four steps—one wall; two steps—the next; then four; then two. I shuffled around it in torn socks. The spy-hole clicked. 'Faster!' shouted the guard. My head began to spin. 'Faster—or do you want a beating?' I bumped painfully into a wall. My eyes stung with sweat. Round and round, round and round. Click! 'Halt, turn about! Walk!' Round, round in the opposite direction. 'Faster!' I stumbled, and picked myself up. Keep moving!' When I fell the guard charged in and cracked me across the elbow with a club as I struggled up. The pain was so agonising that I fell again. 'Get up! Get moving! This is the *manège!*'

Nearly everyone had to go through the *manège,* or training ring as it was known. Hours went by before you got a cup of water or anything to eat. The thirst drove out hunger. It was even fiercer than the stabbing of hot knives that ran up your legs. Worst of all was having to start walking again after being allowed a few minutes rest, or a few hours at night in a stupor on the floor. Stiff joints, cracked muscles, lacerated feet would not support the body's weight. You clung to the walls, while guards screamed orders. When you could no longer stand, you went on all fours.

I do not know how many days and nights I spent in the *manège*. I began to pray for the guards as I moved. I thought of the Song of Songs, in which we are told of the holy dance of the Bride of Christ in honour of her bridegroom. I said to myself, 'I will move with as much grace as if this were a dance of divine love, for Jesus.' For a while it seemed to me that I did. If a man wills to do everything that he has to do, then he does only the things which he wills—and the hardest trials, being voluntary, become easier. And as I went round and about, it seemed as if everything was revolving around me. I could no longer distinguish one wall from another, or a wall from the door, just as in divine love one does not distinguish between good and evil men and can embrace everyone.

17

I had been virtually without sleep for a month when the guard fixed a pair of blacked-out goggles over my eyes and led me to a new interview office. It was a large, bare room. Behind a table sat three or four figures whom I saw only dimly because of the blinding light of the reflectors in my face. I stood before them handcuffed and in bare feet, wearing only a torn, filthy shirt. Familiar questions were repeated. I gave the same replies. This time there was a woman among the inquisitors. At one point she said shrilly, 'If you don't answer properly, we'll have you stretched on the rack.' The machine used last in England for forced confessions 300 years ago had been added to the Party's weapons of persuasion! I said, 'In St. Paul's Epistle to the Ephesians it is written that we must strive to reach the measure of the stature of Christ. If you stretch me on the rack you'll be helping me to fulfil my purpose.' The woman banged the table and there was a discussion behind the dazzle of the reflectors.

Sometimes, a ready answer has the effect of deflecting a blow. I was not 'racked'; instead, we went back to the Inquisition, to the bastinado.

I was taken to another cell. A hood was pulled over my head. I was ordered to squat and place my arms around my knees. A metal bar was thrust between elbows and knees and then lifted on to trestles, so that I swung head down, trussed, with my feet in the air. They held my head while someone flogged the soles of my feet. The blows were like explosions. Some fell on my thighs and the base of my spine. I fainted and was revived by drenchings in cold water. Each time they said that if I gave just one of the names they wanted, it would stop. When they took me down from the spit I had to be carried to my cell.

On every journey to this room I wore the blacked-out goggles which prevented me from learning the prison layout. Sometimes the goggles were kept on while I was beaten. When you see a blow coming, you tense yourself to receive it. But blinded, not knowing where it will fall, or when, the fear is redoubled.

I passed through other tortures. Brinzaru had a nylon whip. After a few strokes with this, I lost consciousness. Once a knife was held to my throat while Brinzaru urged me to talk, if I wished to stay alive. Two men held me down. I felt them tighten their grip and the blade pierced the skin. Again I fainted, and woke to find my chest covered with blood. Water was poured down a funnel into my throat, until my stomach was bursting; then the guards kicked and stepped on me. I was left in a cell with two wolf dogs who were trained to leap forward, snarling, at the slightest movement; but not to bite. Some bread would be placed nearby, but you dared not touch it. In time you realised that the dogs would not attack; but often their teeth snapped inches from your face. I was also branded with a red-hot iron.

In the end I signed about myself all the 'confessions' they wanted: that I was an adulterer and at the same time a homosexual; that I had sold the church bells and pocketed the money (although our church was a prayer-house without bells); that under cover of work for the World Council of Churches, I had spied with the object of overthrowing the régime by treachery; that I and others had infiltrated in times before the Party organisation under false pretences and revealed its secrets.

Brinzaru read these confessions and asked; 'Where are the names of those you passed the secrets on to?'

He was pleased when I gave him a score of names and addresses. It would certainly earn him a bonus and promotion. A few days later I received another flogging. The names had been checked. They were those of men who had fled to the West or who had died. But in the respite I recovered a little strength.

Perhaps waiting was the worst torture: to lie there, listening to screams and weeping, knowing that in an hour it would be my turn. But God helped me never to say a word which harmed another. I lost consciousness easily, and they wanted me alive. Every prisoner could be a source of further information, of use in some later twist of Party fortunes, no matter how long he was kept. A doctor was present at torture sessions to take the pulse and check that the victim was not about to escape into the next world while the Secret Police still had need of him. It was an image of Hell, in which the torment is eternal and you cannot die.

It was hard to remember the Bible. Notwithstanding, I always tried to keep in mind how Jesus could have come to earth as a king, but chose instead to be condemned as a criminal and whipped. A Roman whipping was horrible, and I thought with every blow I received that He also knew such pain, and there was joy in sharing it with Him.

The mockery and humiliation were also more than many could support. Jesus often said that he would be scourged, mocked and crucified. I used to think that mockery, compared with scourging and crucifixion, was nothing. That was before I knew that a man could be forced to open his mouth so that others could spit or urinate in it, while our masters laughed and jeered.

It is not easy to believe, but just as the officers of the Spanish Inquisition thought it a sacred duty to burn heretics, so many Party men believed that what they did was justified. Colonel Dulgheru seemed to be one of these. He used to say, 'It is in the vital interests of society that men should be maltreated if they withhold information needed to protect it.' Much later on, when he saw me reduced to a wreck, weeping from nervous fatigue, he said with something like pity, 'Why don't you give in? It's all so futile. You're only flesh and you'll break in the end.' But I had proof of the contrary: had I been just flesh I could not have resisted. But the body is only a temporary residence for the soul. The Communists, relying on the instinct of self-preservation, thought a man would do anything to avoid extinction. They were mistaken. Christians who believed what they said in church knew that to die was not the end of life but its fulfilment; not extinction, but the promise of eternity.

18

I had been seven months in Calea Rahova prison. It was October and the winter was already on us. We suffered much from cold now, as well as hunger and ill-treatment, and months of winter lay ahead. Gazing from my window at the sleet falling on the prison yard, I shivered, yet my spirits were not low. Whatever I could do for God by patient love in jail would be small, I thought, but the good in life always looks small in comparison with the amount of bad. While evil in the New Testament is depicted as a huge beast with seven horns, the Holy Spirit descended as a little dove. It is the dove which will defeat the beast!

One evening, a plate of savoury goulash appeared, with four whole slices of bread. Before I could eat it, the guard returned and made me gather up my things and follow him to a place where other prisoners were lined up. Thinking of my lost goulash I went by truck to the Ministry of the Interior. This splendid building is much admired by tourists, who do not know that it is built over an extensive prison with a labyrinth of corridors and hundreds of helpless inmates.

My cell was deep underground. A light bulb shone from the ceiling on bare walls, an iron bedstead with three planks and a straw pallet. Air entered through a pipe high in the wall. I saw there was no bucket and I would have to wait always for the guard to take me to the latrine. This was the worst imposition for every prisoner. Sometimes they made you wait for hours, laughing at your pleadings. Men, and women too, went without food and drink for fear of increasing their agony. I myself have eaten from the dish in which I fulfilled my needs without washing it, because I had no water.

The silence here was practically complete—deliberately so. Our guards wore felt-soled shoes and you could hear their hands on the door before key found lock. Now and again there was the far-off sound of a prisoner hammering steadily on his door or screaming. The cell allowed only three paces in each direction, so I lay down and stared at the bulb. It burnt all night. Since I could not sleep, I prayed. The outside world had ceased to exist. All the noises I was used to, the wind and rain in the yard, steel boot-studs on stone floors, the buzz of a fly, a human voice, were gone. My heart seemed to shrink, as if it, too, would stop in this lifeless silence.

19

I was kept in solitary confinement in this cell for the next two years. I had nothing to read and no writing materials; I had only my thoughts for company, and I was not a meditative man, but a soul that had rarely known quiet. I had God. But had I really lived to serve God—or was it simply my profession?

People expect pastors to be models of wisdom, purity, love, truthfulness; they cannot always be genuinely so, because they are also men: so, in smaller or greater measure, they begin to act the part. As time passes, they can hardly tell how much of their behaviour is play-acting.

I remembered the deep commentary which Savonarola wrote on the fifty-first Psalm, in prison, with his bones so broken that he could sign the self-accusatory paper only with his left hand. He said there were two kinds of Christian: those who sincerely believe in God and those who, just as sincerely, believe that they believe. You can tell them apart by their actions in decisive moments. If a thief, planning to rob a rich man's home, sees a stranger who might be a policeman, he holds back. If, on second thoughts, he breaks in after all, this proves that he does not believe the man to be an agent of the law. Our beliefs are proved by what we do.

Did I believe in God? Now the test had come. I was alone.

There was no salary to earn, no golden opinions to consider. God offered me only suffering—would I continue to love Him?

My mind went back to one of my favourite books, 'The Pateric', concerning certain fourth-century saints who formed desert monasteries when the Church was persecuted. It has 400 pages, but the first time I picked it up I did not eat, drink or sleep until I had finished it. Christian books are like good wine—the older the better. It contained the following passage:

> A brother asked his elder, 'Father, what is silence?' The answer was, 'My son, silence is to sit alone in your cell in wisdom and fear of God, shielding the heart from the burning arrows of thought. Silence like this brings to birth the good. O silence without care, ladder to heaven! O silence in which one cares only for first things, and speaks only with Jesus Christ! He who keeps silent is the one who sings, "My heart is ready to praise Thee, O Lord!" '

I wondered how you could praise God by a life of silence. At first, I prayed greatly to be released. I asked, 'You have said in Scripture that it is not good that a man should be alone; why do You keep me alone?' But as days passed into weeks my only visitor was still the guard, who brought wedges of black bread and watery soup, and never spoke a word.

His arrival reminded me daily of the saying, 'The gods walk in soft shoes': in other words, the Greeks believed that we cannot be aware of the approach of a divinity. Perhaps in this silence I was coming closer to God. Perhaps, too, it would make me a better pastor; for I had noticed that the best preachers were men who possessed an inner silence, like Jesus. When the mouth is too much open, even to speak good, the soul loses its fire just as a room loses warmth through an open door.

Slowly, I learned that on the tree of silence hangs the fruit of peace. I began to realise my real personality, and made sure that it belonged to Christ. I found that even here my thoughts and feelings turned to God and that I could pass night after night in prayer, spiritual exercise and praise. I knew now that I was not play-acting, believing that I believed.

20

I worked out a routine to which I kept for the next two years. I stayed awake all night. When the 10 p.m. bell signalled time to sleep, I began my programme. Sometimes I was sad, sometimes cheerful, but the nights were not long enough for all I had to do.

I began with a prayer in which tears, often of thankfulness, were rarely absent. Prayers, like radio signals, are heard more clearly by night: it is then that great spiritual battles are fought. Next, I preached a sermon as I would in church, beginning with 'Beloved brethren', in a whisper which no guard could hear, and ending with 'Amen'. At last I preached with complete truth. No longer need I care what the bishop would think, the congregation say, or spies report. I was not preaching to a void. Every sermon is heard by God, his angels and saints; but I felt that among those around me listening were those who had brought me to faith, members of my flock, both dead and living, my family and friends. They were the 'cloud of witnesses' of which the Bible speaks. I experienced the 'communion of saints' of the Creed.

Every night I talked to my wife and son. I pondered on all that was fine and good in them. Sometimes my thoughts reached Sabina over the prison walls. She has a note in her Bible from this time: 'Today I saw Richard. I was lying in bed awake and he leaned over and spoke to me.' I had concentrated all my power to transmit a message of love to her. We were richly rewarded for a few minutes' thought towards each other, every day; while so many marriages were destroyed by prison, ours held firm and was fortified.

Thinking about my family could also wound. I knew that Sabina would undergo intense pressure to divorce me. If she refused, and carried on her Church work as well, they would almost certainly arrest her. Then Mihai, who was only ten years old, would be left alone. I lay face down on the pallet and hugged it as if it were my son. Once I leapt up and smashed my fists on the steel door, shouting, 'Give me back my boy!' The guards ran in to hold me down, while I was given an injection which made me unconscious for hours. When I awoke, I thought I might be going mad. I knew many who had done so.

It gave me courage to think of Jesus's mother, who stood at the foot of the cross with no word of complaint. I wondered whether we were right to interpret her silence as sorrow unalloyed: surely she was proud, too, that He was giving his life for man? In the evening of that day, being Passover, she must have sung God's praises, according to Jewish ritual. I, too, must thank God for the suffering through which my little son might pass. Again, I took hope: even if Sabina had gone, we had friends who would surely care for Mihai.

One of my constant spiritual exercises was to imagine as if in a picture that I was surrendering all my life to Christ: past, present, future; my family, my church, my passions, my secret thoughts; every member of my body. I confessed my past sins to Christ without reserve and saw Him wipe them out with his hand. Often I wept.

In the first days, I spent much time searching my soul. It was a mistake. Love, goodness, beauty are shy creatures who hide themselves when they know they are observed. My son had given me a lesson on this point when he was five. I had reproved him, 'Jesus has a big exercise book and one of the pages bears your name. This morning he had to write that you disobeyed your mother. Yesterday you fought another boy and said it was his fault, so that went down, too.' Mihai said, after thinking a minute, 'Daddy, does Jesus write only the bad things we do, or the good things as well?'

My son was so often in my mind! I remembered with delight how he had taught me theology. When I read from the epistle to the Corinthians, 'Examine yourself to see whether you are holding to the faith,' he asked, 'How should I examine myself?'

I replied, 'Thump your chest and ask, "Heart, do you love God?" ' I gave my chest a blow as I spoke.

'That's not right,' said Mihai. 'Once the man at the station who hits train wheels with a hammer let me try, and he said, "You only give them a little tap in case they break, not a big thump." So I don't have to give myself a thump either to see if I love Jesus.'

Now I knew that the quiet 'Yes' of my heart when I put the question, 'Do you love Jesus?' was enough.

Each night I passed an hour living in the minds of my chief adversaries—Colonel Dulgheru, for instance! Imagining myself in his place, I found a thousand excuses for him; in this way I could love him and the other torturers. Then I considered my own faults from his point of view and found a new comprehension of myself. It is easier to console others than to comfort oneself, just as we can read with calm sympathy of the guillotine's victims, but are shocked when a revolution threatens us. So now, I went on to reverse events in time, to think of the present as if it were happening in some previous era and about the past as if it were happening today. In this way one can even hope to meet the saints of old.

I thought what I would do if I were a great statesman, a multimillionaire, the Emperor of China, the Pope. I dreamt of what life would be if I had wings or the cloak of invisibility, and decided that I had chanced on a definition of the human spirit as an invisible, winged force which can transform the world. These were diverting fantasies, but time-wasting. A busy architect does not speculate about what he might do with non-existent materials—weightless stone, elastic glass. Meditation, like architecture, should be constructive. But such digression helped me to see how opposed entities can unite in the life of the spirit, and now I understood how Christ can contain all things, be lion of Judah and lamb of God.

Nor did I lack amusement in my empty cell. I told myself jokes and invented new ones. I played chess with myself, using pieces made from bread: Black versus Less-Black, with chalk from the wall. I could divide my mind so that Black should not know Less-Black's next move, and vice-versa, and since I did not lose a game in two years, I felt that I could claim to be a master.

I found that joy can be acquired like a habit, in the same way as a folded sheet of paper falls naturally into the same fold. 'Be joyful', is a command of God. John Wesley used to say that he 'was never sad even one quarter of an hour'. I cannot say the same of myself, but I learnt to rejoice in the worst conditions.

21

The Communists believe that happiness comes from material satisfaction; but alone in my cell, cold, hungry and in rags, I danced for joy every night. The idea came to me with boyhood memories of watching dancing dervishes. I had been moved past understanding by their ecstasy, the grave beauty of these Moslem monks, their grace of movement as they whirled and called out their name for God, 'Allah!' Later I learnt that many others—Jews, Pentecostals, early Christians, people in the Bible like David and Miriam, altar-boys in Seville Cathedral celebrating Easter, even today, also danced for God. Words alone have never been able to say what man feels in the nearness of divinity. Sometimes I was so filled with joy that I felt I would burst if I did not give it expression. I remembered the words of Jesus, 'Blessed are you when men come to hate you, when they exclude you from their company and reproach you and cast out your name as evil on account of the Son of Man. Rejoice in that day and leap for joy!' I told myself, 'I've carried out only half this command. I've rejoiced, but that is not enough. Jesus says clearly that we must also leap.'

When next the guard peered through the spy-hole, he saw me springing about my cell. His orders must have been to distract anyone who showed signs of breakdown, for he padded off and returned with some food from the staff room: a hunk of bread, some cheese and sugar. As I took them I remembered how the verse in St. Luke went on: 'Rejoice in that day and leap for joy—for behold your reward is great.' It was a very large piece of bread: more than a week's ration.

I rarely allowed a night to pass without dancing, from then on; although I was never paid for it again. I made up songs and sang them softly to myself and danced to my own music. The guards became used to it. I did not break the silence, and they had seen many strange things in these subterranean cells. Friends to whom I spoke later of dancing in prison asked, 'What for? What use was it?' It was not something useful. It was a manifestation of joy like the dance of David, a holy sacrifice offered before the altar of the Lord. I did not mind if my captors thought I was mad, for

I had discovered a beauty in Christ which I had not known before.

Sometimes I saw visions. Once as I danced I seemed to hear my name called—not 'Richard', but another name which I cannot reveal. I knew that it was I who was called under my new name and it flashed into my mind, I don't know why, 'This must be the Archangel Gabriel'. Then the cell was full of light. I heard no more, but I understood that I was to work together with Jesus and the saints to build a bridge between good and evil; a bridge of tears, prayers and self-sacrifice for sinners to cross over and join the blessed. I saw that our bridge had to be one that even the weakest in goodness could use. Jesus promised that at the Last Judgment those who have fed the hungry and clothed the naked will sit at his right hand, while wrong-doers will be cast into the outer darkness. Now every man, surely, sometimes helps others and sometimes fails to do so: the body is one, but the spirit is not. The Bible speaks of the 'inner' man, and of the 'outward' man; of the 'new', and 'old'; of the 'natural', and 'spiritual' man. It is the inner, spiritual man who may achieve happiness in eternal life.

I saw that I must love men as they were, not as they should be. Another night I became aware of a great throng of angels moving slowly through the darkness towards my bed. As they approached they sang a song of love that Romeo might have sung to Juliet. I could not believe that the guards did not hear this marvellous, passionate music which was so real to me.

Prisoners who are long alone often have visions. There are natural explanations for such phenomena which do not invalidate them. The soul uses the body for its own purposes. These visions helped to sustain my life: that is enough to prove that they were not mere hallucinations.

22

One night I heard a faint tapping on the wall beside my bed. A new prisoner had arrived in the next cell and was signalling to me. I answered, and provoked a flurry of fresh taps. Presently I realised that my neighbour was conveying a simple code: A—one tap; B—two taps; C—three taps.

'Who are you?' was his first message.

'A pastor,' I replied.

From this cumbersome start we developed a new system: one tap to indicate the first five letters of the alphabet, two taps for the second group of five, and so on. Thus B was a single tap, followed by a pause, then two more taps; F was two taps followed after a space by one. Even this code did not satisfy my new neighbour. He knew Morse and passed on the letters one by one until I had learnt them all.

He signalled his name.

'Bless you,' I replied laboriously. 'Are you a Christian?'

A minute went by. 'I cannot claim so.'

He was a radio-engineer, it appeared, awaiting trial on a capital charge; aged fifty-two and in poor health. He had lapsed from faith some years before, having married an unbeliever, and was in deep depression. I spoke to him through the wall every night, growing fluent in the use of Morse.

Before long, he tapped: 'I should like to confess my sins.'

It was a confession broken by many silences. 'I was seven . . . I kicked a boy . . . because he was a Jew. He cursed me . . . "May your mother . . . not be able to see you . . . when she dies." . . . Mother was dying . . . when they arrested me.'

When the man had unburdened many things from his heart he said he felt happier than he had been for years. We became Morse friends as others become pen-friends. I taught him Bible verses. We exchanged jokes and tapped out the movements of chess games. I sent him messages about Christ, preaching in code. When the guard caught me at it, I was transferred to another cell, with another neighbour, and there began again. In time, many of us learnt the code. Prisoners were often moved, and more than once I was betrayed by an informer, so I tapped out only Bible verses and words about Christ: I was not prepared to suffer for political arguments.

Men were forced by solitary confinement to delve into deeply-buried happenings. Old betrayals and dishonesties returned with inescapable persistence. It was as if they came into your cell and looked at you in reproach: Mother, father, girls long ago abandoned, friends slandered or cheated of their due. All confessions I heard in morse began, 'When I was a boy', 'When I was at school . . . !' The memory of old transgressions stood like savage watchdogs before the sanctuary of God's peace. But when all other gates to heaven are shut for a man, the Kabala tells us that there remains the *bab hadimot,* the gate of tears, and it was through this gate that we prisoners had to pass.

23

One morning, when a neighbour tapped that it was Good Friday, I found a nail in the lavatory and wrote 'JESUS' on my cell wall, hoping it might comfort those who came after me. The guard was angry. 'You're for the carcer!' he said.

I was taken down the corridor to a cupboard built into a wall, just high enough to stand in and twenty inches square, with a few small airholes and one for food to be pushed through. The guard thrust me in and closed the door. Sharp points stung my back. I jerked forward, to be pierced again in the chest by a second set of spikes. Panic went through me,but I forced myself to stand still. Then, moving cautiously in the dark, I felt the sides of the cupboard—all were studded with steel projections. Only by standing rigidly upright could I avoid impalement. This was the carcer.

My legs began to ache. By the end of an hour every muscle seemed to hurt. My feet, sore from the *manège*, were swelling up. When I collapsed, lacerating myself on the spikes, they let me out for a rest, then put me back. I tried to keep my mind on Christ's sufferings, but my own were too strong. Then I remembered that my son Mihai, when very young, had asked, 'What shall I do, Daddy? I'm bored.' I said, 'Think about God, Mihai!' He replied, 'Why should I think about Him? I've only a small head: He has a great big head, so He ought to think about me.' So now I told myself, 'Don't try to think about God. Don't think at all.' In that suffocating darkness I reminded myself that Indian yogi clear their minds of thought by repeating a secret formula, over and over again. Much the same method is used by monks on Mount Athos with their interminable 'prayer of the heart', in which a word is said for every heart-beat: 'Lord Jesus Christ, Son of God, have mercy upon me!' I knew already that Christ was merciful, but just as I used to tell my wife every day that I loved her, so I thought, 'I'll do the same with Jesus'. I began to repeat, 'Jesus, dear bridegroom of my soul, I love you.' The quiet beating of a loving heart is a music that carries far, so I said this phrase to the same rhythm. At first I seemed to hear the devil sneering, 'You love Him, and He lets you suffer. If He's all-powerful, why doesn't He take you out of the carcer?' I continued to say quietly, 'Jesus, dear bridegroom of my soul, I love you.' In a short time the significance of the words was blurred and then lost. I had ceased to think.

Later I was often to practise this detachment in bad moments. Jesus says in the Gospel according to St. Matthew, 'For in such an hour as ye think not the Son of Man cometh.' This has been my experience of Him. Don't think—and Christ will come, taking you by surprise. But the clarity of His light is hard to bear. Sometimes I reversed the process and fled from it to my own thoughts.

24

I spent two days in the carcer. Some were kept in it for a week or more, but the doctor warned that my condition had become dangerous. Already I was living in a borderland between the living and the dead. As a result of my long confinement, and the lack of sun, food and air, my hair had ceased to grow. The barber did not need to shave me for days. My finger-nails were pallid and soft as a plant kept in the darkness.

Hallucinations began to possess my mind. I stared at my tin cup of water to convince myself in moments of despair that I was not in Hell, where there is no water—and then it turned into a helmet. I saw delicious dishes laid out on a table that stretched out far beyond the cell. From a long way off my wife approached; she carried a plate piled high with smoking sausages, but I snarled at her, 'Is that all? How small they are!' Sometimes my cell expanded into a library, with shelf after shelf of books in bindings reaching up into the darkness: famous novels, poetry, biography, religious and scientific works. They towered up above me. At other times, thousands of faces turned eagerly towards me: I was surrounded by huge crowds, waiting for me to speak. Questions were shouted. Voices answered them. There were cheers and counter-cheers. A sea of faces stretched into infinity.

I was also troubled by dreams of violence against those who had put me in prison, and tormented by erotic fantasies. This is a Hell which is not easily understood by those who have not dwelt in it. I was thirty-nine when I entered prison, healthy and active, and now the return of tuberculosis brought increased sexual desire. Lying awake, I had hot sweaty dreams of sensual pleasure with women and girls, then—although I tried to drive them out—came visions of perversions and exaggerations of the act of love. Frustration and the sense of sin caused me horrible suffering: sometimes sharp and searing, at others dull, but always present.

I found a way of shaking off such hallucinations by treating them as hostile intruders, like the T.B. microbes in my body: so far from blaming myself for their inroads, I claimed credit for resisting them. Once I regarded the hallucinations not as sins but as enemies, I could plan how to destroy them. Evil thoughts can be subdued by reason, if their consequences are calmly considered. I did not try to drive them out, knowing that they would slip in again by a side door; instead, I let them stay while I worked out the cost in real life if I surrendered to them. To give way to such temptations would surely bring misery to other families and my own. My wife would have to divorce me. My son's future would be wrecked. My parishioners would lose faith. And then, despised by all, I should still have to answer to God for the harm I had caused. As doctors employ one virus to fight another, so we can use the Devil's maxim, 'divide and rule', to defeat him. The devil of pride—the fear of losing face—can be turned against the devil of lust. The devil of avarice hates vices that cost money!

25

One day, our latrines being blocked, they took me to the toilet used by the guards. There was a piece of mirror on the wall over the washbowl, and for the first time in two years I saw myself.

I had been young and healthy on entering jail. I had been considered handsome. Now, as I looked at what I had become, I laughed: sad laughter, Homeric laughter. So many had admired and loved me: now if they could see the fearful old man who stared back at me they would be appalled. It was a lesson to me that what is really fine in us is invisible to the eye. I would become uglier still—a skeleton and a skull; and, remembering this, my faith and desire to keep to the spiritual life were strengthened.

There was a torn newspaper in the toilet, the first I had seen since my arrest. It contained the news that Premier Groza had firmly decided to wipe out the rich, which struck me as funny—a Government bent on liquidating the wealthy, while the rest of the world was trying to end poverty. I looked for Patrascanu's name, in case he had been reinstated, but it was not among the Ministers in the Chamber where Groza's speech was made.

On my way back to my cell under escort, I heard a woman weeping and crying out in a crazed way. Her shrieks seemed to come from a level of the prison below us; they rose to a paroxysm, then were suddenly stopped.

A few days later a new prisoner was put in the cell next to mine. I tapped out a 'Who are you?' message and received a prompt reply. It was Ion Mihalache, who had been a member of several pre-war governments and a colleague of the great political leader Iuliu Maniu. When the Party terror began, Mihalache joined a group which tried to flee abroad. He was arrested at the airport and, in October 1947, sentenced to life imprisonment. Mihalache was over sixty. 'All my life I have struggled to help my countrymen, and this is my reward' he said.

'When you will all that happens, then what happens is only what you will,' I signalled. 'Renunciation is the way to peace.'

He tapped back, 'There is no peace without liberty.'

I said, 'In a country where tyranny reigns . . . prison is the place of honour.'

He said that God was lost for him.

I signalled, 'God is never lost for any man . . . We are the lost ones . . . If we find ourselves . . . we find the Godhead within us . . . Prison can help us in this search.' He said that he would try again.

Before Mihalache was moved on two days later he told me that the woman whose screams we heard was the wife of a former Prime Minister, Ion Gigurtu. The way her cries stopped showed that they were giving her injections to silence her. When I rapped on the wall next there was no reply. Mihalache was gone.

26

Soon after this, my interrogation was resumed. It was usually conducted by Lieutenant Grecu, a tough young man, intelligent and self-assured, who had been indoctrinated with the belief that he was making a better world. His questioning brought us back once more to the famine relief which I had undertaken for the Scandinavian church mission. Did I still deny, he asked, that the funds were used for spying?

I said, 'I can understand your suspecting the British and Americans of spending money for espionage here, but what interest could Norway or Sweden have in such activities?'

He retorted, 'Both are tools of the imperialists.'

'But Norway is famous for its democratic spirit, and Sweden has had a socialist government for forty years.'

'Nonsense!' he said. 'They're as fascist as the rest.'

At our next meeting, Grecu said he had checked and thought I might be right.

He enquired next about the distribution of the Gospel in Russian. I suggested that a director of the Bible Society called Emile Klein might be behind it. He asked why I had made repeated vists to the town of Iasi (one of the centres of this work). I said I had a standing invitation to call on the actual Patriarch.

Next morning I was called again. Grecu was at his desk, with a rubber truncheon in his hand.

'Your story was lies,' he shouted. 'Emile Klein died before you were arrested. That's why you named him. They've checked the dates of your trips to Iasi—the Patriarch Justinian was hardly ever there.'

He pushed back his chair. 'Enough! Here's some paper. We know you've communicated in code with other prisoners including Mihalache. Now we must know exactly what each of them said. We want to know your other breaches of prison rules. And tell the truth. If you don't . . . '

He cracked the truncheon on the desk. 'You have half an hour,' he said, and left the room.

I sat down to write. The first word had to be 'Declaration'. I had trouble in starting: it was two years since I had held a pen. I admitted that I had broken rules. I had tapped the Gospel message through the walls. I had hoarded pills to kill myself. I had made a knife out of a piece of tin, chessmen out of bread and chalk. I had communicated with other prisoners, but did not know their names. (I did not mention that I had received confessions and even brought men to faith with Morse.) I wrote, 'I have never spoken against the Communists. I am a disciple of Christ, who has given us love for our enemies. I understand them and pray for their conversion; so that they will become my brothers in the Faith. I can give no statement about what others may have tapped to me, for a priest of God can never be a witness for the prosecution. My calling is to defend, not to accuse.'

Grecu returned on time, swinging his truncheon. He had been beating prisoners.

He picked up my 'Declaration' and began to read. After a while, he put the truncheon aside. When he came to the end he looked at me with troubled eyes. He said, 'Mr. Wurmbrand (he had never called me 'Mr.' before), why do you say you love me? This is one of your Christian commandments, that no one can keep. *I* couldn't love someone who shut me up for years alone, who starved and beat me.'

I said, 'It's not a matter of keeping a commandment. When I became a Christian it was as if I had been reborn, with a new character which was full of love. Just as only water can flow from a spring, so only love can come from a loving heart.'

For two hours we talked about Christianity and its relation to the Marxist doctrines on which he was brought up. Grecu was surprised when I said Marx's first work was a commentary on St. John's Gospel; nor did he know that Marx, in his foreword to 'Capital', wrote that Christianity—especially in its Protestant form—is 'the ideal religion for the renewal of lives made wretched by sin'. Since my life had been made wretched by sin, I said, I was simply following Marx's advice in becoming a Protestant Christian.

After this meeting Grecu called me to his office almost every day for an hour or two. He had confirmed the quotations. This became the pretext for long discussions about Christianity, in which I stressed its democratic and revolutionary early spirit.

Repeatedly, Grecu said, 'I was brought up an atheist, and I'll never be anything else.' I told him, 'Atheism is a holy word for Christians. Our forefathers when they were thrown to the wild beasts for their faith, were called atheists by Nero and Caligula. So if anyone calls himself an atheist, I respect him.'

Grecu smiled. I went on, 'Lieutenant, one of my ancestors was a rabbi of the seventeenth-century. His biographers record how he met an atheist and said, "I envy you, dear brother! Your spiritual life must be so much stronger than my own. When I see a man in trouble I often say, "God will help him", and pass on. You don't believe in God, so you have to take on his burdens and help everyone you meet."

'Christians don't criticise the Party for atheism, but for producing the wrong type of atheist. There are two sorts: those who say, "There is no God, so I can do all the evil I like", and those who reason, "Since there is no God, I must do all the good that God would do if He existed." The greatest of all atheists in this second sense, was Christ himself. When he saw men hungry, sick and in distress, he didn't pass on, saying, "God will help them". He acted as if the whole responsibility were his own. So people began to ask, "Is this man God? He does God's work!" That is how they discovered that Jesus was God. Lieutenant, if you can become this sort of atheist, loving everyone and serving everyone, men will soon discover that you have become a son of God; and you yourself will discover the Godhead in you.'

These arguments may shock some people. But St. Paul tells us that missionaries must be Jews among the Jews, Greeks among the Greeks. I had to be a Marxist with the Marxist Grecu and speak the language he understood. The words went to his heart. He began to think and to love Jesus. Two weeks later, in his khaki uniform with the blue tabs of the Security Police at his collar, Grecu confessed to me in my patched prison rags. We became brethren.

From now on, he bravely helped prisoners as best he could,

through difficulties and dangers. He still gave lip-service to the Party and played an outward role, but one day he disappeared, and no one knew what became of him. I made cautious enquiries among the guards, who thought he had been arrested. To hide a true conversion is not easy.

27

I met other secret believers among the Secret Police, and some still go about their duties. Don't say a man cannot torture and pray at the same time! Jesus tells us of a tax-gatherer (whose work in Roman times went hand-in-hand with extortion and brutality) who prayed for mercy as a sinner, and went home 'justified'. The Gospel does not say that the man immediately abandoned his unpleasant job. God looks into the heart and sees in a good prayer the promise of a new life in the future.

During my second year of confinement, one of these divided souls was put in my cell. All the time he stayed with me, his hands were chained behind his back. I had to feed him and do everything for him.

Dionisiu was a young sculptor, full of new ideas in a world which asked only flattering busts of Stalin. He had no money to buy bread, so he took a post with the Secret Police which obliged him to beat prisoners; but at the same time he ran great risks to warn them of informers. Finding himself under suspicion, Dionisiu decided to flee the country; then, when close to freedom, was compelled by some inner urge to return and give himself up. These split personalities are found everywhere under Communism. Dionisiu had been pulled in two directions all his life.

For ten nights, all through the night, I taught Dionisiu from the Bible. His sense of guilt was driven out. Before they moved him from my cell he said, 'If one of the fifteen priests in my little town had stopped to talk to me when I was younger, I should have found Jesus long ago.'

28

Interrogation did not cease with Lieutenant Grecu's departure, but God granted me the gift of being able to forget the names of all for whom I could cause trouble. Although in prison I composed more than 300 poems, totalling 100,000 words, and wrote them all down on my release, I could make my mind a blank during interrogation. So a new device was tried.

On the pretext that my tuberculosis had worsened—and, indeed, my coughing was almost continuous—the doctors ordered me a new drug: a yellow capsule which brought long sleep filled with delightful dreams. When I awoke I was given another. I remained unconscious for some days, awakened only by guards bringing meals which had become light and wholesome.

My recollection of the resumed questioning is hazy. I know that the drug did not make me betray my friends, because when I was put on trial later, I was tried alone. No grand trial of the men behind the World Council of Churches' 'spy net' ever took place. The drug was used on Cardinal Mindszenty, the Trotskyists and many others. It weakens will-power until the victim goes into a delirium of self-accusation. Later, I was to hear men who were taking the course banging on cell doors and demanding to see the political officer so that they might make new charges against themselves. The treatment can also have long-term effects: men who had taken it months before later confessed to me sins they had no chance of committing. Perhaps the tuberculosis in my body counteracted the drug. Perhaps I had received a too big dose of it. At all events, by God's grace, I was saved from treachery.

29

I became still weaker after the drugging, and one day collapsed completely. But although I could rise from bed only with extreme effort, my mind remained alert for a time. I was even afraid of its lucidity.

It is no myth that the great St. Anthony, Martin Luther and many other more ordinary men have seen the Devil. I saw him once, as a child. He grinned at me. This is the first time I have spoken of it in half a century. Alone in the cell, now, I felt his presence again. It was dark and cold, and he was mocking me. The Bible speaks of places 'where satyrs dance', and this had become such a place. I heard his voice day and night, 'Where's

Jesus? Your Saviour can't save you! You've been tricked, and you've tricked others. He isn't the Messiah—you followed the wrong man!'

I cried aloud, 'Then who is the true Messiah who will come?' The answer was plain, but too blasphemous to repeat. I had written books and articles proving Christ was the Messiah, but now I could not think of one argument. The devils who made Nyils Hauge, the great Norwegian evangelist, waver in his faith while in jail, who made even John the Baptist doubt in his dungeon, raged against me. I was weaponless. My joy and serenity were gone. I had felt Christ so close to me before, easing my bitterness, lightening the darkness, but now I cried, 'Eli, Eli, lama sabachthani?' and I felt utterly forsaken.

During those black, horrible days, I slowly composed a long poem which may not be easily accepted by those who have not known any similar physical and spiritual state. It was my salvation. By word, rhythm and incantation, I was able to defeat Satan. Here is an unrhymed and unmetrical version which gives the exact meaning of the Rumanian:

> From childhood I frequented temples and churches. In them God was glorified. Different priests sang and censed with zeal. They claimed it right to love You. But as I grew, I saw such deep sorrow in the world of this God that I said to myself, 'He has a heart of stone. Otherwise He would ease the difficulties of the way for us.' Sick children struggle with fever in hospital: sad parents pray for them. Heaven is deaf. The ones we love go to the valley of death, even when our prayers are long. Innocent men are burnt alive in furnaces. And heaven is silent. It lets things be. Can God wonder if, in undertones, even the believers begin to doubt? Hungry, tortured, persecuted in their own land, they have no answers to these questions. The Almighty is disgraced by the horrors that befall us.
>
> How can I love the creator of microbes and of tigers that tear men? How can I love Him who tortures all his servants because one ate from a tree? Sadder than Job, I have neither wife, child nor comforters, and in this prison there is neither sun nor air and the régime is hard to endure.

From my bed of planks they will make my coffin. Stretched upon it, I try to find why my thoughts run to You, why my writings all turn towards You? Why is this passionate love in my soul, why does my song go only to You? I know well I am rejected; soon I will putrefy in a tomb.

The bride of the Song of Songs did not love when she asked if You are 'rightly loved'. Love is its own justification. Love is not for the wise. Through a thousand ordeals she will not cease to love. Though fire burns and the waves drown her, she will kiss the hand that hurts. If she finds no answer to her questions she is confident and waits. One day, the sun will shine in hidden places and all will be made plain.

Forgiveness of many sins only increased Magdalene's burning love. But she gave perfume and shed tears before You said Your forgiving word. And had You not said it, still she would have sat and wept for the love she has towards You, even being in sin. She loved You before Your blood was shed. She loved You before You forgave. Neither do I ask if it is right to give You love. I do not love in hope of salvation. I would love You in everlasting misfortune. I would love You even in consuming fire. If You had refused to descend to men, You would have been my distant dream. If You had refused to sow Your word, I would love You without hearing it. If You had hesitated and fled from the Crucifixion, and I were not saved, still I would love You. And even if I found sin in You, I would cover it with my love.

Now I will dare to say mad words, so that all may know how much I love. Now I will touch untouched strings and magnify You with a new music. If the prophets had predicted another, I would leave them, not You. Let them produce a thousand proofs, I will keep my love for You. If I divined that You were a deceiver, I would pray for You weeping and, though I could not follow You in falsehood, it would not lessen my love. For Saul, Samuel passed a life in weeping and severe fasting. So my love would resist even if I knew You lost. If You, not Satan, had risen wrongly in revolt against Heaven and lost the loveliness of wings and fallen like an archangel from high, hopeless, I would hope that the Father would forgive You and that one day You would walk with Him again in the gold streets of Heaven.

If You were a myth, I would leave reality and live with You in a dream. If they proved You did not exist, You would receive life from my love. My love is mad, without motive, as Your love is, too. Lord Jesus, find some happiness here. For more I cannot give you.

When I had completed this poem, I no longer felt the nearness of Satan. He had gone. In the silence I felt the kiss of Christ, and everyone is silent when he is kissed. Quiet and joy returned.

PART TWO

After nearly three years of solitary confinement, I was close to death. I spat blood often.

Colonel Dulgheru said 'We're not murderers like the Nazis. We want you to live—and suffer.' A specialist was called. Anxious to avoid infection, he made his diagnosis through a spy-hole in the cell door. Orders were given for my transfer to a prison-hospital.

They carried me up from the underground cells, and in the yard of the Ministry of the Interior I saw moonlight and stars again. Lying in an ambulance, I caught familiar glimpses of Bucharest. We were moving in the direction of my house and for a moment I thought I was being taken home to die. When we were almost there, the ambulance turned off and began to climb a hill on the outskirts of the city. I knew then that we were going to Vacaresti, one of the great monasteries of Bucharest which during the last century had been turned into a jail. The fine church and chapel-of-ease had become store sheds. Many walls had been knocked down between monks' cells, making them into big rooms in which prisoners lived by the score. A few cells remained in which men could be isolated.

A sheet was wrapped around my head before the guards lifted me out of the ambulance. They gripped me under the arms and I was half-carried across the courtyard, up some stairs and along a balcony. When the sheet was removed, I was alone in a narrow, bare cell. I heard an officer talking to a guard on the verandah outside.

'No one is allowed to see this man except the doctor, and then you must be there,' he said. My continued existence was to remain a secret.

The guard, a grizzled little man, was made curious by these precautions. When the officer had left he asked what I had done. I said, 'I am a pastor and a child of God.'

He whispered, bending over me, 'Praise be to the Lord! I'm one of Jesus' soldiers!' He was a secret member of 'The Army of the Lord', a revivalist movement which had branched off from the Orthodox church. In spite of being persecuted by Communists and clergy alike, it had spread rapidly through the villages, gathering hundreds of thousands of followers.

The guard's name was Tachici. We exchanged Bible verses and he helped me as much as he dared—warders had been sentenced to twelve years for giving an apple or a cigarette to a prisoner. I was too weak to leave the bed, and often I lay in my dirt. For a short spell in the morning, I could think clearly, then I tossed and turned in delirium. I slept little. But there was a small window through which I could see the sky again. And in the morning I was awoken by a strange sound—it was so long since I had heard the song of the birds!

I told Tachici, 'Martin Luther, when he walked in the woods, used to raise his hat to the birds and say, "Good morning, theologians—you wake and sing, but I, old fool, know less than you and worry over everything, instead of simply trusting in the heavenly Father's care." '

The window revealed a corner of grass and yard, usually empty. Sometimes white-coated doctors scurried across, afraid even to glance up. They had to practise medicine 'in the spirit of the class-war'.

I could hear men talking when they were out for exercise. In the past I had sometimes longed for the sound of a human voice, but now it was an irritation. Men spoke nothings. Their thoughts seemed trivial and false.

An old man's voice came from the next cell one morning. 'I'm Leonte Filipescu. Who are you?'

I recognised the name of one of Rumania's first Socialists, a brilliant man whom the Party had used and then discarded. 'Fight your illness,' he called. 'Don't give in! We'll all be free in two weeks' time.'

'How do you know?' I asked.

'The Americans are driving the Communists back in Korea. They'll be here in two weeks.'

I said, 'But even if they meet no opposition, it will surely take them more than a fortnight to reach Rumania?'

'Bosh! Distance is nothing to them. They have supersonic jets!'

I did not argue. Prisoners lived on their illusions. If the daily gruel was a little thicker, it implied that an American ultimatum had frightened Russia, and so our treatment was being improved! If someone was knocked down by a warder, it meant the Communists were making the most of their last days of power. Men came back in high spirits from the exercise yard: 'King Michael has broadcast that he will be back on his throne next month!'

No man could bear to think that he would really spend the next ten or twenty years in prison. Filipescu was still hopeful of early release when he was moved out, a month later, to another prison-hospital, where we were to meet again. In his place came a leader of the Fascist Iron Guard, Radu Mironovici, who claimed to be a fervent Christian but was always spouting hatred of the Jews.

I asked Tachici to help me up in bed and called to Mironovici, 'When you take Holy Communion in your Orthodox church, are the bread and wine transformed into the actual body and blood of Jesus Christ?' He answered that they were.

'Jesus was a Jew,' I said. 'If the wine becomes His blood, then that blood is Jewish, isn't it?'

Reluctantly, he supposed so. I went on: 'Jesus says that whoever eats His body and drinks His blood will have eternal life. So, to have eternal life, you have to add to your Aryan blood a few drops of Jewish blood. How then can you hate Jews?'

He had no answer. I begged him to see that it was absurd for a follower of Jesus, who was a Jew, to hate Jews—just as it was absurd for the Communists to be anti-semitic, since they believed in a Jew called Karl Marx. Mironovici was presently moved to a distant cell but he told Tachici: 'A part of my life which was false has fallen away. I was a Christian who was too proud to follow Christ.'

2

On a day when I was running a high temperature and feeling sick and faint, the guards came for me again. They draped a sheet over my head and led me along a corridor. When the sheet came off, I was in a large, bare room with barred windows. Four men and a woman sat facing me behind a table. This was my trial and they were my judges.

'A lawyer has been nominated to defend you,' said the president of the court. 'He has waived your right to call witnesses. You may sit down.'

Guards held me on a chair, while I was given an injection to steady me. When the waves of nausea and dizziness cleared, the prosecutor was on his feet. He was saying that I stood for the same criminal ideology in Rumania as Josef Broz Tito did in Jugoslavia. I thought I must be delirious. At the time of my arrest Marshal Tito was held up as a model Communist—I did not know that he had since been revealed as a deviationist and traitor. He continued his interminable speech about my guilt: spy work through the Scandinavian church missions and the World Council of Churches, spreading imperialist ideology under cover of religion, infiltrating the Party under the same pretence, with the real purpose of destroying it, and so on. As the voice continued, I felt myself slipping from the chair, and proceedings were delayed while I received another injection.

The defence lawyer did what he could. It was not much.

'Have you anything to say?' asked the president. His voice seemed far away and the room was growing dark. Only one thing came into my confused brain.

'I love God,' I said.

I heard my sentence: twenty years' hard labour. The trial had taken ten minutes. As I left, the sheet was wrapped around my head again.

3

Two days later, Tachici whispered to me, 'You're leaving. God be with you!' Another guard followed and, between them, they carried me to the main gate. I had a view of Bucharest spread below—the last time I was to see it for six years. Regulation chains weighing fifty pounds were hammered into place around my ankles. I was lifted into a truck in which there were already some forty men and a few women. All, even the sick, were chained. Near me, a girl began to weep. I tried to comfort her.

'You don't remember me?' she sobbed.

I looked more closely, but her face meant little.

'I was one of your congregation.' After my arrest, poverty had turned her to theft, she told me, and now she had to serve three months. 'I'm so ashamed.' Her voice was full of tears. 'I was in your church, and now you're a martyr and I'm a thief.'

'I'm a sinner, too, saved by the grace of God,' I said. 'Believe in Christ and your sins will be forgiven you.'

She kissed my hand, promising that on her release she would let my family know that she had seen me.

At a railway siding, we were loaded into a special wagon for transporting prisoners. The windows were tiny and opaque. As we rattled slowly across the plain and into the Carpathian foothills, we found that all of us had tuberculosis and decided that we must be bound for Tirgul-Ocna, where there was a sanatorium of sorts for T.B. prisoners. For some 400 years convicts had worked at the local salt mines, and thirty years ago a famous doctor, Romascanu, built the sanatorium and gave it to the state. It had an excellent reputation before the Communists took over.

After a 200-mile journey, which took a day and night, we came to the station of Tirgul-Ocna, a town of 30,000 people. With six other men unable to walk, I was laid on the back of a cart. The others hauled us, while the guards looked on, to a big building at the edge of the town. As I was carried in, I saw a familiar face. It was Dr. Aldea, an ex-fascist who had been converted and become a family friend. When I had been helped to a bed in the quarantine room, he examined me.

'I'm a prisoner myself,' he said, 'but they let me work as a doctor. There are no nurses and only one physician, so we must look after each other as best we can.'

He took my temperature and made his check.

'I won't deceive you,' he said. 'There's nothing we can do. You may have about two weeks to live. Try to eat what they give you, although it is not good. Otherwise . . .' He touched my shoulder and moved on.

During the next days, two men died who had been in the cart from the station. I heard another of them pleading hoarsely with Aldea, 'I swear I'm better, doctor. The fever's going, I know. Listen, please! Today I coughed blood only once. Don't let them put me in Room No. 4!'

I asked the man who brought my watery gruel what happened in Room No. 4. He put the plate down carefully and replied, 'That's where you go when they know there is no hope.'

I tried to eat the gruel but could not. Someone fed me with a spoon. The food would not stay down. Dr. Aldea said, 'I'm sorry, but they insist. You'll have to go to Room Four.'

I rejoined my companions from the cart.

4

I might already have been dead. Prisoners crossed themselves as they passed the foot of my bed. I lay most of the time in a coma. If I groaned, others turned me on my side or gave me water.

Dr. Aldea could do little. 'If only we had some modern drugs,' he said. A new American discovery, streptomycin, was rumoured to be doing wonders against tuberculosis; but the Party line ruled that this was all Western propaganda.

During the next fortnight, four men who entered the room with me died. Sometimes I was not sure myself whether I was alive or dead. At night I slept in snatches, woken by stabs of agony. Other prisoners turned me on my side an average of forty times to ease the pain. Pus was running from a dozen sores. My chest was swollen with it, and the spine was also affected. I spat blood constantly.

My soul and body were linked by the feeblest ties, and I moved to the borders of the physical world. I put a question to my guardian angel: 'What kind of guardian are you who cannot keep me from this suffering, nor even from un-Christian thoughts?' And in a flash of dazzling light that seemed to last a thousandth part of a second, I saw a being who was many-armed as Krishna and heard his voice: 'I cannot do all I should for you. I, too, am a convert.'

I didn't know the Bible, neither dogma at that time. My mind didn't work so I couldn't judge the objective value of the vision. Vaguely I remembered that Orthodox mystics speak about isolated cases when black angels have been brought back to God's service. However, conversion can't change completely the character of those who have been very evil, even when the repentance has been deep. In any case, under those circumstances, the vision offering some explanation for things through which I passed helped me greatly then.

I survived the first crisis. Dr. Aldea's look of pity began to change to puzzlement as I clung to life. I received no medicine, but for an hour in the morning the fever fell slightly and my mind was clearer. I began to look round and take stock of my surroundings.

5

The room contained twelve beds, close together, and some small tables. The windows were open and I could see men working in a vegetable patch, and beyond them high walls and barbed wire. It was very quiet. There were no alarm bells here, no shouting warders—indeed, no warders. They feared infection and kept away from the patients as much as possible. So Tirgul-Ocna was administered from a distance, and through neglect and indifference became one of the less rigorous prisons. Scarcely anything was provided or done for us. We wore the clothes in which we had been arrested, patched together over the years with whatever could be found.

Food was brought by common-law criminals to the door of the political section, and carried from there to the cells. Those who could walk, went for their ration; the rest were given it in bed. There was watery cabbage soup, a few haricot beans, or a thin skilly made of barley or maize.

A few prisoners who were well enough dug the plot outside the building. The rest lay on their plank beds and gossiped the hours away. But in Room four the atmosphere was different. Because no one ever left it alive, it was known as 'The death room'.

Scores of men died, and their places were taken by others in the thirty months I lay in this room. But here is a remarkable fact. Not one died an atheist. Fascists, Communists, saints, murderers, thieves, priests, rich landowners and the poorest peasants were shut together in one small cell. Yet none of them died without making his peace with God and man.

Many entered Room four as firmly convinced unbelievers. I saw their unbelief collapse, always, in the face of death. I have heard it said: 'If a cat crosses a bridge, it doesn't mean the bridge is sound; but if a train crosses, then it surely is.' So if a man calls himself an atheist as he sits with his wife over tea and cakes, that is no proof of atheism. A true conviction must survive enormous pressure, and atheism does not.

6

Old Filipescu often recited passages of Shakespeare, whom he loved, or told us stories from his life to pass the time. He had been a revolutionary for fifty years. The first of his many arrests for political agitation was in 1907. But in 1948, the Secret Police came for him. 'I suffered for Socialism before you were born,' he told them. They retorted that he should have joined the Communists, in that case, and shared the fruits of victory.

'I told these youths, "Socialism is a living body with two arms—Social Democracy and revolutionary Communism. Cut off one and Socialism is crippled!" They laughed.'

Filipescu was sentenced to twenty years. 'A warder told me, "You're going to die in prison!" I replied, "I haven't been sentenced to death, so why do you want to kill me?" '

He told us how he had started life as a shoemaker, but had

given himself an education and learnt to appreciate the beautiful in life. He accepted Marxist teachings on religion—that the church was on the side of the oppressor, that the clergy were kept by the rich to persuade the poor that their reward would come in Heaven.

But no one knows the depths of his own heart. Just as many think themselves religious and are not, so some think they are atheists, without being so. Filipescu denied God; but he was denying only his primitive conception of the word, not the realities of love and righteousness and eternity.

I suggested this to him.

'I believe in Jesus Christ and love Him as the greatest of human beings,' he said, 'but I cannot think of Him as God.'

His condition was growing steadily worse. Within a fortnight, after a series of haemorrhages, the end came. He spoke his last words to me. 'I love Jesus,' he murmured. There had been several deaths that week, and he was thrown naked into a common grave which the prisoners had dug.

General Tobescu, a former chief of the Gendarmerie, raised his voice from the corner when he heard this: 'That is the fate the Socialists in the West are preparing for themselves when they make allies of the Communists.'

The Abbot Iscu of Tismana, my neighbour, crossed himself. 'At least we may be grateful that he came to God at the end,' he said gently.

Sergeant-Major Bucur disagreed, from across the room. 'Nothing of the sort! He told us he couldn't think of Christ as God.'

I said, 'Filipescu will have found out the truth by now in the other world, for he loved Jesus, who will never reject anyone. The robber converted on Golgotha to whom Jesus promised paradise also called him simply man. I believe in the Godhead of Jesus—and also in His love towards those who cannot see it.'

Bucur loved no one, but he worshipped his conception of the state, with himself as viceroy of the village where he had dispensed his own brand of justice. He was fond of telling everyone how, as gendarmerie sergeant, he had beaten thieves and beggars, beaten his own men when they dared to answer back, and—especially—beaten Jews. 'Not a mark on any of them,' he would say proudly. 'You put sacks of loose sand across their backs first. It hurts just as badly, but they can't complain, because they've nothing to show!'

Bucur could not understand why he had been deposed under the new régime. He was ready to thrash anti-Communists with as much relish as anyone else in the way of duty.

Although he was very ill, Bucur would not admit it. When Dr. Aldea was examining him one evening, he burst out, 'Why are you keeping me here? There's nothing much wrong with me. I'm not like these others!'

Aldea looked at the thermometer and shook his head. 'No,' he said. 'You're much the worst. You should stop arguing and think about your soul.'

Bucur was furious. 'Who do you think you are?' he shouted after the doctor's retreating back.

'I suspect Aldea has Jewish blood,' he added—it was the worst that Burcur could think of anyone.

Bucur liked to quarrel with Moisescu, a small, middle-aged Jew whose bed was close to his.

'The Iron Guard knew how to deal with you,' he said.

'Do you know,' said Moisescu mildly, 'that it was as a member of the Iron Guard that I was arrested?' A laugh went round the room.

'It's true,' he protested. 'After the Iron Guard were overthrown, it was a terrible crime to have a green shirt in your possession because it was regarded as their uniform. We Jews had lost so much during their reign that I thought, "Here's a chance to get some of our own back. Buy up all the green shirts left unsold, dye them blue and sell them." My house was crammed with all the green shirts in Bucharest when the police came for a search. They wouldn't listen to my explanation, so I was labelled as an Iron Guard. So a Jew was sent to prison as a Nazi sympathiser!'

Although Bucur loudly declared that he was a militant Christian, his whole life had been a quarrel with God. He went to church, but found no guide. The priests of his village were not ministers of religion, but masters of ceremonial. He could not understand, now, why he was suffering and dying, nor what true faith meant.

I told him: 'You feel now that you have no reason to hope. But the night is darkest before sunrise. Christians believe that the dawn will come. Faith can be put in two words: "though" and "yet". In the Book of Job we read, "Though the Lord slay me, yet I will trust Him." Many times these words come together in the Bible. They tell us to have faith in the darkest moments.'

Bucur was pleased that someone should take an interest in him. But he showed no remorse for the cruelty and evil of his past; until the day on which he realised that Dr. Aldea had been right. His life was ebbing quickly. He said, in a frightened voice, 'I'm dying for my country.'

For hours he was unconscious. When he awoke, he said, 'I want to confess—before you all. I have sinned so much. I cannot die thinking of it.' His voice gained a strange calm. He told us how he had killed scores of Jews, acting not under orders, but because he knew he would never be punished. He had murdered women, and a boy of twelve years. He had been thirsty for blood, like a tiger.

At the end of the recital, he muttered, 'Now Mr. Wurmbrand will hate me.'

I replied, 'No—you yourself hate this creature who killed. You have reviled and rejected him. You are no longer that murderer. A man can be born again.'

Next morning he still clung weakly to life, 'I did not tell everything yesterday,' he said. 'I was afraid.'

He had shot children in their mother's arms. When his ammunition had gone, he had clubbed them to death. His terrible story seemed endless, but when at last it was over, he fell into a sleep. His breathing was hoarse and irregular. His breast rose and fell as if he could never have enough air. We were all silent. His hands clenched and unclenched on the soiled blanket, and then clasped themselves around the small cross at his neck. There was a tortured rattling from his throat and the breathing stopped.

Someone called out to a prisoner in the corridor. Two men came to take Bucur's body. The morning sun poured through the open windows on to his face, but now that the eyes were closed and the hard lines of the mouth relaxed, his features in death showed a great peace, such as he had never known in life.

7

Prisoners from other wards came often to Room Four to pass the night with us, helping the dying and offering comfort.

At Easter, a friend brought something wrapped in a twist of paper for Valeriu Gafencu, a former Iron Guard trooper. They came from the same town. 'It's been smuggled in,' he said. 'Open it!'

Gafencu undid the paper and revealed two lumps of a glittering white substance—sugar! None of us had seen pieces of sugar for years. Our wasted bodies craved for it. All eyes were on Gafencu, and the prize in his hand. Slowly he wrapped it up again.

'I shall not eat it yet,' he said. 'Someone might be worse off than I during the day. But thank you.' He put the present carefully beside his bed, and there it stayed.

A few days later, my fever increased and I became very weak. The sugar was passed from bed to bed until it came to rest on mine.

'It's a gift,' said Gafencu. I thanked him, but left the sugar untouched in case someone needed it more next day. When my crisis passed, I gave it to Soteris, the elder of two Greek Communists whose condition was grave.

For two years the sugar went from man to man in Room Four (and twice it returned to me); each time the sufferer had the strength to resist it.

Soteris and Glafkos were Communist guerrillas who had fled to Rumania at the end of the Greek civil war. They had been arrested, like many of their comrades, for fighting poorly; now they never tired of boasting of their exploits before the tide of battle turned against them. They had raided the famous monasteries of Mount Athos, looting all they could carry, smashing what they had to leave. Women are forbidden on Athos and many of the 2,000 monks had not seen one for years. 'We took a band of girl partisans with us,' Soteris said. 'You should have seen those old boys run!'

Soteris was proud of his atheism while he could joke and hope for life: but as death approached he cried out for help from God. Only the priest's murmuring voice, promising heavenly forgiveness, could quieten him. Then he, too, found the great moral force to renounce the two pieces of sugar.

His body was prepared for burial by a prisoner from outside who often came to help us. He was known, respectfully, as 'The Professor' and his name was Popp. Rarely did his stooped and scholarly figure appear unaccompanied by someone to whom he was teaching history, French or some other subject.

I asked once how he managed without writing materials. He explained: 'We rub the table with a piece of soap and scratch the words with a nail.' When I admired his persistence, the innocent blue eyes sparkled. 'I used to think I taught for a living. In prison I've learnt that I teach because I love my pupils!'

'You have a vocation, as the priests say?'

'Well,' he replied, 'here we are shown what we are worth.'

When I asked if he was a Christian he looked upset. 'Pastor, I have had too many disappointments. At my last prison, Ocnele-Mari, the church was turned into a store-room and they asked for someone to tear down the cross on the steeple. No one cared to do it. In the end it was a priest who volunteered.'

I said that not every man in holy orders has a priestly heart, nor were all who called themselves Christians disciples of Christ in the true sense of the word. 'A man who visits a barber to be shaved, or who orders a suit from a tailor, is not a disciple, but a customer. So one who comes to the Saviour only to be saved is the Saviour's customer, not his disciple. A disciple is one who says to Christ, "How I long to do work like yours! To go from place to place taking away fear; bringing instead joy, truth, comfort and life eternal!" '

Popp smiled. 'But what of those who become disciples at the eleventh hour? I have been puzzled to see so many convinced atheists turn into believers at the end.'

I said that our minds do not always work on the same level. 'A genius can talk nonsense at times or bicker with his wife, but he is not judged by that. We should respect our minds, like his, when they are at their best—when they are straining to find a way out at the moment of supreme crisis. It is when the mind has to pass through the gap of death that the façade of atheism nearly always collapses.'

'And why do you suppose that a man like Sergeant Bucur longs to confess his crimes publicly?'

I said, 'Once I lived near a railway and never noticed the trains by day because the town was noisy. But at night I heard their whistles clearly. So the clamour of life can deafen us to the quiet voice of conscience. It is when death approaches in the silence of the prison, where there are no distractions, that men hear the voice who never have before.'

The Abbot said: 'In my last prison, at Aiud, there was a poor murderer in solitary confinement. He kept waking in the night and shouting, "Who's that in the next cell? Why doesn't he stop knocking on the wall?" '

'Well?' said Popp.

'The next cell was empty.'

'I can cap that,' offered Moisescu. 'In my last place there was an Iron Guard who had killed a rabbi. He was sure the rabbi was riding on his shoulders and digging spurs into his flesh.'

8

Since I had no strength to wash myself, Professor Popp took on the task. I asked whether there were showers in his part of the prison.

'Yes!' he said. 'In the People's Republic of Rumania we have the most modern equipment. Only it doesn't work. The showers have been dry for years.' He straightened his back and went on:

'Have you heard of the Communist and the Capitalist who died and met in Hell? They found two gates. One was labelled "Capitalist Hell" and the other "Communist Hell". Although the men were class enemies they put their heads together to decide which would be better. The Communist said, "Comrade, let's go into the Communist department. There, when there's coal, there'll be no matches. When there are matches, there'll be no coal. And even when they have both coal and matches, the furnace will break down!" '

The Professor continued to wash me while the others laughed. Aristar the farmer said, 'The first Communists were Adam and Eve.'

'Why?' asked the obliging Popp.

'Because they had no clothes, no house, they had to share the same apple—and still thought they were in paradise.'

The telling of jokes and stories was important to us. Men lay all day with only their miseries to think of, and anyone who could help them to forget was doing an act of mercy. I talked often for hours on end, although ill and dizzy with hunger: a story, as much as a piece of bread, could sustain the life of man. When Popp urged me to save my strength, I said I had enough for one more anecdote that morning.

'The Talmud tells us of a rabbi walking in the street when he heard the voice of the prophet Elijah saying, "Although you fast and pray, never have you deserved the high place in Heaven which awaits those two men on the other side of the road." The rabbi ran after the strangers, and said, "Do you give much to the poor?"

'They laughed. "No, we are beggars ourselves."

' "Then do you pray continuously?"

' "No. We are ignorant men. We don't know how to pray."

' "Then tell me what you do."

' "We make jokes. We make people laugh when they are sad." '

Popp looked surprised. 'Are you telling us that those who make men laugh may have greater honour in Heaven than those who fast?'

'That is the teaching of the Talmud, which is a book of Jewish wisdom. But we can also read in the Bible—the second Psalm—that God himself laughs sometimes.'

Popp said, helping me back into my clothes, 'He wouldn't find much to laugh at here—but where is God, pastor, and why does He not help us?'

I said, 'There was a pastor called to a man's deathbed. He found the mother trying to comfort her sobbing daughter. The girl said, "Where is the protecting arm of God you preach about, pastor?" He replied, "It is on your shoulder, in the shape of your mother's arm." '

'Christ is with us in prison in many ways. Firstly, he can be seen in our Christian doctors, who are beaten and bullied but go on helping us. Some official doctors in Vacaresti have also smuggled in drugs and earned themselves ten years in jail.

'Secondly, Christ is here in the priests and pastors who work to ease others' burdens, and in the form of all Christians who give food, clothes and help to men worse off than themselves. Thirdly, He is with us in the form of those who teach about God, and also of the story-tellers. And you have Him with you not only in the person of those who serve you, but also in the shape of those whom you can serve.

'Jesus tells us that, at the Last Judgment, God will separate the good from the bad, on His right hand and His left. Jesus will say to those on the right, "Come, enter and possess the kingdom that has been ready for you since the world was made. For I was hungry and you gave me meat; I was a stranger and you took me in; naked and you clothed me; sick and you visited me; I was in prison and you came to me." The good will ask, "Lord, when did we do all this?" And Christ will reply, "Inasmuch as you have done it to the least of my brethren, you have done it for me." '

9

Gafencu had spent his whole adult life in prison, but like other Iron Guard followers in whom Christian belief had prevailed, he could not do enough to make up for his mistakes. Every day, he set the example of putting aside part of his meagre ration to help build up the weakest among us. His anti-semitism had been left behind, and when some of his old Fascist friends came to see him in Room Four, he suddenly came out with a remark which shocked them: 'I'd like to see the country ruled entirely by Jews.'

His comrades stared at him in horror.

'Yes,' said Gafencu calmly, 'Prime Minister, legislators, civil servants—everyone. I'd make only one condition. They must be men like the old Jewish rulers, like Joseph, Moses, Daniel, St. Peter, St. Paul and Jesus himself. Because if we have any more Jews over us like Ana Pauker, then Rumania is finished.'

Gafencu had been jailed when he was nineteen. His youth had gone by without his ever knowing a girl. When others talked about sex, he asked, 'What is it like?'

He told me one day, 'My father was deported from Bessarabia by the Russians. We never had enough to eat. I was beaten in school, then put in jail for running away and joining the Iron Guard. I'd never met a single good, truthful, loving person. I said to myself, "It's just a legend about Christ. There isn't anyone in the world like that today and I don't believe there ever was." But when I'd been in prison a few months I had to say that I was wrong. I met sick men who gave away their last crust. I shared a cell with a bishop who had such goodness that you felt the touch of his robe could heal.'

Gafencu had been in Room Four for a year, and in all that time he had not been able to lie on his back. It gave him too much pain. He had to be propped up continually. Every day he had a little less control over his body, often fulfilling his necessities where he lay; then having to wait, sometimes at night for hours, until someone came to clean him.

Stronger patients from outside had to take over the washing for those of us who could not help ourselves, scrubbing shirts, underwear, pillow-cases, sometimes twenty sheets a day, although they had to break ice in the yard to reach the water. My own things were always stiff with pus and blood, but when I tried to stop a friend from washing them he was angry.

Gafencu never complained. He sat very still in bed, sometimes moving his head a little to nod agreement or convey a word of thanks. When it was known that he had not long to live, his old friends and new ones gathered around his bed with tears in their eyes. His last words were, 'The spirit of God wishes us jealously for Himself.'

When he had gone, the others knelt and prayed. I said, 'Jesus tells us that if a seed does not fall into the earth and die, it cannot bring forth fruit, and that as a seed is reborn in a beautiful flower, so man dies and his mortal body is renewed in a spiritual body. And his heart which has come to be filled with the ideals of Christianity will surely bear fruit.'

After a priest had said a prayer, Gafencu was wrapped in his sheet and carried to the mortuary. During the night he was buried in a common grave by criminal convicts, who always performed this task.

10

A steady flow of new arrivals at Tirgul-Ocna kept us informed of events outside, and sometimes it seemed that we in prison were hardly worse off than the 'free' workers and peasants. Wages had never been so low. An eight-hour day had been proclaimed, but you might work twelve before completing your 'norm', and then 'voluntary' work and Marxist lectures left no time for family life; in any case, every apartment housed two or more families.

Strikes were illegal. One newcomer, a gnarled old trade unionist called Boris Matei, told me; 'It's forty years since I was jailed for fighting for the eight-hour day, and now that there's a Communist government I'm working fourteen hours in prison.' His crime was to write an anonymous letter to Comrade Gheorghiu-Dej, the Party boss, protesting on behalf of his workmates against the severity of their conditions and saying they would be entitled in any capitalist state to withdraw their labour. The Secret Police came to his rolling-stock depot and took handwriting samples from the 10,000 workers. After weeks of investigation, Boris was accused of trying to foment a strike and given fifteen years for attempted sabotage.

Boris remained unshaken in his Marxist creed. He had no sympathy for the dissenting groups who had been herded with him into prison: freemasons, rotarians, theosophists, spiritualists. Nor could he feel for the poets and novelists who had been locked up for their independent outlook: they had been summoned in turn to Party H.Q. to be given their orders, and should know better than to chase the will-o'-the-wisp of objective truth.

Boris argued that Lenin had underlined in his books the importance of finding and clinging to one point of view in life.

'The Party line?' I said. 'But this doctrine reverses all philosophical concepts. If I look at the cell from my bed I see only the window. If I look from where you're sitting, I see the door. If I look at the floor, the room has no ceiling. Every viewpoint is in reality a point of blindness, because it incapacitates you totally from seeing other points of view. It is only when we abandon all "points of view" and accept our intuition of the whole that we find truth. St. Paul says "Love believes everything"—not just the creed of this group or that.'

But talk of religion made Boris angry. 'There is no God, no soul! Only matter exists. I defy you to prove otherwise.'

I said he must take his arguments from a Communist textbook in which I had seen the following definition of a kiss: '"A kiss is the approach of two pairs of lips, with reciprocal transmission of microbes and carbon dioxide." The love, the longing, or the falsity of the kiss has no place in your philosophy. This impoverishment of spiritual values affects the material side of life, which you consider all-important. It takes the heart out of the workers, so that the poor quality of goods from Communist countries has become a byword.'

Boris said, 'I know the saying that the Sabbath is made for man, not man for the Sabbath, but we all exist to benefit the state. The loss of individual liberty and private property are steps on the way to world freedom.'

I thought that even a dog will fight with anyone who tries to take his bone, but if a fifteen-year sentence had not cured Boris of his illusions, arguing was unlikely to do so. He might also be one of the latest crop of informers.

Informing had spread like a disease. You might be denounced for speaking of God or praying aloud; even for learning or teaching a foreign language. Often the man who pointed the finger might be a friend, inside or outside prison, a son, father, wife, husband. The pressure to inform was cruelly strong. Indeed, the informer was probably a worse menace for 'free' men than for those already behind bars, and in Room Four we exercised more free speech than was heard anywhere else in Rumania, since none of us was going to live.

II

It was the anniversary of the 'ten days that shook the world'—the Russian revolution of November 1917—and Professor Popp commemorated it with an anecdote.

On the first anniversary of the triumph of Bolshevism, he said, the new rulers held a hunting party in the forest outside Moscow. Later, they rested by the fire and Lenin asked, 'Tell me, comrades, what you consider the greatest pleasure in life.'

'War,' said Trotsky.

'Women,' said Zinoviev.

'Oratory—the power to hold a vast crowd under your spell,' said Kamenev.

Stalin, as always, was taciturn, but Lenin insisted: 'Tell us your choice!'

At last, Stalin said: 'None of you knows what real pleasure is. I will tell you. It is to hate someone, and to pretend for years that you are his best friend, until one day he rests his head trustingly on your breast. And then to plunge the knife into his back. There is no higher pleasure in the world than this!'

There was a long silence. Already, at that time, we knew something of Stalin's ruthlessness: the rest, to be made known after his death by his own companions, proved the truth of this chilling story.

To raise the temperature a few degrees, I told another Stalin tale, set nearer home.

The devout women of our Banat province were praising the Communist take-over of Rumania. One said, 'Comrade Stalin has transformed our lives.' Another added, 'He has relieved us of the burden of tending our animals by putting them all in the collective.' And a third, 'It's certainly easier to betray a husband who's in jail than one at home.' They decided to make him a thanksgiving present on his seventieth birthday. They wove two yards of a costly material which is used only for making Rumanian national costume, and posted it to the Kremlin. Stalin was overjoyed.

'How these Rumanians love me!' he told Molotov. 'To reward them I shall have my picture in Rumanian dress published on May 10, their great feast day. I've taken their country—now I'll win all their hearts!'

But when the Kremlin tailor saw the cloth, he shook his head.

'Comrade Stalin, you're such a big man, and it's a complicated coat with many pleats and folds. I must have at least two more yards for the trousers.'

'What! You dare haggle with me?' Stalin cried. 'Get out and make it!'

Since he could not, the tailor was shot. One after another, all the tailors in Moscow told Stalin that for such a big man as he, two yards were not enough. After a hundred tailors had been shot, Molotov ventured a word: 'Comrade Stalin, our Marxist theories contain all the wisdom in the world, but I have heard that certain rabbis have a wisdom that is out of it. Let's ask one of them.'

A rabbi was brought and said at once, 'I know the very tailor for you. His name is Isaac Cohen and he lives in New York.'

'Call him here!' said Stalin.

'He won't come; he's far too clever,' the rabbi answered.

'Well,' thought Stalin, 'for the sake of winning the hearts of the whole Rumanian people, I shall go over to New York.' And at 356 Broadway he found Cohen's neon sign. He went in and told the story.

'I'll pay anything you like,' he promised. 'After all, it's not coming out of my pocket—the people of Rumania will pay.'

Isaac ran the tape-measure over him. 'Listen, mister. I'll make you a complete national costume with a spare pair of pants *and* give you back half a yard.'

Stalin was astounded. 'How can you do that when all my own tailors have said I'm such a big man they can hardly make the coat alone from two yards?'

Isaac Cohen replied, 'You may be a big man in Russia, but here with us you're so small that two yards are more than enough.'

PART THREE

FOR some time there had been frightened talk of a system of 're-educating' prisoners, which was practised at Suceava and Piteshi jails. It was carried out not with books, but by beating. The tutors were usually turncoat Iron Guards, who had been formed into an 'organisation of prisoners with Communist convictions' (PCC). We heard the names of Turcanu, Levitkii and Formagiu as the organisers of these groups. They seemed to be behaving like savages.

We feared that the process would be introduced among us; but Boris scoffed. He could not believe that his former associates of the Left would allow atrocities.

He said, 'They know that "terror can never uproot ideas". That's what Karl Kautsky, the Social Democrat thinker, wrote at the start of the Russian revolution.'

I said, 'Yes. I remember what Trotsky, who was War Minister, replied. "Mr. Kautsky, you do not know what terror we will apply." It's ironic that Trotsky's own ideas have been as effectively uprooted by terrorism in Russia as has Capitalism.'

The Abbot said. 'I fear that terror and torture, applied ruthlessly and long, may crush any man's resistance, without a miracle of God.'

'I don't believe in miracles,' said Boris. 'I'll get along without them, thanks. Nothing has touched my convictions yet.'

The prison's atmosphere grew worse after a brief visit by the 're-education' leader Formagiu, from Piteshi, with instructions to inaugurate the system. Up to now, although you were tormented for most of the day, you knew that sooner or later the guards would go to eat or sleep. Now the 'prisoners with Communist convictions' moved in with us. They had the power to beat and bully at will, and had rubber truncheons for their work. They had been hand-picked by the authorities from the worst and most violent prisoners, and there was no escape from them: to every fifty prisoners there was a group of ten or twenty 'PCC' men, and the number grew steadily. Those who declared themselves ready to become Communists had to prove their conversion by 'converting' others in the same way.

Crude violence was punctuated by sessions of more refined cruelty, under medical supervision to ensure that prisoners did not die. Doctors were often PCCs themselves. I knew a Dr. Turcu who, after examining a cell-mate, would advise a pause, give the man an injection to increase his resistance and tell the re-educators when to start again. It was Turcu who decided when the man had reached his limit and might be thrown back into his cell until next day.

A wave of madness swept the prison. Tuberculosis patients were stripped, laid on the stone floors and drenched with buckets of freezing water. Pigs' swill was thrown on the ground before men who had been starved for days; with hands tied behind their backs they were forced to lick it up. No humiliation, however vile, was spared. In many prisons men were made by the PCC bullies to swallow excrement and drink urine. Some wept and begged at least to be given their own, not that of others. Some went crazy and began to scream for more. Convicts were also made to perform sexual perversions publicy. I had not thought that such mockeries of body and soul were possible.

Those who clung to their faith were the worst treated. Christians were tied for four days to crosses, and daily the crosses were placed on the floor. Then the other prisoners were ordered to defecate on their faces and bodies. After this, the crosses were put up again.

A Catholic priest brought into Room Four told us that in Piteshi jail, on a Sunday, he had been pushed into the latrine cesspit and ordered to say Mass over excrement, and give men Communion.

'Did you obey?' I asked.

He buried his face in his hands and wept. 'I've suffered more than Christ,' he said.

These things were done with the encouragement of the prison administration, on orders from Bucharest. Turcanu, Formagiu and the other specialists were taken from jail to jail, recruiting PCCs and seeing that the campaign did not flag. Party leaders, even men from the Central Committee, like Constantin Doncea and the Under-secretary of the Interior Ministry, Marin Jianu, came to watch the sport. Boris, who had worked with Jianu, broke through the guards to protest, but if Jianu recognised his former colleague he did not admit it. 'We don't interfere when one swine beats another!' he said; in other words, the Party disassociated itself from the torturers, but allowed them to torture. 'Take him away,' said Jianu. Boris was beaten until he screamed for mercy.

The old union fighter broke down completely. Exposed to humiliation and torture day and night, something had burnt out in him. He crawled to kiss the hands of the men who beat him.

'Thank you, comrade,' he said. 'You have brought me to the light.' Then he began to prate about the joys of Communism, and how criminal he had been to persist in error. After such a collapse his self-respect demanded a total shift of loyalty; otherwise he would have appeared ridiculous in his own eyes. Boris joined the PCC group. One of the first he used his truncheon on was Dr. Aldea.

The re-education system—imported from Russia—brought incredible results. Victims blurted secrets they had kept back under months of interrogation. They denounced friends, wives, parents. So thousands more arrests were made.

2

During this time a group of sick men from the lead-mines were brought to a special cell at Tirgul-Ocna. They were joined by other prisoners who, finding that some of the newcomers were priests, confessed to them and so gained their confidence. The men from the mines spoke freely of their secret religious and political activities. Then they were moved to a larger cell, for re-education—and learnt that they had been talking to informers.

One of them was carried bruised and bloody into Room Four. He told us that the 're-educator' in charge was a well-built young man with a set smile, who made jokes all the time. 'Does that hurt?' he would ask. '*So* sorry! Let's try something new. Did you enjoy that?'

'If I ever get my hands on that man,' said the victim, 'I'll skin him alive.'

'That's right,' crackled the old farmer Badaras. 'Put salt and pepper on, that's the spirit!' Badaras had a daily prayer; 'In the name of the Father, the Son and the Holy Ghost, God destroy the Communists, make them suffer, hurt them, the pigs!'

'Why say such things?' I asked him. 'That's not what is expected of a Christian.'

He shook his fists to Heaven in invocation. 'I say them because God will not let anyone into paradise who does not curse the bastards!'

Many like Badaras lived for the day on which they could torture their torturers; believing in Hell, so that the Communists might fry there.

'We mustn't give way to hatred,' I said. 'These men like Boris have broken under terrible pressure.'

But Boris was now a sore topic in Room Four. An attempt to prove his Communist conversion by beating Dr. Aldea—who made very plain his contempt for Turcu and the other PCC doctors—had made Boris one of the most hated men in prison. Aldea suffered great pain from boils on his back and shoulders, and Boris had beaten him on the back. Prisoners would have given their lives for Aldea, who was giving his for them. After the beating, the doctor was found a bed in Room Four. Then someone came to say that a seriously ill prisoner was asking for him.

'The doctor is too sick to move,' said the Abbot.

Aldea asked, 'Who is it?'

'Boris,' said the man.

Aldea climbed painfully out of bed and no one spoke as he walked from the room.

3

Abbot Iscu spoke sometimes of his experiences in the slave camps at the Danube–Black Sea canal, where thousands were dying of ill-treatment and hunger. The canal had been begun largely on Russian instigation—since it would help them to drain Rumania of her produce even faster than they were already doing—and also as a prestige project for our government. It was an immense scheme, and it had become such a symbol of Communist achievement that when a group of engineers warned that the river was unlikely to supply enough water for both the canal and its irrigation network, they were shot as 'economic saboteurs'. Rumania's resources were thrown prodigally into the plan, and over 200,000 political and common-law prisoners laboured to build it between 1949 and 1953.

The Abbot found himself at Poarta Alba, one of the penal colonies along the route. Living in ramshackle barracks, behind wire, 12,000 people had each to move by hand eight cubic metres of earth a day. They pushed wheelbarrows up steep inclines, under the blows of guards. Temperatures fell to minus 25 Centigrade in winter, and water, brought in barrels, froze solid. Disease was rife. Many prisoners broke through into the forbidden areas around the camp, hoping to be shot.

The most brutal criminals were put in charge of 'brigades' each of a hundred or so prisoners and paid on results, in food or cigarettes. Christians were herded into a so-called 'Priests' Brigade' where, if a man as much as made the sign of the cross—a reflex action among the orthodox—he was beaten. There was no day of rest, no Christmas, no Easter.

Yet at Poarta Alba, the Abbot said, he witnessed the most noble acts. A young Catholic, Father Cristea, incurred the hatred of an Orthodox priest turned informer, who asked him, 'Why do you close your eyes so often? Is it in prayer? I challenge you to tell the truth: do you still believe in God?'

To answer 'yes' would mean, at least, a flogging.

Father Cristea considered. 'I know, Andreescu, that you tempt as the Pharisees tempted Jesus, to accuse me. But Jesus told them the truth and I will tell it to you. Yes, I believe in God.'

'Well! Do you believe in the Pope, too?' Andreescu went on.

Cristea replied, 'I believe in the Pope, too.'

Andreescu hurried to the political officer, who came over and called the young man out before the others. Cristea was thin, exhausted: he shivered in his rags. The officer was well-fed, wrapped in a greatcoat and wearing a Russian fur hat. 'I hear that you believe in God,' he said.

Father Cristea opened his mouth to answer, and in that moment one could understand why it is written in the Gospel according to St. Matthew, before the Sermon on the Mount, that Jesus 'opened his mouth and spoke'—surely a strange thing, for no one speaks with a closed mouth. Now Cristea had only parted his lips to speak, but everyone sensed that a great pearl could come from his mouth at this moment of decision. The Christians there were overcome with awe.

Cristea said, 'When I was ordained, I knew that thousands of priests, throughout history, had paid for their faith with their lives. And as often as I went to the altar I promised God, "Now I serve Thee in beautiful robes, but even if they should put me in prison, I will serve Thee still." And so, lieutenant, prison is no argument against religion. I believe in God.'

The silence that followed was broken only by the sound of the wind. The lieutenant seemed at a loss for words. At last he said, 'And do you believe in the Pope?'

The answer came, 'Since St. Peter there has always been a Pope. And until Jesus returns there will always be one. The present Pope has made no peace with Communism; and nor will his successors. Yes, I believe in the Pope!'

The Abbot ended his story and said, 'I found it hard to forgive my Orthodox brother who had turned informer, and I am no follower of Rome, but at that moment I felt like crying "*Viva il Papa!*"'

'What happened to Father Cristea?' someone asked.

'He was locked for a week in the carcer, where you stand and never sleep; then beaten. When he still refused to deny his faith, he was taken away. We never saw him again.'

4

Re-education was claiming new victims every day, and the feeling grew that unless something was done soon we should all be 'converted' or killed. A rumour reached Room Four that some kind of protest was brewing among the Communist prisoners, who were the boldest among us: the guards were more careful with them, for those who were in jail today had been in power yesterday and might again be tomorrow.

Christians debated what we should do: if there were a riot, should they join in? Or was it a time to 'turn the other cheek'? Several prisoners argued against a fight.

I said, 'Jesus is usually portrayed as "meek and mild"—but he was a fighter, too. He drove the merchants from the temple with a whip and gave as guide to his first followers the Old Testament with its fire and fierceness.'

We decided to work with the rebels. Little could be done in secret because of the many informers among us and the suspicions between anti-semite and Jew, peasant and landowner, Orthodox and Catholic.

In the town of Tirgul-Ocna, the one relaxation was a weekly football match in a stadium which was near the prison. On May 1, which coincided with a savage new outburst of re-education, we heard that a Labour Day game would be played in the stadium, at 5 p.m., and the whole town would be there. It was our chance for a demonstration. The signal was to be the smashing of a window.

Soon after the game began there was a faint tinkle of breaking glass somewhere, and the whole prison burst into bedlam. Windows shattered. Plates and mugs were hurled out. Chairs were smashed. Someone started a steady chant: 'Help us! Help us!' From higher windows overlooking the stadium men cried, 'We are tortured here! Your fathers and brothers and sons are being murdered!'

The game came to a stop. The crowd was on its feet and soon hundreds had gathered in the road below the walls. Inside, one of the prisoners had cut his wrists and the guards began lashing out with clubs. The crowds in the street were quickly driven away by troops wielding rifle-butts. There remained the task of putting the prison to rights and counting the casualties. Among them was Boris, who had been knocked down and badly hurt while trying to rescue another prisoner from under the feet of the guards. Again Dr. Aldea had to tend him. We sent friendly messages, but there was no reply. Then we learnt he had been moved to another jail.

News of the revolt spread rapidly through the country. There were no outright reprisals; only a stiffening of the régime. Those suspected of being ringleaders were moved out to other prisons; deprived of such medical attention as they received at Tirgul-Ocna, many of them died.

5

Abbot Iscu was coughing for longer spells each day. His body, wasted by years of starvation and exposure at the canal, was racked by terrible bouts. We lay and watched him dying. Sometimes he did not recognise friends who came to help him. When he was conscious he passed hours in whispered prayer, and always he had words of comfort for others.

Other survivors from the canal had come to Tirgul-Ocna, and their stories of its horrors made it sound like the slavery of Israel in Egypt, with the added bitterness that the oppressed had to praise their oppressors. A famous composer among the prisoners had been forced to write hymns exalting Stalin, and to their accompaniment the brigades marched to work.

Once, when a man collapsed and a doctor pronounced him dead, Colonel Albon, the hated Poarta Alba commandant, shouted, 'Rubbish!' He gave the corpse a kick. 'Put him to work!'

My bed was between those of the Abbot and young Vasilescu, who was a canal victim of a different kind. Vasilescu was a common-law criminal who had been put in charge of the Priests' Brigade. He had worked them until they dropped. But for some reason Colonel Albon took a dislike to him and he was treated in turn so brutally that he was also dying. His tuberculosis was well advanced.

Vasilescu was not an inherently bad young man. He had a rough-hewn, square face with dark curly hair that grew low on his forehead, making him look like a bewildered young bull. Tough, ignorant, he was too fond of what he thought the good things in life to settle down to a steady job; and he had had a hard life. He was like the hired murderer in 'Macbeth'—'One whom the vile blows and buffets of the world hath so incensed that I am reckless what I do to spite the world.'

He told us, 'Once you get in those camps you'll do anything to get out, anything! And Albon said if I did what he told me, they'd let me go free.' He wanted clothes, a girl to take to a dance. And the Party offered him the choice of joining the tortured or the torturers.

'They took a crowd of us to a special camp where they train secret police,' he said. 'And one of the things we had to do was shoot cats and dogs and then finish off the ones still living with steel spikes! I said, "I can't do that!" And the chap said, "Then we'll do it to you!"'

Vasilescu was sorry for himself now. He told me again and again of the terrible things he had done at the canal. He had not spared the Abbot. Vasilescu was obviously dying and I tried to give him a little comfort; but he couldn't rest. One night he woke up gasping for breath. 'Pastor, I'm going,' he said. 'Please pray for me!' He dozed and woke again, and cried, 'I believe in God!' Then he began to weep.

At dawn Abbot Iscu called two prisoners to his bed and ordered, 'Lift me out!'

'You're too ill to move,' they said. The whole room was upset. 'What is it?' said voices. 'Let us do it!'

'You cannot do this,' he said. 'Lift me out!'

They picked him up. 'To Vasilescu's bed,' he said.

The Abbot sat beside the young man who had tortured him, and put a hand gently on his arm. 'Be calm,' he said soothingly. 'You are young. You hardly knew what you were doing.' He wiped sweat from the boy's forehead with a rag. 'I forgive you with all my heart, and so would other Christians too. And if we forgive, surely Christ, who is better than us, will forgive. There is a place in Heaven for you, also.' He received Vasilescu's confession and gave him Holy Communion, before being carried back to his bed.

During the night both the Abbot and Vasilescu died. I believe they went hand in hand to Heaven.

6

Dr. Aldea said I should have a pneumothorax. It could be done in a few minutes and consisted of running a hollow needle into me which allowed air to enter and cushion the lung. It was relatively painless and afterwards I fell asleep. When I awoke I was very happy to find Professor Popp sitting by my bedside. He had been away for months in Jilava prison, and he too had suffered much under the 're-education' system. We talked for hours.

The professor told me that there had been many suicides at Jilava. It was the same in other prisons. At Gherla and Piteshi men threw themselves down from the upper floors until the spaces between the landings were covered with wire to stop them. Some cut their wrists with glass, some hanged themselves, some died after drinking cleaning fluid. One poor old Orthodox father had thrown himself down from a top bunk to the floor, cracking his skull. He had done this several times before he succeeded in killing himself.

'He'd been tortured,' the professor said. 'He was afraid that if the re-educators started on him again he would break down and betray his faith. He was a very rigid man—a prisoner confessed to him that he'd once worked for the Communists, and Father Ioja forbade him to take Communion for fifteen years!'

Some of the suicides were famous men, like George Bratianu, a great pre-war figure in Rumanian politics. He found no other means of taking his life than to starve himself to death, unnoticed among prisoners who neither knew nor cared. The leader of the Liberal Party, Rosculet, had killed himself at Sighet jail: he was one of those who had thought that 'local' Communists were not like the Russian variety; but after using his name as Minister of Cults, the Party imprisoned him as a counter-revolutionary.

The brutalities of 're-education' caused unrest in many prisons, and rumours spread across the country. Then two unconnected incidents brought the truth into the light of day.

During an inspection at Tirgul-Ocna, a hated Secret Police colonel, Sepeanu, spotted a new fence. 'Why did you build this?' he asked Commandant Bruma. 'The wood might have been better used to beat these counter-revolutionaries.' He laughed heartily.

The story caused wild rage. The atmosphere of revolt was still simmering in Tirgul-Ocna. A former major shouted, 'Something must be done!' And he decided that he was the man to do it. When Sepeanu had gone, the major asked that an interrogator be brought specially from Bucharest to hear a secret which he had failed to confess.

The interrogator came. The major told him, 'You know that I am serving twenty years as a war criminal for executing Russian prisoners. As Brigade Major, I did not shoot these men myself. I can tell you who did. He was a lieutenant named Sepeanu, who today is a Secret Police colonel.'

So Sepeanu was also tried for war crimes and sentenced to twenty years. During the trial he spoke about what was happening in the prisons under the 're-education' system.

The second incident involved another Secret Police chief. Colonel Virgil Weiss had been a friend of Ana Pauker and others in the Government. Then he fell foul of them, and at Piteshi jail he came into the hands of Turcanu, leader of the 'Prisoners of Communist Convictions'.

A man who helped Turcanu to torture victims told me later that Colonel Weiss fainted three times in an hour while they worked on him. They brought him round with cold water. He said, 'All right—I'll tell everything I kept back—and let us see if your bosses can stand it.' Turcanu believed he had stumbled on secrets that would bring him at last the release he had been promised. 'If you lie now, I'll kill you,' he warned. Weiss said, 'I have important things to say, but not to you. They concern traitors in high places.'

He was taken to Bucharest, where he spent several weeks in

hospital. Members of the Party's Central Committee, rivals of the Pauker clique, interviewed him there. He revealed that Pauker, Luca and Georgescu, the ruling ministers, had enlisted Weiss's aid in obtaining false passports, with which they could, if need be, leave Rumania quickly. They had also transferred large sums of money to Swiss banks.

The information was passed to the Party Secretary-General, Gheorghiu-Dej, chief schemer against the Pauker group.

Colonel Weiss told the story of re-education and showed Dej's friends its effects on his own body. They were alarmed. Another reversal of Party fortunes lay ahead: they might soon face the same treatment. Some had been unaware of the excesses, and others pretended not to have known; but now inquiries were begun. The leading 're-educators' were interrogated at Secret Police headquarters and several of them, Turcanu included, were sentenced to death.

The re-education scandal was used as a weapon against the Ministry of the Interior, which was headed by Theohari Georgescu, and in the political purge of 1952 the triumvirate which had ruled Rumania since the Communist take-over was overthrown. The other Ministers involved in Colonel Weiss's charges, Vasile Luca and Ana Pauker, were made scapegoats for the catastrophic inflation and the disasters brought by collectivisation.

7

Many of those who came to help us in Room Four were farmers who had rebelled against forcible collectivisation of their land. The prisons of Rumania were full of them. Thousands more had been put before firing squads.

They told some terrible stories. Their property had been seized, and under the 1949 'land reform' law, they received no compensation. Turned overnight into vagabonds who had nothing to lose, they fought back. Officials were liable to be shot, beaten or burned alive with petrol. It was all for nothing. The farmers lacked organisation. Their rebellions occurred at different times and in different regions so the government could always stamp them out.

A leathery old sheep farmer called Ghica told me, 'The Secret Police showed me two rusty rifles. "We dug them up in your barn," they said. "If you join the collective, you might avoid a trial." Well, I agreed. But when they came to take my animals, I lost my head and tried to stop them. They beat me up—and here I am serving fifteen years. I've lost everything. Land, sheep, wife, children!' All farmers lamented their losses in that order.

Another told how he had been deprived of his flock. He begged at least to keep the bells from their necks. The officials laughed but let him have his way. He took the bells up to his loft and tied them to a rope. All night he sat there, ringing the bells from time to time. When morning came, he ran through the village to the Party headquarters and stabbed the secretary to death.

A third farmer had two plough-horses. His greatest pleasure was to feed and groom them. When they were taken he burnt down the stables of the collective farm.

That year, fewer countryfolk came into prison. Gheorghiu-Dej, while retaining the Party leadership, made himself Prime Minister in 1952, and sought popularity by slowing down collectivisation. Luca, Pauker and Georgescu were all dismissed from their posts.

Winter came on, with heavy snowstorms. Thick icicles hung from the roof, and hoar frost patterned the window-panes. Outside the cold made you gasp. By December the snow was six feet deep. It was the coldest winter for a hundred years, so they said. There was no heating, but until now we had two or three blankets each, instead of the regulation one, for every time a man died in Room Four we took his bedclothes. Then there was a check—and we were left with a single covering each. We slept in our clothes all winter. Often we were without bread. The soup, made of carrots too rotten to be sold, became still thinner.

On Christmas Eve, prison talk became more serious. There were few quarrels, no swearing, little laughter. Every man thought of those he loved and there was a feeling of communion with the rest of mankind, which was usually so remote from our lives.

I spoke of Christ, but all the time my feet and hands were cold as steel, my teeth chattered, and an icy lump of hunger in my stomach seemed to spread through my body until only the heart lived. When I stopped, a simple farming lad took up where I had left off. Aristar had never been to school. Yet he talked so naturally, describing the scene of the nativity as if it had happened in his own barn that week, that there were tears in the eyes of all who listened.

Someone began to sing in the prison that evening. At first his voice was quiet, and hardly came in among the thoughts that occupied my mind, of my wife and my son. But gradually the voice swelled wonderfully in the crisp, clear air until it echoed through the corridors and everybody stopped what they were doing.

We were very quiet when he ceased. The guards, huddled in their quarters around a coke stove, did not stir all evening. We began to tell stories, and when I was asked for one, I thought of the song, and told them this old Jewish legend:

King Saul of Israel brought David, the shepherd honoured for killing Goliath, to his court. David loved music, and he was delighted to see a harp of great beauty standing in the palace. Saul said, 'I paid much for that instrument, but I was deceived. It gives forth only ugly sounds.'

David took it up to try, and drew from it music so exquisite that every man was moved. The harp seemed to laugh and sing and weep. King Saul asked, 'How is it that all the musicians I called brought discord from this harp, and only you could bring out music?'

David, the future king, replied, 'Before me, each man tried to play his own song on these strings. But I sang to the harp its own song. I recalled how it had been a young tree, with birds that chirped in its branches and limbs green with leaves that blossomed in the sun. I reminded it of the day when men came to cut it down; and you heard it weep under my fingers. I explained then that this is not the end. Its death as a tree meant the start of a new life in which it would glorify God, as a harp; and you heard how it rejoiced under my hands.

'So when the Messiah comes, many will try to sing on his harp their own songs, and their tunes will be harsh. We must sing on His harp His own song, the song of His life, passions, joys, sufferings, death and resurrection. Only then will the music be true.'

It was a song like this we heard that Christmas in the jail of Tirgul-Ocna.

8

Aristar died in February. We had to dig through deep snow and break ground like iron to bury him in the prison yard, alongside Abbot Iscu, Gafencu, Bucur and a score of others he had known in Room Four. His bed was taken over by Avram Radonovici, who had been a music critic in Bucharest.

Avram knew long passages from the scores of Bach, Beethoven and Mozart, and could hum them for hours—it was as good as a symphony concert. But he had brought a more precious gift with him. Because of his tuberculosis, which had affected his spine, he was encased in a plaster cast when they brought him to Tirgul-Ocna, and as we watched he pushed a hand into the breast of this grey shell and extracted a small, tattered book. None of us had seen a book of any kind for years. Avram lay there quietly turning the pages, until he became conscious of the eager eyes fixed on him.

'Your book,' I said. 'What is it? Where did you get it?'

'It's the Gospel according to St. John,' said Avram. 'I managed to hide it in my cast when the police came for me.' He smiled. 'Would you like to borrow it?'

I took the little book in my hands as if it were a live bird. No life-saving drug could have been more precious to me. I, who had known much of the Bible by heart and had taught it in the seminary, was forgetting it every day. Often I had tried to remind myself of a great advantage in this lack of a Bible—while reading what God told prophets and saints, we may forget to listen for what He has to say to us.

The Gospel went from hand to hand. It was difficult to give it up. I think prison was harder for educated men. Factory workers and farmers found more varied society than they had known before, but the reading man was like a fish thrown on the sand.

Many learnt the whole Gospel by heart and we discussed it

every day among ourselves; but we had to be careful which prisoners were let into the secret. This Gospel helped to bring many to Christ, among them Professor Popp, who, by being near to many living Christians, had come steadily closer to faith. The words of St. John were completing the work, but there was a last barrier.

'I've tried to pray again,' said the professor. 'But between reciting the Orthodox formulas I learnt as a boy and demanding favours of the Almighty to which I have no claim, there is nothing much to say. Like the king in "Hamlet", my words fly up, my thoughts remain below.'

I told him of a pastor who was called to an old man's deathbed. He went to sit in an armchair close to the bed, but the old man said, 'Please don't sit there!' So the pastor pulled up a stool, heard his confession and gave him Holy Communion.

The old man revived and said, 'Let me tell you the story of that armchair. Fifty years ago, when I was a lad, the old pastor here asked if I said my prayers. I replied, "No. I have no one to pray to. If I shout at the top of my voice the man on the floor above doesn't hear, so how will God in Heaven?" The old pastor replied mildly, "Do not try to pray then! Just sit quietly in the morning with another chair before you. Imagine that sitting in it is Jesus Christ, as he sat in so many homes in Palestine. What would you tell him?" I said, "If I were honest, I'd say I didn't believe in him." "Well," said the pastor, "that shows at least what's really in your mind. You could go further and challenge him: if he exists, then let him give proof of it! Or if you don't like the way God runs the world, why not tell him so? You wouldn't be the first to complain. King David and Job told God they thought he was unjust. Perhaps you want something? Then say exactly what it is. If you receive it, give him thanks. All these exchanges are in the realm of prayer. Don't recite holy phrases! Say what is really in your heart!" '

The dying man went on, 'I didn't believe in Christ, but I did in the old pastor. To please him, I sat before that armchair and pretended Christ was in it. For a few days it was a game. Then I *knew* that He was with me. I spoke to a real Jesus about real things. I sought guidance and received it. Prayer became dialogue.

Young man, fifty years have passed and every day I speak with Jesus in that chair.'

The pastor was there when the man died, stretching out a hand with his last gesture towards the unseen friend in the armchair.

The professor asked, 'Is that how you pray?'

I said, 'I like to think that Jesus stands near me, and that I can talk to Him as I do to you. People who met Him in Nazareth and Bethlehem didn't recite prayers to Him. They said what was in their hearts, and so ought we.'

Popp said, 'Why do you suppose that many who did talk to him in Palestine 2,000 years ago didn't become his followers?'

I said: 'For centuries the Jews prayed for the coming of the Messiah, and none more loudly than the Sanhedrin, the supreme council. But when he came, they mocked and spat and sent him to his death, for the last thing they wanted was someone who would upset their comfortable routine. That's true of many of all nations today.'

Professor Popp became a Christian. He told me, 'When I first saw you I had a premonition that you had something to give me.' Such intuitions are not uncommon in jail. When the outer world is cut off from sight, a new sense opens for the unseen.

We became very close. Sitting together in silence sometimes, he would say the thought that was stirring in my mind. So it should be, but rarely is, between friends, and between man and wife.

9

A thaw came in March. The icicles melted and the snow lay in patches against the wall. Buds appeared on the bare trees and we heard the birds sing. Through our chilblained hands, our feet wrapped in rags, our faces stiff with cold, we felt life start again.

News galvanised the prison. A prisoner had been taken to the hospital in town, where a woman scrubbing the floor had wept. 'What's wrong?' he asked. 'Our father Stalin is dead,' she sobbed. 'It's in the newspapers.' We shed no tears. Everyone speculated excitedly on what it would mean.

Popp, said, 'If Stalin is dead, so is Stalinism; a dictatorship doesn't survive its dictator.'

'But Communism has survived Lenin,' said someone.

A few days later we heard train whistles blowing and bells tolling to mark Stalin's funeral in Moscow. The prison echoed with laughter and curses. The guards looked surly and the officers were nervous. No one knew what might happen next.

After weeks of uncertainty, a high official came from the Legal Department and we understood that he had been sent to study prison conditions. Silence greeted him as he went from cell to cell asking for complaints. Many thought it was a trick. When he reached Room Four I said. 'I have something to say, but I won't start unless you promise to hear me to the end.'

'That's what I've come for,' said the official politely.

I said, 'Prosecutor, you had a renowned predecessor in history, called Pontius Pilate. He was asked to handle the trial of a man he knew to be innocent. "Never mind," said Pilate to himself. "Am I to risk my career for a Jew and a carpenter?"

'Although 2,000 years have passed, this betrayal of justice has not been forgotten. In any church you enter throughout the world, you hear it said, in the Creed, that Jesus was crucified under Pontius Pilate.'

The others in Room Four were looking worried for me.

I said, 'Look into your heart and you'll see that we are the victims of injustice. Even if we're guilty in the Party's eyes, we were to purge our crimes in prison—but this is a long-drawn death sentence. Before you make your report, look at our food, the lack of heating and simple medicine, the dirt and disease. Ask about some of the barbarities we've suffered. Then write the truth. Don't wash your hands of helpless men as Pilate did.'

The prosecutor looked at me sombrely, turned on his heel and left without a word. The news that he had heard me out spread through the prison and encouraged others to speak. Before he left, we heard that there had been angry words in the commandant's office. Later that day the guards became polite, almost apologetic. A week afterwards the commandant was dismissed.

With the improvements in prison routine I began to get out of bed and walk a few paces each day. Dr. Aldea brought the official doctor to see me.

Aldea said, 'We can't make you out. Your lungs are like a

sieve, the spinal vertebrae are affected; I couldn't put you in plaster and there's been virtually no surgical intervention. You're no better, but you're getting no worse, and so we're going to move you out of Room Four.'

My friends there were very happy. They took courage from the fact that, after two and a half years, I was the first man to leave the cell alive.

'How's it done, pastor?' said one, jokingly. 'Why doesn't that old body of yours obey doctor's orders and die?'

I said, 'I expect you could find a medical reason if you tried. But in the war I learnt a lesson about looking for explanations. I met some Party men who had been in Russia. When I asked why the Soviet Union had eased its campaign against religion at the time, one man said, "You tell us." I replied that I thought it was a concession to Britain and America, who were helping to keep Russia in the war. The official smiled. "That's the explanation which I would give, as a Communist. If I were a Christian I'd say it was God's answer to prayer." I was silent, because he was right. In the Bible, it is said that an ass once reprimanded a prophet. So I say to you now, that if I have recovered, it is a miracle of God and an answer to prayer.'

I knew that many people—prisoners I had met, as well as my congregation—prayed for me; but not for many years did I learn how many thousands around the world had joined in their prayer.

PART FOUR

ROOM 4 had been like an altar on which men were transformed and transfigured for their faiths. I was glad to be still alive, but leaving it was a descent. From an atmosphere of nobility and self-sacrifice, I returned to the world of quarrels, vanity and pretences. It was sad and comic to see how many of the old upper-class clung to their illusions. Grubby 'excellencies' wished each other good-day. Starved 'generals' inquired after one another's health. Endlessly, they discussed the return of their vanished affluence.

One of these, Vasile Donca, accepted from me a piece of string to hold up his trousers. String was a precious thing in jail. But when, next day, I spoke to him I was ignored—I had failed to address him as 'brigadier'.

Donca, like many others, would do anything for a cigarette. The guards were the only source of tobacco, and although they were forbidden to hand it on, they smoked a lot at night, littering the yard with butt-ends. Cell leaders and informers were let out first in the morning so that they had a monopoly of butt collecting. But sometimes another prisoner would make a find, and his friends would stand in a circle with him, smoking it on the end of a pin.

One morning a guard lit a cigarette as he lolled by the cell door near my bunk. Donca edged his way round the cell and began to talk to him in a low, urgent voice.

'Guard! What do you want for that cigarette?'

The guard grinned. 'What have you got to offer, Brigadier?'

Donca had nothing, but he tried to bluff. 'I am not without friends in high places. You shall be rewarded for any attention you show me!'

'Influential friends?' said the guard. 'So you are really a Communist after all, Brigadier?'

'I am a loyal Rumanian, Sergeant.'

'Well, if you were a loyal Rumanian Communist, Brigadier, I might give you this cigarette.'

Donca hesitated and looked furtively around. The guard moved as if to go away.

'Wait! Of course I'm a loyal Rumanian Communist!'

The guard beckoned to his comrades to come and share the joke.

'So you dance to a Russian tune, Brigadier? Give us a dance! Dance like a Russian bear!' He held out the cigarette.

With his arms spread and a pained grin on his face, Donca began to hop from foot to foot. The guards collapsed into laughter. The prisoners averted their faces as Donca rooted among their legs for the discarded cigarette.

When Donca moved elsewhere, his bunk was taken by another former member of the Staff, General Stavrat. Epaulettes no more make the officer than the habit makes the monk, and Stavrat was everything that Donca was not. Though short in stature, he dwarfed his fellow-prisoners by sheer strength of personality. Crusty, quick to despise weakness, yet full of kindness and good sense, he liked to address the cell at large as 'Men!'

Juliu Stavrat was a general without boots. He had given his away. We shared my pair, going out in them on alternate days for exercise in the yard. Soon after his arrival, the first food parcels were allowed and one was delivered to General Stavrat. He opened it before an excited audience. A gasp went up. Ham, smoked sausage, fruit-cake, chocolate—what sacrifices his wife must have made to buy such things! Stavrat, who had lived on scraps for eight years, wrapped up the parcel again and came over to my bed. 'Pastor,' he said, 'be good enough to divide this among the men.'

Stavrat was a Christian before he was a soldier. When we heard that Russia had exploded her first A-bomb, he said, 'Then we must no longer look for full-scale American military intervention: it is better for us to rot in jail than for millions of people to die in an atomic war.'

'You think it would destroy humanity?' I asked him.

'The future of humanity and its past as well,' he said. 'There will be no one left to know our struggle and progress through the ages.' Stavrat had a deep feeling for history. He could talk eloquently of Rumania's past.

'But if nuclear war solves nothing,' he added, 'and civilisation and Communism cannot live together, I don't know what the answer is.'

'It's Christianity,' I answered, 'in a vital form. It can change the lives of great men and lesser. Remember the many barbarian rulers like Clovis of France, Stephen of Hungary, Rurik of Russia, who were converted and made their countries Christian. It can be done again. Then we'll see the Iron Curtain melt.'

'Shall we start with Gheorghiu-Dej?' smiled Stavrat. 'A tall order!'

2

Gheorghiu-Dej, his rivals all eclipsed, was now our dictator. He admitted freely that grave mistakes had been committed, and among the gravest was the Danube-Black Sea Canal project. After three years in which millions of pounds had been wasted and thousands of lives lost, only five of its projected forty miles had been completed. Leading engineers and camp administrators were accused of sabotage. Three were sentenced to death, two summarily executed. Thirty others were given prison terms from fifteen years to life. A fresh survey now proved that the Danube could not supply sufficient water for the project—exactly what the engineers consulted at the start were shot for saying. The canal was abandoned. All that remained of use in Rumania's major investment of time and money in the first decade of Communist rule were the labour camps. These could now accommodate the overflow from the prisons.

While we were talking about the fiasco, Professor Popp took

me aside. He said, 'I have been keeping something from you since my return to Tirgul-Ocna. Dr. Aldea thought it might be too much of a shock for you in your condition. Your wife is now in prison, and she has been at the canal.'

Popp had pieced the facts together from various prisoners who had worked there. Sabina had been arrested two years after me. No charge was brought against her. She led the women in the church as a deaconess and was told what to preach, but that was not her way. At Poarta Alba, she was put among women who had to shovel earth into wheelbarrows and cart it great distances. Those who did not fulfil their quota were kept without bread. There were schoolgirl patriots and prostitutes, society women and women suffering for their faith. At Camp Kilometre 4, Commandant Kormos was later sentenced to hard labour for raping thirty girl prisoners: the charge was 'damaging the prestige of the régime'.

My wife came under the orders of a notorious figure, Colonel Albon, the Poarta Alba chief. She ate grass like an animal: rats, snakes, dogs, everything was eaten. Some of those who had eaten dog said it was good. I asked them, 'Would you eat it again?' 'Oh, no!' they said. Sabina was tiny and fragile, so a favourite joke of the guards was to throw her into the freezing Danube and fish her out again. But she survived. Her life was saved by the collapse of the project. She was sent with other prisoners to a state farm where pigs were bred, and there, too, the work was hard.

The Professor said that a prisoner from Vacaresti had spoken with my wife in the hospital there.

'She has been very ill,' said Popp, 'but she will live. She knows that you are safe. The women around her spoke of a pastor who was supposed to be dying, and who preached from behind the walls. They told your wife that they stopped hearing your voice in 1950—that you must have died. But she said no, that she believed you to be alive, whatever the evidence against it.'

This news almost shattered my self-control. I tried to pray, but a black gloom settled on my mind. For days I spoke to no one. Then one morning in the prison yard I saw a very dignified old priest by the guard-room, his white beard blowing in the cold wind. He had just arrived and they had left him there. Several officers were standing about.

'What's this old priest doing here?' asked one of them.

'He's come to confess them,' mocked another.

That is what Father Suroianu soon did. There was such an aura of holiness around him that you felt a great impulse to tell this man the whole truth. I, too, although not believing in sacramental confession, revealed to him my sense of despair, and sins which I had never before told. The roots of evil are not often laid bare in the confessional. But the more I accused myself, the more Father Suroianu looked at me not with contempt but with love.

Suroianu had more reason to mourn than any of us. Tragedy had struck his whole family. One of his daughters, a cripple, had been deprived of her husband, who was in Tirgul-Ocna with us. Another daughter, and her husband, had been sentenced to twenty years. One of his sons had died in prison. The second, on whom Suroianu had set great hopes as a priest, had turned against him. His grandchildren had been driven out of school or had lost their jobs because of their parents' 'anti-Party activities'. Yet Father Suroianu, a simple, self-educated man, spent his day encouraging and cheering others.

He never greeted people with 'Good morning', but always with the Biblical 'Rejoice!' He told me, 'The day you can't smile, don't open your shop. It takes seventeen muscles of the face to smile, but forty-three to frown!'

I asked him, 'You've had so much misfortune—how can you "rejoice" always?'

'Why, it's a grave sin not to do so,' he said. 'There's always good reason to rejoice. There is a God in Heaven and in the heart. I had a piece of bread this morning. It was so good! Look now, the sun is shining! And so many here love me! Every day you do not rejoice is a day lost, my son! You will never have that day again.'

3

I, too, could rejoice, in the sense at least that I was now fulfilling the wish I had cherished since being ordained—to be a prison pastor. In everyday life one rings the bells and waits for people to come to church; but here my parishioners were 'in church' with me, not on one morning in the week, but all day and every day. They had to listen, if not always willingly.

Lazar Stancu, a clever linguist whose crime had been to work for a foreign news agency, broke in to say, 'Not more about Christianity, please! There are other interesting religions.'

'Well,' I said. 'I know something about Confucius and Buddhism.' And I told one of the lesser-known New Testament parables.

'Fascinating!' Stancu exclaimed, and praised its beautiful and original thought.

'I'm glad you think that,' I said, and explained that it was really Christ's teaching. 'Why do you run after other religions?' I asked. Was it the case of an old Rumanian proverb, 'Your neighbour's hen is always a turkey?' Or simply the restless intellectual's search for novelty?

Stancu said, 'Bernard Shaw once suggested that people are so inoculated in childhood with small doses of Christianity that they seldom catch the real thing.'

One evening, a young prisoner jumped up and cried, 'Stop it! Stop it! Stop it!' There was a silence. He was a new arrival and the others looked at him surprised. He turned and ran to his bunk, where he flung himself down. I went over to him. He had a fine sensitive face, but his jaw and neck were covered by improvised bandages. He gave me a tearful glare and turned his back. Feeling that I would only upset him further by trying to talk at the moment, I did not persist.

Dr. Aldea told me his name was Josif. 'A nice lad', he said, 'but he'll be scarred for life by an ulcer on the face. He's another bone tuberculosis case.' He told me that four years before, when only fourteen, Josif had been arrested while trying to reach Germany, where his sister was living. The Secret Police put him under the guard of trained dogs, which leapt at him if he moved, snapping at his throat. Shock and fear had filled his mind; he talked again and again of the hours he had spent on the frontier at the mercy of the dogs. Next, suspected of being a pawn in some political game, Josif was taken to Bucharest and tortured for information which he did not possess. Then he was sent with a forced labour gang to the canal, where he starved and fell victim to T.B.

I watched Josif as he settled down among us. He had a native honesty and openness that life had not corrupted. At times, forgetting his troubles, he threw back his dark shock of hair and roared with laughter at some ancient prison joke. But often his hand went to his damaged face. It hurt him: but worse was the thought that his good looks were gone for life.

Sure that I could help him, I bided my time.

4

For a few months after Stalin's death, monthly parcels from home were permitted. We looked forward keenly to these. On the postcards they gave us I wrote asking, in addition to food, for cigarettes and 'Doctor Filon's old clothes'.

Smoking I dislike, but since men were so desperate for cigarettes I always asked for my full quota to give away. The result was that those for whom I had none were resentful and those to whom I gave often suspected me of giving more to others.

The request for Dr. Filon's clothes puzzled my family. The doctor was a small man. I was very tall. I hoped that they would guess that what I really wanted from him was streptomycin. Aldea told me that Socialist medicine now conceded that the drug, discovered in America ten years before, had value. If I received some, he could treat me; but we were not allowed to ask for it in our parcels.

Apart from tuberculosis, I was suffering also from one of the frequent bouts of toothache which plagued us all. Teeth decayed quickly for lack of food and treatment, or were broken in beatings. Sometimes I had fifty-pound chains around my ankles and could not even walk a few steps to ease the pain. But never was it worse than during this spell at Tirgul-Ocna. An upper tooth had me in agony all day; then at sunset the pain moved down to the lower jaw. We had no dentist and no hope of relief. Pascal is said to have combatted toothache with mathematical problems, so I tried to compose sermons; but pain must be more amenable to calculation than composition, for they were miserable sermons. I began poems, but they were poems of desperation.

I tried to forget the pain by talking to Josif. I sat by him and asked why he had been so angry when I spoke.

He said, 'I hate God! If you go on I'll call the guards.' His eyes began to fill with tears. 'Leave me alone!'

But the boy's good nature always broke through, and a day or two later he was telling me of his hopes of meeting his sister in Germany and going on together to join relations in America.

'You must start to learn English, then,' I said.

'I'd love to, but who'll teach me, here?'

I said I could give him lessons if he wished.

'Could you? Really?' He was overjoyed, and he proved a bright pupil, although we had no books, paper or pencil.

I told him of books in English I had read, and had him repeat after me passages which I knew by heart from the Bible.

5

Josif was not the only prisoner who threatened to report me, but the real danger in our midst was the hidden informer. Often such men used the pretence of patriotism to serve their purpose, especially with the young.

The partisans who held out for years in the mountains of Rumania inspired many youngsters to form their own anti-Communist groups, so that boys and girls of seventeen and eighteen were arrested and herded into jail: there was even a fourteen-year-old with us at Tirgul-Ocna. They loved to hear the stories which a former intelligence colonel called Armeanu used to tell of our King Stephen the Great and other patriot-heroes who had struggled against foreign domination.

General Stavrat, who had known Armeanu before, said, 'I don't trust that man. We must keep an eye on him.'

Later that day, I walked by slowly while Armeanu was with a young partisan called Tiberiu. 'They got me,' Tiberiu said, 'but others are carrying on the fight . . .' When I walked past again, I heard him say that a young girl was among them. Armeanu, seeing me near, clapped him on the shoulder and went off.

I asked Josif to listen; Armeanu would take even less notice of him. Indeed, a few evenings later, he heard snatches of conversation.

'Hasn't a good-looking chap like you got a girl?' Armeanu was asking Tiberiu. 'Of course you have—I bet she's pretty, too. What's her name? . . . Maria—and where does she come from? . . . Yes, I know the place. In fact, I was friendly with a family called Celinescu who had a daughter of the same name . . . Ah your Maria is a Miss Cuza. And her father? An army captain, eh? Not in the 22nd regiment by any chance? . . . Oh, the 15th. Yes, yes.'

After this report, I agreed that Armeanu was probably an agent and that the girl Maria would be arrested in a few days. General Stavrat wanted to confront him at once, but I knew that we could prove nothing against the man. When next I found Armeanu alone, I struck up a conversation. He asked why I was in prison and I saw a desperate chance.

'For spying,' I said, adding that I knew I could speak freely to a nationalist like him. 'My arrest doesn't matter. I'm only a minor cog in the organisation.' I dropped further hints and allowed him to wheedle names and addresses of my 'contacts'. I saw a look of cunning triumph in his face: he thought he had the information which would secure his release.

As soon as the cells opened next day, Stavrat saw Armeanu whispering to the guard. Immediately afterwards the colonel was called for a 'medical inspection'—this was a frequent pretext for consulting informers. Then I was sent for by the political officer. He must have imagined an extra star on his shoulder already, for without any attempt to shield Armeanu he at once demanded the full story of the great international spy-network I had mentioned.

'Lieutenant,' I replied, 'if you pass on the information which I gave Armeanu yesterday it will start a furore in Bucharest. That's why I advise you not to do it. You'll only harm yourself.'

'What do you mean?' he asked.

I said, 'I invented the whole thing. I wanted to check my suspicions about Armeanu. Now I know.'

The officer stared at me in disbelief. Then, he burst out laughing.

I went back and told Stavrat. He tackled Armeanu. 'Brave men have died under your command,' he said, 'and now you turn to treachery!'

Armeanu tried to bluster, but he was an outcast from that day. I heard years later that he had died in prison. All his betrayals brought him only shame.

6

My next month's parcel included 100 grams of streptomycin. The hint had been taken! Thinking of the men I had left behind in Room Four, I asked General Stavrat to offer it to the most serious case there.

'That's Sultaniuc,' he said with distaste. 'A thorough-paced Iron Guard Fascist. He's at death's door, though he won't admit it. Much better take the stuff yourself . . . Very well, if you insist.'

Stavrat was soon back. 'He wanted to know where the drug came from, and when I told him it was yours he said he wouldn't take anything from an opponent of the Iron Guard. There's nothing to be done with a fanatic like that.'

I thought there might be a way around. When Stavrat had left, I asked Josif—whom no one would suspect of duplicity—to act as a go-between.

'Tell Sultaniuc the general was mistaken. Say it's a gift from Graniceru. He's an Iron Guard man too, and I hear he recently received some drugs.'

Josif was unsuccessful. 'Sultaniuc doesn't believe that Graniceru would give him anything. He won't look at the powder unless you swear on your oath that it doesn't come from you.'

'Why not?' I said. 'I've given him the drug and I can give him an oath to go with it. The streptomycin is really not mine, but God's. I gave it to Him the moment it arrived.'

Dr. Aldea, who was busy elsewhere when the streptomycin arrived, was speechless when he heard what had become of it. Even Stavrat was puzzled at my giving 'a false oath'. He said, 'I thought you clergy always insisted on the whole truth and nothing but the truth.'

Stavrat soon had an example of what 'the whole truth' can cost when two new prisoners, one of whom had testified against the other, were put into our cell. The first was a Catholic bishop, who wanted Rome to know how bitterly his Church was being persecuted. The second was a lawyer who delivered the bishop's letter of complaint to the Papal Nuncio—when there was still one in Bucharest—for transmission to the Vatican. As the lawyer left the Nuncio's palace, he was arrested and, having denied delivering a letter, confronted by the bishop. The bishop said, 'I cannot lie. Yes, I did give him a letter.'

Both men were tortured and ended up in Tirgul-Ocna, where they argued over which was right. The bishop expected my support, but I could not give it. I said, 'If a man refuses to tell a lie, well and good, but then he should keep dangerous questions in his own hands. If he decides to risk someone else's safety, he must defend him at all costs.'

The bishop protested, 'The whole affair has brought me much sorrow, but how could I say something which was untrue?'

I replied that if we do good to our enemies, surely we should help our friends. 'If my hostess has spent all day preparing a disastrous dinner, I still feel obliged to compliment her: that's not a lie, it's simple courtesy. When men here ask, "When will the Americans come?" I tell them, "It can't be too long now." It's not the truth, I'm afraid, but it's not a lie either. It is a word of hope.'

The bishop was unconvinced. I continued, 'If you submit to the purists, all art becomes a lie. Faust didn't really sign a contract with the devil, you know; it's just that liar Goethe at work. Hamlet never existed—that's a Shakespearean lie. The simplest jokes (I hope you laugh at jokes) are a fabrication.'

'That may be so,' the bishop replied, 'but here is a personal issue. When *you* are interrogated by the Communists, Mr. Wurmbrand, do you not feel that you must tell the truth?'

'Of course not. I have no qualms about saying the first thing that comes into my head, so long as it misleads those who are trying to trap my friends. Am I to give these people information which they can use to attack the church? I'm a minister of God!

'The world uses fine words for ugly things. Fraud becomes

cleverness. Meanness is called economy. Lust wears the crown of love. Here the ugly word "lie" is used for something which instinct tells us is right. I respect truth, but I'd "lie" to save a friend.'

When we were alone, Josif asked me, 'What do you call a lie, then?'

'Why should you expect a definition from me? Your own conscience, if guided by the Holy Spirit, will tell you in every circumstance of life what to say and what to leave unsaid. You don't think the oath you carried to Sultaniuc about the streptomycin was a lie, do you?'

'Oh no,' said Josif, with his sweet smile. 'That was an act of love.'

7

Josif's bitterness was eased, and one day after our English lesson I asked him, 'Why do you say that you hate God?'

'Why? he echoed. 'You tell me first why God created the T.B. microbe.' He considered that that should end the conversation.

'I can explain,' I said. 'If you will listen quietly.'

He replied woefully, 'I'll listen all night if you can do that.'

I warned him that I would keep him at his word. It was a problem, I said, which went to the root of human suffering, and evil. Josif was not the only one to ask why such things could happen under the eye of a merciful God; probably all of us in prison had asked the same question, and there was not one answer, but several.

'Firstly, we tend to confuse the unpleasant with the bad. Why is the wolf bad? Because it eats sheep, and this upsets me. I want to eat the sheep myself! And whereas the wolf must eat the sheep to live, I have no need to do so, for I can eat other things. Worse still, the wolf has no duty towards the sheep, whereas we rear it all its life, feed and water it, and when it puts its full trust in us, then we cut its throat. No one thinks we're bad.'

Josif sat watching me, his head propped in his hand.

'It's the same with bacilli. One bacillus lives—and makes dough ferment; another lives—and damages a child's lung. Neither germ knows what it does, but I approve one and condemn the other. So things are not good or bad in themselves—we label them according to whether they are convenient to us. We want the whole universe to conform to us, although we are an infinitesimally small part of it.'

The cell was dark, and unexpectedly quiet. 'Secondly,' I said, 'what we call "bad" is often simply unfinished good.'

'That will take some proving,' Josif put in, 'in my case.'

I said, 'You had a namesake 4,000 years ago, who was sold into slavery by his brothers, and suffered many other injustices in Egypt. Then he rose to be Prime Minister and so he was able to save the land, and his own ungrateful brothers, from starving in a famine. So until, like Joseph, you reach the end of the story, you can never know if what has happened so far will prove good or bad. When a painter starts a portrait, all you see is a blur of colour. It takes time for the sitter to emerge. Everyone admires the portrait of Mona Lisa, but it took Leonardo forty years to finish. The ascent of a mountain is hard going before you can enjoy the view from the summit.'

'But the men who die here in prison,' Josif said, 'may never see the view.'

'On the other hand, a spell in jail may help them to the summit. Would Comrade Gheorghiu-Dej have come to power in Rumania if he hadn't been in prison like us?'

'And those who don't live to see freedom again?'

'Lazarus died in poverty and sickness,' I said, 'but Jesus tells us in a parable that the angels took him into eternal blessedness. After death there comes to all of us a compensation. Only when we see the end of everything can we hope to understand.'

Josif promised to think about it.

8

One rapid cure for toothache is good news, and the letter which came for me raised my spirits to the skies, for it said my wife was free. She was still confined to Bucharest, but my son would shortly be allowed to visit me! The letter ended there: it was all the information they allowed.

I had left Mihai at the age of nine, and now he was fifteen. I could not imagine my son so grown up. We had always been so close. I began to worry about the meeting day and night. At last they led me into a large hall, where I had to sit in a box with a window blocked by three iron bars, so small that the visitor opposite would see only a small part of my face. The guard shouted, 'Mihai Wurmbrand!' and he came and sat down before me. He was pale and thin and hollow-cheeked, with the beginnings of a moustache.

He said with a rush, in case he was cut off, 'Mother says even if you die in prison you must not be sad because we'll all meet in paradise.'

Consoling first words! I did not know whether to laugh or cry. I pulled myself together. 'How is she? Have you food at home?'

'She's well again,' he said. 'And we have food. Our Father is very rich.'

The guards assigned to listen to us grinned. They thought my wife had re-married.

To every question, Mihai found some reply in a verse from the Bible, so that in the few minutes which were allowed I received little family news; but he did tell me he had left a parcel with the guards at the gate.

I received the parcel next day, in excess of my allowance, because Mihai had addressed it to 'Richard Wurmbrand'. The others had gone to my prison self, Vasile Georgescu. Shortly afterwards, restrictions were fully restored: no visits, no parcels, no letters.

9

Before the easier times ended, a warder dragged a basket into the cell. It contained sheets and towels, and more than enough of these unimaginable luxuries for all.

'There's been a miscount,' said Emil, a tailor. 'Let's cut up the extra ones for clothes! I can run up some warm shirts out of this stuff.'

Ion Madgearu, a lawyer, said uneasily, 'It would be stealing state property.'

'Who's to know? There's no inventory!'

'I'm a political prisoner, not a criminal.'

'You're a fathead!'

Sides were taken and the argument raged. Josif appealed to me.

I said, 'All this "state property" is stolen from us. We've been reduced to rags and we are entitled to take back what we can. We owe it to our families to do all we can to survive the winter. It's just the same as when the guard comes in half asleep in the morning to ask "How many are you in this cell today?" We try to exaggerate our numbers to get a little extra bread—and quite right too!'

Madgearu said, 'I prefer to abide by the law.'

'But every law is unfair to someone,' I replied. 'The law tells a millionaire, who lacks nothing not to steal, and it says the same to you and men, who have nothing. Jesus excuses David for doing unallowed things when he was very hungry.'

Madgearu fell in with the rest of us eventually, but later he told me he had a special reason for wishing to make no compromise of this kind.

'I used to be a state prosecutor and in my time I've sent hundreds to jail. I thought, "Well, it makes no difference what I say; the Party will send them to prison in any case." When later I became the scapegoat for some mistake and received a fifteen-year sentence myself, I was stunned. They sent me to the lead-mines at Valea Nistrului. There, a Christian prisoner befriended me. He shared his food and was my good shepherd. I felt we'd met before, so I asked why he was in jail. "Oh," he said, "I helped a fellow in trouble, like you. He came to my farm, seeking food and shelter. Then he was arrested as a partisan and I got twenty years." I said, "Disgraceful!" and he gave me a strange look . . . Then it came back to me. I had been the prosecutor in his case. The man never reproached me, but his example of returning good for evil decided me to become a Christian.'

10

Josif sang as he tried on the shirt which Emil had made him out of the surplus towelling. It was like a tunic, with a hole for his head, but he was happy to have something fresh near his skin. 'State property! Everyone steals these days,' he said cheerfully.

Stavrat said, 'He takes it for granted. In ten years we've turned into a nation of thieves, liars and petty spies. Farmers steal from land they once owned; farm-workers steal from the collective; even the barber steals a razor from his own shop which the co-operative has seized. Then they have to cover their thefts. Did you, pastor, make absolutely accurate tax returns?'

I admitted that I saw no reason to give the parishioners' money to the atheistic Party.

'Stealing will be a subject taught at school, next,' said Stavrat.

Josif put in, 'I didn't listen to anything at school. The teachers said that Bessarabia, which everyone knows was stolen from us, had always been part of Russia.'

'Good lad!' said the general.

'I hope you'll reject their teaching against religion, too, Josif,' I added, and told him about a professor I knew who had to lecture regularly on atheism. 'After crossing himself alone in his room, asking God's forgiveness, he would go out and tell the students that God did not exist.'

'Well, of course,' said Josif, 'they would be spying on him.' He could not imagine a world in which you did not have to look around before opening your mouth.

The talk turned to a new informer called Jivoin who had deserted from the Jugoslav army and been arrested on the border as a spy. Now, to ingratiate himself with the prison authorities, he played the anti-Titoist and got the guards into trouble by reporting them if they relaxed the rules.

'Some of us have decided to give Jivoin a shock,' Josif said. 'If we all jump on him together they can't punish us too badly.'

'Wait a day,' I said. 'I've an idea which may work better.'

Since Jivoin was used to the cell turning its back on him, he was flattered when I sought him out and asked about his homeland. Soon he was repeating Croat jokes and Serbian proverbs, and recalling the beauty of Montenegro, its songs and dances. He grew steadily more excited under my prompting.

'And what's your new National Anthem?' I asked.

'Oh, it's magnificent—haven't you heard it?'

'No, I'd like to, very much.'

Delighted, Jivoin jumped up and raised his voice in song. The guards outside did not recognise the Titoist hymn until he came to the chorus. Then Jivoin was seized and rushed off to face a wrathful political officer.

'Well, that's the end of him,' said Josif. We began to laugh.

Not long after Jivoin was neutralised, a former Iron Guard man, Captain Stelea, was moved to our cell from one further down the gallery. There he had left, with regret, an old wartime comrade.

'What was his name?' General Stavrat asked.

'Ion Coliu,' Stelea replied. 'He was put in with me the night after my arrival at Tirgul-Ocna and we had a wonderful talk about old times.'

Stavrat asked whether Stelea had told Coliu any secret which he had held back under interrogation and torture.

'Yes, everything,' said Stelea. 'He's been my closest friend for years. I'd stake my life on him.'

When Stavrat told Stelea that Ion Coliu had become the most reviled stool-pigeon in Tirgul-Ocna, he could not believe it. I was asked to confirm the fact. For hours Stelea sat on his bunk like a shell-shocked soldier. Then he leapt up and began to shout and fight with us hysterically, until the guards carried him off.

A room is set aside in every prison for those who break down. They are left to rave and scream, excrete on the floor and fight among themselves, sometimes to death. Food is pushed through a hatch and left. No guard risks his life among them.

11

Josif's sentence had only weeks to run. He was planning for the future, he told me. 'My sister in Germany will work for a permit for us to go to America. I'll perfect my English and learn a trade!'

But still he hated his disfigured face. One evening, I told him how Helen Keller, although blind, deaf and dumb, became one of America's great personalities. He was fascinated as I described how she taught herself to become a fine pianist, aided only by a piece of sounding wood held in her teeth, the other end of which was fixed in the piano; and how her work brought Braille to thousands of blind people.

'She wrote, in one of her famous books, that although she had never seen the starry Heaven, she had Heaven in her heart. That is why she could spread before a world that has these senses, but often fails to use them, the beauty of God's creation.'

I told him that Helen Keller came from a wealthy family. If she had been 'lucky' like other girls in having all her senses, she might have frittered away her life in trivialities. Instead, she used what men called 'evil' as a stimulus to reach new heights of achievement.

Joseph pondered. 'Helen Keller must be a case in a thousand,' he said.

'No. There are many like her. The Russian writer Ostrovsky was blind, paralysed, and so poor that he had to write his novel on wrapping paper. It is world-famous today. Great men have often been sick men. Schiller, Chopin, Keats were tubercular like us. Baudelaire, Heine and our own poet, Eminescu, had syphilis. Scientists tell us that the microbes of such diseases excite our nervous cells and so they heighten our intelligence and perception, although they may bring madness or death in the end. T.B. may make a bad man worse, but good ones become better; they see their lives running out and want to do all the good they can in the time left to them.'

Josif helped often in Room Four. I said, 'Haven't you seen the special serenity, gentleness and lucidity which comes to some of those who suffer from tuberculosis?'

His eyes lit up. 'That's true. How strange!'

I said, 'For thousands of years men regarded fungus—mould that grows on walls—as bad. Then twenty-five years ago Sir Alexander Fleming found the good in it, and penicillin, which heals so many diseases, was discovered. Until its real use was known, this mould was evil. It may be that we have yet to learn how to put the T.B. microbe to work for us. When once this incurable disease of ours has finally been conquered, our children will perhaps be inoculated with small doses of the germ to enliven their intelligence.

'God made Heaven and earth, and your life, and so much beauty, Josif! There is sense in your suffering, as there was in Jesus's, for it was His death on the cross which saved mankind.'

Josif was shivering in his new shirt, which was already growing threadbare.

I took the woollen jacket which my relatives had sent and tore out the lining, for myself. I persuaded him to take the jacket. He clasped his arms over his narrow chest to show how warm he was.

Josif's conversion began on that day. Yet something was needed to lift him into faith.

It happened during the distribution of the bread rations. They were laid in rows on a table each morning. Each portion was supposed to be three and a half ounces, but some were a shade larger, some smaller. There were often disagreements over whose turn it was for first choice, and quarrels over who had to be last. Men asked each other's advice: which was the biggest portion left? Having acted on it, they suspected they were being misled, and friendships turned sour over a mouthful of black bread. When a surly prisoner called Trailescu tried to cheat me, Josif was watching.

I told Trailescu, 'Take mine, too. I know how hungry you are.' He shrugged and stuffed the bread into his mouth.

We sat translating New Testament verses into English that evening and Josif said, 'We have read nearly everything Jesus said now, but still I wonder what He was like to know as a man.'

I said, 'I'll tell you. When I was in Room Four there was a pastor who would give away everything he had—his last bit of bread, his medicine, the coat from his back. I have given these things also sometimes, when I wanted them for myself. But at other times when men were hungry and sick and in need I could be very quiet; I didn't care. This other pastor was really Christ-like. You felt that just the touch of his hand could heal and calm. One day he talked to a small group of prisoners and one asked him the question you have asked me: "What is Jesus like? I've never met anyone like the man you describe, so good and loving and truthful." And the pastor replied, in a moment of great courage, simply and humbly, 'Jesus is like me.' And the man, who had often received kindness from the pastor, answered, smiling, "If Christ was like you, then I love Him." The times when one may say such a thing as that, Josif, are very rare. But to me that is what it means to be Christian. To believe in Him is not such a great thing. To become like Him is truly great.'

'Pastor, If Jesus is like you, then I love Him, too,' Josif said. There was innocence and peace in his gaze.

The moment passed and we went on with our lesson. I told him how Jesus answered the Jews who asked for a sign so that they might believe him. 'Our ancestors,' they said, 'had bread from Heaven. Moses got it for them.' And Jesus replied, 'I am the bread of life. Whoever comes to me shall never be hungry or thirsty. Your forefathers ate, and are dead. I speak of bread which comes from Heaven, which a man may eat and never die.'

Next day Josif worked in Room Four, as he often did now. When we met in the evening he said, 'I want to be a Christian more than anything.' I baptised him with a little water from a tin mug, saying 'In the name of the Father, and the Son and the Holy Ghost.' The bitterness left his heart completely before he was released.

On the day of his departure, he embraced me. There were tears in his eyes. He said, 'You've helped me as though you were my own father. Now I can stand by myself, with God.'

Years afterwards we met again. He was a Christian. But now he was proud to bear the scar he had hated once.

12

Our prison administrators soon got over their fright at Stalin's death. There had been serious trouble in the slave-camps of Siberia, and they were determined to show no weakness. Old restrictions were revived, new ones created. The windows were closed and painted over, despite the doctors' protests, and we could open them only an inch at night when the guards were not looking. In summer the heat and stench were horrible.

Outside, too, the sufferings of the Church increased. We heard, from newly arrested Orthodox priests, how Patriarch Justinian had become wholly a tool of the Party.

One of his worst acts was his treatment of Mother Veronica, a nun venerated throughout Rumania. Years before, as an unlettered peasant girl, Veronica claimed to have had a vision of the Virgin

Mary, who appeared to her in a field and said a convent must be built on the spot. After several such apparitions had been recorded, contributions poured in, and 200 young girls took the veil. In the years that followed the Holy Virgin's shrine became a place of pilgrimage like Lourdes, and after the Communist take-over the legend that she would redeem Rumania acquired a new meaning. One day Justinian arrived in a glossy black car and began his ministrations by excommunicating the priest of the convent church. Then, as head of the Church, he told the nuns that they were wasting their time preparing for an after-life; much better go out and take their pleasures in the world—why should they forego their sexual rights for an illusion of future bliss? The nuns closed their ears to him. They refused to leave their refuge. So Justinian's visit was followed by a Security Police raid. The sisters who would not break their vows were shamefully ill-treated, and finally the convent was shut down.

The news shocked Rumania: for a time the Party was worried. Mother Veronica was subjected to intense pressure in a secret prison and made to confess that her vision had been a delusion. After her release she married and had children. That was the end of the Rumanian Lourdes.

Another blow for the faithful was the fate of Petrache Lupu, known as 'the shepherd saint' from Oltenia. While tending his flock many years before, he had seen the figure of an old man. The old man introduced himself as God, declaring that more churches must be built and money given for the poor. Although Lupu was a hereditary syphilitic who could hardly speak intelligibly, his story was believed. Thousands came to see him. When war broke out, and he was flown to the front to inspire the troops, the soldiers competed to kiss his hand. He went from one sector to another telling them that God wanted them to kill more Russians. On his arrest by the Communists, Petrache Lupu asked his fellow-prisoners when the Americans would rescue them. 'Why wait for the Yanks?' they said. 'Your "Old Man" will surely free you soon enough?' Lupu cackled, 'He'd like to, but he hasn't got a gun!'

The Orthodox priests sadly quoted another instance: that of a wonder-working monk, Arsene Boca, whose followers said they did not need to confess to him because he knew their sins at a glance. Boca spent a spell in prison. Then he gave up his habit, married and lived as other men.

Many of the blows the Party struck at religion simply lopped off branches of credulous superstition, leaving true faith sounder than ever. But human nature is such that if religious superstition is too drastically shorn it may be replaced by atheist superstition. Instead of excessive veneration for holy images we then have the idolatry of Stalin, the mass murderer, and the second devil is worse than the first.

13

A new batch of prisoners came in and one of them who had been beaten badly asked for me. I went with Professor Popp along the passage.

It was Boris. The old trade unionist had been in several prisons since re-education ended. He lay on the stone floor where the guards had thrown him. The others from the cell were out on exercise and no one had given him any help until Popp came past. We eased him on to a plank bed. His grubby shirt was stuck to him with congealed blood. Slowly and painfully we soaked it off, revealing a back criss-crossed with lash strokes, fresh and old. It was his reward for co-operating with the re-educators, and the reward of all his companions who had thought to win favour with the Party by wielding a truncheon.

The prisoners began to file in from exercise, and many cast looks of hatred and contempt at Boris.

'I asked for it,' said the old fellow as Popp and I cleaned the wounds.

'You got it!' said someone.

Boris clutched my arm. 'I met someone you know. Patrascanu gave me a message for you.'

Boris said that Lucretiu Patrascanu, the former Communist Minister of Justice who had shared my cell after our arrest in 1948, was dead. During the year of uncertainty which followed Stalin's end, the Party bosses were as fearful as our guards that they might be submerged in a counter-revolution. They saw the imprisoned Patrascanu as a man with a popular following who might lead a liberalising movement and take revenge on them. After six years in jail, he was given a rushed trial and death sentence.

Boris had been with him briefly. He said that Patrascanu, who had done so much to bring Communism to power, was tortured before he died. He complained of the cold and they gave him heavy clothes and put him in chains. 'Still cold?' they said, and heated the cell until, gasping and soaked in sweat, he begged them to turn off the steam heat. They did so, after stripping him to his shirt, and then let the cell temperature fall to freezing. So Patrascanu was alternately roasted and frozen, and since he did not die, he was taken out and shot.

Boris said, 'He told me, "If you meet Wurmbrand again, tell him he was right."'

Dr Aldea came. 'We'll have to take you to Room Four,' he said to Boris.

14

I spent all the time I could with Boris in the 'death room', and after a few days he seemed to be on the mend. Although his pride would not let him admit it, he was happy to be back in an atmosphere of human kindness.

He nodded towards his neighbour, a Jehovah's Witness. 'Old Losonczi's praying for me. He says enough prayers for both of us.' Raising his voice, he said, 'Losonczi, you tell God everything, don't you?'

The old fellow said, 'I ask good for us all.'

'You haven't had an answer yet,' said Boris. 'He's pulling your leg, perhaps; trying you out, like Job!'

He caught hold of my wrist. 'It's something to explain, isn't it? Year after year, men pray for liberty, for news of their families, for one single meal they might enjoy. What do they get? Nothing!'

Boris went on. 'I was in Jilava, the worst prison in Rumania. My friends were praying, "God, if you love us, give us something to eat without worms in it."'

'And did the food get better?' Losonczi asked.

'No, it got worse!'

I said, 'When the doctor treats you, doesn't he often have to cause you pain?' Think for a moment of animals that die in scientific experiments. If there were a dog that knew that what it went through might save the lives of millions of higher beings, might it not accept pain willingly, even death? I believe that what we suffer may be serving future generations. Jesus bore His pain, knowing that it would save mankind.'

Losonczi intervened. 'All over the world, every day, people say "Our father" and declare that His Kingdom shall come, and it does not come. But I think I know why. It's because the people who pray don't really want it to! They say, "Thy Kingdom come" but it's not a prayer from the heart. What they really want is the Iron Guard back, or the Americans to come, or the King to return, or anyone else to come who will help them.'

Boris was listening seriously.

'But the last thing in their minds, be sure, is the Kingdom of Heaven, though they could have it for certain if they thought and worked for it. In my village we had a service to pray for the poor. Everyone was there except one rich farmer, whose pew was empty. While we were thinking how much better we were than he, his son arrived with four sacks of wheat. He put them down at the church door, and said, "My father has sent his prayer". That man *did* something to create the Kingdom of God.'

I said, 'You're answered, Boris! The Bible promised that the Jews would come from the ends of the earth and be given their kingdom in Palestine—but the prophecy might not have come true for another 1,000 years if men like Herzl and Weizmann had not worked and struggled to fulfil it.'

Others nearby, gaunt, earnest men in this room of death, asked me questions about the meaning of prayer and how it could help. I spoke aloud my thoughts. 'Many look on God as if He were a rich man to whom they appeal for favours. Many cling to superstition. But Christians in prison know that we must try to achieve a purer form of religion, even though it is not for everyone. Our prayers take the form of meditation, acceptance, love.

'Millions call on the Father daily. But since we on earth are the children of God, and children share their father's responsibilities, then these prayers are turned to us, too. Is not the Father to whom all pray in my heart?

'So, when I say "Hallowed be Thy name", I must hallow God's name. "Thy Kingdom come," so I must fight to end the rule of mad beasts over a great part of the world. "Thy will be done," and the will of good men, not bad. "Forgive us our sins," so I must also forgive. "Lead us not into temptation," so I must keep others from being tempted. "Deliver us from evil," so I must do all I can to free man from sin.'

Losonczi and I became friends. He was an interesting man, a farmer, whose simple good sense shone through the strange views he held as a Jehovah's Witness. I found that the sect had chosen him, not he the sect. Disillusioned with the Orthodox Church, and seeking religion because of a personal crisis in his life, he had embraced the first faith he met. There were many of these 'refugees' from the larger confessions. Had Losonczi been drawn into a legally approved sect such as the Baptists or Adventists he would not have been serving a twenty-year sentence as one of the outlawed Witnesses.

One day, as I was talking to him, he asked me, 'Do you know why I am really here?' It was not, he said, only because the Party hated the Witnesses for their rigid attitude. 'Years ago I committed a great sexual sin. I repented and asked God to let me suffer and atone for it. I am still atoning.'

Losonczi was not in a state to listen to another doctrine now. He was dying.

'Even the saints had difficulty in subduing their carnal nature,' I said. 'Jesus knew this. He has atoned for our sins, and there's no need for you to go on atoning by yourself.' He replied, 'I can't forget'.

A few days later I came into the room and found Losonczi's bed empty. He had died during the night.

15

The old man had died thinking of a sexual sin in his youth, and here he did not suffer alone. Sex was an abiding torment to everyone in jail. Prisoners sat gazing at nothing, their heads filled with fantasies of men and women in the act of sex, and in every perversion of it. They tried to find relief in endless talk and often in baiting me with provocative questions.

Married men, thinking of what their wives were doing, suffered most of all. A good half had already been divorced in their absence; the pressure to divorce 'counter-revolutionaries' was strong, and wives who had left their imprisoned husbands for other men had no reason to resist it.

A leader in the obsessive sex-talk had once owned a department store and—according to his own account—seduced many pretty girl assistants. A fleshy man of middle age, Nicolas Frimu took pride in his prison nickname, 'The Great Lover'. He boasted often of the young actress wife who, he said, adored him.

When he was called to the Commandant's office, he expected to hear the result of his appeal against sentence. 'I'll soon be out now,' he said. 'And then—!' he kissed his fingers loudly.

He was back soon, flushed with rage. 'My appeal's been rejected—and she's divorced me and re-married!' he exploded. For several minutes, without pause, he described the revenge he would take on the woman and her new husband—a director of the State theatre. Other discarded husbands urged him on, shouting and laughing bitterly as they invented still more atrocious punishments.

I said, 'But how many of us would be faithful to our wives if we were free and they in jail?'

'Don't start lecturing!' shouted Frimu.

I said: 'I'm sorry about your bad news. But you're always talking about the girls you've led astray: how can you expect women to be pure, with men like you about!'

Novac, a dean who was usually reserved and shy, surprised us by saying, 'The husband is not always to blame. I tried to make my wife happy. I thought I had. When I went home after my first prison term, my front door was opened by a stranger. My wife came out and said, "I'm married to him—so please go!" I tried to speak to her, but she wouldn't listen. "I've had enough trouble, I want no more counter-revolutionaries in my home," she shouted. So I spent my first night of freedom in a railway station waiting-room.'

'More fool you!' said Frimu.

Petre, an airman, asked, 'How about the second night?'

The dean flushed and turned away.

Emil, a farmer, trembled with anger as he told how he had returned after a previous sentence. 'My dog scented me from half-way down the street. She tore her chain from the fence and rushed to greet me, and when I bent down she jumped up to lick my face. Then I went into the house, and found my wife in bed with another man.'

He glared round at us. 'Which of the two was the dog, Pastor?'

16

The Communist Party worked deliberately to corrode morality. But, putting this factor aside, was Christian teaching in sexual matters respected? It seemed unlikely from the talk in prison, and a handful of Christian prisoners tried to find out by asking for a truthful answer to a simple question: 'Have you always obeyed the basic rules of the Christian church in remaining chaste in word thought and deed before marriage, and faithful thereafter?'

Of 300 prisoners, all nominal Christians, two men answered yes. One was saintly old Father Suroianu, and the other a boy of fifteen.

We sat comparing notes. General Stavrat said, 'The church will have to think again. An army cannot go into battle with orders which no one obeys.'

'To preach what nobody practises devalues all a priest may have to say,' remarked Stancu, the journalist.

'We cannot go against the Bible,' objected Dean Novac.

'Surely not,' I said. 'But though we cannot compromise with sin, we must have more understanding for the sinner. In Biblical times women wore veils and dresses like tents. You had to be a virtuoso of vice then to lead a girl astray. Nowadays their clothes are designed to lure the male, and opportunities abound.

'We can remember how Jesus treated the woman taken in adultery. Nobody there could cast the first stone. They crept away and Jesus asked, "Woman, has no one condemned you? Go, and sin no more."'

The dean was worried. 'Young people have so much licence today. They need guidance.'

I agreed, but added, 'We must also teach that sex is a gift that God gives mankind. We must tell the whole truth to free it from any taint of obscenity. There is divinity here. The world's oldest religious book, the "Maneva-Darma Sostra", says: "Woman is an altar to which man brings as a pleasing sacrifice to God, his seed." '

'Most of us look at a woman in a more humdrum way,' complained Stancu. 'She's something to be used. An object of pleasure, or a well-dressed doll to be seen about with. A slave to clean and cook, or an idol in whose service a man can lose himself. Nobody seems to regard her as an equal, even in sexual enjoyment.'

'The main thing is to choose a partner who can make you happy,' said the dean.

'Or vice-versa,' I suggested. 'One of the happiest men I knew chose the plain girl of the village because he thought she would find no one else to marry.'

'What a romantic!' scoffed Stancu. 'Marriage is only a contract. When my parents found a nice girl with the right size of dowry, the deal was done. We've been quite content, going our own ways.'

'So you're not really married at all,' I said.

'The knot was tied in church!'

'I consider a marriage for material interest is invalid in God's sight, even if it's blessed by the Pope in Rome.'

Stancu laughed. 'Then there must be plenty of invalid marriages about. Boys sell themselves to rich girls, just as poor girls are sold to rich men. Isn't it more unreasonable to be valued for good looks, which don't last, then a solid bank balance, which does?'

I answered by telling Stancu about a young woman whose parents had made her marry a wealthy man. After years of unhappiness she fell in love with the tailor who made her clothes, and went to live with him. Many church-goers would have nothing to do with her. To live with a man out of wedlock is sin, but I tried to understand her position. Her parents, by beatings and other means, had forced her into this marriage. The best thing was not to despise this woman, but to help her by encouraging her to put things which were irreversible in order legally. I asked my people not to judge her hastily.

'The young woman came in tears to thank me. I said that the register of church members was not the same as the register God keeps in Heaven. "God has understanding even if not approval for the feelings which brought you to the arms of another man. God continues to love you." She flung her arms round my neck and kissed me, and at that moment my wife came in.'

The others roared with laughter. Stancu asked, 'And how did you explain the situation to her?'

'There was nothing to explain,' I said. 'The woman lived happily with the tailor, and when he died, years later, I told my wife what had happened.'

17

Prisons are supposed to encourage homosexuality, but we saw no evidence of this, perhaps because of the illness, the exhaustion, the overcrowding we had to live with. Professor Popp spoke strongly against one or two suspected instances.

I said that we should condemn the sin, but try to understand these often unhappy men and forgive their failings, as we did other human faults, and try to cure them. Many great men had been homosexual—Alexander, Hadrian, Plato, Leonardo; and many had shown a deep Christian feeling in their work, from Socrates—who was called 'a Christian before Christ'— to Michelangelo and, in our own time, Oscar Wilde and André Dunant, who founded the International Red Cross.

'Yes, I know their honours list,' said Popp, 'but so many of them, in the theatre and so on, flaunt their problem and turn a private matter into a public one. Since society condemns this tendency, they should at least practise a little pudency.'

A rabbi recalled a word of advice from that book of great practical wisdom, the Talmud. 'It says that if a rabbi cannot conquer a bad impulse, he should at least avoid scandal, put on a veil and go to another town; and then return to preach the law.'

Paul Cernei, a young man who had once been in the Iron Guard, had been lying on a nearby bed. Now he swung his feet to the floor and said, 'I'll put a real problem to you. One that wrecked my life . . . Some years ago I met a girl—let's call her Jenny. We fell in love. She would never let me take her home, so in the end I decided to ask her father's approval of our marriage. When I found the house and gave my name, he came out and said, "My son, Jenny has told me all about you!" I looked at him in horror. He was a rabbi, with a Star of David on his breast. I was an anti-semite. I didn't know what to do. I mumbled that I had no idea Jenny came from a Jewish family, and walked away.'

He paused. 'I never saw the girl again. I never married. I couldn't forget her. I've heard that she's still single, too.'

Cernei told the story movingly. Stavrat said, 'When you get out, it may not be too late . . .'

'But if we could get married,' Cernei asked, 'who should change religions? I'm Orthodox and she's a Jewess.'

I said, 'Either your faith has meaning for you, and then you can't change it for anything in the world; or it doesn't, and then you might as well abandon it. But since you love each other, why can't you both keep the religion of your choice?'

'I'd want children,' he replied. 'We should have to bring them up in one religion or another.'

I thought that as the children grew up, Cernei and his wife could both explain their beliefs—each respecting the other's—and let the children choose for themselves later on. 'You could make your love a means to bring her, with meekness, to the truth.'

'Her parents would never approve her change of religion,' Cernei said.

'She should listen to them, certainly, but she shouldn't submit if she knows they're wrong.'

Stavrat shook his head. 'Honour thy father and thy mother,' he quoted.

'But, general,' said Cernei, 'my father left the house while I was still in the cradle. My mother went off with someone else. I was brought up in an orphanage.'

No one could find an answer to that.

'I wish I'd stopped to think before I walked away that day,' Cernei said.

How often I heard prisoners speak words like that. We are like cars with headlights behind. Looking back, we see the damage we have done and the people we have hurt. We realise too late that if we had only stopped to count the cost to our families, our health or simply our self-respect, we would not have acted as we did.

When Cernei left us, the general said, 'He's a decent young man. People always blame a bad upbringing when men go wrong these days, but bad blood matters too. We take care in breeding animals, but degraded, worthless criminals are not discouraged from breeding their kind.'

Christians cannot ignore this fundamental problem of heredity. We try to reform the adult, or punish the criminal, but we never ask would-be parents to consider whether something in their descent may harm the unborn. Sex does not exist only to bring babies into the world: it has its own value in making life nobler and happier. And this is our excuse when we bring children into the world casually, for a moment's pleasure, and forget that procreation is a sacred act.

Most prisoners, who are always short of food, put sexual need on an equal footing. At the Last Judgment men will be reproached for failing to feed the hungry; and they will be reproached, too, some say, if they have not satisfied their partners' thirst after love, whenever they could have done, ennobling their partners and making them happier.

There is sexual injustice, of course, just as there is social and economic injustice. It is one of the great causes of human suffering. But then every law, even divine law, has unavoidably an element of injustice in it in giving the same tasks to unequal men living in unequal conditions. The law lays down the same rules for rich and poor, for under-sexed and over-sexed, for the ignorant and the intellectual.

Marriage must be a question of honour. It is a duty you take upon yourself—to be faithful. Love is a sentiment, and all sentiments change: nobody loves or is angry for ever in equal measure. It is a law of nature that passion lowers in intensity as one grows older, so it cannot be a guarantee of a happy marriage, either. There must be something else: the decision to be loyal, the decision to make the other happy.

Since it is obviously impossible to satisfy everyone's sexual need, we discussed chastity as an alternative. The Catholics spoke up in favour of celibacy for the priesthood.

I said, 'If celibacy is imposed, and marriage forbidden by vow, then failure to abstain may damage a priest's faith.'

'It can become a great creative force,' the professor said. 'It's doubtful whether Spinoza, Kant, Descartes, Newton, Beethoven ever knew a woman in the Biblical sense.'

I thought the chief aid to be given was to teach men to sublimate this natural drive into works useful to society and God. Chastity, in my view, was for the few. Yet we must understand more and more that our bodies are not ours to misuse for selfish pleasure, but temples of God, to be consecrated to His service.

18

Popp and I took turns to look after Boris, who lay in Room Four, coughing weakly. Dr. Aldea said, 'If he eats, he may last ten days. My visits are not really helping him. He's filled with remorse over that beating he gave me. It harms him to see me.'

I asked if the man could be moved into my cell. Aldea arranged it. So Boris was carried to the bed next to mine, and I nursed him through the last week of his life.

He withered away under our eyes. His hair was reduced to a few strands, his cheeks were sunken. He sweated feverishly, as I sponged him down, day after day.

'All over soon,' he murmured. 'A priest once told me "You'll rot in hell". So be it!'

'What made him speak like that?' I asked.

'I was cursing God for my sufferings. He said I'd be punished for eternity.'

A pastor named Valentin intervened: 'Men curse the Communist Party, but eventually it may release them. If hell were endless, then God would be worse than our Secret Police.'

Boris opened his eyes. 'Do you mean you don't believe in Everlasting Fire?'

'The Biblical doctrine of the endlessness of hell is true subjectively, no doubt, but what *is* hell? Dostoievsky calls it a state of conscience, and he was an Orthodox believer. In the "Brothers Karamazov" he wrote of hell, "I believe it is the suffering of being unable to love." '

'I don't think I'd mind that sort of hell,' said Boris.

I said, 'Perhaps you've never known what it may be to live where there is no love. When the bad have only the bad for company, imagine what it will be like! It is said that when Hitler went to hell he looked about until he found Mussolini. "What's it like down here?" he asked. Mussolini replied, "Not so bad, but there's a lot of forced labour." Then he began to sob. "Come, Duce," said Hitler, "let's know the worst." "Well, then, it's this—Stalin's in charge of the working party!"

Boris smiled. 'I'd certainly hate to find my old boss Ana Pauker down below.' He lay thinking. 'That Catholic priest who told me I'd burn for blasphemy was a good man. He never harmed anyone, but he still thought that, simply for revenge, God would torture me endlessly. The God he believed in was worse than he.'

Pastor Valentin said, 'I don't doubt that those in hell feel it as an eternal punishment. In this sense the Bible calls it endless, as prison seems endless to us. But, even under the worst conditions, we see men coming to love God and to realise they have done wrong. Dives, in Jesus's parable of poor Lazarus, shows signs of a change of heart in hell! He had been an egotist, now he is concerned about his brothers. Nothing is fixed anywhere in nature. If there is some evolution in hell towards goodness, then it opens a door to hope!'

Boris called weakly to prisoners on bunks nearby, 'Good news, my lads! Pastor Valentin says we may not fry for ever, after all!'

There was laughter. Frimu, Stavrat and others came across to us.

'Well,' asked Frimu, 'what's going to be my punishment?'

Frimu was a gluttonous man. I said, 'The early Christians used to tell of a man who went to hell and was surprised to find a banquet laid. He recognised many historical figures around the table. "Do you always feast like this?" he asked. "Certainly, we may order whatever we wish!" "Then what is your punishment?" "It is that we can never bring the hand which holds the food to our mouths." The newcomer saw a way out. "But can't each of you feed your neighbour and let him feed you?" "What!" cried the other. "Help *him*? I'd rather go on starving!" '

General Stavrat said 'I was taught at school and in church that God will punish eternally those who die unrepentant and without faith. It is the received dogma.'

'Received in your mind, but not, perhaps in your heart, general. We see men around us cursing God and denying his existence because they suffer unjustly. They will surely be judged according to their deeds and words and thoughts. And then? Suppose you see a stranger in danger of being killed—you'd be the first to run and help him. And if a Christian really believed that his neighbour will be tortured in all eternity in hell, he should try day and night to persuade him to repent and believe. How sad that this doesn't happen.'

19

Boris's old prejudices fell away one by one, but instead of becoming cheerful he grew depressed. 'I feel I've wasted my life,' he said. 'I thought myself clever. I've misled a great many people in the last fifty years. If your God exists, he won't want me in Heaven! So down I go to join that old sow Pauker—I'm really scared now!'

Often when he could not sleep he asked me to talk to him.

'Who's going to pray for me when I'm gone?' he asked. He thought Lutherans forbade prayer for the dead. I said that Luther simply did not want people to suppose that, however much they sinned, they might pay a priest to pray them out of purgatory.

Pastor Valentin said: 'We pray for our fellow-prisoners, who are dying every day. It wouldn't be an act of love to stop praying just when the soul leaves the body—because Catholics and Protestants quarrelled about public prayer 400 years ago.'

'And does prayer help them?'

'Yes,' he said. 'Before God all are living—and so they are for me. And if they are living, I am sure prayer can help them.'

'If I were you, I wouldn't waste prayers on me.' He laughed a little at this, and brought on a fit of coughing.

Valentin said, 'I'm sure you've done much good. There are

certainly many worse men. But I pray for the worst of all—Stalin, Hitler, Himmler, Beria.'

'What do you pray?' Boris asked me with a weak voice.

I said: 'God, forgive the great sinners and criminals and, among the worst of men, me also.'

I sat with Boris a long time. It was so quiet that we could hear Frimu's boastful voice in the next cell. There was laughter and giggling over his sexual exploits.

For some hours, Boris was silent. I thought he was asleep. Suddenly he murmured, 'What can it be like?'

'What?' I asked him.

'The judgment of God. Does he sit on a tall throne, saying "Hell, Heaven . . . Hell, Heaven" as the souls come before him? I can't see it, myself.'

I told him how I imagined it.

'God sits on a throne with a great curtain behind Him and, one by one, we come before Him. Then God makes a sign with His right hand, and from behind the curtain come beings each more beautiful than the other: so splendid that we cannot bear to look at them. Each of these beings stands before one of those to be judged. We who are accused ask, "Who is this beautiful being with me?" God answers, "That is you, as you would have been if you had obeyed Me." And then comes, for the disobedient, the eternal hell of remorse.'

'Remorse,' Boris whispered.

During the night he had a haemorrhage. I had a difficult time with him; then he fell into a coma. He lay quietly, his eyes staring blindly at the ceiling for an hour. His pulse was weak but still present under my fingers. Suddenly he pulled his hand away and half sat up. He gave a cry which seemed to tear soul from body, 'Lord God, forgive me!'

Some of the prisoners around us awoke and muttered angrily, before going back to sleep.

When dawn came, I began to wash the body and prepare it for burial, and while I was doing this, someone informed the Orthodox bishop in a cell down the corridor that a man had died. He came along and began the ritual. I went on with my work. Now and then the bishop interrupted himself to hiss at me, 'Stand up!

Show some respect!' but I did not look up. When the ritual was finished, the bishop upbraided me again.

I said, 'Where were you when this man was dying all last week? Did you hold a cup to his mouth when he wanted water? Why do you come only now to perform a ceremony which meant nothing to him?'

We were both angry. His ritual seemed such a hollow thing beside that simple cry from the depths of the heart, 'Lord God, forgive me!'

20

Spring, 1955, brought signs of a political thaw. A number of prison commandants were arrested for 'sabotage'. To Tirgul-Ocna came many of the slave workers who had been victims of the 'saboteurs'. Beds had to be found for them, and I was among a group who were ordered in early June to get ready for transfer to another jail.

Dr. Aldea said, 'You're not fit to move, but there's nothing we can do. Take care of yourself. And if you lay hands on any more streptomycin—don't give it away!'

I said goodbye to my friends amid many tears.

'We'll meet again: I know it,' said Professor Popp.

I heard my name shouted, and joined a line of men out in the yard. We were a bizarre gathering, with our shaven heads and suits of many patches, each clutching a bundle of rags—all that we possessed. Some could hardly walk; nevertheless, those of us serving long sentences were ordered to march a step forward and then lie on the ground while our ankles were chained.

The political officer stood over the blacksmith as he moved from man to man. When my turn came, the officer smiled unpleasantly.

'Ah, Vasile Georgescu! Surely you have something to say about being put in irons?'

Lying on my side, I looked up and replied, 'Yes, lieutenant, I can answer you in song.'

He folded his hands behind his back and said, 'Oh, please! I'm sure we'd all like to hear you.'

I sang the opening words of the Republic's anthem, 'Broken

chains are left behind us . . .' The blacksmith's hammer finished the task in a few more blows, and in the uneasy silence I added, 'You sing that broken chains are left behind—but this régime has put more people in chains than any other.'

The lieutenant had not found a reply when a shout from the guard-room announced the arrival of transport. We were taken to the station and herded into wagons. There we lay for hours before the train began to creak and rattle across country. Through holes in the tiny, painted-out windows, we glimpsed forest land and mountains. It was a warm and beautiful summer's day.

PART FIVE

THE journey across the plains westwards from Bucharest was about 200 miles, but there were so many stops and starts that it took almost two days and nights. Word of our destination went round even before the thick, 100-year-old walls of notorious Craiova Prison came into sight.

Our chains were struck off in the stone-flagged courtyard, and we were goaded with blows along dark passages thick with dirt. We were thrust, in small groups, into cells along a gallery. Loud protests came from inside them: 'There's no room here! We're suffocating already!' The guards squeezed the new arrivals in forcibly. It was like rush hour on the underground railway, with the porters wielding truncheons.

A push in the spine sent me stumbling forwards and the door banged behind me. The stench in the cell made me feel sick. At first I could see nothing. I felt about, and my hand drew back from an almost naked, sweating body. Slowly, as I grew used to the dim light from a ceiling bulb, I saw rows of bunks rising in tiers, packed with men who lay gasping for breath. More men, also half-naked, sat on the floor, or leant against the walls. No one could move without waking a neighbour, whose curses aroused everyone else.

My stay in this cell over the next two months was broken only by journeys to the stinking sump outside, carrying lavatory pails.

I told the prisoners I was a pastor, and said a brief prayer. A few swore at me, but many listened quietly. Then someone called my name from an upper bunk hidden in the darkness.

'I recognise your voice,' he said. 'I heard your speech at that Congress of Cults many years ago.'

I asked who he was. He replied, 'We'll speak tomorrow.'

The long night ended at 5 a.m., when reveille was sounded by a guard who beat on a dangling piece of railway line with an iron bar. The man from the upper bunk, a little fellow with a twist of cloth around his head, came down to shake my hand.

'It's as well I knew your voice in the dark,' he said, gazing at me with bloodshot eyes. 'I wouldn't have recognised you by sight. The Party has had its revenge for your protest, I see. How thin you are!'

He was a hodja called Nassim, who had represented the small Moslem community at the 1945 Congress of Cults.

Our friendship began while I was trying to eat my first meal at Craiova. The vile, greasy smell of the soup preceded its arrival in the cell. Shreds of rotten cabbage and unwashed offal floated in a scum. But to eat was a duty and I emptied my dish.

'How can you?' asked the hodja, whose stomach had revolted.

It was a Christian secret, I said. 'I think of St. Paul's words "Rejoice with those that rejoice." Then I remember friends in America who are now eating grilled chicken, and I thank God with them as I take the first mouthful of soup. Next, I rejoice with friends in England who may be eating roast beef. And I get down another mouthful. So, by way of many friendly countries, I rejoice with those that rejoice—and stay alive.'

The Hodja and I had to share a bunk through the hot, stuffy nights. I was lucky not to be on the floor.

'You lie very still,' he said as others coughed and fidgeted around us. 'What are you thinking? Does St. Paul help you now, too?'

I replied, 'Yes, for now I rejoice with those in the West by thinking of their comfortable homes, and the books they have, the holidays they can plan, the music they hear, the love they have for their wives and children. And I remember the second part of the verse, from the Epistle to the Romans, "And weep with those that weep". I am sure that in the West many thousands think of us and try to help us with their prayers.'

2

All men in prison feel a need to assert themselves. They like to argue. They flare up at a word. And when they find someone who does not return insult for insult, they torment him all the more. In the conditions of Craiova the difficulties I faced were almost insuperable. When I preached I had to raise my voice over groans and pretended snores. The prisoners were desperately bored. They had no inner resources and they longed for their familiar distractions. I found that sermons turned into discussions, and then into quarrels. But anyone who could tell a story, particularly a crime story, was sure of an audience. So I told them thrillers of my own invention, in which the Christian message played a central but inconspicuous part.

My most popular hero was a bandit called Pipa, whose name everyone in Rumania knew. I described how my mother, as a girl, had once seen him in court and had never forgotten his savage, hunted looks.

Pipa's parents were wealthy. They died while he was still a boy, leaving him in the care of a guardian, who cheated him of his property. Pipa took work at an inn, where the owner promised to keep his wages for him until he returned from military service, so that he could set up his own business. When Pipa returned from the army, the inn-keeper denied their agreement, and in blind fury the youth stabbed him to death.

Pipa became an outlaw. From his mountain lair he made a series of raids—all on inns. Over the years he killed thirty-six inn-keepers. (Amazed whistles from my listeners at this point.) He did not lack company. With two other outlaws, all in their best stolen clothes, he went down to a village and persuaded three girls to dine with them. They drugged the wine and carried the girls to their cave.

So much was fact; but at this point in my version the girls, awakening, kept their captors at arm's length by telling them stories, in the style of the 'Thousand and One Nights'. These romances ended with the prettiest girl relating the story of the Gospel and winning the outlaws over.

'Pastor,' said a forester called Radion, 'I've heard many crime stories, but none like yours, which always end with the criminal, the victim and the policeman all going to church together.'

Well received also was an epic account of Dillinger, whose progress from hungry down-and-out to America's worst gangster was the pattern for many lives in the cell. A ruined childhood, or social injustice, are the usual preludes to a criminal career, and Dillinger had begun his by robbing a cinema cashier of a few dollars.

When we understood how Pipa and Dillinger had become what they were we could pity them, I said; and from pity came love, and love among mankind was the chief aim of Christianity. We condemn men, but how rarely we offer the love which might save them from crime.

I could have spoken for twenty-four hours a day without exhausting the demand for stories. I began to draw on classics with a Christian viewpoint: Dostoievsky's 'Crime and Punishment', Tolstoy's 'Resurrection', told in episodes.

Often the other prisoners told their own stories, farcical, tragic or both. Radion, tall and lean as the trees he used to tend, had led an uneventful life, until the day when he passed through a wood with two friends and looked back to see the forest in flames.

'When we reached the next village we were arrested and charged with starting the fire,' he said. 'We were beaten until we confessed that we'd done it to sabotage the local "collective". But at our trial the real culprit came forward, and we were acquitted.

'We were not freed. They took us back to the police station and said, "Now confess what else you have done!" Under torture, we confessed to a sabotage plot that was a complete invention. I would have said anything to stop the pain!' They were sentenced to fifteen years each.

There were many stories like this at Craiova. Before long we knew each other inside out. It was a nervous, highly-charged atmosphere. No one could bear contradiction, and all sense of proportion or logic was lost.

When I re-told Knut Hamsun's novel 'Hunger', many eyes were bright, and a prisoner called Herghelegiu told me, as the group broke up for supper, how touched he had been. I suggested that he might offer a little of his bread to the hodja, who feared that the food might contain pig-fat, forbidden by the Koran. But if Herghelegiu was moved to the heart, he was not moved to the stomach. My proposal was ignored.

The intellectuals were prisoners of words. If someone mentioned an American scientific discovery, it was scoffed at as US propaganda. If someone talked of a modern Russian writer, he would be dismissed as a state-subsidised hack. Catholics rejected unheard the wisdom of Jewish philosophers. The Jews knew little of the thought of the church.

Once I described a religious book I had been thinking out at nights. Judgment was instantly passed. 'Riddled with Lutheranism!' cried one Orthodox listener. 'It's easy to see you're a Protestant,' said another. Some days later, during a conversation with the same couple, I quoted extensively from 'The Problem of Truth', by a 'great Rumanian writer' called Naie Ionescu. The reception was rapturous. I decided that if ever I wanted a fair hearing for my views, they had better be published anonymously, since both books were the same.

Alexandru, a student, raised patronising smiles when he recited some verses of his own. I quietly suggested that he should read another one, which was announced as a Shakespearian sonnet. 'Superb!' the critics chorused. Without revealing Alexandru's secret, I told them one should not be over-awed by famous names. Shakespeare, Byron,—to take English poets only—often exalted unworthy ideas.

An old cavalry officer disagreed. 'I'm no literary man,' he said, 'but I've always admired Gunga Din. Kipling created a soldier's hero there!'

I said, 'Gunga Din may have been a better man than I am, but he gave his life fighting for the British against his own people. What would you say of a Rumanian who died fighting for the Russians against his countrymen?'

An English scholar championed Shakespeare's nobility of thought.

I answered that when Shakespeare was writing, the problems of the Reformation and Puritanism were drawing even street-sweepers into excited argument—yet a historian who had only Shakespeare's plays to read would hardly know that Christianity had reached England.

'In all his plays there is not a single Christian character,' I said, 'except, perhaps, for poor Cordelia. Claudius slays his rival. The Queen weds her husband's murderer. Hamlet dreams of revenge, will not act and cannot forgive. Polonius is an intriguer. Ophelia's only escape is into insanity. Othello is a professional killer. Desdemona merely plays cow to his bull. Iago is a monster of cynicism and deceit . . . Shakespeare was a magnificent poet and a born psychologist, but he had no idea of Christian character.'

The scholar said, 'Perhaps there's really no such thing as "Christian character" to describe.'

I told him that I knew he had been in prison only a few weeks; when he had been there longer, he would know better. He would see some of the goodness which I had experienced: the sinners who confessed with their last breath, the saints who forgave their murderers, as we hope to be forgiven in the end. And I quoted to him some lines which showed how great a Christian poet was lost in Shakespeare:

They say the tongues of dying men enforce attention like deep harmony,
Their words are scarce, they're seldom spent in vain
For they breathe truth that breathe their words in pain.

How well he could have applied this passage to the last words of Jesus on the Cross.

3

The little hodja had much to teach about submission to the will of God. He often reminded us that every chapter of the Koran, the most widespread book in the world after the Bible, begins with the invocation, 'In the name of Allah, the Merciful, the Compassionate', and he tried to make this precept a part of everyday life. Five times a day, Nassim knelt on the hard floor and made obeisance in the direction of Mecca.

Men made fun of him. I told them: 'When an Englishman asks for bread, a German for *brot,* an Italian for *pane,* they are all asking for the same thing. Gheorghe is a Catholic, so he makes the sign of the Cross like this. Carol, an Orthodox believer, makes it like that. Ion, a Baptist, clasps his hands. So why shouldn't Nassim address his prayers to the East? We all approach God differently, but He sees past our gestures of love and honour into the heart. That is where we should look, too.'

Nassim and I had many talks, sitting alongside on a low bunk amid the squalor and confusion of the cell. He spoke of his faith—which Moslems believe was revealed to the Prophet by the Angel Gabriel—with a fervour that momentarily transformed that dismal place. To my surprise, he talked of Jesus with great love.

'Jesus is for me a most holy and wise prophet, who speaks the language of God himself. But he cannot in our view be the Son of God. I hope I haven't offended you.'

'By no means,' I replied. 'In fact, I agree with you.'

'How can a Christian say that?'

'I say it because a son results from a man and a woman making love. No Christian believes in that sense that Jesus is the son of God. We call him "Son of God" in another, unique sense, as an emanation from the Creator. He is the Son because he bears the very stamp of God, as a man does of his father. He is the Son in the way he brims over with love and truth. In those ways we have no doubt of it.'

'In that way I, too, can accept,' said Nassim, with his grave Muslim smile.

Jesus turns away nobody who loves him, even if a man does not know the true title of the One he loves. The penitent thief spoke of Him only as a man, but Jesus promised that he should sup in paradise.

4

Prisoners came and went; only the air never changed. Each time men left, others took their place, and I started my 'parish work' again.

Among newcomers was General Calescu, a former head of Military Justice who loved to fight his battles over again. Most had taken place, he admitted, in the 'boudoir', and his best days were during the war. 'So many pretty spies—I always tried to let them off if they were kind to me!'

When Calescu was not talking of women, it was food. One evening, he announced, 'Today's my birthday: I invite you all to dinner!' And since he had spent many happy anniversaries in Paris as a young man—'We shall repair to Maxims. Be my guests!' For an hour or two, regardless of expense, he regaled us on the best the house could offer. 'Maître d'hôtel!' he called. 'What do you recommend? A *bouillabaise* of every fish, swimming in rich saffron sauce? Perhaps too much to start with? How about *foie gras,* with truffles, from Périgord, with hot toast and fresh Normandy butter? All quite simple! Then *canard à l'orange*—you like duck, don't you, pastor? Or a *coq au vin*? And, for the hodja, *shaslik* on a flaming sword!'

Each dish was accompanied by an elegaic list of wines: Burgundy and Hock, a magnum of champagne, a golden Château Yqem, liqueurs and old brandy. Cigars were chosen: Henry Clay, Romeo y Julietta. There was no stopping this panorama of pleasures. Then the door opened, and in came the usual barrel of rotting tripe and cabbage.

In this talk of food, as in day-dreams of sex, imagination took over. Simpler souls than Calescu invented fantasies of chicken stuffed with bananas, potatoes piled with strawberry jam and many other dishes now fortunately lost to mind. In fact, the food at Craiova was the worst I encountered anywhere—except for one day, when, to our complete and unbelieving surprise, the guards brought in a canister of onion soup, another of stew with real meat, white mashed potatoes, fresh carrots, two bread rolls for each man and a big basket of apples. We almost expected one of Calescu's cigars to complete the meal.

What did it mean? Prisoners see great significance in the slightest change in their routine, and we hoped for new wonders. During the afternoon General Calescu called excitedly from the window, 'Women, dammit—and they're leaving!' A crowd gathered round the bars and peered down. Half-a-dozen well-dressed women were being led towards the gate by the commandant. They were, said a guard, a delegation of 'democratic women' from the West, leaving after an hour, with comments on the excellence of the food.

The meals were even worse during the following week. Later we heard that the visitors' eye-witness reports on Rumania's model prisons were circulated in Britain, France and the United States.

5

There were several of these guided tours at the time. When the Russian leadership changes hands there is usually a brief thaw, and now, after a hidden struggle among Stalin's successors, Marshal Bulganin emerged as Chairman of the Council of Ministers.

Calescu said that the rise to power of this former War Minister meant that 'the Americans would have to fight at last'. Prison rumour supported his opinion. President Eisenhower's 'very words' on the question were quoted: 'I have only to do up the last button on my uniform and the captives of Eastern Europe will be free!'

Calescu's dream was that once the Red armies had been routed, the king would return to his throne. This faith in the monarchy was shared by the majority of farmers and landworkers. Their reasoning was simple: 'When the king was here, I had my field and my cattle. Now he's gone I have nothing.'

On Rumania's former national day, many in the cell joined in a service which included prayers for King Michael and the Royal family. The informers decided that it would be safer to look the other way. But our cell republican, the schoolmaster Constantinescu, argued against the monarchy and its 'futile ceremonial'.

Radion, the forester, said, 'Pomp and glory may mean nothing to you, but to a king they come naturally. He doesn't need to strive for them. He's not like a politician, who has to make a name with wars and revolutions, and does so always at our expense. He leaves us in peace. That's why I'm for the king!'

Radion also bested General Calescu, who liked to joke about religion.

'If Jesus could really turn wine into water,' Calescu said, 'why didn't he set up shop and make a fortune?'

Radion said, 'No-one alive can prove that the Saviour performed this miracle, surely. But I can give you the evidence of my own eyes that He can turn wine into furniture.'

'Amazing!' tittered Calescu.

'Yes,' said Radion. 'Before my conversion I used to spend every penny on drink, and my wife didn't have so much as a chair to sit on. When I gave it up, we saved the money and furnished our home instead.'

The spring brought news, this time official, which put an end to General Calescu's war games. The Russians had promised to withdraw their troops from Austria, and the first 'summit meeting' between East and West after ten years of cold warfare was to take place in Geneva.

Soon 'peaceful co-existence' was all the rage. Constantinescu was full of it. 'Why shouldn't the West live harmoniously with the Communist East?' he demanded.

I said, 'I'm no politician, but I know that the Church, at least, can never make peace with atheism, any more than police can make peace with gangsters, or disease with health.'

'You hate atheists, then?' said Constaninescu.

I replied, 'I hate atheism as a creed, but I love atheists, just as I hate blindness, but love the blind. Since atheism is a form of spiritual blindness, it must be fought.'

Constantinescu's long face registered mock surprise. 'You talk of fighting, pastor? I thought Christians turned the other cheek. Didn't St. Francis save a wolf from those who wanted to kill him, and say, "Don't kill brother wolf, he is one of God's creatures."'

'I admire St. Francis deeply,' I replied, 'but if I don't shoot brother wolf he will eat sister sheep. My duty to kill the wolf if I can't control him is inspired by love. Jesus told us to love our enemies, but He himself used force when there was no other way. God takes thousands of lives daily: it is in His nature to give death, as well as life.'

A newcomer to Craiova, the engineer Glodeanu, said he had heard BBC broadcasts which took the line that the Western powers should no longer try to interfere in the internal affairs of the Communist bloc.

I objected, 'But if I start to knock a hole in a boat which we are sharing, and say, "Don't interfere—this is my side of the boat", will you agree? No! The hole in my side will end by drowning us all!' The Communists, I went on, had seized whole countries and tried to poison youth with hatred. Their plan to overturn the established order all over the world was not an internal affair.

'It's international banditry!' said Calescu.

Constantinescu rallied. 'The West can't always be right, general,' he said, 'and Stalin wasn't wholly evil. He could say, "Man is our most precious capital." '

'So that's why we're kept locked up,' snorted Calescu. But Constantinescu insisted that there had been industrial, and even cultural, progress under Communism. 'You can't deny that,' he said.

I replied, 'A visitor to Egypt in ancient times would have been amazed by Pharaoh's monuments, but God did not admire them. They were the work of slaves, whom God sent Moses to free. In Russia and the satellites today, slave labour is building the houses, factories and schools you talk about. And what is being taught in the schools? Hatred of everything Western.'

'The Communists say they plan for the future,' said Constantinescu. 'A generation or two may be sacrificed, but the basis is being laid for the future good of mankind.'

I said, 'To make future generations happy, men must be good themselves. But Communist leaders are constantly denouncing one another as the worst of criminals. The most powerful men in the Soviet Union have been murdered by their own comrades. What Communist can be happy, knowing he may fall in the next Party purge?'

'There is good in them,' Constantinescu objected. 'No man is entirely bad, and Communists are men, who keep something of God's image.'

My reply was: 'I agree. There was even good in Hitler. He improved the lot of most Germans. He made his country the strongest in Europe. His death with Eva Braun in the bunker, his marriage with her at the last moment, might be considered moving. But who would make this point, when he murdered so many millions? Hitler gained the world for Germany, and destroyed its soul, even before his defeat. Communist successes have also been made at the expense of the soul, by crushing man's most vital element, his personality.'

'You cannot tar all Communists with the same brush,' said Constantinescu. 'Tito, for instance, is regarded as a mild dictator.'

'But they all have one aim: to carry the Communist revolution through the world, and uproot religion. "Mild" Tito has killed thousands of enemies, and jailed his friends.'

'I still say there's been progress,' said Constantinescu.

'For my part, I admire no progress that is bought with tears and blood, however impressive it may look from outside. Never has any people chosen Communism in a free election, or got rid of it with another.'

'The world wants peace; what's your alternative—atomic war?'

I said, 'Nuclear war is not the alternative; nobody wants that. The world has a great problem with drug addiction, but we don't think of adopting Hitler's solution of herding the addicts into gas chambers. All the same, we can't settle down to "peaceful co-existence" with the dope traffic; a solution must be found, even if we have to struggle for fifty years. How can we live peacefully with people who cannot stay at peace among themselves, because all their leaders want is power and then more power? The Communists lull our suspicions while they plan their next grab.'

I could make no impression on Constantinescu's resolve to take Soviet gestures at their face value. Leaning out from my bunk, I snatched his pillow—the small, lumpy bundle of personal things he used as a head-rest. His skull hit the wall. He was furious.

'But why can't you co-exist peacefully with me?' I asked. 'I'm ready to be friends, now I've stolen all you have.'

But I had to restore his property before the talk turned to other things.

Constantinescu was a victim of wishful thinking about Communism. Men trained in the school of Lenin and Stalin see goodwill as weakness to be exploited. For their own good we must work for their defeat. Love is not a universal panacea; it does not take the place of corn plaster. Communist rulers are criminals on an international scale, and only when the criminal is vanquished does he repent; only then can he be brought to Christ.

In the Roman Senate, whenever a problem was raised, Cato would reply, 'First destroy our enemy Carthage and then all things can be arranged! *Delenda est Carthaga!*' I was sure that the fate of the West was either to destroy Communism or be destroyed by it.

6

A desire to show Communism in a better light before the summit meeting diminished some of the worst excesses in the prison system. At Salcia, where punishments had included hanging prisoners by the heels and plunging women in icy water for hours, the whole staff was arrested. Official evidence said fifty-eight people had died in the competitions between 'brigade leaders' to see who could work to death the most prisoners—in fact, Salcia survivors who came to Craiova said there had been at least 800 deaths.

With a show of judicial indignation, the Salcia staff were given long sentences, and the purge had a chastening effect in other jails. Beatings stopped. Guards became carefully polite. When the Jilava commandant, Colonel Gheorghiu, asked for complaints, and had a plate of barley thrown at him, the culprit suffered nothing worse than a day in solitary confinement.

The reforms were short-lived. Soon beatings and insults became routine once more; and a year or so later, when the trials had been forgotten abroad, the mass-murderers of Salcia were reinstated, with promotion. Only the common law criminals, who had acted as their tools in torturing others, stayed in prison.

During this shake-up in the jails, I was moved several times. These nightmare journeys have merged into one in my mind. I close my eyes and see a frieze of stubble-chinned, shaven-headed convicts, jogging gently with the movement of the train. Always we wore fifty-pound chains, which chafed us through our clothes and made sores that took months to heal in our under-nourished state.

On one journey we came to a halt during the night, and the silence was broken by a wail of anguish: 'I've been robbed!'

I sat up to find little Dan, a petty crook from Bucharest, moving from one prone figure to the next, shaking everyone awake. Dan was cursed and cuffed, but he went on howling, 'I had 500 lei hidden away and it's gone! It's all I had in the world!'

In the hope of quietening him, I said, 'My friend, I hope you don't suspect a pastor of stealing, but if you do you may search me to the skin.'

The others also allowed Dan to search them for the sake of peace, but nothing was found. The train moved off at last and, one by one, we fell asleep. I was awakened at dawn by a new and worse uproar. All the other eighteen prisoners had been robbed as well.

'I knew we had a thief among us!' Dan cried.

Days later, at Poarta-Alba, our next stop, I told the story to a man serving a year for theft. Bursting with laughter, he said, 'I've known Dan for years. He simply wanted to find out where each of you kept anything worth lifting!'

There were many 'Dans' at Poarta-Alba, where 'politicals' and common criminals were held together. Once I dozed off while a group were playing with home-made dice. A tickle on my foot awoke me. I sat up rubbing my eyes, to find a prisoner unlacing one of my shoes. The other was already off.

'What are you doing with my shoes?' I demanded.

'I've just won them at dice,' he grinned, and was offended when I would not give them up.

It is a world apart, the world of thieves. I found that they like to talk of their exploits, the riskier the better. They loved the excitement as other men love drink, gambling or women. I wondered at the dedication they brought to their work.

One evening, when most prisoners were outside, the door crashed open and the guards flung in a pickpocket, known to everyone as 'Fingers'. He rolled on the floor, gasping and groaning, as I helped him to his bunk. Soaking a rag in water, I began to wash the blood from his swollen mouth. It seemed he had been pilfering from the kitchen.

'You're not a bad sort, pastor,' Fingers said. 'When I get out and make my next good haul, I won't forget your share.'

I said I hoped he would find a better means of living. He

laughed. 'They're wasting their time beating me,' he said. 'I love my work. I'll never give it up.'

I put my arm around his shoulder and told him, 'Thank you. You've taught me a great lesson.'

'What do you mean?' Fingers asked.

'If beatings don't persuade you to give up your ways, why should I listen to those who want me to change mine? I must put at least as much thought into winning a soul as you do into pulling off your next coup. The more I listen to the stories which you and your friends tell, the more I learn.'

He grinned painfully, 'You're joking, pastor'.

'No,' I said. 'For example, you work at night, and if you fail the first night, you try again the next. So I, as a pastor, should spend my night in prayer, and if I don't get what I want, I shouldn't give up. You steal from others, but there is honesty among thieves: we Christians should be as united among ourselves. And although you risk your liberty and lives for money, as soon as you get it you throw it right and left; we should not overvalue money, either. You thieves don't let punishment deter you; nor should we shrink from suffering. Just as you hazard everything, so too, should we, knowing there is a paradise to win.'

The prison at Poarta-Alba consisted of the remains of the labour camp beside the canal project on which my wife had been forced to work. I knew that now she was living somehow in Bucharest. No hour passed without thoughts of her. We lived in long, bare huts which held fifty men each. All around were derelict barracks and vegetable patches which Sabina must have known. This melancholy comfort was taken from me when, after a few weeks, I was told to prepare for another move.

Fingers came up to say good-bye. With him was an associate called Calapod, a villainous bandit who had been feared throughout the countryside. He slapped me on the back, shouting, 'So this is the Holy Reverend who likes thieves and robbers!'

'Mr. Calapod,' I said, 'Jesus did not mind comparing himself with a thief. He promised, "I will come as a thief in the night". Just as those whom you have robbed never knew you were coming, so one night Jesus will come for your soul, and you will not be ready.'

7

Weeks in the dank chill of Craiova and Poarta-Alba, and on journeys in chain-gangs, worsened my tuberculosis. I arrived at my next prison at Gherla, in the Transylvanian mountains, in such a state that I was put into one of a group of cells known as 'the hospital'. Our doctor, a young woman called Marina, said this was her first post. Other patients told me that on her first day she had turned pale as she went from cell to cell. Nothing in her training had prepared her for the dirt, the hunger, the lack of simple medicines and equipment, the uncaring cruelty. They thought she was going to faint, but she carried on.

Marina was a tall, fragile girl with fair hair framing an exhausted face. After an examination, she told me, 'You need good food and plenty of fresh air.'

I could not help laughing. 'But don't you know where we are, Dr. Marina?'

Tears rose in her eyes. 'That's what I learnt at medical school.'

Some days later, high-ranking officers came on a visit. Dr. Marina tackled them in the gallery outside our cells. 'Comrades, these men haven't been sentenced to death. The state pays me to keep them alive, just as it pays you to keep them safe. I only ask for conditions which will allow me to do my job.'

A man's voice said, 'So you side with convicted outlaws!'

'They may be outlaws to you, Comrade Inspector,' she replied, 'but to me they are patients.'

Conditions got no better, but instead we had news that was worth all the drugs in the pharmacopoeia to me. Before the summit meeting at Geneva, visits by relatives were to be allowed.

Excitement mounted high. We were all nervous. At one moment a man would be filled with joy; at another, near to tears. Some had been ten or twelve years without news of their families. I had not seen Sabina for eight.

The day came, and when my name was called I was marched into an echoing hall and made to stand behind a table. Some twenty yards further on, I saw my wife, behind another table. The commandant, flanked by officers and guards, stood near the wall between us, as if ready to umpire a tennis match.

I gazed at Sabina, and it seemed to me that in the years of her suffering she had achieved a peace and beauty such as I had never seen before. She stood there with folded hands, smiling.

Gripping the table, I called, 'Are you well at home?'

My voice sounded strange in the room. She replied, 'Yes, we are all well, thank God.'

The commandant broke in, 'You are not allowed to mention God here.'

'My mother is still alive?' I asked.

'Praise God, she is alive.'

'I HAVE TOLD YOU THAT YOU ARE NOT ALLOWED TO MENTION GOD.'

Then Sabina asked, 'How is your health?'

'I am in prison hospital—'

The commandant: 'You are not allowed to say where you are in prison.'

I tried again, 'About my trial, is there hope of an appeal?'

The commandant: 'You are not allowed to discuss your trial.'

So it went on, until I said, 'Go home, Sabina, dear. They won't let us speak.'

My wife had brought a basket of food and clothes, but she was not allowed to give me as much as an apple. As they took me away I looked over my shoulder and saw her being escorted by armed guards through the door at the further end of the hall. The commandant lit a fresh cigarette, his thoughts elsewhere.

That evening, Dr. Marina stopped at the foot of my bed. 'Oh dear!' she said, 'and I thought your wife's visit would do you so much good.'

We became friends. She told me that she had been taught nothing about religion, but supposed herself to be an atheist. 'Isn't everyone, these days?'

One day, when alone with Marina and another Christian prisoner in the little cubicle which served her as a surgery, I mentioned that it was the day of Pentecost.

'What is that?' she asked. A guard on orderly duties was going through the files, so I waited until he left with the card he wanted. Then I replied, 'It's the day on which God gave us the Ten Commandments, thousands of years ago.'

I heard the guard's returning footsteps and added loudly, 'And it hurts here, doctor, when I cough.'

The guard returned the card to the files and moved off again, so I continued, 'Pentecost is also the day on which the Holy Spirit came to the Apostles'.

Again the warder's footsteps, so I continued hastily, 'And at night the pain in my back is terrible'.

Dr. Marina bit her lips to stop laughing. I went on with my interrupted sermon, while she tapped my chest, and told me to cough and peered down my throat, until at last she burst into laughter. 'Do stop!' she gasped, holding a handkerchief to her mouth as the guard's stolid face again appeared in the doorway. 'Tell me later.'

I told her the story of the Gospel in the weeks that followed, and when I, and others at Gherla, had brought Dr. Marina to Christ she took even greater risks to help us.

Years later, in another prison, I heard that she had died of rheumatic fever which had affected her heart. She had always overworked herself.

8

I was moved back to Vacaresti, the prison-hospital where I had spent a month after my solitary confinement in the cells beneath the Ministry of the Interior. The place was more crowded than ever. Tubercular patients had to share rooms and exchange infections with sufferers from other diseases.

Two Secret Police officers who came to interrogate me asked quizzically what I thought of Communism now. 'How am I to say?' I replied. 'I know it only from the inside of its prisons.'

They grinned, and one said, 'Now you can learn about it from a VIP: Vasile Luca—the old Minister of Finance—is in your cell'.

Luca's dismissal for currency scandals in March 1953 had helped to bring down the Ana Pauker clique. With Theohari Georgescu, Minister of the Interior, he had been expelled from the Party, and now all three were in various prisons with the victims of their five-year reign. In his days of power, Luca was much flattered, but little loved. Now guards and prisoners took the chance to show their contempt. Luca sat alone, in a corner of our cell, biting his knuckles and muttering to himself; old, ill, and unrecognisable as the man whose photograph had appeared so regularly in the newspapers.

Luca could find no relief from his sufferings. A Christian, whatever his troubles, knew that for his faith he was treading the road that Christ had trod, but Luca, who had worked all his life for Communism, had neither hope nor belief left. If the Nationalists came to power, or the Americans arrived, Luca and his comrades would be the first to hang. In the meantime, they were punished by their former Party friends. Luca was close to breaking point when we met.

After his political disgrace, he told me, he was forced to confess under torture to absurd charges. A military court condemned him to death, but the sentence was commuted to life imprisonment.

'They knew I wouldn't last for long,' he said, coughing.

He was given to outbursts of rage against his Party enemies. One day, when he could not eat the food pushed into our cell, I offered him my bread. He took it hungrily.

'Why did you do that?' he growled.

'I've learnt the value of fasting in prison.'

'And what might that be?'

I said, 'Firstly, it shows that the spirit is master of the body. Secondly, it saves me from the quarrels and hard feelings over food which are so common. Thirdly—well, if a Christian does not fast in jail, what means has he of helping others?'

Luca admitted that the only help he had been given since his arrest had come from Christians. Then his bile rose again.

'But I know far more clergymen who are first-rate scoundrels. As one of the Party's Central Committee I kept a firm hand on sects and religions. My department had a file on every priest in the country—including you. I began to wonder if there was a priest in Rumania who wouldn't soon be knocking at my back door after dark. What a band of brothers!'

I said that man might degrade religion, but religion ennobled man much more. This was shown by the host of saints: not only those of old, but the many great Christians who could be met today.

Luca grew angry. His spite against the world would not allow him to admit goodness in anyone. He recited familiar atheist arguments about the Church's persecution of science. I reminded him of the great scientists who have been Christians—from Newton and Kepler to Pavlov and the discoverer of anaesthetics, Sir James Simpson.

Luca said, 'They conformed to the conventions of the time.'

I said, 'Do you know the declaration of Louis Pasteur, who discovered microbes and vaccination? "*Je crois comme une charbonnière le plus que je progresse en science.*" He believed like a coalminer, like a woman coalminer of the last century. This man who spent most of his life at the head of a body of scientific studies had the faith of the simplest human creature.'

Luca said indignantly, 'What of all the scientists the Church has persecuted?'

I asked if he could name them.

'Galileo, of course, who went to prison. Giordano Bruno, whom they burned . . .' He stopped.

I said, 'So you can only find two cases in 2,000 years! That's a triumph for the Church by any human standards. Compare the Party record in the last ten years, here in Rumania alone. Many thousands of innocent people shot, tortured and imprisoned; you yourself sentenced on the strength of perjured evidence obtained by threats and bribes! How many miscarriages of justice do you think there have been in all the countries under Communist rule?'

One evening I spoke of the Last Supper, and Jesus's words to Judas, 'What you have to do, do quickly'.

Luca said, 'Nothing will make me believe in God, but if I did, the one prayer I'd make to Him would be, "What you have to do, do quickly".'

His condition worsened. He spat blood, and in his fever a cold sweat broke out on his forehead.

At this time I was moved to another prison. Before I left, he promised to give thought to his soul. I have no way of knowing what happened, but when a man starts to argue with himself, the chances of finding the truth are small. Conversions are usually instantaneous. The message pierces the heart, and from its depths something new and healing breaks out at once.

I met many like Luca at that time, and often discussed with friends how Communist leaders and their collaborators should be dealt with when Communism fell. Christians opposed revenge but were divided among themselves: some who thought that forgiveness should be complete, and those who said that Jesus—in telling Peter to forgive men who had wronged him 'Not seven times, but seventy times seven'—had fixed a limit which the Communists had long over-stepped.

My view is that, having judged each man singly, with understanding of the evil forces that made him, we have only the right, without being vindictive, to put the wrong-doer into a position where he can do no further harm. Communists already spend much time and effort in punishing each other. Stalin poisoned Lenin, it is said. He had Trotsky murdered with an ice-pick. Khrushchev so hated his 'comrade' that he destroyed his reputation and despoiled his tomb. Luca, Theohari Georgescu, Ana Pauker and so many more were victims of their own cruel system.

9

My next journey was by road, in a truck labelled 'State Food Trust'. Security vans often bore such signs so that people should not know how many were on the move, and perhaps also for fear of rescue attempts. Two men were with me. One was a former Iron Guard leader serving a twenty-year sentence. The other, a minor thief, was due to be freed shortly after doing six months.

'I won't see these again,' said the Iron Guard cheerfully, shaking his shackles. Then, turning his back to me, he told the thief that it had been agreed to free all 'politicos' before the summit meeting, and that he would be among the first to be released. The thief explained in turn that all he wanted was a decent job, but nobody would give him one.

The Iron Guard sympathised. Then, seizing his neighbour by the sleeve, he said, 'I've an idea! Why can't we help each other? Now the Russians have given way, the Americans will be here within the month. I have influential friends among them. Supposing we changed identities—at the next stop, you answer to my name and I to yours. As soon as they let me go in your place, I'll start preparing the way for the American take-over. You, bearing my name, will be released as a political prisoner on the day they arrive. Leave the rest to me—your future will be made!'

The thief was enraptured. When the van pulled up in the prison yard, the two men answered to each other's names and were marched to different compounds. Ten days later, the Iron Guard who had gone to the short-service section was released. The thief saw weeks and months go by without news of the Americans. Faced by the prospect of fulfilling the other man's sentence to the end, he told the commandant the truth. The Iron Guard was hunted down, and the thief expected to be freed at last. Instead, he was tried for helping a Fascist criminal to escape and was given a twenty-year sentence of his own. So the two men had to go on living together—like so many others who had wronged one another.

The new prison was called Jilava, which means 'wet place' in Rumanian. It was justly named. To enter it, the truck drove down a steep ramp, and we sank below the earth into darkness. The deepest levels of Jilava were more than 30 feet below ground. It had been designed as a fortress, with trenches around, and strangers could pass by unaware of its existence. Sheep grazed above it, and we felt buried alive, under thousands of tons of earth. Jilava was intended to hold 500 troops, but now it had to keep 2,000 prisoners in a series of ill-lit cells and tunnels which now and then widened out into small courtyards where men exercised. At some points streams ran down the walls, which were stained with great patches of green damp.

The man in the next bunk to me, a former police chief from Odessa, Colonel Popescu, said conditions were far worse when he arrived. A hundred men had been crushed together in our small cell with the windows boarded up, and some had died from suffocation.

Popescu told me he had hidden from the Russians for twelve years after the war in a cave with the entrances blocked up. He slept on straw and ate what friends pushed in through a small hole. But in the end, the Secret Police found him. Crouching in that cramped space so long, his legs had become paralysed. It was months before he could walk.

It was plain from Popescu's ribald talk that religion had been outside his thoughts for many years. I asked how he had passed the time in his lonely cave.

'I composed a novel,' he said. 'If I wrote it down, it would run to 5,000 pages. But no one would dare to publish it.'

I saw why, when Popescu recited bits of it. Never have I heard such a torrent of obscenity.

Our meal was announced by a shout from the corridor. I took my rotten-carrot soup over to a neighbour's bunk, and we sat talking for a while. He was a young radio engineer who had sent information to the West for a patriotic group, and he mentioned that he had been brought to Christ through his knowledge of Morse.

'It happened five or six years ago. I was interrogated in the cells of the Ministry of Interior and, while I was there, an unknown pastor next door tapped Bible verses to me through the wall.'

When he told me the position of his cell, I said, 'I was that pastor.'

With his help I built up a nucleus of Christians who spread their influence through the prison. But there was one man whom everyone left alone.

Gheorge Bajenaru was the son of an Orthodox bishop. He was known as 'the wickedest priest in Rumania'. He forged his father's signature to honours and degrees. He embezzled the funds from a school where his wife was headmistress. When she committed suicide to conceal his guilt, Bajenaru showed no remorse. He even informed on his own father for money. Then he went to the West, posing as a refugee. He was made a bishop, with charge over all Rumanian Orthodox exiles. He obtained funds from them, and from the World Council of Churches. Meanwhile the Communists waited.

Bajenaru had been a worldly, arrogant man, built like a bull, but now he was thin and shrunken. He told me what had happened. He had gone to Austria for the wedding of a wealthy Rumanian, and stayed on a few days. Leaving a restaurant in the French sector one night, he heard steps behind him. A club came down on his head. Bajenaru recovered in a moment, and turned to fight. Four men grappled with him. He felt a needle jab into his leg.

'I woke up in the Soviet zone. There was a looking glass on the wall, and I didn't know the man who looked back at me. My black beard had gone. They had cropped my hair and dyed it red. My skin had been bleached to go with it. I was flown to Moscow. Interrogators in the Lubianka prison thought I might be a key figure in the Anglo-American spy world. They wanted to know what the World Council of Churches was planning to do behind the Iron Curtain and about the intrigues of Rumanian exiles in the West. I could tell them nothing. I had merely been enjoying myself. The Russians wouldn't believe me. "Very well, Your Grace," they said, "we shall stimulate your memory in the surgery."

Bajenaru held up his hands to show that the finger-nails were gone.

'They broke them one by one,' he said. 'The doctor was in white. So were the two nurses. There was every scientific aid you can think of, except anaesthetics.'

Bajenaru was tortured for weeks. He was close to insanity when the Russians, deciding that he had nothing for them after all, passed him on to the Secret Police in Bucharest. There he was again tortured.

At Jilava his interrogation was still going on, and when he returned to our cell from questioning, prisoners accused him of informing. In fact, he wished only to atone for what he had done. Suffering had purified him. But the others could not believe it, although Bajenaru showed his change of heart in many ways. Once, when he held a public liturgy, praying aloud for the king and the royal family, someone told the guards. He was sent to the 'Black Room' with myself and some other clergy who were among the informer's victims.

We were driven down a steep flight of steps to a windowless, underground chamber in the depths of the fort, which was probably an old ammunition store: no shell could penetrate there. Water, dripping from the roof, kept the floor of the 'Black Room' awash, and even in summer it was bitterly cold. 'We must keep moving,' said a voice in the pitch darkness. So we began to walk in a circle, slipping on the slimy floor, and we kept on until many hours later, exhausted and bruised from falls, we were let out.

Others said we had been lucky. Men were often stripped to the skin before being locked in the 'Black Room'. The story of how one group of eighteen had survived in it for two days was still told. They were all middle-aged or elderly members of the National Peasant Party. To avoid freezing to death they formed themselves into a human snake in the darkness. Each man clung to the one in front for warmth as they stamped around in an endless circle, splashed from head to foot in filth. Often a man collapsed, but the others always dragged him up from the water and forced him on.

Bajenaru continued to pray for the king. When at last he was sent for trial, he returned to say calmly that he had been sentenced to death. He had achieved humility. I have noticed that humble men, who have sinned grossly, can often resist persecution better than Christians of high spirituality. St. John Chrysostomos, who lived in the days of the Roman chariot races, once said, 'If a car drawn by the horses of Righteousness and Pride were matched with another drawn by Sin and Humility, I believe the second chariot would reach Heaven first.'

Colonel Popescu suggested to Bajenaru that he should appeal for mercy. Bajenaru replied, 'I do not recognise these judges. I obey God and the king'.

When Bajenaru had been moved to the condemned cell, Popescu said, 'Perhaps we were wrong in trying to be his judges, too'.

We heard nothing of him for four months; then he returned to our cell, his sentence commuted to life imprisonment. Although his whole character had changed, the majority of prisoners would not accept him. 'Another trick, you devil!' they said. It was unjust. Bajenaru had been offered release if he agreed to work for the Secret Police. He replied, 'I'll leave prison when the last priest goes free'.

His reprieve was regarded as suspicious because it was commoner for a sentence to be increased than lessened. At any time, under Communism, the state can obtain a more severe penalty for a sentenced man. In fact, a prisoner who had served twelve years of a life sentence had been told, without explanation, that his sentence had been reviewed. He was shot next day.

Bajenaru was shifted to another cell, where he was kicked and beaten by the prisoners. Twice he attempted suicide. Then he was transferred to another jail, where he died.

10

The first execution while I was at Jilava was of two brothers, named Arnautoiu. They had lived in the forest for years as partisans, until a woman who visited their hideout was trailed by soldiers and they were caught.

Executions were conducted with grim ceremonial. At dawn, guards lined the corridors, and from the cells hundreds of eyes watched through cracks and spyholes as the commandant led a small procession out into the yard. Two senior officers came first; then the brothers carrying their chains, each gripped by a guard on either side, and followed in turn by a doctor and guards with machine guns. We heard the clang of hammer blows in the cold, morning air, as the men's chains were struck off. Sacks were pulled over their heads and they were pushed into the car which drove them a short distance to a field, where they were shot in the back of the head at point blank range. We heard the shooting.

The executioner was a man of gipsy blood called Nita, who received a bonus of 500 lei on each occasion. He was the best-mannered guard we had: they called him the Black Angel of Jilava.

'I always give them a last cigarette in the cell before their time comes,' he told us. 'I try to keep their courage up, and it's not so hard as you might suppose, because every one of them thinks to the last moment that he'll be saved.'

This happened in the instance of a youth of nineteen, called Lugojanu. His father, a former government minister, had been tortured to death in prison. The boy, aided by some friends, made a series of attacks on militiamen in revenge. One of the raiders talked, on being captured, so Lugojanu and eight accomplices were sentenced to die.

The first two were marched out into the yard, then a second pair. The others heard their chains being removed. They heard the shots. They heard the guards coming to fetch the rest. One of them told me later, 'I felt perfectly calm. I saw the Holy Virgin and she spoke to me so gently. I was confident that I should be reprieved.' The door of the cell opened. It was the commandant. Word had come from Bucharest that the sentences on the remaining men had been commuted. Many times in jail I saw at work this mysterious power which sustains men in their last moments.

The Black Angel's politeness was by way of an apology for his hideous job. 'I'm no monster,' he said, in effect. The other guards, and their trustees among the prisoners, felt no such need.

The spirit in Jilava was particularly bad. It was a transit jail, where men often met old enemies. Many prisoners were former policemen. The old police hands, even those who had worked against Communism, had been kept on for two years to train the Party's candidates. These experienced men were then ordered to arrest some of their own comrades. Then they, in turn, were arrested by the men whom they had trained. After sentence, scores of these police had to share the same cell, for in the end no officer of the old régime escaped the purge.

One day, recriminations were suspended in favour of a new focus for the hatred which festered in them all.

He was thrown into our cell from another—bruised, dishevelled, dirty, his jaw hanging loose. He gazed around in terror. Then a roar went up: 'Albon!'

The commandant of Poarta-Alba, who was responsible for the deaths of thousands, had been made a scapegoat for the failure of the canal. We remembered how Colonel Albon had greeted new arrivals at his camp. 'Professors, doctors, lawyers, priests—all my clever friends! Here we've no use for brains; only for hands, your gentlemanly hands! For your labour, you are paid with the air you breathe. Don't think you'll be freed except by death—or when they stop work on the canal and lock me up!'

Now Albon looked at us like a hypnotised rabbit. A prisoner seized him by the collar and dragged him to his feet. Another swung him round. A third kicked him in the groin. Albon went down under a torrent of blows, shrieking hysterically.

I tried to save him. The men turned on me: 'So, you side with this murderer!'

Albon struggled up, streaked with blood and dust, amid laughter, jeers and boos. He fell again on his way to the door, cutting himself on the sharp corner of a bunk. In a fresh scrimmage, the shirt was torn from his back. He held his hands before his face to shield it. Finally, he collapsed and lay still on the floor.

Albon was treated like this in cell after cell until he was moved to Ocnele-Mari prison, which the authorities reserved for disgraced officers and officials.

Days later, I recognised another familiar face. Colonel Dulgheru, who had questioned me for a week in solitary confinement, had landed in jail. I told him what happened to Albon, and he tried to keep out of trouble, but it was inevitable that someone else would soon spot him.

He told me he had been accused of being a police spy in pre-Communist days—the usual charge when the Party wanted to incriminate one of its own men—and described how he had been arrested. He went to the cells to interrogate someone, with his retinue of three subalterns. They opened a cell door politely and ushered the colonel in, then closed it again behind them. Dulgheru found himself locked in an empty cell. He banged on the door demanding to be let out. His men laughed. He heard one of them say, 'This time, you're the one to stay there!'

When Dulgheru's identity was discovered at Jilava he also was set upon by the prisoners and had to be removed to Ocnele-Mari. The Party prison soon became as overcrowded as the rest.

Soon after his departure, I was sent for interrogation to Bucharest. Shields like motor-goggles were placed over my eyes before I was taken by car the few miles to the capital. At Secret Police H.Q. the questions of a uniformed colonel seemed designed to sound out my attitude to the régime rather than to get information. He gave me no clue to his real purpose in seeing me.

The place was crowded and 'secret' prisoners were sharing cells. I was put with a thick-set, sullen man. He was Vasile Turcanu the chief 're-educator', who had been sentenced to death by the régime which had once given him licence to kill. The Party had kept him alive for three years, intending, in the usual way, to announce his execution when some need for a political distraction arose.

Turcanu described how they had arrested Teohari Georgescu, Minister of the Interior, during the 1953 purge. He was sitting in his office before a row of telephones when three of his own security officers stalked in with revolvers. They made Georgescu face his own portrait, hanging on the wall in its gold frame, while he dropped his trousers for a search.

I tried to bring some Christianity into Turcanu's life in the few hours I was with him, but little could be done for a man so deeply ensnared in doctrines of violence.

The most startling news I gleaned from the cells at Secret Police H.Q. was that Stalin had been denounced as a murderer and tyrant by his successor Khrushchev. The first reports of how Beria and six of his top men were executed on Christmas Eve, 1953—along with thousands of lesser Soviet secret agents—had just been published, and the process of discrediting Stalin had begun in Rumania. Gheorghiu-Dej, the new Rumanian dictator, was introducing a more popular policy. Dej liked to live well himself, and his temperament, at least, was an improvement on that of the Pauker circle.

II

The news I took back to Jilava threw the cell into uproar. Everyone was delighted that Stalin had been pushed from his pedestal. They hoped it would hasten their own release.

But Popescu said, 'I know the Party. They'll denounce the robber—and they won't repay the robbed.'

'Anyway, Stalin's finished,' another prisoner said.

'May he burn in hell!' shouted a second.

Amid laughter, cheers and jeers, two prisoners waltzed round together, screaming obscene remarks about 'Uncle Joe'. Only the guards were silent. Stalin's denunciation left their future unsettled.

Popescu called to me, 'You're not looking so happy, pastor!'

I said, 'I can't take pleasure in explosions of hatred towards anyone. We do not know Stalin's fate. He may have been saved at the last hour, like the thief on the cross.'

'What! After all the crimes Stalin had committed?' asked someone.

'Perhaps he is like the rich man who had only moments of repentance in his life, and yet ended in Heaven,' I said.

I told them how a man who had lived by exploiting the poor developed a great hatred for the village minister, simply because he was good. When they met in the street, the man spat in the minister's face; and he let him do it, thinking, 'This is a pleasure for the poor creature'. Once a year, however, the rich man, who was called Bodnaras, went to church. It was always on Good Friday, and as he heard the story of the Crucifixion, two tears would roll down his fat cheeks. He wiped them away quickly and left before the collection was taken.

One Good Friday, a large congregation waited for the service to begin. The minister did not appear, and nor did Bodnaras. An hour passed. At last someone looked behind the altar. There was the pastor, stretched on the floor, breathing calmly, his eyes closed and with such a look of bliss on his face that the people saw he was transfigured by a holy ecstasy.

That morning Bodnaras had died and gone to judgment and when the devils placed all his bad deeds upon the scales, his guardian angel had nothing to put on the other side except the two tears he had shed every year. Yet those tears weighed exactly as much as all the evil deeds together.

What could be done? Bodnaras began to sweat and tremble. But just at that moment God looked away and the rich man snatched a few bad deeds off the scale. The balance swung up on the side of Good.

But God sees even when he looks away. He said sadly to the rich man, 'Never in all creation has anyone tried to cheat Me on the Day of Judgment'. And looking around Heaven, he asked, 'Who will defend this man?'

The angels were silent. 'Come,' said God, 'this is not the People's Republic of Rumania. We can't condemn someone without a defence.'

Even the rich man's guardian angel shrank from the task. 'But,' he added, 'there is a minister in his town of so saintly a character that he might be willing to speak for him.'

So the minister was brought to Heaven, while his body remained below. Bodnaras thought his last chance had gone when he saw the man he had often humiliated, but the pastor accepted the brief at once.

'Heavenly Father,' he began, 'which of us is better, you or I? If I'm better than You, come down from Your throne and let me take Your place, for every day I allowed Bodnaras the joy of spitting on me, and was free of bitterness. Certainly if I can forgive him, so can You.

'My second plea is that Jesus died on the Cross for the sins of man, and although in our unhappy country we may now be punished many times for the same crime, it is not right that Bodnaras should suffer again for his sins, when they have been punished already in Jesus's body.

'And thirdly, God, a practical question—what do You lose if he goes to Heaven? If paradise is too small, You can enlarge it. If You do not wish to put evil among the good, then make another Heaven for lost souls—give them a little happiness, too.'

These words were so pleasing to God that He called at once to Bodnaras, 'Go now to Heaven!' The rich man scuttled off. Then God turned to the minister, deeply moved, and said, 'Stay here a while, and talk with Me.'

'Thank You,' said the pastor, 'but I haven't taken service yet, and everyone in church is waiting to get home to dinner. I must go back and do my duty, and tell men to beware of sin. But I shall teach them also that You fulfil your duty, forgiving us, for Your love is given even to the worst of sinners. If You began to judge man according to his deserts, none of us would escape.'

The cell heard this story in silence.

'And would you,' Popescu asked, 'defend Stalin before God?'

'Who knows if Stalin has not wept over his sins?' I said. 'Psychologists say that the worse a man's crimes, the less he is responsible for them. A maniac like Hitler, who burns in ovens millions of harmless people he has never met; a mass-murderer like Stalin who kills thousands of his own comrades—such men are not normal, and we cannot judge them by standards we apply to others.'

Colonel Popescu said, 'I've heard many Christian teachings in this cell, but this is the best—and the hardest to put into effect.'

12

In the spring of 1956 some swallows nested high up in the roof of the cell, near the window. One day a chirp announced that the eggs had hatched. A prisoner stood on another's shoulders and peered in. 'Four of them!' he called. The parent birds never seemed to rest. It made a change from talk about our release to count the times they darted in and out to feed the chicks—250 trips a day! An old countryman said, 'They'll fly in twenty-one days'. The others laughed. 'You'll see,' he said. On the twentieth day nothing had happened, but on the twenty-first, with cheeps and flutterings, the young birds flew. We were so pleased. 'God has arranged their schedule,' I said. 'He can do as much for us.'

The weeks passed, and it seemed that the denunciation of Stalin did indeed herald another 'thaw'. It could not last; yet many prisoners were being released under the terms of an amnesty. Would I be one of them? The thought only saddened me: if they let me go now, what use would I be? My son had grown up and could hardly remember his father. Sabina was used to going her own way. The Church had other pastors, who made less trouble.

Early one morning, a voice broke into these thoughts: 'Interrogation, at once! Move!'

Back to the bullying, the fear, the questions to which I had to find false answers! I started to gather my things, while the guard bellowed, 'Come on, come on! The car's waiting.' I hurried with him through the corridors and across the yard. One after another the steel gates were unlocked as we climbed the steps. Then I was outside.

There was no car in sight, only a clerk who handed me a slip of paper. I took it. It was a court order and it declared that, under the amnesty I was free.

I stared at it stupidly. All I could say was, 'But I've only done eight and a half years and my sentence is for twenty'.

'You're to leave at once. This comes from the highest tribunal.'

'I've got nearly twelve years yet to serve.'

'Don't argue! Get out!'

'But look at me!' My ragged shirt was grey with dirt. My

trousers were a map of coloured patches tacked together. My boots might have been borrowed from Charlie Chaplin. 'I'll be arrested by the first policeman.'

'We've no clothes here for you. Do get off!'

The clerk turned back into the prison. The gate clanged and its bolt was driven home. Outside the prison walls there was not a soul to be seen; I was alone, in an empty, summery world. The warm June day was so quiet that I could hear insects buzzing about on their business. A long, white road stretched away under trees of an amazing deep green. In the shade of a grove of chestnuts, cows were browsing. How still it was!

I called out, so that the guards could hear behind their walls, 'God, help me not to rejoice more because I'm free than because You were with me in prison!'

It is three miles from Jilava to Bucharest. I heaved my bundle on my shoulder and set off across the fields. It was only a collection of smelly rags, but they had been so precious to me in jail that I never considered leaving them. Soon I left the crown of the road to walk in the deep grass and touch the rough bark of the trees as I went along. Sometimes I stopped to gaze at a flower or a budding leaf.

Two figures came towards me—an old country couple. They stopped me and said curiously, 'You come from *there*?' The man brought out a leu, a coin worth about a penny, and gave it to me. I looked at it in my hand, and almost wanted to laugh. No one had ever given me a leu before.

'Give me your address, so that I may repay you,' I said.

'No, no, keep it,' he urged me, using 'thou', as people do in Rumania to children and beggars.

I went on with my bundle. Another woman stopped me. 'You come from *there*?' She hoped for news of the priest of Jilava village, arrested months before. I had not met him, but explained that I was a pastor myself. We sat on a wall by the roadside. I was so happy to find someone who wanted to talk about Christ that I felt in no hurry to get home. When I went on at last, she, too, brought out a leu: 'For the tram fare.'

'But I have a leu already.'

'Take it for Our Lord's sake, then.'

I walked on until I reached a tram stop on the outskirts of the capital. People crowded around me, knowing at once where I had come from. They asked after brothers, fathers, cousins—all had someone in prison. When I boarded the tram, they would not let me pay. Several stood to offer me a seat. Released prisoners in Rumania, far from being outcasts, are highly respected men. I sat with my bundle on my knees, but just as the car started I heard cries from outside. 'Stop! Stop!' It was my heart that nearly stopped. We jerked to a halt as a militiaman's motor-cycle swerved in front. There had been a mistake—he was coming to take me back! But the driver turned and shouted, 'He says there's someone standing on the steps.'

Next to me was a woman with a basket of fresh strawberries. I looked at them unbelievingly.

'Haven't you had any this year?' she said.

'Not for eight years,' I replied.

She said, 'Go on, take some!' and filled my hands with the soft, ripe fruit. I ate them in hungry mouthfuls, like a child.

At last I reached my own front door and hesitated a moment. They were not expecting me, and I was a fearful sight in my filth and rags. Then I opened the door. In the hall were several young people, among them a gawky young man who stared at me and burst out: 'Father!'

It was Mihai, my son. He was nine when I left him: now he was eighteen.

Then my wife came forward. Her fine-boned face was thinner, but her hair was still black; I thought she was more beautiful than ever. My eyes blurred. When she put her arms around me, I made a great effort and said, 'Before we kiss, I must say something. Don't think I've simply come from misery to happiness! I've come from the joy of being with Christ in prison to the joy of being with Him in my family. I'm not coming from strangers to my own, but from my own in prison to my own at home.' She sobbed, and I said, 'Now if you wish, you may kiss me.' Later, I sang softly a little song I had made for her years before in prison to sing if we ever met again.

Mihai came to say that the place was full of visitors who would not leave without seeing me. Members of our church had been telephoning all over Bucharest; the door-bell rang continuously. Old friends brought new ones. People had to leave so that others could find standing room. Every time I was introduced to a woman, I had to bow politely in my absurd trousers, held up by string. By the time all were gone it was nearly midnight and Sabina pressed me to eat something, but I felt no hunger. I said, 'Today we have had happiness enough. Let's make tomorrow a day of fasting in thankfulness, with Holy Communion before supper.'

I turned to Mihai. Three of our visitors—one a philosophy professor from the university whom I had not met before—had told me that evening that my son had brought them to faith in Christ. And I had feared that, left without father or mother, he would be lost! I could find no words for my happiness.

Mihai said, 'Father, you've gone through so much. I want to know what you've learnt from all your sufferings.'

I put my arm around him and said, 'Mihai, I've nearly forgotten my Bible in all this time. But four things were always in my mind. First, that there is a God. Secondly, Christ is our Saviour. Thirdly, there is eternal life. And, fourthly, love is the best of ways.'

My son said, 'That was all I wanted.' Later he told me that he had decided to become a pastor.

In my clean, soft bed that night, I could not sleep. I sat up and opened the Bible. I wanted the Book of Daniel, which had been a favourite, but I could no longer find my way to it. My eye was held instead by a line in the Epistles of St. John, 'I have no greater joy than to hear that my children walk in truth'. I had this joy, too. I went into my son's room, because I had to be sure that he was really there. In prison I had dreamt so often of this, only to wake in my cell.

It was two weeks before I could sleep regularly. By then I was being treated in the best-placed bed of the sunniest ward of the best possible hospital. As an ex-prisoner, everyone wanted to help me—in the streets, the shops, everywhere—and the stream of visitors began again.

PART SIX

Now that I was free, I longed in the depths of my heart for quietness and rest. But Communism was working everywhere to complete the destruction of the Church. The peace I desired would have been an escape from reality and dangerous for my soul.

I returned to a poor home, but I was luckier than many. We had a tiny two-roomed attic, with hardly any furniture. I slept on an old wooden bed with a soft mattress lent by a neighbour; the bed had a cushion to extend it for my length. Water came from the basement, three floors down, and the nearest lavatory was in another building. I expected nothing better. We all knew in prison of the housing and food shortages, and of church buildings closed or taken over, as ours had been.

Our comfortable flat had been confiscated on my wife's arrest. Because she refused to divorce me after her release, she could not get work and lived in extreme poverty, darning women's stockings and living on the kindness of friends. She said that it would have gone hard for them but for Mihai.

When he was thirteen, Mihai had been allowed to visit his mother during her three years of forced labour on the canal. Deprived of both parents, living on charity, he felt bitter.

'I borrowed the money to go to the camp,' he said. 'We met in a place where there were two sets of iron bars dividing us. Mother was in prison uniform, dirty and thin. She was half-crying, and had to shout to make me hear. She said, 'Mihai, believe in Jesus and be faithful!' I answered, 'Mother, if in a place like this you can still believe, then so must I.'

On her return to Bucharest Sabina found that Mihai had become a piano-tuner after being taken on as an apprentice by a tuner at the Opera House: his ear was so true that he was able to work at this craft by himself from the age of eleven. Soon he earned enough to help his mother and send himself to school. It was a poor life, but he had bread.

Mihai's troubles with the Party began early when he won the right granted to model pupils to wear a red tie—and refused to do so because it was 'the symbol of the oppressors'. Publicly expelled, he was quietly taken back to the school when the fuss died down because his teachers gave only lip-service to the régime. At fourteen, he was expelled again for saying that he had read the Bible for himself and that attacks on religion in the school books were based on falsehoods. Now he was trying to continue his studies in evening classes.

Mihai was a Christian, with no love of Communism. But a song-bird with a nest near a family of crows will fall into discordant notes, and Mihai had heard little else. On the day after my return I had to tell him that he was mistaken in believing that the workers in capitalist countries were dying of hunger. His student friends took it for granted, and one girl told me that she had wept in school over the starving children of America.

Even the best young people seemed confused and disorientated. Not only were they deprived of the chance of reading great Christian authors, but you could not buy the works of thinkers like Plato, Kant, Schopenhauer and Einstein. Mihai's friends said their parents told them one thing, their professors another, and often they asked for my advice.

A young theology student from the university of Cluj wanted help in his thesis.

'What is the subject?' I asked.

'The history of liturgical song in the Lutheran church.'

I said, 'You should begin by writing that we should not be filling young men's heads with historical trivialities, when tomorrow they may face death for their faith.'

'What should I be studying, then?' he asked.

I replied, 'How to be ready for sacrifice and martyrdom.'

I told him some of the things that I had seen in prison, and soon he was bringing his friends. All had the same trouble as they tried to chart a course. I questioned them about their studies.

One of them said, 'Our theology teacher says that God gave three revelations. The first was to Moses. The second was to Christ. And the third was to Karl Marx.'

'What does your pastor think of that?'

'The more he talks, the less he seems to say.'

The upshot of these conversations was that I agreed to go to Cluj and preach in the cathedral there. The students wanted my books, but all my writings had been banned.

Before I went I had a call to pay, in fulfilment of a promise made in prison to members of the Army of the Lord, a sect which is not unlike the Salvation Army and which was being harassed unrelentingly by the Secret Police. It was several years since I had met the Patriarch Justinian Marina, and I thought that he might help. The harm he had done to the Church was great; it was also in his power to do some good.

I found him walking in the grounds behind his palace. I suspect he chose to see me in the garden because it was free from microphones and away from his eavesdropping clerks. I said, 'You are Patriarch and men come to you for places and pensions, and everywhere you must preach and sing—so I thought that I should come and sing to you. It's a song of the Army of the Lord, which I learnt in prison.' I sang it, and asked him to do something for these good and simple people: 'They must not sit in prison for ever, merely because they belong to a certain sect.' He said he would try, and we had a long talk.

I tried to call him back to God. I said, 'In the Garden of Gethsemane, Jesus called even Judas "friend", opening the way to salvation.' I wanted to plant a seed from which a change of heart might grow. He listened quietly, and even with humility, but said he could do little because at his side had been put the Metropolitan of Iasi, Justin Moisescu; if he went too far or resigned, Moisescu would replace him as Patriarch and things would be worse. Justinian had kept a kind of respect for me, but although his divided heart did not love what his hand did, his waverings always ended in submission to the Party's demands.

Later I heard he had raised the matter of the 'Army' in the Holy Synod, where he was opposed by the Metropolitan—who (above all men in Rumania!) had become accepted as Orthodox representative for the World Council of Churches. Next, he was reproved by the Ministry of Cults for receiving me—his secretary, of course, had reported my visit, just as the Patriarch always reported on his secretary. Justinian had agreed to meet representatives from the 'Army', but when they arrived he sent them packing, 'So Wurmbrand told you to come, did he? It's time he was back in jail again!'

2

The news that I had promised to deliver a series of talks at Rumania's ancient university town was at once reported to the authorities, with the warning that my real purpose was to attack Marxism and make trouble among the students under the guise of lecturing on Christian philosophy. The zealous informer in this case was a Baptist minister, who told me to my face what he had done.

His action did not surprise me. I had met many of his colleagues since my release—priests, pastors, even bishops, who put in such reports to the Ministry of Cults. Usually, the reports concerned their own flocks, and usually the clergy were ashamed and sorrowful at what they did. They said it was not so much for their own safety, but to save their churches from being closed down. Every town had its Secret Police representatives from the Ministry of Cults, who questioned ministers regularly on the conduct of their congregation; quite apart from politics, they wanted to know which parishioners were frequent communicants, which of them tried to obtain converts, what sins people confessed. Those who refused to answer such questions were dismissed, and if there was no one 'suitable' to take over, their churches were shut. So by now Rumania had four categories of ministers: those in prison, those who informed under pressure and tried to keep things back, those who shrugged and did what they were told, and those who had acquired a taste for informing. These were only a few. The more honorable official pastors who did not collaborate soon lost their licence to preach. But traitors, like street-walkers, thrive by being brazen, and my Baptist colleague was such a man.

His warning was taken up at once by an official spy called Rugojanu. The Ministry of Cults, too, had its categories. Some of the employees were slack, others used their power to extract 'protection money' from the clergy, but Rugojanu was a fanatic who went from church to church, tirelessly sniffing out 'counter-revolutionaries'. He attended my lectures himself.

At Cluj, on the first evening, there was a group of fifty students and a few teachers of theology. As Darwin and his evolutionary theories were always to the fore in theological classes, I tried to deal with them. I said that the new Rumania, advanced and Socialist, rejected all capitalist ideas; was it not odd that an exception was made for the English bourgeois, Sir Charles Darwin?

Rugojanu, hunched forward in a pew, was staring at me. I looked back at him as I went on, 'A doctor's son wants to be a doctor, a composer's son a musician, a painter's son an artist, and so on. If you believe you were created by God, then you will try to become Godlike; if you prefer to believe that you spring from a tribe of apes, you are in danger of turning into a beast.'

I started my lectures on a Monday. On Tuesday the audience had doubled. By the end of the week more than a thousand faces looked up at me—the whole university, it seemed, was crowding into the cathedral. I knew that many of them were eager to hear the truth, but feared the consequences of embracing it; so I told them of the advice given me by a pastor who died for his faith at the hands of the Fascists. He said, 'You give your body as a sacrifice to God when you give it to all who wish to beat and mock you. Jesus, knowing his crucifixion was near, said, "My time is at hand". His time was the time of suffering, and it was His joy to suffer for the salvation of mankind. We, too, should regard suffering as a charge given us by God. St. Paul wrote, in the Epistle to the Romans (xii. 1): "My brothers, I implore you by God's mercy to offer your very selves to Him: a living sacrifice dedicated and fit for His acceptance." '

I looked out at the silent congregation. It was, for a moment, as if

I were back in my church during the war on the day when the Iron Guard bullies filed in with their guns. Menace was around us; not only in the place where Rugojanu, was taking notes.

I continued: 'Don't let suffering take you by surprise! Meditate on it often. Take the virtues of Christ and His saints to yourself, by thought. The pastor I spoke of, my teacher who died for his faith, gave me a recipe for a tea against suffering, and I will give it to you.'

I told them the story of a doctor of early Christian times who was unjustly imprisoned by the emperor. After some weeks his family were allowed to see him, and at first they wept. His clothes were rags, his nourishment a slice of bread with a cup of water every day. His wife wondered and asked, 'How is it you look so well? You have the air of one who has just come from a wedding!' The doctor smilingly replied that he had found a remedy for all troubles, and his family asked him what it was. The doctor told them, 'I have discovered a tea which is good against all suffering and sorrow. It contains seven herbs, and I shall number them for you.

'The first herb is called contentedness: be satisfied with what you have. I may shiver in my rags as I gnaw on a crust, but how much worse off I should be if the emperor had thrown me naked into a dungeon with nothing at all to eat!

'The second herb is common sense. Whether I rejoice or worry, I shall still be in prison, so why repine?

'The third is remembrance of past sins: count them, and on the supposition that every sin deserves a day in prison, reckon how many lives you would spend behind bars—you have been let off lightly!

'The fourth is the thought of the sorrows which Christ bore gladly for us. If the only man who ever could choose his fate on earth chose pain, what great value He must have seen in it! So we observe that, borne with serenity and joy, suffering redeems.

'The fifth herb is the knowledge that suffering has been given to us by God as from a father, not to harm us, but to cleanse and sanctify us. The suffering through which we pass has the purpose of purifying us, and preparing us for heaven.

'The sixth is the knowledge that no suffering can harm a

Christian life. If the pleasures of the flesh are all, then pain and prison bring an end to a man's aim in living; but if the core of life is truth, that is something which no prison cell can change. In prison or out of it two and two make four. Prison cannot stop me from loving; iron bars cannot exclude faith. If these ideals make up my life, I can be serene anywhere.

'The last herb in the recipe is hope. The wheel of life may put the emperor's physician in prison, but it goes on turning. It may put me back into the palace, and even put me on the throne.'

I paused for a moment. The crowded church was still.

'I have drunk barrels of this tea since then,' I said, 'and I can recommend it to you all. It has proved good.'

As I finished speaking, Rugojanu stood up and pushed his way out of the cathedral without a backward glance. I came down from the pulpit and the audience broke into a babble of talk. Outside, students applauded and cheered and tried to take my hands. I telephoned Sabina, who was glad at what I had done, although she knew reprisals would follow.

Next day I was summoned by my bishop, who told me that Rugojanu was making trouble. While he was telling me about protests from the Ministry of Cults, Rugojanu himself strode into the room. 'Ah, you!' he cried. 'What excuses are you trying to make? A torrent of sedition—I heard it!'

I asked the man what in particular had displeased him. Everything had—but particularly my cure for suffering.

'But what was wrong with my poor tea?' I asked. 'Which herb did you not like?'

He said violently, 'You told them the wheel always turns. But in this counter-revolutionary outburst, you are mistaken. The wheel will not turn, my friend; Communism is here for ever!' His face was distorted with hatred.

'I didn't mention Communism,' I replied. 'I said simply that the wheel of life keeps turning. For instance, I was in prison, now I am free. I have been ill, now I am better. I lost my parish, now I may work . . .'

'No, no, no! You meant that Communism would fall, and they all knew what you meant. Don't imagine you've heard the last of this!'

Rugojanu called church leaders to a meeting at the bishop's palace in Cluj, where I was denounced for trying to poison youth with concealed attacks on the government. 'You may be sure that he will never preach again,' shouted Rugojanu, working himself into an ugly rage. At the end he cried, 'Wurmbrand is finished, Wurmbrand is finished, Wurmbrand is finished!' He gathered up coat and hat and walked out of the building.

A hundred yards from the door a car, swerving to avoid a dog, mounted the pavement and crushed him against the wall. He died on the spot.

The story of Rugojanu's last words and their sequel spread through the country. Often during these years God showed His sign.

The revocation of my licence as a pastor did not stop me from preaching, but now I had to work as secretly as I did among Soviet soldiers after the war. A new danger was presented by visits from old prison friends asking for advice and help. Some of whom, having turned informer, were trying to provoke me. These unhappy men had expected too much from release; on finding their domestic world turned upside down, they had turned to the pursuit of sexual pleasure to win back their lost youth. This usually cost more than they could afford; and the short cut to a new start with the régime and quick profits lay in providing the Party with information. Their freedom was more tragic than their confinement.

Our best safeguard against informers lay in the warnings we received from friends in the Secret Police. Many of our followers held Party jobs of one kind or another. One young couple who spent their days in the propaganda department passed their evenings praying with us, and more than once we met in the home of a leading Secret Police officer while he was away, his maid being one of us. At other times we met in basements, attics, flats, country homes. Our services were as simple and as beautiful as those of the first Christians 1900 years ago. We sang aloud; if questions were asked, it was a birthday celebration; Christian families with three or four members had thirty-five birthdays a year! Sometimes we met in open country. The sky was our cathedral; the birds supplied our music, the flowers our incense, the stars our candles, the angels were the acolytes who lit them, and the shabby suit of a martyr just freed from prison meant far more to us than the most precious priestly robes.

4

I knew, of course, that sooner or later I would be re-arrested. After the revolution in Hungary the situation grew more difficult with every month. Khrushchev announced a new seven-year plan, 'to eradicate the vestiges of superstition'. Churches were closed or converted for use as Communist clubs, museums, grain stores. Those whom the Party newspapers reviled as 'swindlers in black soutanes' were rounded up in thousands.

I prayed, 'God, if You know men in prison whom I can help, souls that I can save, send me back and I will bear it willingly.' Sabina sometimes hesitated, then said, 'Amen'. There was at this time an inner joy about her, which came from knowing that we would serve Christ more fully soon. Once more, I wondered if our image of the Mother of the Lord, standing grief-stricken by the Cross, is not mistaken; was she not also filled with joy that her son would be saviour of the world?

They came for me at 1 a.m. on January 15, 1959. Our little attic was turned inside out in a search that lasted four hours. My son saw a belt of his behind a dislodged cupboard. 'And yet people say the Secret Police are useless!' he remarked. 'I've been looking everywhere for that.' Next day he was barred from night-school for his insolence.

When they had taken me away, Sabina picked up my Bible. She found, on a scrap of paper, a sentence I had noted down from the Epistle to the Hebrews (xi. 35) which said 'through faith . . . women received back their dead raised to life'. I had written below it, 'I have such a woman for my wife.'

5

It was still dark and the streets were covered with icy slush when we reached Police Headquarters in Bucharest. I went through the familiar reception processes before guards led me to a cell. Here I found a man of about thirty named Draghici, one of the hated re-education leaders at Piteshi. Each time the cell door opened he jerked round. He said, 'I'm sorry to be so jumpy. I never know if they're coming to take me out for a bath or to be shot. I've been under sentence of death for four years.'

Draghici told me his life story. As a boy he had revered the local priest, who one day said, 'Your father's a watchmaker—ask him to repair the church clock, cheaply.' Draghici persuaded his father to do the work for nothing. The priest then asked for a receipt for 500 leu, so that he could pocket the money, which he debited to the church. Draghici sneered as he added, 'I might have grown up as a Christian and given the Church a lot of money over the years, except for that'.

His father, a drunkard, disappeared with the family savings, and at fourteen the boy enlisted in the Iron Guard for the sake of the green shirt, the marching songs, the admiration of the girls. A few months later, the Guard was overthrown. Draghici went to prison, and when the Communists took power was automatically sentenced to eleven years as an active Fascist. After serving seven years he was promised at Piteshi, 'Beat the other prisoners, and you'll be freed.'

He told me, 'I was now twenty-one. I didn't want to stay in jail, so I did what I was told. I believed them, and now I have to die for it.'

It looked to me as if he were dying already, of tuberculosis. 'It's no more than I deserve,' he said.

I lay awake, listening to Draghici coughing and I thought: if God called me now and asked, 'After fifty-six years on earth, what do you think of man?' I should have to reply, 'Man is a sinner but the guilt is not his. Satan and his fallen angels are at work to make us wretched as they are themselves.'

For ten days and nights I reasoned with Draghici. 'It is not of your free choice that you became a criminal,' I said, 'but your sense of guilt demands atonement. Jesus has taken on himself this punishment you feel that you deserve.'

On the tenth evening, Draghici broke down in tears. We prayed together, and his remorse and fear were lifted. So my request to be allowed to help other prisoners was answered in my first days back in prison.

6

I was taken next for interrogation at Bucharest's Uranus jail. A Secret Police major tried to make me name 'counter-revolutionaries' I had met.

I said that I should be glad to name counter-revolutionaries: in Russia as well as at home. Several thousands of them had been killed in the Soviet Union during the 'thirties by Yagoda, then Minister of Interior, but in the end the real counter-revolutionary was revealed as Yagoda himself. Then, under his successor, Beria, the Soviet secret police drove hundreds of thousands to their death, until Beria, too, was shot. I added that the supreme enemy of the revolution, the killer of millions, was Josef Stalin, who had since been turned out of his tomb in the Red Square. So it would be best, I suggested, to look elsewhere than in my poor church for counter-revolutionaries.

The officer ordered me to be beaten and kept in solitary confinement. There I stayed until my trial. It was a ten-minute re-hearing, in secret session, of the previous trial ten years before. My wife and son were present this time to hear me denounced.

I waited in a cell later for transport to the next prison. While I spoke to the others about Christ, an officer came in to announce the new court decision. I thanked him, and went on with what I was saying. The sentence had been increased from twenty years to twenty-five.

PART SEVEN

THERE were other newly-sentenced clergy with me in the Secret Police truck. After a short journey it descended a steep ramp and halted. My heart sank, for I knew that I was back in the underground prison of Jilava. Voices shouted, 'Get them out!' and the van doors burst open.

A party of baton-swinging guards drove us with blows along the passage. They had been drinking and at the sight of priests there was a whoop of joy. Grey, grubby prison uniforms were flung at us. Those who were slow in changing had the clothes torn from their backs. Beards were cut off amid roars of laughter. Heads were roughly shaved. Bleeding and half-naked, we were driven into a large cell.

We sat on the stone floor, huddling together in the February cold. Presently a guard lurched in, bawling, 'All priests outside'. There were suppressed giggles and snorts from beyond the door. We filed out, and into another gauntlet of baton-blows, through which we ran, protecting our heads with our arms as best we could. Those who fell were kicked by heavy boots, and spat on.

Half an hour later all priests were again called out. No one moved. Guards rushed into the cell, lashing out indiscriminately.

I tried to comfort those near me. One man had lost some teeth and his lip was badly split. As I cleaned the blood from his face he said, 'I'm Archimandrite Cristescu'.

We had met, years before. I had been waiting to see the Orthodox patriarch. Miron Cristescu was working in his office, so I had told him about our troubles. He had placed his hands on my shoulders and said, 'Brother, Christ will come again: we hope for it'—something a man of God should say often, yet rarely does. I did not forget him. But shaven, with his face streaked by blood and dirt, he was unrecognisable.

The hours passed as we sat and shivered. Miron Cristescu talked of how he and others around the Patriarch had tried to save the Church from becoming an instrument of the state. They thought they could work on the Patriarch's better nature. But Gheorghiu-Dej had chosen well. Justinian was sent on a visit to Moscow, where his head was further turned. He delivered blow after blow at the Catholics, the Uniates and all within his fold who would not compromise.

'Here I am like all the rest,' said Archimandrite Cristescu. 'I was mistaken to try—I should have resisted from the start.'

'Don't let such thoughts sadden you too much,' I said.

He raised his fine eyes to my face and answered, 'Brother Wurmbrand, I know only one sadness, the sadness of not being a saint.'

Spoken from a pulpit this would have been just a beautiful phrase; in that horrible cell, after a ferocious beating, the words showed his true greatness.

2

Miron was with me when a few days later I joined a convoy that headed into the mountains. After many hours the Transylvanian town of Gherla and its largest building, the prison, came into view. Here my wife had visited me during my two-months' stay in 1956. It had other memories for me, too. From the upper windows of the jail, which was built during the reign of Empress Maria Theresa in the eighteenth century, you could see the old gallows, now no longer used; for the Communist method of execution is a shot in the back of the head. Beyond the high walls we saw life going on in the town. Prisoners gazed out at the passing scene and dreamed. But at noon no one could bear to watch. It was then that the children came from school, shouting and laughing as they chased each other home, and every man thought of his own family.

Some 10,000 prisoners were packed into primitive accommodation intended for 2,000, and the régime was as harsh as in the worst days of the re-education campaign. The previous summer there had been serious rioting at Gherla. Prisoners had barricaded themselves into a wing in protest at the nailing up of shutters which kept out light and air. The doors were smashed down by warders. A running fight began. The militia were called in and opened fire, killing and wounding many prisoners. As a punishment food was reduced to starvation level; and hundreds of convicts were dispersed to other jails.

We, priests and pastors, soon took their place, along with thousands of other political prisoners caught in the new wave of arrests—landowners, army officers, doctors, shopkeepers, artisans who would not be herded into co-operatives, farmers who opposed the final seizures of land which the Party was then preparing. After two disastrous Five-Year Plans, Dej had announced a Sixteen-Year Plan, which would last until 1975—'If anyone remains at liberty to operate it,' a prisoner said to me.

The cells were long, dark, echoing barrack-rooms, each containing eighty to 100 men but only fifty to sixty bunks. Many shared a bed. Sleep was difficult. Apart from the usual night-long procession to the lavatory buckets, which soon overflowed, we had a dozen regular snorers: each performed an individual tune; and if one stopped another joined the resonant chorus. Nor could you rest by day, when discipline was enforced by whips and studded boots. The guards made surprise 'security visits' to the cells, banging the iron bars across the windows with their batons to ensure that they had not been filed. At the same time the prisoners lay face down on the floor in rows, to be counted. The guards walked on each man in turn as his name was called.

The slighest breach of the rules brought a minimum of twenty-five lashes, with a doctor standing by—for men had died under such castigation. There was scarcely a man in the prison who had not been flogged, and some had received 'the twenty-five' several times. We agreed that rods hurt more than sticks or batons. The blows burnt like fire: it was as if your back were being grilled by a furnace, and the shock to the nervous system was great. Very noticeable, too, was the brutalising effect these floggings had on the guards, our masters. Blood and power seemed to affect even the best among them, like drink; and they carried the poison of cruelty from the jail out into society every day.

There was one flush-toilet on each landing and to this Miron and I carried the lavatory buckets every day. We had to queue with other prisoners waiting their turn to pour the contents down the drain. The Archimandrite was a fastidious and cultured man, but he forced himself to these chores. One morning he slipped on the greasy stone floor and some liquid splashed a warder's boot.

'Cretin!' the man yelled, striking Miron a vicious blow on the shoulder. 'You'll end up in Rozsa Sandor!'

As we spooned up our gruel later, he asked me what this meant.

'The graveyard,' I replied. 'They always say that—take no notice.'

Rozsa Sandor was the prison cemetery; its grey headstones, deep in weeds, could also be seen from the windows. It was named after a murderer who, during the last century had been sentenced to twenty years, when he was nineteen years old. Looking down through the bars of Gherla he saw in a garden a woman with a baby in her arms. Day after day he watched them. The priest called to baptise the girl child; her first communion party was held; she went to school, and grew into a young woman. All the time Rozsa Sandor watched. She became his life: he decided that they would marry when he was free. At last the day came and he emerged from jail. He hurried over the road and found a party in progress—a wedding feast. She had thought to receive him in this way! He ran up to her and said, 'I cannot tell you how happy I am that you will be my wife today.' The girl stared at hideous, toothless Rozsa Sandor and began to laugh. 'What can the silly old man mean?' she asked. Then, taking the hand of the young man beside her, she said, 'This is my bridegroom.' Rozsa Sandor gaped at the couple. In a fit of rage and madness he snatched up a carving-knife and stabbed them both to death. He was hanged for the murders and buried in the prison cemetery which was called now after his name.

'You'll end in Rozsa Sandor!'

The shouted threat was a daily reminder that we were growing older. Prisoners never realise how time is passing. To themselves they remain the same age as when they entered prison; they dream of the young wives and sweethearts they have left, never the careworn women to whom they will return.

Even the clock over the main gate at Gherla had stopped. It never moved in the six years I was to spend there.

3

The prison commandant was a gross, red-faced little Nero who could not stop eating. Prisoners brought before Major Dorabantu were startled when, in the middle of some tirade, his hand burrowed into a drawer and emerged clasping a garlic-sausage roll or an apple.

My first meeting with him was typical. I stood at attention listening to a rambling, muddled hymn of hate. It seemed that there were only two things Dorabantu did not hate; food and the sound of his own voice.

'So, Wurmbrand!' he cried, showering the table with a mouthful of cakecrumbs. 'A monk, huh!'

I said that I was a pastor.

'Pastors, priests, monks! All the same to me. Grinding the faces of the poor to feather your own nests. I know!' He waved his arms clownishly as he told stories of his wretched boyhood. He had kept his father's sheep near one of the richest monasteries in Rumania; when they strayed on to Church land, the monks had thrashed him brutally.

'Ever seen a priest firing a double-barrelled shotgun at a hungry child, Wurmbrand? A pretty holy picture!'

Dorabantu also complained that he had been exploited as a factory worker in later life. So now he was making good use of his opportunity to pay back the capitalists and priests.

There were some tough characters in my cell, murderers and thieves who were nominally political prisoners because they had killed a Communist or because thieving was sometimes called economic sabotage. Others were war criminals serving life sentences for massacring Russians and Jews. They were bitter, angry men, and all my attempts to offer religious consolation were shouted down. Those in particular who had killed Jews were very bitter against me, because I am myself of the Jewish race. I never hid this fact, and often when I was questioned about it, I expressed the natural love I had towards my nation, although using every man's right to choose his faith. I have chosen another faith than that of most of my people. When I began speaking quietly to a single man in a corner, others formed a menacing circle around us.

'We told you to shut up!' snarled the leader. I stood up and someone pushed me. Another put a leg out and I landed on my face. I felt a violent kick in the ribs. But as the pack fell on me, there was a shout of warning.

A warder, peering through the peep-hole, had seen the struggle and was calling for help. The crowd scattered. When the cell door opened everyone was in his bunk.

'Wurmbrand!' The commandant, prowling the corridors, had heard the story. The guard had recognised me as the tallest in the room, but in the half-darkness he could not identify the attackers.

'Wurmbrand, who did it?'

Nursing a cut lip, I said I could not answer.

'Why not?'

'As a Christian I love and forgive my enemies, I don't denounce them.'

'Then you're an idiot!' snapped Dorabantu.

'There you are right,' I said. 'Anyone who is not a Christian from all his heart is an idiot.'

'Are you calling me an idiot?' thundered the commandant.

'I didn't say that—I meant *I* was not as good a Christian as I should be.'

Dorabantu smote himself on the forehead with the palm of his hand. 'Take him away. Thirty strokes!'

He waddled off, growling, 'Crazy monks!'

When I returned the guards were still questioning prisoners. Since no information was forthcoming, no one else was punished. But after this there were few interruptions when I tried to preach.

4

At times, prison quarrels were comic, although those involved rarely thought so. I lived in several different cells, never with less than sixty men, always with two narrow, barred slits for windows. Should they be open, so that we lay freezing in our beds, or closed, making the air stuffy and evil-smelling, so that we woke each morning with a headache? The topic was debated, literally for hours, day after day, as though we were in Parliament. There were two parties. Those away from the window said, 'Fresh air harms no one.' Those near it replied, 'Thousands die from pneumonia every year.'

'If powerful material interests dictate that twice two should be something other than four, then it will be,' is an axiom of Lenin. We saw this proved in prison. The guards grew bored as we exercised. 'The hour's up—everyone inside!' they shouted. We protested, 'We've not had fifteen minutes yet.' Both sides believed they were right; self-interest dictated our sense of time.

The common criminals quickly settled in, as much at home here, almost, as outside. They had their routine, their order of precedence, their own slang. They were wonderfully clever at smuggling scraps of food. They called the warders by nicknames and tried to cadge cigarettes through the spyhole in the door. They got the positions of trust, leaving the dirty work to the politicals—and the dirtiest to the priests and practising Christians.

Owing to the overcrowding, I was edged in a bunk between two men who quarrelled like moulting birds of prey locked in the same cage. Tall, emaciated ex-Sergeant Grigore had shot Jews by the hundred, in obedience to orders. His enemy Vasile, an 'economic saboteur', made Grigore the scapegoat for all his wrongs. Vasile, who was small and scrawny, quickly found his adversary's weak spot. His face contorted with triumph as he spat out the word, 'Murderer!' Grigore cringed and could not answer.

I told Vasile, 'Why say this? He's old and ill, and we don't know where he will spend eternity: if it's with Christ you're abusing a future citizen of Heaven; and if it's in hell, why add curses to his suffering?'

The thief looked surprised. 'Don't you know how many Russians and Jews that rat killed?'

'That happened during a horrible war twenty years ago,' I replied, 'and he's paid for it with fifteen years of hunger, beatings and prison. Do you call me a clown because I used to turn cart-wheels in the middle of the room when I was three? Or illiterate because I couldn't read when I was four? Those days are past.'

Vasile was annoyed. Next day, a group began talking close to me of how they would treat the Russians if they had the chance.

'Hanging's too good for them,' Vasile screeched. 'They should be flayed alive . . .' Eventually I could not bear it any longer and objected that neither Russians nor anyone else should be treated thus.

'But yesterday,' protested Vasile, 'you defended a man who killed hundreds of Russians, and now you say killing Russians is wrong!'

Grigore was deeply unhappy over the memory of his crimes, and he asked me, 'Have I atoned if I suffer like this—when suffering is forced on me?'

'Yes—the Bible says that he who has suffered in the body has finished with sin.' I told him of poor Lazarus who suffered and went to Heaven. 'If you believe in Christ, you will be saved,' I said.

'People think differently,' he said. 'Look at Eichmann, the man they want to hang in Israel.'

'There's no evidence that he's suffered—but in any case I don't think a man should be accused of crimes committed so long ago. He may not be the same man. I know I am not,' I said. 'And I'm sure that many Jews would agree.' (It was not until years later that I heard that Martin Buber, the great Jewish thinker, had objected to Eichmann's sentence.)

Grigore said, 'I'm not the same because I've repented for what I did; but others might be ready to do it again.'

'Nobody can be punished for what he may possibly do wrong in the future. Wickedness is only a part of us all. Some of the worst men also have great virtues. And so have you, Grigore.'

At this thought he cheered up a little.

There was no lack of laughter in the cell. Gladness, in the Acts of the Apostles, is called a witness to the existence of God; and without such a belief the presence of joy in prison is inexplicable.

Some could laugh at their sufferings. Major Braileanu was one: a short, spry ex-officer with a boyish quiff of hair, he brought a new rumour to the cell. There was to be another summit conference that spring of 1959, between the Soviet Foreign Minister Gromyko and Western representatives. It was said that the meeting would be held on May 10. Prisoners adopted a new greeting—they held up all ten fingers to indicate the hoped-for day of release.

On the day of the conference the guards did, in fact, open the cell and call out four men, Major Braileanu among them. Were they the first to be released? We watched them enviously. But soon we heard shrieks of agony coming from the small recess at the end of the corridor where floggings took place. It was impossible to shut out the sound. Three men were beaten; but when the fourth's turn came he did not utter a murmur under the usual twenty-five blows. Braileanu followed the others back to the cell, pale and unable to speak. He pulled himself up. 'Gentlemen,' he said. 'I give you our new salute.' He held up two fingers of his right hand, five of his left, to signal twenty-five.

Stories and riddles were told by the hour. Everyone had to contribute. There was a certain kind of nonsense that made us laugh better than anything.

'What has three colours, hangs on trees and sings tara-boom-cha-cha?' asked Florescu, a half-gipsy thief. No one could answer. 'A herring.' 'A herring hasn't three colours!' 'If I paint it, it has.' 'They don't hang on trees, either.' 'They do if I tie them on.' 'They don't sing "tara-boom-cha-cha"!' 'I only said that so that you wouldn't guess.'

Gaston, a thin-faced Unitarian pastor who wore thick spectacles, posed another riddle: 'A man travelling on a train has a wife called Eve and they live in a red house: what's his name?' There was puzzlement on all faces—if a man went by train and shared a red house with his wife Eve, how did that help to know his name? 'Easy,' said Gaston, 'it's Charles.' 'But how do you know?' 'I've known him for years, he's my best friend.'

Archimandrite Miron told what he swore was a true story

about the commandant: strolling down a line of convicts on parade, he asked each man the same question: 'What is your crime?'

'I've done nothing sir, and I've got ten years.'

Dorabantu moved on. 'And what is your crime?'

'Nothing sir, and I've got twenty years.'

'Lying swine,' said Dorabantu indignantly. 'Nobody in the People's Republic gets more than ten years for nothing!'

The small thieves and pickpockets were the best story-tellers. They lived, outrageously, on their wits. Florescu said he had robbed a jeweller in Carol Street, Bucharest, which was lined with jewellers' shops. He told the story like this:

Mr. Hershcovici, courtliest of jewellers, welcomed an elegant young couple to his premises. 'Good morning,' said the man, who was, of course, Florescu. 'This is my fiancée, the sweetest girl in Bucharest!' And one of the richest, too, according to their chatter. 'We've come to choose the ring—diamonds, of course . . . Oh no, those are too small.' From rings they proceeded to a jewel-faced watch for the girl's mother, an alligator dressing-case for her father, and then the girl broke in with, 'Oh dear, we mustn't forget the bishop. He's my uncle, so he won't accept a fee for the service and you know our tradition: a service not paid for is not acceptable to Heaven.' 'True, true, but what does one give a bishop?' And at this moment the eyes of both turned to a showcase which held a complete set of gilded episcopal robes. 'Just the thing!' cried Florescu. 'But, dear,' said the girl, 'we don't know whether they'll fit him.' Florescu looked the jeweller up and down. 'They're just the same build!' And Hershcovici, hoping to sell the costly robes, allowed himself to be draped in a golden cassock. They tied the belt around his waist and jammed a glittering mitre on his head. 'A perfect fit!' said Florescu. 'Just hold this sceptre!'

With that, the couple swept the jewellery into the alligator case and ran from the shop. Hershcovici was paralysed with shock; then he followed, screaming, 'Thieves! Stop them! Help!' The Jewish merchants ran to their doors and saw Hershcovici galloping down an empty street in the full regalia of an Orthodox metropolitan. 'Hershcovici's gone mad!' they shouted. Three of them brought him down and held him as he struggled and protested. 'No, no! What are you doing? The thieves are escaping!' So they did, up a side street, never to be caught.

When the laughter stopped, Pastor Gaston said, 'But they caught you in the end, Florescu.' The thief did not want to discuss that episode.

'Well, suppose you tell us why you're here, Pastor?' he said.

'Very well,' said Gaston. 'It's a funny story too. I was given seven years for a Christmas sermon on the flight of the Holy Family into Egypt.'

Gaston had been denounced by one of his congregation. At his trial it was said that in deploring Herod's attempt to kill the child Jesus in the massacre of the innocents, Gaston was really attacking the Communist campaign against religion; while his references to Egypt revealed to his hope that Nasser would join the imperialist camp.

Pastor Gaston asked an interrogator afterwards what he had really done to upset the Party. 'I always sided with the workers,' he protested. 'I started a school and a co-operative. I doubled my congregation.'

The officer laughed. 'The kind of priest we want is the man in the next parish to yours—a lecherous old drunkard whose church is always empty.'

Gaston sometimes spoke to me about his poor childhood. He was always hungry, and he had stolen when there was nothing to eat. 'Once I raided a hencoop,' he said. 'They paraded me through the village with a notice round my neck saying "Thief!" ' He grew up 'wanting to overturn the world'.

He studied various systems of politics and philosophy and joined the Unitarian Church. When the police came, they found among his hundreds of books a copy of Adler's 'Individual Psychology'.

'Aha!' said a detective. 'An individualist!' and carried the book off as evidence.

5

In a batch of new prisoners I was shocked to see Professor Popp. He looked ill, and he moved like an old man. We had not met after the amnesty of 1956 and my letters had gone unanswered. Popp explained why that evening.

Like many other released prisoners he had plunged into a hunt for pleasure. 'I felt starved,' he said. 'I was afraid life had passed me by. I had to prove that I could enjoy myself again. I spent lavishly, I drank too much, I left my wife for a younger woman.

'Then I was sorry. I hadn't forgotten my Christian vows. I wanted to see you, but you were far away. I told everything to another pastor, and blamed Communism for destroying the country. He listened—and then denounced me.'

Popp had been given another twelve-year sentence. His first prison term had brought out all the strength and goodness in him. He had been like a seabird that rises highest on its wings in the face of the wind, and falls as the wind falls. Now his will was weak. I tried to bring him back to God, but life seemed empty of meaning to him.

He said that, soon after his sentence, he had been informed of his 'civil burial'. This was a new feature of life in the People's Republic. When a counter-revolutionary went to jail, his colleagues, friends and family were gathered together by a Party official who told them, 'Comrades, this man is dead for ever and for everyone. We are here to bury his memory'. One by one, his offences against the State had to be denounced by the 'mourners'. Popp's widowed daughter spoke with the rest. Had she refused, she might have lost her job, and she was the mother of three young children.

Popp was put to work with me on the second day. We had to clean the floor of the large cell, scrubbing it from end to end. A prisoner elected by the guards as a room leader walked up when we were almost finished and kicked over the bucket of dirty water, saying, 'Now do it again!' Finally a guard came to inspect. He grabbed the room leader, bringing his face down towards some mud he had brought in on his own boots. 'Filthy!' he yelled. We scrubbed for another hour, to the accompaniment of kicks and insults from the room leader. There is no oppressor worse than the oppressed.

This experience left Popp shaking with exhaustion. As a

distraction, I introduced him over the meal to Pastor Gaston. A look of shock passed over Gaston's face. Popp simply turned away and closed his eyes.

As the days passed, the professor withdrew further into himself. We had to urge him to eat and help him get ready each morning. He neither laughed, nor wept, nor joined in the life of the cell. But one morning, stung by some jeering remark from the room leader, he seized the man's throat, clinging to it like a madman until two guards clubbed him down. He was carried unconscious to the hospital wing; next day we heard that he was dead.

6

The tragedy filled the cell with sorrow. While others prayed for Popp's soul, according to the Orthodox habit, Gaston lay in silence on his bunk, and when I spoke of eternal life he rose and moved away.

There was talk in the cell that evening of life after death. Gaston was asked what he thought on the question. 'Progressive Unitarians don't believe in a supernatural survival,' he said.

'But we are not talking to Progressive Unitarians,' I replied. 'We are talking to you. Let's have the courage to be ourselves. Not always "we Catholics, we Protestants, we Rumanians . . ."'

'Speaking personally, then, I don't believe in it.'

'If you are speaking personally,' I said, 'that is the first step to believing, for personality is God's greatest gift to man, the one thing that remains as your body changes. The atoms of oxygen and hydrogen in my body are the same as in yours. My body's heat can be measured on the same instrument as yours. All bodily energies—chemical, electrical—are alike from man to man. But my thoughts, my feelings, my will are my own. Physical energy is like a poker chip, which has no mark on it. Spiritual energy is like a coin that bears the head of a king. Why, then, should it share the body's fate?'

Florescu, who had drawn up a stool, said—with an obscenity, 'I believe in what I can see, taste and feel. We're all matter, like this bit of wood I'm sitting on, and when you're dead, that's it.'

I went over and kicked the stool from under him. It shot across the floor, and Florescu went down with a bump. He scrambled up furiously and made for me, but the others held him. 'What's the idea?' he snarled.

I replied mildly, 'But you said you were matter like the stool. I didn't hear the stool complain!'

There was some laughter, in which even Gaston joined.

'I'm sorry, Florescu,' I said. 'I just wanted to prove that since matter does not react with love or hate, it is, after all, different from us.'

Florescu sulked for a while, then interrupted again:

'I might believe if the dead ever came back to talk to us.'

'I am sure that men have been in touch with the dead,' I replied. 'Great scientists from Newton to Sir Oliver Lodge have believed in spiritualism. The Bible describes the evocation of the dead King Saul. Scriptures forbid it but say it is possible.'

The row over the stool had brought others to listen, and I began to preach earnestly about life after death. It was for us no academic matter, but a topic of burning and immediate interest. Men died every day in Gherla.

'If God had made us for this life only,' I said, 'he would first have given us age with its wisdom, then youth with its vigour. It seems senseless to gather knowledge and understanding simply to take it to the grave. Luther compares our life on earth to the life of an unborn child: he says that if the embryo could reason in the womb it would wonder why it grew hands and feet, and it would surely come to the conclusion that there must be another world to come in which it would play and run and work. Just as the embryo is preparing for a future state, so are we.'

I forgot the guards and raised my voice to preach to prisoners lying in bunks that rose in tiers to the ceiling. Eyes watched me in the dim light which the weak bulb hanging above us seemed to make still more dismal.

I said, 'Suppose I argue that there is room in a pint bottle for ten pints of milk. You would say I am mad. Yet I can have together in my head thoughts of an event like the Flood, which happened thousands of years ago, of my wife and son in the room where I left them, of God and the devil. How does it happen that within the narrow limits of my head there are encompassed the daily things of life, and the infinite and the eternal? The illimitable must be contained by something illimitable: this is the spirit. When your unfettered spirit can go anywhere in time or space, do you believe that it can share the fate of this husk which is the body?'

While I spoke of these things there was a silence such as there never is in church. No one yawned or fidgeted, no thoughts strayed. The prisoners, in soiled clothes, their cheeks hollow and their eyes big with hunger, received the thought of survival after death as thirsty soil receives rain.

7

Next day before reveille I awoke to find Gaston's bunk empty. Then I saw the outline of his frail body at the window. I threw a blanket round my shoulders and joined him. We looked down through the bars. The light was ashen. Mist hung in the yard, but we could see a row of black coffins lying by the main gate. They contained men who had died in the last twenty-four hours: one would be Popp. This was a daily scene at Gherla, and I wondered why Gaston had chosen this day to rise and watch. I tried to get him back to bed, but he would not move.

Under our eyes, a guard crossed the yard and raised the lids of the coffins, exposing the bodies. Behind him came a hulking figure with a steel stake in his hand. He lifted it and plunged the steel into each corpse in turn.

'God rest their souls,' I said.

The guards were making sure that no life remained and that no would-be escapees had replaced the bodies. Gaston was trembling. I put the blanket around him, but he continued to stand watching while the coffins were closed and loaded on to the lorry which would take them to Rozsa Sandor cemetery.

For days after this, Gaston brooded. Whatever was on his mind he would not reveal it to us. He rebuffed all my attempts to break into his misery. In the evenings he would listen to the others exchanging stories, but only once did he contribute one himself.

The prisoners exchanged glances; he had been silent and morose so long that they did not know what to expect.

He said: 'I was sitting in a restaurant just before my arrest. I thought it would raise my spirits to have a good meal. So I hung my overcoat by a corner table and ordered all the things I liked. Another customer nearby looked at me in a worried way and rose to speak, but I waved him away. "Please," I said, "we all have our troubles and I should like to dine in peace." The meal was good. I lit a cigar and I thought I should apologise for being uncivil: I asked the man's pardon and said perhaps he would like to tell me the trouble now. "Too late," he said, "the stove's burnt a hole in your overcoat." '

Gaston's story won some laughter, but he went back to his bunk and lay down in the darkness. At one period Gaston had spent hours telling us how he honoured Christ as the greatest teacher, but not as God, and what the Unitarians accepted as true in the Bible and what not. Their reappraisal did not leave much to hold on to. They were not over-concerned with eternal life, he said. But now he began to talk again about Professor Popp. What proof was there that anything remained after the horrible scene we had watched together that dawn? The male human creature, he said, needed four things to survive: food, warmth, sleep, a woman companion. 'And the last can be dispensed with,' he added. 'My wife's gone to live with another man. Our two children are in a state home.'

'You yourself don't believe this,' I said. 'We live here on the very minimum of these things, yet every day you hear laughter and men singing. Their bodies have nothing to sing about. It's something else in them that sings. You believe in the soul, don't you? What the ancient Egyptians called *kaa*, the Greeks *psyche*, the Hebrews *neshama*? Why else do you worry about your children's upbringing? If it will all be over for them in a few decades, what do any of us want with religion, morals, or decency?'

'It's too late,' he said. 'I can't change now. My life has been smouldering away, like my coat in that restaurant, and people have tried to warn me before; but it's gone too far at last. I've nothing to live for, and the only thing that keeps me from suicide is that I'm scared of dying. I kept a piece of glass the other day —I meant to slash my wrists; but I didn't have the courage.'

I said, 'Suicide proves nothing except that the soul is strong and independent enough to kill the body for its own reasons. Even if you were free and had all you wanted, you might feel this way. It's terrible about your wife and children: but I feel there is something else troubling you, something you have not told anyone.'

Gaston was silent.

I continued, 'I knew a prisoner who knowingly starved himself to give bread to his son who was in jail with him, until he died of malnutrition. That's how strong the soul is. A man like Kreuger, the Swedish match millionaire who had everything the body can possibly need, killed himself, leaving a note that spoke of "melancholia". He had had something else than the body; the soul for which he had not cared. But you have inner resources, you have Christianity, to help you. Speak to Jesus: He will give you comfort and strength.'

Gaston sighed in the darkness. 'You make it sound as if He was here with us, alive.'

'Certainly he's alive,' I said, 'Don't you believe even in the Resurrection? Tomorrow I'll prove it to you!'

'How you persist!' he said. 'You're worse than a Communist!'

8

While the prisoners were talking next evening I reminded them that Easter was approaching—my second in Gherla.

'If we had any hard-boiled eggs we could dye them red and crack them together, following the Orthodox custom,' I said. I held out my hand as if offering an Easter egg, and said, 'Christ is risen!'

Old Vasilescu, one of the farmers, hit my fist with his own and cried, 'He is risen indeed!' A chorus of voices echoed the traditional response.

'That's a strange thing to say!' I said, turning to the others. 'Surely Christ died on the Cross? What proof have you that He is risen?'

There was a silence. Vasilescu tugged at his heavy moustaches. 'I'm a simple farmer, but I believe it because my father and mother and his father and all our priests and teachers told me so.

I believe it because I see how nature is resurrected every year. When the snow is on the ground, you can't ever believe that the fields will bear crops in spring. But the trees bud and the air grows warm, and the grass green. If the world can come alive again, so can Christ.'

'A sound answer,' said Miron.

'But in a world where every Christian assertion is challenged, that's not enough,' said Gaston.

'We need the strongest proofs, I agree,' I said, 'and they exist. Mommsen, the great historian of the Roman Empire, calls the Resurrection the best-proven fact in history. Do you believe the classical historians were largely truthful?'

No one argued.

'They were usually courtiers, the flatterers of kings, men who praised for profit or to please powerful protectors. How much more should we believe Paul, Peter, Matthew, Andrew, Apostles who died a martyr's death to spread the truth!'

I asked Major Braileanu, 'When you served on courts-martial, did you take account of a witness's character as well as his words?'

'Of course,' he replied. 'In a clash of evidence it is all-important.'

'Then we must credit the Apostles on that ground, for they spent their time doing and preaching good.'

'It's miracles like the feeding of five thousand with five fishes that stretch my belief,' said the major.

'What is a miracle?' I asked. 'Missionaries from Africa say they are at first received as miracle workers; the primitive tribesman is astounded to see a match struck. Pearl Buck told women in a remote part of China that in her own country carriages moved without horses. "What a liar!" they whispered. So a miracle is simply something a superior creature can do, and Jesus was a man of exceptional powers.'

Gaston objected, 'A primitive man might accept such a thing. It remains hard for a rationalist.'

'It is rational to believe that Christ rose from the dead; otherwise we must accept the impossible—that the church, which has survived the external assaults and internal corruptions of 2000 years, is built on a lie. Only consider that Jesus in his lifetime organised no church, wrote no books. He had a handful of poor disciples and one of these betrayed him for money, while the rest fled or denied him when the test came. He died on the Cross crying, "My God, my God, why hast Thou forsaken me?" His tomb was closed with a huge stone.'

'Not a hopeful start,' said Braileanu.

'Then how do you explain that it led to a world religion?'

'The disciples came together again,' said Gaston doubtfully.

'But what gave them the power to preach and to die for their faith?'

'They overcame their fear in time, I suppose.'

'Yes, they say how they mastered it: on the third day Christ appeared in person and gave them courage. Peter, who had been frightened by a housemaid, stood in Jerusalem and declared that he and his brethren had seen and spoken with Christ; that He had risen indeed. Peter said they might kill him before he denied it again. So the Romans did.'

'Was it rational to believe', I asked, 'that Peter and the disciples went to be crucified for a liar? Peter gave his first sermon about the Resurrection 500 yards from the empty tomb. He knew that the facts could not be contradicted, and no one among Christ's enemies attempted to do so.'

'Why was Saul of Tarsus so easily converted by his vision of Christ reproaching him, on the road to Damascus? Saul was the scourge of Christianity,' I said.

'It may have been an auditory and visual hallucination,' said Braileanu.

'Paul knew about these things. An apparition is no argument to an expert like him. He yielded so quickly and completely because, as a member of the Sanhedrin, he knew the great secret–that the tomb was empty!'

Archimandrite Miron had sat sewing a patch on his trousers as we talked. He raised his intense luminous eyes to Gaston and said, 'Years ago I had a postcard from my brother in New York, who had been to the top of the Empire State Building. He didn't investigate the foundations first, Pastor Gaston. The fact that it had been there forty years is proof that the foundations are good. The same with the Church, which has rested 2000 years on the truth.'

Our arguments had an effect on Gaston. His pain was eased and his faith deepened. The wish to kill himself faded as the weeks passed; but still he seemed to carry a load of guilt.

The summer brought a fresh influx of prisoners. We were moved into different cells, and I lost sight of him.

9

Months went by, and I preached and worked in a dozen cells at Gherla. I was often punished, and it was because of a beating that I met Gaston again.

We were playing chess in the cell with figures made out of pieces of bread one day when Dorabantu, who still prowled the corridors burst in. 'I'll have no gambling!' he bellowed.

I suggested that chess was a game of skill, not chance.

The commandant expanded his chest, 'Tcha! Ridiculous! Skill is also a matter of chance!'

Pleased with this answer, he strutted away. When he had gone the prisoners burst into laughter and started to mimic his voice. The door crashed open again. Dorabantu had been eaves-dropping.

'Wurmbrand—out you come!' Others were ordered out with me.

'You'll laugh on the other side of your faces this time,' shouted the commandant.

We received twenty-five strokes each and afterwards were moved to an isolation cell. There, alone on a bunk, lying face down, I found Gaston. He, too, had been beaten. His back was a mass of bloody wounds. We tried to ease the pain with applica-tions of a shirt soaked in water, and when the worst had passed, I examined the raw flesh for splinters of wood. His body shook as if in a fever. He could not speak much at first, but slowly, in broken phrases, he explained that he had been punished for preaching. A prisoner had informed on him.

He said, 'I want to tell you something . . .'

'You mustn't talk.'

'Now or never. About Professor Popp—and the pastor who betrayed him . . .' He stopped, his lips trembling.

'You needn't tell me,' I began.

'I couldn't stand the pressure! I've suffered. When he died . . .' He began to sob.

We prayed together. He said that he could never forgive himself.

'The professor didn't; how could anyone?' he asked.

'Of course they can. So would Popp if he had known everything,' I said. 'Let me tell you about a man who was far worse than you. It will help us to pass the night. He was the murderer of my wife's family. She forgave him, and he became one of our closest friends. There are only two men my wife kisses—her husband, and the man who murdered her family.' I told Gaston the story.

When Rumania entered the war on Germany's side, a pogrom began in which many thousands of Jews were killed or deported. At Iasi alone 11,000 were massacred in a day. My wife, who shares my Protestant faith, is also of Jewish origin. We lived in Bucharest, from which the Jews were not deported, but her parents, one of her brothers, three sisters and other relatives who lived in Bucovine were taken to Transmistria, a wild border province which the Rumanians had captured from Russia. Jews who were not murdered at the end of this journey were left to starve, and there Sabina's family died.

I had to break this news. She recovered herself and said, 'I will not weep. You are entitled to a happy wife, and Mihai to a happy mother, and our Church to a servant with courage.' If she shed tears in private I do not know, but from that day I never saw Sabina weep again.

Some time later our landlord, a good Christian, told me sadly of a man who was staying in the house while on leave from the front. 'I knew him before the war,' he said, 'but he's changed completely. He has become a brute who likes to boast of how he volunteered to exterminate Jews in Transmistria and killed hundreds with his own hands.'

I was deeply distressed and I decided to pass the night in prayer. To avoid disturbing Sabina, who was unwell and who would have wished to join in my vigil in spite of that, I went upstairs after supper to the landlord's flat to pray with him.

Lounging in an armchair was a giant of a man whom the landlord introduced as Borila, the killer of Jews from Transmistria. When he rose he was even taller than I, and there seemed to be about him an aura of horror that was like a smell of blood. Soon he was telling us of his adventures in the war and of the Jews he had slaughtered.

'It is a frightening story,' I said, 'but I do not fear for the Jews—God will compensate them for what they have suffered. I ask myself with anguish what will happen to the murderers when they stand before God's judgment.'

An ugly scene was prevented by the landlord who said that we were both guests in his house, and turned the talk into more neutral channels. The murderer proved to be not only a murderer. Nobody is only one thing. He was a pleasant talker, and eventually it came out that he had a great love of music.

He mentioned that while serving in the Ukraine he had been captivated by the songs there. 'I wish I could hear them again,' he said.

I knew some of these old songs. I thought to myself, looking at Borila, 'The fish has entered my net!'

'If you'd like to hear some of them,' I told him, 'come to my flat—I'm no pianist, but I can play a few Ukrainian melodies.'

The landlord, his wife and daughter accompanied us. My wife was in bed. She was used to my playing softly at night and did not wake up. I played the folk-songs, which are alive with feeling, and I could see that Borila was deeply moved. I remembered how, when King Saul was afflicted by an evil spirit, the boy David had played the harp before him.

I stopped and turned to Borila. 'I've something very important to say to you,' I told him.

'Please speak,' he said.

'If you look through that curtain you can see someone is asleep in the next room. It's my wife, Sabina. Her parents, her sisters and her twelve-year-old brother have been killed with the rest of the family. You told me that you had killed hundreds of Jews near Golta, and that is where they were taken.' Looking into his eyes, I added, 'You yourself don't know who you have shot, so we can assume that you are the murderer of her family.'

He jumped up, his eyes blazing, looking as if he were about to strangle me.

I held up my hand and said, 'Now—let's try an experiment. I shall wake my wife and tell her who you are, and what you have done. I can tell you what will happen. My wife will not speak one word of reproach! She'll embrace you as if you were her brother. She'll bring you supper, the best things she has in the house.

'Now, if Sabina, who is a sinner like us all, can forgive and love like this, imagine how Jesus, who is perfect Love, can forgive and love you! Only return to Him—and everything you have done will be forgiven!'

Borila was not heartless: within, he was consumed by guilt and misery at what he had done, and he had shaken his brutal talk at us as a crab its claws. One tap at his weak spot, and his defences crumbled. The music had already moved his heart, and now came—instead of the attack he expected—words of forgiveness. His reaction was amazing. He jumped up and tore at his collar with both hands, so that his shirt was rent apart. 'Oh God, what shall I do, what shall I do?' he cried. He put his head in his hands and sobbed noisily as he rocked himself back and forth. 'I'm a murderer, I'm soaked in blood, what shall I do?' Tears ran down his cheeks.

I cried, 'In the name of the Lord Jesus Christ, I command the devil of hatred to go out of your soul!'

Borila fell on his knees trembling, and we began to pray aloud. He knew no prayers; he simply asked again and again for forgiveness and said that he hoped and knew it would be granted. We were on our knees together for some time; then we stood up and embraced each other, and I said, 'I promised to make an experiment. I shall keep my word.'

I went into the other room and found my wife still sleeping calmly. She was very weak and exhausted at that time. I woke her gently and said, 'There is a man here whom you must meet. We believe he has murdered your family, but he has repented, and now he is our brother.'

She came out in her dressing-gown and put out her arms to embrace him; then both began to weep and to kiss each other again and again. I have never seen bride and bridegroom kiss with such love and passion and purity as this murderer and the survivor among his victims. Then, as I foretold, Sabina went to the kitchen to bring him food.

While she was away the thought came to me that Borila's crime had been so terrible that some further lesson was needed. I went to the next room and returned with my son, Mihai, who was then two, asleep in my arms. It was only a few hours since Borila had boasted to us how he had killed Jewish children in their parents' arms, and now he was horrified; the sight was an unbearable reproach. He expected me to accuse him. But I said, 'Do you see how quietly he sleeps? You are also like a newborn child who can rest in the Father's arms. The blood that Jesus shed has cleansed you.'

Borila's happiness was very moving: he stayed with us that night, and when he awoke the next day, he said, 'It's a long time since I slept like that.'

St. Augustine says, '*Anima humana naturaliter Christiana est*'—the human soul is naturally Christian. Crime is against one's own nature, the result of social pressure or many other causes, and what a relief it is to cast it off as he had done!

That morning Borila wanted to meet our Jewish friends and I took him to many Hebrew Christian homes. Everywhere he told his story, and he was received as the returning prodigal son. Then, with a New Testament which I gave him, he went to join his regiment in another town.

Borila later came to say that his unit had been ordered to the front. 'What shall I do?' he asked. 'I'll have to start killing again.'

I said, 'No, you've killed more than a soldier needs to already. I don't mean that a Christian shouldn't defend his country if it is attacked. But you, personally, shouldn't kill any more—better allow others to kill you. The Bible doesn't forbid that!'

10

As I told the story, Gaston grew quieter. At the end, he smiled and reached out to clasp my hand; and so he fell into an untroubled sleep.

In the morning we were moved back together into another

cell. Among the prisoners, I found Grigore, who was also a war criminal responsible for massacring Jews. He knew Borila.

I told Gaston, 'There's an epilogue to the story of the man who killed my wife's family. This man can tell you it.'

Grigore explained how he had served with Borila in Transmistria, where they had massacred the Jews. 'When we went to Russia again, he was a changed man,' he said. 'We couldn't understand it. He put aside his weapons and instead of taking lives, he saved them. He volunteered to rescue the wounded under fire, and in the end he saved his officer.'

II

The months turned into years: two had gone by, and except that the faces came and went, all else remained the same. Prison made of some men saints, and of others brutes, and it was difficult to tell who would be saint, and who brute; but one thing was sure—that the majority of prisoners would go on living, as it were, in a vacuum. They sprawled on their bunks, hour after hour with nothing to do. Talk became the whole of life. I wondered what would happen if science should ever make work unnecessary. There is a limit to innovation in sex, films, and other drugs; and so many have nothing else in their minds.

As my third year in Gherla progressed, things eased a little. We gained a little more freedom of speech, a few mouthfuls more of food. Conditions outside were changing again, we gathered. We did not know in what way, nor that the greatest trial still lay ahead.

PART EIGHT

On a morning of March 1962, the guards burst into the cells, shouting 'All priests outside!' The others gathered their few belongings and filed dutifully into the corridors. I did not stir.

We had a new commandant, a martinet called Alexandrescu. This move, whatever its purpose, meant more trouble, and I wanted to work and preach without fresh hindrance. It turned out that the whole jail was being divided into class groups: 'intellectuals' in one cell, peasants in another, military men in a third, and so on. Overcrowding and the stupidity of the guards led to muddles. A member of a sect called 'Students of the Bible' was placed in a cell of writers and teachers; he was an ignorant labourer, but to the officials, all 'students' were intellectuals.

When the clergy had departed, a guard asked me what I was. 'A pastor,' I replied in a country accent. So I was placed in a cell with shepherds and farm hands. 'Pastor' is the usual word for a shepherd in Rumanian.

I escaped segregation for a few weeks. Then an informer betrayed me, and I was taken, after a beating, to the cell in which priests had been gathered. It was to be my home for the rest of my stay in Gherla—cavernous, with walls of grey, dirty cement. The only light was from two narrow windows. Bunks were closely packed in tiers four-high. There were some low benches, and a table. The prisoners—mostly clergy, but with other

Christian believers—numbered about 100. There was always a queue waiting to use the lavatory bucket.

As I entered, a deep voice cried, 'Welcome, welcome!' It was old Bishop Mirza, an exemplar of the Orthodox faith and a man of great goodness. His rusty black pullover was full of holes. He had sad gentle eyes and an aureole of white hair.

Heads were raised and I greeted men I knew—including Archimandrite Miron, who had a bunk above the bishop and Gaston.

That evening, in the hour which the priests' room had set aside for prayer, Catholics collected in one corner, the Orthodox occupied another, the Unitarians a third. The Jehovah's Witnesses had a nest on the upper bunks; the Calvinists assembled down below. Twice a day, our various services were held: but among all these ardent worshippers I could scarcely find two men of different sects to say one 'Our Father' together.

Far from fostering understanding, our common plight made for conflict. Catholics could not forgive the Orthodox hierarchy for collaborating with Communism. Minorities disagreed about 'rights'. Disputes arose over every point of doctrine. And while discussion was normally conducted with genteel malice, as learnt in seminaries on wet Sunday afternoons, sometimes tempers flared.

When mass was celebrated a few feet from his bunk day after day, the evangelical pastor Haupt evoked some words of Martin Luther.

'What's that?' one of the Catholics demanded.

Haupt raised his voice obligingly: 'I repeated the words of Luther; "All the brothels which God condemns, all murders, thefts, adulteries do not make so much harm as the abomination of the Papal mass".'

After the service had broken up, one of the Catholics, Father Fazekas, said: '*Dear* brother, have you not heard the saying, "Mankind has suffered three great catastrophies—the fall of Lucifer, and of Adam, and the revolt of Martin Luther'?"

Father Andricu, an Orthodox priest, joined in the counter-attack: 'Luther and Lucifer,' he put in, 'are one and the same!' So Catholic and Orthodox followers became temporary allies.

But before nightfall, they were squabbling over the supremacy of Rome.

Fazekas was of Hungarian origin, and this was held against him even by his fellow-Catholics. When he prayed aloud to the Virgin Mary as 'patron of Hungary', general displeasure was shown.

'Isn't the Blessed Virgin Rumania's patron, too?' asked a patriotic Orthodox priest.

'Certainly not, she is Hungary's patron.'

Gaston ironically wondered if the Virgin was not patron of Palestine, since it seemed treacherous to leave the country of her birth to become patron of another.

'Perhaps you haven't heard that the Jews murdered her son?' said Fazekas.

Bishop Mirza, smiling gently, tried to calm everyone down. 'The Virgin is not bound to any one country,' he said. 'She leads the Church, she is Queen of Heaven, she moves the planets and heads the choirs of angels!'

I said that didn't leave God much to do.

Other Protestants supported me but in a manner which I disliked. 'Why should I venerate Jesus's mother like this?' said one. 'She cannot save.'

Fazekas replied, 'Poor man! Do you venerate only those who will save you? The mother of the Lord sings in the Magnificat, "All generations will call me blessed". They do so because she was Jesus's mother, not because she distributes favours.'

It was a good answer, yet, much as I honour the Virgin Mary, I believe her role has been exaggerated by her following, and that this distortion began in ancient times. When Christians first thought about Heaven, they had visions of an oriental court: a place of luxury, music and sweet scents. A man requiring a favour from the sultan found a friend, who said a word to a vizier, who might pass it on to the sultan's favourite wife, and she to her husband. It created the idea of a spiritual hierarchy, in which simple men put their requests to priests, priests to the saints, the saints to the Virgin.

The bedrock of my faith is that a man may speak directly to God, but there are times when argument only encourages anger.

I told the others of the two martyrs of different confessions who were sent together to the stake. They were asked if they had a last wish before the fire was lit. Both said, 'Yes! Tie us back to back so that I don't have to see that damned heretic as I die.'

Sometimes I too could not hide my feelings. For hours I listened to Father Ranghet, a Dominican in the bunk below, telling his beads.

At last I said, 'Why do you have to appeal a thousand times a day to the Virgin? Is she deaf, or indifferent or reluctant to hear? When I ask someone here for a favour he grants it if he can; but I do not keep on asking, if he doesn't.'

Ranghet was cross. 'Since you Lutherans have no belief in the infallibility of the Holy Father, you have still less cause to believe in your own,' he said. 'What's wrong in your impaired sight is right in mine.' And he went back to repeating 'Hail Mary . . .' rather louder than before.

'You speak often of the "Holy Father"—do you mean God?' I asked.

'I mean His Holiness the Pope!' he answered.

'To me it seems blasphemy to use divine titles for a human being,' I replied. 'You call him Christ's Vicar on earth, which means his substitute—but I cannot accept such a substitute, any more than I could allow my wife to have a substitute for me.'

'You go too far!' he cried.

And I had thought it was he who went too far! Only that day Father Ranghet had said that all the sacrifices, of life, of liberty, offered by all men, were as nothing compared with the offering he made at the altar when he sacrified the son of God. I could not accept that a priest made God from a piece of bread, or that there was any need for such a thing. I could not believe that my eternal destiny depended on absolution from a man who might not be too sure of Heaven himself.

I looked for topics on which we could agree. When Pastor Weingartner, a modernist Protestant, took issue with Catholics on the Virgin Birth, I felt bound to take their side.

Weingartner said he could not accept such a scientific improbability.

I replied, 'It is too late to make an historical inquiry into the

Virgin Birth, but it is also too early to dismiss it as scientifically impossible. An American biologist called Loeb has already produced a birth without male seed in infra-organisms. What a biologist can do for a small being surely God can do for man?'

'But the history of religion is crowded with virgin births,' said Weingartner. 'It can only be a myth.'

I answered by telling the story of a famous rabbi who lived in the Ukraine in Czarist times, and was once called upon to give evidence in defence of a follower. The noble looks and spirituality of Rabbi Hofez Haim impressed the court, but the old man refused to take the oath; he was unwilling, he said, to involve God's name in his evidence. The prosecution protested, 'We must have a guarantee that he is telling the truth.'

The defence lawyer rose. 'Your honour,' he said, 'may I mention something which will prove the character of my witness and show that we can accept his evidence, even if, for religious reasons, he cannot be put on oath? Rabbi Hofez Haim often goes from shop to shop collecting money for the poor. One day a thief knocked him down and snatched the purse containing the collection. The rabbi was upset—not so much at the loss of the money, which he instantly decided to replace from his own small savings at home—but at the harm done to the thief's soul. He ran after him calling, 'You have no guilt before God, it is my money and I give it to you freely! The money for the poor is safe at my house! Spend what you have taken with a clear conscience!'

The judge gazed sternly at the lawyer. 'Do you believe this story?' he asked.

'No, I don't.'

'Then why tell us stories you don't believe?'

'Your honour, has such a story ever been told of you, or me or my friend, the prosecutor? They say instead—of course it's quite untrue—that we are too fond of women, or drink, or gambling. What a saint this man must be to have such legends woven around his name!'

Weingartner said, 'Very amusing—but I don't know if the story about the rabbi was true, and I cannot believe the story of the Virgin Birth either.'

'Christians believe the word of God,' I said. 'But if it were a myth, as you call it, don't scoff. Myths have a profound place in human thought. They are often the measure of a man's greatness.'

'You mean that people must have thought Jesus very great to believe that he was not born like other men?' he said.

'My own son, when he was very young, asked me how Jesus was born,' I said. 'So I told him again the story of the manger. "No," he objected, "that's not what I want to know. Sometimes people say, 'What's born of a cat eats mice,' and if Jesus had been born like us, he would have been bad like us".'

Bishop Mirza had been listening to us. 'A child spoke like that!' he said.

'You have a point,' admitted Pastor Weingartner. 'We must try harder to understand each other's views.'

I said, 'I confess that I would have accepted Christianity in another form than Lutherism, if it had been so presented to me at the time of my conversion. What matters is respect for the Scriptures as the only rule, and salvation by faith in Jesus. The names and forms don't count.'

Next morning a pleasing thing happened. Bishop Mirza came to me and said, 'I thought in the night of the Lord's Prayer which tells us to say, "Our Father which art in heaven . . . forgive our trespasses". Jesus did not tell us to confess to a priest, or receive absolution from him—he told us to pray for it to the Father. Of course the question is not a simple one, but if I were a Protestant, I should use this argument. So I thought that in friendship I would make you a present of it in exchange for your defence of the Virgin Mary.'

The bishop had set us an example. If we failed to live in peace together, we fell into the trap which the Communists had laid: by locking us up together, they deprived the other prisoners of spiritual guidance while we vitiated our cause with quarrels. But what else did they have in mind?

Electricians had been working in the prison for some time, and in many cells loudspeakers had been fitted, one to each wall. So we were to have broadcasts.

Gaston said, 'It won't be light music.'

2

When the entire prison had been divided into classes, a series of lectures began. They seemed absurd. A brash, young political officer would explain that an eclipse of the sun was about to occur, but there was no cause for alarm—socialist science had freed us from superstition. He proceeded to explain the workings of a solar eclipse to a yawning audience of dons and doctors. The event was to take place on February 15, and since it was the duty of the People's Republic to broaden our views, we could watch from the courtyard.

Weingartner's hand went up. 'Please, if it rains can we have the eclipse in the hall instead?'

'No,' said the lecturer seriously, and began his explanation again from the start.

The indoctrination lectures lasted for hours. The same points were driven home over and over again. At the end of the day, exhausted and ill-tempered, we were left to our own disputes.

These were often started by Father Andricu, to whom Luther and Lucifer were as one. His extremism swung him between a crusade against the Russians during the war to championship of Communist ideas after it was over. He had travelled the country preaching in favour of the Party until his former comrades decided that 'the Red Priest' had outlived his usefulness, so he was arrested, beaten and sentenced to ten years for his wartime activities. Now he was an all-too-vociferous champion of the Orthodox faith. 'It's the only true religion!' he would trumpet. 'The rest are frauds and mockeries!'

Once I asked: 'When you were baptised, Father Andricu, was it in the Orthodox Church?'

'Of course! By a bishop!' he answered.

'And you studied religious doctrine at an Orthodox school?'

'The finest in Rumania!'

'Then you won't be upset if I give you the one honest, logical reason why you're an Orthodox believer? It is that fifty years ago a Rumanian Orthodox man copulated with a Rumanian Orthodox woman.'

Andricu was furious; but I said that this principle was true for most of us. We are put in a mould from earliest youth and taught only the arguments which favour our parents' religion. Yet we are convinced that we have thought it all out for ourselves.

I went on, 'Once I overheard the inmates of a stable discussing their beliefs. The lambs said the only true religion was to say, "Baa, baa!" Calves said the correct ritual was to say "Moo!" Pigs asserted that the right song of praise was "Honk! honk!" '

'Don't put us on a level with the animals,' Andricu protested. 'I may be a simple priest, but I have studied other faiths besides my own.'

I said that we had all done that, but from a viewpoint which is ours through the accident of birth. Turning to a group of Protestants, I asked at random, 'How many of you know the ninety-five theses which Luther nailed on the church door at Wittenburg?'

They all did. Pastor Haupt quoted Luther's words, 'Here I stand; I can do no other!'

I asked if the Protestants could also repeat from the Papal Bull the reasons for Luther's excommunication. 'Leo X was no madman,' I said; 'we ought to know his reasons.' But not one of them had read that great historical letter.

Father Andricu was by now arguing with a rabbi who turned on him to say, 'Are you by any chance acquainted with our Talmud?'

Andricu retorted: 'Have *you* looked into our New Testament?' The answer in each case was clearly 'No'.

To avert another clash, I asked the company, 'Do you know Tolstoy's story of how he once explained his faith point by point to a rabbi: meekness, humility, patience . . . "We don't need the New Testament for these virtues; we too honour them," said the rabbi. Finally Tolstoy said, "Jesus has taught us one thing which Jewish religion does not. He tells us to love our enemies." "This we do not practise," the rabbi admitted, "but neither do you Christians".'

3

As the prison lectures continued, I saw that although they were in themselves ridiculous, there lay behind them a clever plan.

The speakers turned from politics to appeals directed at the pleasure-seeking, irresponsible side in all of us which Freudians called the Id. They told us how much we were missing in the world. They talked of food, drink, sex—subjects with which they were more at home than Marxist dialectic, although that was not forgotten. One talk took us again among Darwin's apes. A young political officer worked his way through a brief on the theory of evolution, and with mangled quotations from Marx, Lenin and Darwin progressed by way of conflict between Christianity and science to its sad consequences in America, where millions were starving.

At first, we were encouraged to argue, and when a lecturer said that 'only a handful of chemicals' remained of the body after death, I asked why, if that were so, some Communists had given their lives for their beliefs: 'For a Christian to sacrifice himself,' I said, 'may be considered wise. To give up the transitory things of life to win eternity is like laying down ten dollars to win a million. But why should a Communist give his life—unless he too has something to gain for himself?'

The political officer could find no reply. So I suggested that the answer had been given by St. Augustine when he said that 'the soul is naturally Christian'.

'Atheism is a mask for your feelings. In the depths of your heart—which is never reached unless a man practises meditation or prayer—you, too, believe there is a reward for living up to ideals. Deep in your heart, you also believe in God.'

'Let us see what Lenin has to say about that!' said the lecturer, and from a well-thumbed booklet, which had often given him inspiration before, he read, ' "Even flirting with the idea of God is unutterable vileness, contagion of the most abominable kind. Filthy deeds, acts of violence and physical contagions are far less dangerous." ' He grinned. 'Any more questions?'

'Have you a child?' I asked.

'I have a daughter in the Young Pioneers.'

'And would you prefer that she should be stricken with a horrible disease rather than come to believe in her Creator? That is what Lenin says—that cancer is better than religion.'

The political officer called me up and slapped my face.

Under this onslaught of indoctrination, a blow seemed a modest price to pay for upholding one's beliefs. Clearly, there was more to come. We had a sense of being constantly spied on. We puzzled over the silent loudspeakers.

Until recently we had been starved, beaten, abused, but no one had cared what we thought. 'Invent all the new Cabinets you like in your cells, you bandits—we have the Government in Bucharest!' Commandant Dorabantu used to say. But he had gone—removed for falsifying the accounts.

The lectures showed how this attitude had changed, following the new policy of Gheorghiu-Dej, Rumania's dictator, who was trying to ease the Kremlin's grip and do business with the West. For this Dej had to show a more 'democratic' façade. The army of political prisoners held in Rumania was an embarrassment to him, yet we could not simply be set free to spread 'counter-revolutionary' beliefs. Our ways of thought were to be altered, by mass brainwashing.

To prisoners in Gherla in 1962, this was one theory among many, and few believed it. There was uncertainty about what actually happened in brainwashing. Feelings were summed up by Radu Ghinda, a well-known author and Christian writer, who had recently joined us: 'If they haven't changed me in fifteen years, how will they do so now?'

We were talking this over when the cell door opened to admit more new arrivals. Among them was a large hangdog figure who took a few halting steps from side to side, as if to escape the stares of prisoners.

Radu Ghinda was the first to recognise him. 'Daianu!' he cried.

The man shuffled over to embrace his friend. Nichifor Daianu had been a great figure in Rumania. Poet, Professor of Mystical Theology, leader of the anti-Semitic 'National Christian Defence League', he had come to Gherla from Aiud jail to continue his twenty-five-year sentence.

At first I hardly recognised the man. His great belly had gone. The skin hung in folds at his chin like a turkey's. The *bon viveur* and lady-killer, whose face had once been slapped in a Bucharest restaurant, had become a trembling, spidery old man.

Fellow-prisoners from Aiud told us what had happened there.

Daianu, who was used to plenty of food, had tried to get a second helping of barley gruel from the cooks. The prison governor had him turned away. On the following day the governor was there again. 'Stop!' he said, 'That man is too fat. Let him wait until tomorrow.' Next day, as Daianu's turn came, the governor said, 'Tell me, Daianu, is there a God?' The cook held the ladle suspended. Daianu mumbled something. 'Speak up, let us all hear!' Daianu said, 'There is no God.' 'Louder,' said the governor. 'There is no God!' shouted Daianu. The governor nodded for him to be served. Daianu stuffed the gruel into his mouth. This spectacle so pleased the governor that he had it repeated every day for the next week. The story was told all over Rumania, and later abroad as well.

But Daianu's gift for writing religious poetry remained. Friends from his Fascist days encouraged him to recite some of the verses he had composed at Aiud. They were songs of grief and repentance, more beautiful than any he had yet written. He had retained, too, his anti-semitism, like his friend Radu Ghinda. Their following among ex-Iron Guard prisoners smuggled scraps of food and even cigarettes to them in the priests' room. Anti-semitism dies hard, and Daianu and Ghinda were martyrs to the cause.

When theories about brainwashing were being discussed one evening, Ghinda scoffed. 'Rubbish! Pavlov played tricks with the behaviour-patterns of dogs, and the Communists in Korea adapted some of his ideas to make American prisoners change sides—but these methods won't work on people of education and intelligence. We're not G.I.s!'

'Nor dogs,' said Daianu.

No one disagreed.

4

Pastor Weingartner told us of a simple personality test he had learnt while studying psychology: you drew a line down the centre of a card, then asked people to make of it the first thing that came into their heads. We used a soaped board and a nail.

One man drew a sword, another a helmet, others a flower, a crucifix, a book, a geometric figure. I said, 'I need another board—this is too small for what I have to draw.'

Not one in ten of us showed in our drawings the touch of mysticism which is at the heart of a priestly nature.

Weingartner laughed. 'No wonder they wouldn't let me try it at the seminary! Perhaps we should all learn to make shoes—for it's the shoemaker among us who seems to have a truly spiritual character.'

He referred to Gelu, a sectarian believer who had a great knowledge of the Bible. This seemed to irritate Daianu.

'My dear man,' he said, 'if you want to tell us about shoes and how to mend them, well and good. But you are among men here who possess theological degrees from the great universities of Europe and need no Bible classes.'

'You're right, professor,' replied Gelu. 'It's I who need instruction. Could you tell me what the Old Testament book of Habakkuk is about?'

'A very minor prophet,' said Daianu. 'Don't worry your head about him.'

'Well, then, the Book of Obadiah?'

Obadiah was another prophet whom shoemakers did not need to know.

'Perhaps you can tell me about Haggai?'

Daianu could not. There was not a theologian in the room who could muster three sentences on the subject. Gelu astonished us by quoting whole chapters from these prophets by heart.

The clergy studied books about the Bible rather than the Holy Scriptures themselves. Another reproach that could rightly be made against them was that they were grounded in dogma and dialectic, but knew next to nothing of the Communist ideology that was working to destroy them.

During 1963 we had news of Pope John's appeal for a reconciliation between the 'separated brethren', and soon we were quarrelling over how unity might be achieved.

'We fight over the Kingdom of Heaven, which none of us has,' I said. 'If we possessed it, we should not dispute. Those who truly love Christ must love one another. Like so many blind men whom Jesus has healed, we discuss how our sight was restored. One says, "It was done by the power of faith". Another, "He touched my eyes". A third, "He rubbed clay mixed with spittle on my eyelids". If Jesus came among us, He would say, "I have made you whole in different ways. Now you should not quarrel, but rejoice!"'

Goethe says that 'colour is the pain of light': passing through a prism, light is torn to pieces. I saw our division in the search for truth as a pain borne by Christ.

5

The loudspeaker on the wall at last crackled into life. 'One-two three-four-testing,' said a voice repeatedly. Then came the words: 'Communism is good. Communism is good. Communism is good.' A pause. More crackling. The voice returned with increased volume, resonance and authority:

Communism is good
Communism is good
Communism is good
Communism is good

It continued all night and into the next day. Soon we were only intermittently conscious of the tape-recorded words, but still they penetrated our minds, and when finally the voice stopped, switched off at a control centre somewhere in the prison, the words rang in my head: 'Communism is good. Communism is good. Communism is good.'

Weingartner said this was the first stage in a long process. 'Our rulers have learnt it from the Russians and the Russians from Peking. Next it will be public confession. Under Mao-Tse-Tung, the Chinese must attend lectures in their factories, offices and streets. Then they are made to denounce themselves, to say how they plotted against the proletariat, five, ten or twenty years ago. If you don't confess you're imprisoned as a stubborn counter-revolutionary: if you do confess, you go to jail for what you have said. So people try to confess and yet not to confess, to admit to treacherous thoughts, while denying they have acted on them. One man denounces another. All trust between friends and in families is destroyed. The same procedure has begun with us!'

Father Fazekas said, 'Satan always apes God. It is a mockery of Christian confession.'

'How long will it last?' asked Gaston.

'Until you believe that "Communism is good"; perhaps for years,' said Weingartner.

Our next lecturer was plump and jolly. He told us of the wonderful, new Rumania which was developing under Gheorghiu-Dej's Sixteen-Year Plan, and of the paradise which those whom the Party considered worthy were already enjoying. He described the privileges granted to loyal workers, the good food, the flowing wine, the glorious holidays at Black Sea resorts with girls in bikinis everywhere.

'But I forget!' he laughed. 'Most of you fellows have never seen a bikini. You don't even know what it is, poor chaps! Let me explain. The best things in life are not left to the decadent West!'

His eyes gleamed and his voice became thick as he began a gloating description of breast and belly and thigh, and mixed the pleasures of wine and travel into his gross talk. I have never seen on human faces such hungry lust as I saw then on most of those around me in the big hall. They were ugly and frightening in their suggestion of animals in heat. Their human decency was stripped away by the man's unbridled talk, and only sensual greed remained.

So much pleasure waited for us outside, the lecturer said. 'There's the door. *You* can open it, if you choose. Throw off the reactionary garbage of ideas which have made criminals of you! Come to our side! Learn to be free!'

Little was said after these talks. No one thought now of the wives and hard work that awaited them outside. The raw desire which is part of our will to live had been skilfully revived.

Protestants and Orthodox priests who had been married suffered surely much more from this appeal to the sex instinct than the Catholic priests who had led a life of celibacy from their very youth.

We had been kept for months past on low rations, and weighed regularly to ensure that we remained forty pounds below normal. Now the food improved, but it had a strange flavour. I suspected the presence of aphrodisiacs, and imprisoned doctors later agreed with me that sexually-stimulating drugs had been added to our meals. Many of the staff left and now the doctors, the clerks who came to read out an announcement or a court verdict were nearly always girls. They wore tight, teasing dresses and used scent and make-up. They seemed to linger deliberately in the cells.

'You've only one life,' the lecturers said each day. 'It passes quickly. How much time have you left? Throw in your lot with us. We want to help you to make the most of it!'

This appeal to the ego, the self-enhancing, self-protective side of one's nature, came when primitive emotions were well in ferment. Finally, as the veneer cracked, came the appeal to the super-ego, our conscience, social values and ethical standards. The lecturers said our patriotism had been false, our ideals a fraud, and in their place they tried to plant the Communist ideology.

'Struggle meetings' was the name given to these mass-suggestion sessions, and the struggle never stopped. 'What are your wives doing now?' asked the jolly lecturer. 'What you'd like to be doing yourselves!' We were exhausted, and hysteria was close. The tape-recorders ground out the message that Communism was good during every hour when lectures were not in progress. Prisoners quarrelled among themselves.

Daianu the poet was the first to break. At the end of a lecture, he jumped to his feet and began to babble about his crimes against the state. 'I see it now, I see it all! I have thrown away my life for a false cause!' He blamed his land-owning parents for putting him on the wrong road. No one had asked him to attack religion, but he repudiated his faith, the saints and sacraments. He ranted against 'superstition' and blasphemed against God. On and on he went.

Then Radu Ghinda stood up and continued in the same vein. 'I have been a fool,' he shouted. 'I have been misled by capitalist and Christian lies . . . Never again will I set foot in a church except to spit in it.'

Daianu and Ghinda called on the prisoners to give up their old beliefs with greater enthusiasm than the lecturers themselves. Both were gifted speakers, and many who heard their eloquent praises of the joy and liberty that Communism brings were deeply shaken, convinced that they spoke from genuine faith.

When Ghinda sat down, a gaunt, trembling old man shouted, 'You all know me—General Silvestru of the Royal Army. I disown my rank and loyalty. I am ashamed at the role I played in making criminal war on our ally, Russia. I served the exploiting classes. I disgraced my country . . .'

The general was followed by an ex-police chief, who 'confessed' that Communism would have come to power sooner had the police not hindered it; as if every man there did not know that Communism had been imposed by the Russians.

One after another, men stood and parroted their confessions. This was the first fruit of months of planned starvation, degradation, ill-treatment and exposure to mass suggestion. The first to give way were those, like Daianu and Ghinda, whose lives were already eaten by private guilt. Daianu had preached asceticism but practised gluttony and pursued women. He told students to give up the world for God, and himself became a propagandist for Hitler. He said, 'Love Jesus'; and he hated the Jews. He thought he was a believer, but what a man believes is shown in his daily life: his poems, fine as they were, expressed aspirations, not fulfilment. Ghinda, too, was torn ideologically by anti-semitism on the one hand, and his faith on the other. And both men were growing old: they had served more than a dozen years in prison, and faced many more.

Others in the priests' room did not yield so quickly, and for them further suffering lay in store. Our quarrels, at least, came to a halt. We learnt that all our denominations could be reduced to two: the first is hatred, which makes ritual and dogma a pretext for attacking others; the second is love, in which men of all kinds realise their oneness and brotherhood before God. At times it had seemed that a mission to priests would be more valuable than any other. More often now it was as if the cell were ablaze with the spirit of self-sacrifice and renewed faith. In such moments the angels seemed all around us.

For the Communion service, bread was needed and many were ready to sacrifice their ration. But the Orthodox ritual requires that the bread be consecrated over an altar containing a relic from the body of a martyr. There was no relic.

'We have living martyrs with us,' said Father Andricu. They

consecrated the bread and a little wine in a chipped cup, which had been smuggled from the hospital, over the body of Bishop Mirza as he lay ill in bed.

6

Soon the prisoners who had been 'converted' were asked to lecture in turn to the others, and they did so with passion, believing that their release depended on their efforts. Then word went around of a terrible sequel to the defection of Daianu and Ghinda. Two members of the Iron Guard stole a chisel from the carpenters' shop, opened their veins and bled to death as protest.

I found Daianu and Ghinda in a corner of the cell. 'What do you think of yourselves now that your betrayal has cost the lives of two men who believed in you?' I asked.

Ghinda said, 'They died so that the people may live!'

'A week ago you were counted among the enemies of the people yourselves,' I said.

Daianu burst out: 'I mean to get out of here, whoever suffers!'

Feeling against them became so strong that they were taken to another cell. Miron said, 'Strange that men who wrote with what seemed deep Christian faith should turn traitor so easily!'

Perhaps the answer was that in their writings Daianu and Ghinda praised Christ for the gifts He gives us—peace, love, salvation. A real disciple does not seek gifts, but Christ himself, and so is ready for self-sacrifice to the end. They were not followers of Jesus, but customers; when the Communists opened a shop next door with goods at lower prices, they took their custom there.

7

I had become very ill again. During 1963 I was moved to the prison hospital. I had been there one week, when every man was ordered up. Some could hardly walk, but we helped each other out into a big yard where the whole prison had been assembled. We stood while an hour-long play was acted by chosen prisoners. The play mocked Christianity and when the officers around the commandant clapped or laughed, the audience did the same.

When it was over, Alexandrescu raised his harsh voice to ask for positive or negative comments. It was not enough to show approval; reasons must be given. Daianu led the way. Ghinda followed. One after another men went up to repeat slogans against religion. As they rejoined the ranks, some embraced me tearfully, and said, 'We *must* say these things until it is over!'

When the commandant called me out, I remembered what my wife had said to me many years before, at the Congress of Cults: 'Go and wash this shame from the face of Christ!'

I was well known at Gherla; I had been in so many cells.

Hundreds of eyes were on me, and they all seemed to ask one question: 'Will he praise Communism too?'

Major Alexandrescu called, 'Go on! Speak!' He did not fear opposition. When the stubborn ones broke—and it was only a matter of time, they thought—it showed the Party's power.

I began cautiously, 'It is Sunday morning, and our wives and mothers and children are praying for us, in church or at home. We should have liked to pray for them, too . . . Instead we have watched this play.'

As I spoke of their families, tears came into the eyes of prisoners. I went on, 'Many here have spoken against Jesus, but what is it that you have against him? You speak of the proletariat, but wasn't Jesus a carpenter? You say that he who doesn't work shall not eat, but this was said long ago, in St. Paul's Epistle to the Thessalonians. You speak against the wealthy, but Jesus drove the moneylenders from the temple with whips. You want Communism, but don't forget that the first Christians lived in a community, sharing all they had. You wish to raise up the poor, but the Magnificat, the Virgin Mary's song at Jesus's birth, says that God will exalt the poor above the rich. All that is good in Communism comes from the Christians!

'Now Marx has said that all proletarians must unite,' I continued. 'But some are Communists and some are Socialists and others Christians, and if we mock each other, we cannot unite. I would never mock an atheist. Even from the Marxist point of view this is wrong, for if you mock you split the proletariat.'

I quoted what Marx says in his introduction to 'Capital', that Christianity is the ideal religion for remaking a life destroyed by sin. I asked if there was anybody, even a Communist, who was without sin—for if he had not sinned against God, he had against the Party. I gave them many quotations from their own authors. Major Alexandrescu shifted in his chair, and kicked the ground with his toe, but did not interrupt.

The prisoners, too, were quiet, and seeing they were moved I forgot where I was and began to preach openly about Christ, and what He had done for us, and what He meant to us. I said that just as no one had heard of a school without examinations, or a factory where work was not scrutinised to see that it was good, so all of us would be judged, by ourselves, by our fellows, by God. I looked at the commandant and said, 'You will be judged, too, Major Alexandrescu.'

He let it pass again, and I told how Jesus teaches love and gives eternal life. At the end prisoners burst suddenly into cheers.

When I returned to my place Miron said, 'You have undone all their work,' but I knew this was untrue: Gaston whispered, 'Did you hear the cheers?'. I answered, 'They were cheering what they had found in their own hearts, not me.'

Until now only a noisy minority of priests had fallen under the influence of brainwashing. We who opposed it openly were also few, but our sympathisers were many, even if they lacked the courage or the wit to fight back.

It was not easy. As a result of this speech I lost my sanctuary in the prison hospital and was sent back to the priests' room.

The political officer told us that Daianu and Radu Ghinda, in their private cells, had volunteered to write about the wonders of the People's Republic, which neither of them had set eyes on for a dozen years. They were given pen and paper and all the Party literature and tourist propaganda they might need. The two men made full use of this chance to prove their new convictions, for some weeks later they were freed. It was a powerful blow against our resistance. They were the first to be released under the new system, and we could not know that they were also to be the last.

Lieutenant Konya, the political officer, brought a newspaper into the priests' room and called to Father Andricu.

'Read this out,' he said, 'so that everyone can hear.'

Andricu read the headline: 'A COUNTRY THAT LAUGHS AND HEARTS THAT SING'. It was an article by Radu Ghinda, with a smiling photograph taken before his arrest.

Lieutenant Konya said, 'We want you to know that every one of you has the same chance of freedom and work, just as soon as you give up your nonsensical, out-of-date beliefs and join the people of the new Rumania!'

Hearts that sing! Everyone remembered Ghinda as a bag of bones. We knew that his family was in distress and his child had been refused education.

Daianu also lent his name to glorifications of freedom in Socialist Rumania, but, like the French medical students who blotted their copy-books and were marked down as '*bon pour l'Orient*'—'good for the East'—the output of Daianu and Ghinda was good only for the West. There they could trade on the ignorance of those who did not know the country. The articles they wrote appeared in special newspapers and magazines sent to thousands of Rumanians abroad, but nobody could get them in Rumania itself.

Everyone was excited at the two men's release. Many who had suffered cruelty and humiliation for years, without giving way, now began to waver. But those who did yield, instead of being freed, had to prove their conversion by volunteering to work fourteen or sixteen hours a day. On returning to their cells they had to attend more lectures, or give them. They had to keep a 'temperature chart of political health'—which meant that everyone had to write about his neighbour's attitude to Communism, whether it was lukewarm, or cold or even hostile.

The authorities cannot have received good reports about me. Lieutenant Konya came to bring me two pieces of news. First, he said that my wife was in prison, and had been for some time. Second, that I was to be flogged at 10 p.m. that evening for my repeated defiance and insolence, culminating in my speech at the 'play'.

The news about Sabina was a terrible shock, and my pain at the thought of it added to my fear of the beating to come. We all dreaded this period of waiting. Time dragged, and then passed all too quickly when I heard footsteps coming down the passage. The tramping boots went by. Someone was taken from the next cell. Presently I heard blows falling and screams from the room at the end of the corridor. Nobody came for me that night.

Next morning I was again warned. For six days the suspense was maintained. Then I was led up the passage. The blows burned like fire. When it was over, Lieutenant Konya, who supervised, shouted, 'Give him some more!' Then I was slow in getting to my feet.' Ten more!' said Konya. I was half carried back to the cell, where the loudspeakers were blaring:

Christianity is stupid
Christianity is stupid
Christianity is stupid
Why not give it up?
Why not give it up?
Why not give it up?
Christianity is stupid
Christianity is stupid
Christianity is stupid
Why not give it up . . .?

Sometimes beatings were administered by warders in the cell, for 'minor irregularities'.

'Drop your trousers for a beating!'

We dropped them.

'Lie on your bellies!'

We lay on our bellies.

'Turn over on your backs, hold your feet up.'

We rolled over.

We went on trying to pray. Sometimes a priest would say, 'I call on "Our Father" but what kind of father, what God abandons me to my enemies like this?' And we urged him, 'Don't give way. Go on saying "Our Father". Be obstinate. By persisting you will renew your faith!' He could listen to us, because we shared his suffering.

When the guards became bored with beating, they grabbed a couple of prisoners. 'Right!' they said. 'Slap your friend in the face!' If the man failed to do so, they said, 'You've lost your chance', and told the second man to strike the first. He hit out blindly. 'Now slosh him back!' They struck at each other's faces until blood flowed. The guards roared with laughter.

One evening Lieutenant Konya told me to gather my things. Since I had not responded to treatment, a spell in the special block might help. There were many rumours about this section of the prison. Those who returned from it were few. They died, or they succumbed to brainwashing and were moved out. Some joined the indoctrination staff and learnt to brainwash others.

We crossed the yard, turned several corners and stopped before a row of doors. One was opened and double-locked behind me.

I was alone in a cell walled in white tiles. The ceiling reflected fierce white light from concealed lamps. It was full summer, but the steam heating—which worked nowhere else in Gherla—was full on. Konya had left me in handcuffs, so that I could lie only on my back or side. I was soaked in sweat. The spy hole clicked open, and the guard outside sniggered. 'Something wrong with the heating?' My stomach ached. There had been a peculiar taste in the food, and I thought it was drugged again. The loudspeakers here had a new message:

Nobody believes in Christ now
Nobody believes in Christ now
Nobody believes in Christ now
No one goes to church
No one goes to church
Give it up
Give it up
Give it up
Nobody believes in Christ now . . .

Konya was back in the morning, letting a flood of cool air through the open door. My handcuffs were unlocked. I stretched stiff arms and obeyed his order to follow him along the corridor.

A new cell awaited me, and fresh clothes. There was a bed with sheets, a table with a cloth, flowers in a vase. It was too much: I sat down and began to weep. When Konya left, I recovered. I looked at a newspaper on the table. It was the first I had seen in all my years of imprisonment. I tried to find in it news of a rumour going around Gherla that the US Sixth Fleet had entered the

Black Sea to demand free elections in the captive countries, but what I found was an item about a Communist dictator who had taken power in Cuba and was defying America on her own doorstep.

My first visitor was Commandant Alexandrescu. He said my new surroundings were a sample of the good life which was open to me. He began to attack religion. Christ, he said, was a fantasy invented by the Apostles to delude slaves into hopes of freedom in paradise.

I picked up the newspaper and gave it to him. 'This is printed on the Party presses,' I said. 'It gives a date in July 1963. That means 1,963 years since the birth of someone who—according to you—never existed. You don't believe in Christ, but you accept him as the founder of our civilisation.'

Alexandrescu shrugged. 'It means nothing; it's customary to count that way.'

'But if Christ never came on earth, how did the custom arise?' I asked.

'Some liars started it.'

I said: 'Suppose you tell me that the Russians have landed on Mars, I need not believe you. But if I turn the radio-knob to hear New York and the Americans congratulate them, then I know it must be true. In the same way, we must accept Christ's existence as a historical fact when it is recognised in the Talmud by his worst enemies, the Pharisees, who also give the names of his mother and some of his Apostles. And again, we must be impressed when the Pharisees attribute miracles to Christ, while protesting that they were worked by black magic. Many heathen writers also recognised Him. Only Communists deny this plain fact of history, simply because it does not suit their theory.'

Alexandrescu did not pursue the argument. Instead, he sent me a book. It was wonderful to have a book in one's hands after all these years, even if it was only the 'The Atheist's Guide'. This manual, unknown in the West, is essential reading for all who want to make themselves careers behind the Iron Curtain.

My copy was well-bound, illustrated and carefully argued. From the origins of religion it made its way through Hinduism, Buddhism, Confucianism and Islam. Then came Christianity, with a chapter for each confession. Catholicism came out badly, Lutherism much better (Luther had defied the Pope), but all were shown to be impostures. Science had proved this, so the Church had always persecuted science. A full chapter portrayed the Church as a tool of capitalism through the centuries; Christ's exhortation to love your enemies meant no more than to bow to the exploiter. A special section was devoted to the corruption of the Russian priesthood (the book had evidently been translated from the Russian). One picture after another was used to show, misleadingly, that Christian rites were based on heathen supersti tion. A last chapter analysed 'Forms of Atheist Propaganda' and concluded with a list of Soviet decrees aimed against religion. Over this I fell asleep.

9

During the next few weeks I alternated between promises and threats, between my flowery private room and the blinding cell with loudspeakers, between good, but probably drugged, meals and starvation, between argument and punishment. While undergoing the heat treatment I was joined one morning by Father Andricu, the former 'Red priest' who had repented. He sat panting until he could bear no more. Then he jumped up and hammered wildly on the door, begging to be let out. Presently the commandant appeared.

'It can be hotter yet,' said Alexandrescu. Or we could be free men if we chose, he repeated. 'But if you were released, how would you act and what kind of sermons would you preach? I want you to write a draft.' He gave us pen and paper and went out.

We sat down and wrote. When I had finished, I gave Andricu my sheaf of paper and took his to read through.

'You can hear sermons like that every Sunday,' he said defensively. 'Progressive, in a scientific, Marxist way.'

I said, 'Don't deceive yourself, Father Andricu. You know this is a recantation of all that you believe. Even if a priest loses his faith, he should be silent. I don't speak of judgment before God. What would your parishioners, your friends, your family think if they heard you preach this stuff? Don't let the Communists cheat you again. They buy you with promises that they never keep.'

I argued for a long time with Andricu, telling him that in his heart he knew still the truth of Christianity. At last he said, 'Give me back the sermons,' and tore them into pieces.

10

A new series of 'struggle meetings' attended by hundreds of prisoners began in the main hall, and we were sent from the special block to hear them. Most lectures were now being delivered by men who, not long ago, were our cell-mates. After instruction, they came back to declaim praises of the Communism that had given them years of suffering. Their attacks on religion were based often on modern theologians who deny the Scriptures: propagandists like those of the 'God is dead' school. 'Study your own thinkers!' we were told. 'They have proved that there is no objective truth in Christianity.'

For ten to twelve hours a day we listened to lectures, joined discussions, absorbed the tape-recorded slogans. The brain-washed lecturers made the appeal to the Id more frequently and more grossly than the official speakers; and their visions of freedom, money, a job with standing—the assault on the Ego—were more convincing.

In each cell, a handful of men reported daily on the 'political health' of the others. Those who truckled to them were fairly safe. Those who did not usually ended in the special block. Informing touched everyone like a fever. A man near me complained to an officer that a guard had searched his bunk without looking beneath it!

On August 23, the anniversary of the armistice with Russia, most prisoners were ready to believe whatever they were told. A large meeting in the hall was addressed by Major Alexandrescu. 'We have good news,' he started.

Peasants whose farms had been seized broke into smiles when he announced that their land was flourishing in the collectives. Former merchants and bankers applauded when he said that trade was beginning to boom.

'Some of you', said the Commandant, 'are seeing reason at last. Others are being very foolish. You idiots! You have sat in prison for ten or fifteen years, waiting for the Americans to come and free you. I have news for you. The Americans are coming—but not to release you. They are coming to do business with us!'

Alexandrescu said the Party, under Premier Gheorghiu-Dej, had taken steps to win commercial favour in the West. Loans were being raised, factories built, nuclear plants operated, all with Western aid.

'You fools!' he spat out the words again. 'You've all been living in illusion. We know the Americans better than you. If you beg, they give you nothing. If you insult and mock them, you get all you want. We've been cleverer than you.'

Somebody laughed, high-pitched laughter, and others joined in. Soon the whole hall was rocking. The noise was becoming hysterical when, with a raised hand, the Commandant quelled it. In good humour, he said that to compensate us all for being unable to join the 'Freedom Day' celebrations, he had arranged that we should watch them—television had been installed for the occasion.

The TV show began with speeches by Gheorghiu-Dej and others on the fall of the Fascist régime in Rumania. None of the orators, of course, mentioned the vital roles played on August 23, 1944, by young King Michael, nor by the National Peasant statesman Juliu Maniu and the Communist Minister of Justice Patrascanu, since the King had been exiled, and the other two had died in jail.

I remembered that during Communism's early days people tried to avoid the anniversary parade, but now when the march-past began I was astonished by the endless columns tramping past the portraits of Marx, Lenin and Dej among the red flags flapping in the breeze. We heard the brassy music, the crowds' cheers, the shouts, 'August 23 brings us freedom!'

'It was never like this in the past,' I said to Father Andricu beside me.

He hissed back: 'The first time a girl is violated, she struggles. The second time she protests. The third time she enjoys it.'

When the performance ended, another began.

'We shall now discuss the celebrations,' Alexandrescu said.

One after another, the audience testified. Ex-soldiers, former policemen, landowners, peasants, industrialists. Each ended his contribution with the cry, 'August 23 has brought us freedom!'

My turn came. I started in the mood of the day.

'If there's anyone to whom August 23 had brought liberty, it is I,' I said. 'The Fascists hated me, and if Hitler had won his war I should be a piece of soap by now. But I'm alive, and the Bible has a saying, "A live dog is better than a dead lion".'

I continued to approving murmurs. 'But in another way, I was free before August 23. Let me tell you how. In ancient times the Tyrant of Syracuse read the book of Epictetus, the philosopher-slave, and admired it so greatly that he offered to set him free. "Free yourself!" replied Epictetus. His visitor protested, "But I'm the king!" The philosopher answered, "A tyrant ruled by his lusts is in bondage; a slave who rules his passions is free. King, free yourself!" '

The hall was quiet now. 'Although I am in prison, I am free. I have been freed by Jesus from my guilt, from darkness in my mind. I can thank the events of August 23 for freeing me from Fascism. But for the other freedom, the freedom from all that is transitory, from death, I thank Jesus.'

The Commandant was on his feet. 'Tell that nonsense to Gargarin. He's been up in space, but he saw no sign of God!'

He laughed. The prisoners laughed with him.

I replied in a matter-of-fact way, 'If an ant walked around the sole of my shoe, it could say it saw no sign of Wurmbrand.'

II

I was punished by another spell in the Special Block, and I was there when Alexandrescu called specially to inform me that the American President had been assassinated.

'What do you think about that?' he enquired.

I said, 'I can't believe it.'

He showed me a newspaper which reported Mr. Kennedy's death in a single paragraph.

'Well?' he insisted. Pursuing questions of this sort was part of the technique to discover how prisoners' minds were working.

When I replied that if Kennedy were a Christian, then he was happy now in Heaven, Alexandrescu walked out.

Later I was in a cell with Father Andricu when the guards came for us. We were blindfolded and handcuffed before being led out —for all we knew, it might have been to execution.

The guards said, 'Turn right here!' and 'Now turn left!'

In a distant part of the prison our blindfolds came off. We were in a suite of clean, warm offices. Andricu was taken off to another part of what must have been the central administration section. I remained outside a door, alone with a guard who, in the past, had listened when I spoke quietly of Christ.

He whispered: 'My poor friend! You're having a hard time, but in God's name, go on!'

He moved some paces away, his face blank, but his words warmed me.

When the door opened, I was led into the presence of a man in general's uniform. It was Negrea, the Deputy-Minister of the Interior, whose intelligence was matched by the energy burning in his strong, gipsy face. The political officer and some officials from Bucharest sat beside him.

Negrea said politely, 'I've been studying your case, Mr. Wurmbrand. I don't care for your views, but I like a man who sticks to his guns. We Communists are obstinate, too. I've often been in prison myself and plenty was done to make me change my mind, but I stood firm.

'I believe it's time we met half-way. If you're prepared to forget what you've suffered, we'd forget what you've done against us. We could turn the page and become friends instead of enemies. So far from acting against your own convictions, you could act upon them and still enter a period of fruitful co-operation.'

A file lay open before him. 'I've even read your sermons. The explanations of the Bible are beautifully put, but you must realise we live in a scientific age . . .'

'What now?' I asked myself, as Negrea went into the Party's science lecture. Had an important minister come 200 miles for this?

Like the Danube, which twists and turns through the plains but reaches the sea at last, his discourse came to an end.

'We need men like you! We don't want people to join us out of opportunism, but because they see the fallacies in their past thinking. If you are prepared to help us in the struggle against superstition, you can start a new life at once. You will have a post with a high salary and your family around you again in comfort and in safety. What do you say?'

I replied that I found joy in the life I was already leading; but as for helping the Party, I had thought of a way of doing so if I were released.

The political officer sat up. Negrea said, 'You mean you'll work for us?'

'I suggest that you send me from town to town and village to village along with the best Marxist teacher you have. First I shall expose my ignorance and the stupidities of my retrograde Christian religion; then your Marxist can explain his theories and the people will be able to make up their own minds between the two.'

Negrea gave me a hard stare. 'You're provoking us, Mr. Wurmbrand. That is what I like about you. It's just the way we Communists used to answer the bosses in the old days. So let's not argue. I'll make you a better proposal still. Nobody wants you to become an atheist propagandist. If you're really so attached to an outworn faith—though I can't understand how a cultured man can accept such nonsense—then keep to it. But also keep in mind that we have the power! Communism has conquered a third of the world; the Church must come to terms with us.

'Let's put our cards on the table, for once. Frankly we're tired of Church leaders who do everything we ask, and sometimes more. They've compromised themselves in the eyes of the people; they're no longer in touch with what's going on.'

One by one, Negrea listed the remaining bishops. All were powerless, he said, or Party men; and everybody knew it.

'Now if a man like you became a bishop you could have your faith and still be loyal to the régime. Your Bible says you should submit to authority because it comes from God, so why not to ours?'

I said nothing. Negrea asked the other officials to leave us alone for a moment. He was convinced that I would accept the offer, and gave me his confidence on something he did not want the others to hear.

'The Party made a mistake,' he began, 'in attacking your World Council of Churches. It began as a spy-ring but the pastors concerned are often of proletarian origin; they aren't shareholders, so to speak, but superior servants. Instead of opposing such men we should win them over to our side so that the council itself becomes our instrument.'

He leant over the desk. 'Mr. Wurmbrand, this is where you can help. You've worked for the World Council of Churches. You're known widely abroad: we still get many enquiries about you. If you became a bishop, you could help our other WCC allies to build a bulwark for us—not of atheism, but of Socialism and peace. Surely you recognise the universal human idealism behind our campaigns to ban the bomb and outlaw war? And you'll be able to worship to your heart's content: there we won't interfere.'

I thought for a moment.

'How far must this co-operation go? Bishops who worked with you in the past have had to inform on their own priests. Will I be expected to do that, too?'

Negrea began to laugh. 'You'd be under no special obligation by virtue of your office,' he said. 'Everyone who knows of any act which may harm the state is obliged to denounce the man who does it, and as a bishop you'll certainly hear such things.

'The present Lutheran Bishop of Rumania is very old. You'd be Bishop-elect and effective Head of your Church in Rumania from the start.'

I asked for time to reflect and Negrea agreed.

'We'll meet before I leave again for Bucharest to put your release papers through,' he said.

I was taken back to an isolation cell and lay thinking for many hours. I remembered the old Jewish story of another man who asked for time to think: a rabbi, facing the Inquisition, who was asked to deny his faith. Next morning the rabbi said 'I will not turn Catholic, but I make one last request—that before I'm burnt at the stake my tongue should be cut out for not replying at once. To such a question "No!" was the only answer.'

But that was only one side of the case: on the other, I knew that the official Church in a Communist country can survive only through some compromise; even by paying taxes to an atheist state a Christian compromises. It was easy to say the Church could go 'underground', but an underground Church needs cover for its work. Lacking this cover, millions of people would be left with nowhere to meet for worship, no pastor to preach, no one to baptise them, marry them, bury their dead—an unthinkable alternative, when I could help to avoid it by saying a few words in favour of collectivisation or the so-called peace campaigns.

And then, I had not seen my wife and child for years; I did not know if they were alive. The political officer had said that Sabina was in prison; what would become of her and Mihai if I refused this proposal?

I needed strength from above to say no, when doing so meant serving eleven years more, with the sacrifice of my family and almost certain death under terrible conditions; but at that moment God's face was veiled and my faith failed me. I saw before me the huge shape of Communism which already covered so much of the world and threatened to cover the rest as well; and my imagination was overcome by the danger of dying, and being beaten again and again, and the hunger and privations to which I was condemning my wife and son. My soul was like a ship driven from side to side, rocked by a violent tempest, one moment plunged into the abyss, the next carried up to Heaven. I drank in those hours the cup of Christ; it was for me the Garden of Gethsemane. And like Jesus, I threw myself with face upon the earth and prayed with broken cries, and asked God to help me overcome this horrible temptation.

After prayer, I felt a little quieter. But still I saw before me Nichefor Daianu and Radu Ghinda and so many more who had harmed the faith, including the Patriarch; they numbered thousands, and now I had become a man mean in faith, and I would be swallowed up like them for my weakness of the flesh. I began to think carefully of all the times I had argued the truth of Christianity. I repeated to myself the simplest questions. Is the way of love better than hatred? Has Christ lifted the burden of sin and doubt from my shoulders? Is He the Saviour? There was no difficulty eventually in answering 'Yes'. And when I had done so, it was as if a great weight had been removed from my mind.

For an hour I lay on my bed, saying to myself, 'I shall try now not to think of Christ'. But the effort failed: I could think of nothing else. There was a void in my heart without Christianity. For a last time my mind went to Negrea's proposal. I thought of the tyrants from Nebuchadnezzar who set a king over the Jews, to Hitler who set his puppets over Europe. My visiting card would read 'Richard Wurmbrand, Lutheran Bishop of Rumania, by appointment of the Secret Police'. I would not be a bishop of Christ in a holy place, but a police spy in a state institution.

I prayed again, and afterwards I felt tranquillity of soul.

Next day I was called again. Commandant Alexandrescu was there, among several others around Negrea, and when I said I could not accept, the whole question was argued again. Only when we reached the subject of the World Council of Churches did Negrea once more ask the rest to leave. Then he urged me to reconsider my refusal.

I said, 'I don't feel worthy to be a bishop—I wasn't worthy to be a pastor, and even to be a simple Christian was too great for me. The first Christians went to their deaths saying "*Christianus sum!*"—"I'm a Christian!"—and I haven't done that; instead, I considered your shameful offer. But I cannot accept it.'

'We'll find another who will,' he warned.

I replied, 'If you believe you can prove that I'm wrong, bring me your atheist arguments! I have the arguments for my faith, and I seek only the truth.'

He asked me, 'You know, of course, what this will mean for your future?'

'I have considered well, and weighed the dangers, and I rejoice to suffer for what I am sure is the last truth.'

Negrea gave me the look of a man who realises he has been wasting time. Polite to the last, he nodded to me, closed his briefcase, stood up and crossed to the window, where he stood looking out while the guards handcuffed and led me away.

12

For a long time I remained in the 'special block'; how long I am not sure. Time has telescoped all days of certain periods in my prison life into one enormous day. The brainwashing increased in its intensity, but changed little in method. The loudspeakers now said:

Christianity is dead
Christianity is dead
Christianity is dead

I recall one day clearly. They had given us postcards to invite our families to come and bring parcels. On the day named, I was shaved and washed and given a clean shirt. Hours passed. I sat in the cell staring at the glittering white tiles, but no one came. Evening brought only a change of guard. I was not to know then that my postcard had never been sent, and the same trick was played on other stubborn prisoners. The loudspeaker said:

Nobody loves you now
Nobody loves you now
Nobody loves you now

I began to weep. The loudspeaker said:

They don't want to know you any more
They don't want to know you any more
They don't want to know you any more

I could not bear to hear these words and I could not shut them out.

Next day brought a brutal 'struggle meeting', confined to the disappointed men. Plenty of other wives had come, the lecturer said. We were the fools. We had been abandoned. Our womenfolk were in bed with other men—at that very moment. He described what was happening between them with all the obscenity at his command. And where were our children? Out in the street, atheists every one! They had no wish to see their fathers. How stupid we were!

In the special block I listened to the speaker, day after day:

Christianity is dead
Christianity is dead
Christianity is dead

And in time I came to believe what they had told us for all those months. Christianity was dead. The Bible foretells a time of great apostasy, and I believed that it had arrived.

Then I thought of Mary Magdalene, and perhaps this thought, more than any other, helped to save me from the soul-killing poison of the last and worst stage of brainwashing. I remembered how she was faithful to Christ even when He cried on the cross, 'My God, why have you forsaken me?' And when He was a corpse in the tomb, she wept nearby and waited until He arose. So when I believed at last that Christianity was dead, I said, 'Even so, I will believe in it, and I will weep at its tomb until it arises again, as it surely will'.

PART NINE

In June 1964 all prisoners were gathered in the main hall. The commandant entered with his officers, and we prepared for a new stage in the 'struggle campaign'. Instead, Major Alexandrescu announced that under the terms of a general amnesty granted by the government, political prisoners of every category were to be freed.

I could not believe it. Looking around, I saw blankness on every face. Then Alexandrescu shouted an order, and the entire hall broke into cheers. If he had told them, 'Tomorrow you will all be shot,' they would still have cheered, and cried, 'Quite right! We don't deserve to live!'

The announcement was not, as we first thought, another trick. The summer of that year saw the release of innumerable thousands of prisoners. For this we had to thank another so-called 'thaw' between East and West, and also—though I did not know it at the time—a true change of heart in our Prime Minister, Gheorghiu-Dej. After many years of doubting Communist dogma, he had returned to the faith in which his mother had raised him and kept all her life. Dej had been converted through a maidservant in his home and her uncle, a good old man who often spoke to him of the Bible. Christianity, although he did not confess it openly, gave him the strength to defy his Soviet masters. Ignoring their threats, he opened new relations with the West, and in doing so set an example to other captive countries. Unhappily, he died a few months later, his end being hastened, it is said, by Soviet agents.

My turn came for release. I found myself among one of the last groups of a hundred or so men gathered in the big hall. We were almost the last prisoners left in Gherla. A strange silence had descended on the corridors. Our hair was cut and we were given worn but quite clean clothes.

While I wondered what had become of the original owner of the suit I wore, I heard a man call, 'Brother Wurmbrand!' He came up and said he was from Sibiu, so I supposed that he was a member of our church there.

'I've heard so much of you from your son,' he added. 'We shared a cell together.'

I said, 'My son—in prison? No, no; you're mistaken!'

'You mean you didn't know?' the man went on. 'He's been in jail six years now.'

I turned away and he left me. The blow was almost more than I could bear. Mihai's health had not been good; it would never stand up to the strain of prolonged prison life.

My mind was still frozen with pain and shock when Commandant Alexandrescu came up. 'Well, Wurmbrand,' he asked in a curious tone. 'Where will you go now that you are free?'

I replied, 'I don't know. I've been told officially that my wife is in prison, and now I hear my only son is, too. I have nobody else.'

Alexandrescu shrugged. 'The boy, too! How do you feel, having a jailbird for a son?'

'I am sure he is not in jail for theft or any other crime, and if he is there for Christ's sake, then I am proud of him.'

'What!' he shouted. 'We spend all this money keeping you for years, and you think it's something to be proud of to have a family in prison for such things!'

'I did not want you to spend anything on me,' I said.

So we parted. I walked out of prison, in another man's clothes. The streets of Gherla seemed dazzling. Cars roared past and I started nervously. The colours of a woman's coat, of a bunch of flowers, shocked my eyes. Music from a radio, coming through an open window, had a texture rich as over-sweetened coffee.

The air smelt clean and new, as if the hay were being carted beyond the confines of the little town. But everything was saddened by the thought of my wife and son in prison.

I went by bus to the nearby town of Cluj where I had friends, but they had moved. I tramped from one house to another in sweltering midsummer heat, until I found them at last. They brought out cake and fruit, all manner of good things. But there was a beautiful brown onion on the table, and it was that I wanted. I had hankered so often for an onion to take away the taste of prison food. Now I did not like to ask for it.

I made a telephone call to a neighbour of ours in Bucharest. The voice that answered was Sabina's!

'It's Richard,' I said. 'I thought you were in prison!'

There was a confused noise. Mihai came on the line. 'Mother's fainted—hold on!' There were more strange sounds. Then he said, 'She's all right. We thought you were dead!'

Miahi had never been in prison. The false news I had been given was a last turn of the screw to test my reactions to brain-washing.

I took the train to Bucharest. As it drew into the station, I saw a crowd of men, women and children. Their arms were full of flowers and I wondered what lucky person was receiving such a welcome. Then I recognised faces, and leaned from the window of the carriage to wave. As I climbed down, it seemed as if all the people of our church were running to meet me, and then my arms were around my wife and son.

That night Sabina told me that she had been given news of my death years before. She refused to believe it, even when strangers called on her who claimed to be ex-prisoners who had attended my burial.

'I will wait for him,' she said.

The years passed and no word came, until my telephone call. It was for her as if I had been resurrected from the dead.

2

One Sunday, months after my release, I took a group of schoolchildren for a walk. The Secret Police dogged us first but seeing that we went into the Zoo they left us.

I led the children to the lions' cage and gathered them around me so that I might speak quietly.

I said, 'Your forefathers in the Christian faith were thrown to wild beasts like these. They died gladly, because they believed in Jesus. The time may come when you also will be imprisoned, and suffer for being a Christian. Now you must decide whether you are ready to face that day.'

With tears in their eyes, each in turn said 'yes'. I asked no other questions in this, the last confirmation class I held before leaving my country.

I have described in the preface why I decided that I must leave my country, and how I came to the West. Now I have only this to add. On the wall of a civic building in Washington, D.C., there is a large plaque containing the Constitution of the United States, skilfully engraved in copperplate. When first you look at it, you see only the engraved words of the Constitution; then, on stepping back, so that the angle of the light changes, the face of George Washington appears, carved into the text.

So it should be with this book, which contains episodes from a man's life, and the story of those who were with him in prison. Behind them all stands an unseen being, Christ, who kept us in faith and gave us strength to conquer.

The author welcomes correspondence concerning the Underground Church and letters should be addressed to him at 24 Elm Grove, Crouch Hill, London, N.8.